D0758240

BAPTIST
LIFE
AND
THOUGHT:
1600-1980

Baptism in the Schuylkill River, 1770

BAPTIST LIFE AND THOUGHT: 1600-1980

A SOURCE BOOK

William H. Brackney, General Editor

Editorial Board
 Clarence C. Goen
 Robert T. Handy
 Eleanor M. Hull
 William G. McLoughlin
 Ellis E. O'Neal
 Vernon F. Snow
 James M. Washington

Judson Press® Valley Forge
in cooperation with
The American Baptist Historical Society

BAPTIST LIFE AND THOUGHT: 1600–1980

Copyright © 1983
Judson Press, Valley Forge, PA 19481

Library of Congress Cataloging in Publication Data
Main entry under title:

Baptist life and thought, 1600-1980.

  Includes bibliographical references and index.
  1. Baptists—United States—History. 2. Baptists—England—History. 3. Baptists—Doctrinal and controversial works. I. Brackney, William. II. American Baptist Historical Society.
BX6235.B34   1983   286'.09   83-11261
ISBN 0-8170-0959-0

The name JUDSON PRESS is registered as a trademark in the U.S. Patent Office.
Printed in the U.S.A. ⊕

Acknowledgments

The quotation from William N. Clarke, *Sixty Years with the Bible: A Record of Experience* (New York: Charles Scribner's Sons, 1909) is reprinted with the permission of Charles Scribner's Sons.

Selections from *Life Under the Peculiar Institution* by Norman R. Yetman are used by permission of Norman R. Yetman.

Material from the Broadmead Baptist Church records and the transcriptions in Roger Hayden, editor, *The Records of a Church of Christ in Bristol 1640-1677* (Bristol: The Record Society, 1974) are used with the permission of the Broadmead Baptist Church and Roger Hayden, respectively.

Quotations from the Andrew Gifford Remains are used with the permission of the officers of the Bristol Baptist College.

Selections from other unpublished sources not acknowledged above are used with the permission of the respective libraries and study centers indicated in the headnotes.

Contents

Preface

The story of this book began after an adjourned meeting of the American Baptist Historical Society in 1953. Now, three decades later, a team of editors has created the present volume with several goals in mind. An overall goal has been to have the book reflect the great diversity among American Baptist scholars and the differing approaches that represent our historiography. The choice of editors intentionally mirrors this goal.

Our first aim is to provide scholars, students, and church professionals with a concise collection of primary sources that illustrate the fullness of Anglo-American Baptist life and thought. At points we rejected some obvious alternatives, favoring instead materials that are not as well known, not recently published, and not readily available elsewhere. Throughout, we have limited the explanatory notes to background, biographical, and source-critical apparatus in order to maximize space for original sources. The outline and organization of sources have been a group decision, originating with proposals from individual specialists.

Second, we intend this book to be an agenda for further scholarly explorations. Much spadework needs to be accomplished in a new generation of research in Baptist history, theology, and polity, and we hope that some of our source selections will raise more questions than they answer. For this reason we have given much attention to specific citation of locations for original materials plus bibliographic essays for each major section. In each case the American Baptist Historical Society has a copy of the full sources included in this book.

Finally, we have been concerned with origins, trends, and larger cultural patterns. We have placed the traditional segments of denominational identity—history, theology, and polity—in the broader socio-political, economic, and religious contexts of England and America. Further, we have not neglected the larger Christian community of which Baptists are definitely a part.

A word about our overall plan of organization. We acknowledge the debt of American Baptists to the seventeenth-century English and Welsh milieus; thus our initial section reveals the story of the early English Baptists to 1800. Section II discovers the uniqueness of Baptists in colonial America while at the same time pointing to their dependence upon the English tradition and other American Protestant developments. The third Section focuses upon the organizational and missional identity of American Baptists as well as those who dissented from the mainstream of denominational life. In Section IV the triumph of the Baptist movement and its response to difficult questions is explored, and in Section V we have wrestled with the multiplicity of forces that have acted upon Baptists in this century.

Specific assignments in the sourcebook are difficult to describe as each specialist added much to the entire work. Yet the following persons capably designed the respective sections: "The English Baptist Heritage," Vernon F. Snow; "Baptists in Colonial America," William G. McLoughlin; "Missions, Organization, and Controversy," Clarence C. Goen; "The Era of Progress and Protest" and "The Modern Era," Robert T. Handy. Valuable aid regarding the role and identity of women was given by Eleanor Hull and regarding nonwhite traditions by James M. Washington. The general editor has reviewed each section, made final revisions, prepared the bibliographic essays, and supervised the research and preparation of original texts. Further, Ellis O'Neal has created the Index and added much helpful stylistic advice.

We wish to express deep appreciation to the many librarians, archivists, and historians who have assisted us in locating obscure resources and in helping to make some difficult decisions. Several persons deserve special gratitude: Paul Fiddes and B.R. White at Regents Park College, Oxford; John Nicholson of Northern Baptist College, Manchester; Sidney Hall of Bristol Baptist College—all in Great Britain; Fred Anderson, The Virginia Baptist Historical Society; Martha Mitchell of Brown University; Mary Riley of Bates College; and Diana Yount of Andover Newton Theological School. Lester B. Scherer, W. Morgan Patterson, Oscar Burdick, and Norman H. Maring made very helpful suggestions.

Susan Eltscher and Arlyce Kretschman of the American Baptist Historical Society provided large amounts of technical assistance; Kathryn Brackney copied and checked many original texts; and Marty Batterson of Colgate Rochester Divinity School typed the manuscript. The administrations of Colgate Rochester, Andover Newton, and Union Theological seminaries provided comfortable and convenient settings for editorial committee meetings and research, facilitating our task in an enjoyable way. Most of all, Harold Twiss, General Manager of Judson Press, has been a patient friend who has enthusiastically supported this project from its inception.

We are also grateful to the John Ben Snow Memorial Trust for a generous grant that has greatly facilitated the publication of this book.

The general editor accepts full responsibility for the ultimate state of the text, especially any shortcomings. In the spirit of documentary historians from Thomas Crosby and Morgan Edwards to the present, the editors trust that the documents will speak for themselves.

William H. Brackney
All Saints' Day, 1982

Abbreviations Used Frequently in This Volume

ABFMS   American Baptist Foreign Mission Society. Founded in 1814 as the General Missionary Convention of the Baptist Denomination in the United States of America for Foreign Missions, it was popularly known as the Triennial Convention because it met in convention nationally once every three years, 1814-1845. Following the departure of the Southern Baptists, the agency was reorganized in 1846 as the American Baptist Missionary Union. In 1910 it became the Foreign Mission Society and in 1972 it adopted a second program title, The Board of International Ministries of the American Baptist Churches in the U.S.A.

ABHS   American Baptist Historical Society, founded in 1853.

ABHMS   American Baptist Home Mission Society. Founded in 1832, it has retained this corporate identity throughout its history. In 1972 the agency adopted the program title, the Board of National Ministries of the American Baptist Churches in the U.S.A.

ABPS   American Baptist Publication Society. Formed in 1824 as the Baptist General Tract Society, its function was broadened in 1840 and it became the American Baptist Publication and Sunday School Society. In 1844 "Sunday School" was dropped from the name; in 1945 the Northern Baptist Board of Education merged with the Society to create the American Baptist Board of Education and Publication. In 1972 the Board adopted the program title, the Board of Educational Ministries of the American Baptist Churches in the U.S.A.

BWA   Baptist World Alliance, founded 1905.

FWB   Freewill Baptists, founded by Benjamin Randal at New Durham, New Hampshire, in 1780. In 1841 the Free Communion Baptists merged with the Freewill group to become the Free Baptists. Free Baptists in the North merged with the Northern Baptist Convention in 1911.

M & M Board   The Ministers and Missionaries Benefit Board was chartered in 1911 and remains with that title at present.

NBC/ABC   The Northern Baptist Convention was formed in 1907. In 1950 the name was changed to the American Baptist Convention. In 1972 another name change occurred and the Convention became known as the American Baptist Churches in the U.S.A.

SBC   Southern Baptist Convention, formed in 1845. The Convention includes the Foreign Mission Board, Home Mission Board, and the Sunday School Board. The Home and Foreign Boards were created in 1845; the Sunday School Board is the result of an 1863 merger of the Southern Baptist Publication Society (1854) and the Southern Sunday School Union (1858).

WABFMS and   Woman's American Baptist Foreign Mission Society (1871) and Woman's WABHMS   American Baptist Home Mission Society (1877, originally the Woman's Baptist Mission Societies of the East and West) were integrated into the respective Foreign and Home Societies in 1955.

General Introduction

W ho are the Baptists?'' or, more appropriately, ''What are the Baptists?'' Either of these questions sparks a lively debate among Baptists and non-Baptists alike. Some maintain that Baptists follow a New Testament pattern of church life and thus ''Baptist'' churches reach back to the Apostolic Era (the Successionist Theory). Still others argue that Baptists were essentially an outgrowth of the Separatist-Nonconformist movement of post-Elizabethan England and that Baptists belong rightly to the Congregational branch of Protestantism. A third school of thought has modified the English origins argument and posits evidence that early Baptists were influenced by the Anabaptist movement through contact with Dutch Mennonites in the early seventeenth century. Since present documentation is scarce, complete validation of any of these theories must await further discoveries of primary source materials; however, in this instance, it is useful to proceed upon the documentary evidence that does exist.

Documentation of the Baptist tradition commences when the first ''baptizing'' congregations, so-called, began to appear about 1608. Through John Smyth and Thomas Helwys a connection with the heirs of the Radical Reformation can be established. As congregations created a clear identity for themselves, a theological distinctive arose delineating General from Particular Baptists, and the two branches grew concomitantly amid eras of intense persecution from the reign of James I to the reign of William and Mary. The chief concerns for English Baptists were thus related to identity: the nature of the gathered church, the ordinances, a learned clergy, and Christian life-style. Later, as the sect generally achieved social and religious recognition, Baptist leaders

15

promoted relationships with other Protestants, within the trans-Atlantic community, and finally with the entire world through the missionary crusade of the late eighteenth century. For Baptists in America the connection with English Baptists cannot be denied; indeed, it was the foundation which English and Welsh congregations laid that led to the origins and growth of Baptist life and thought in America.

The American frontier provided Baptists with an ideal environment in which to expand in numbers and persuasions. The English General/ Particular divisions when transplanted to America led to a wide variety of ecclesiological traditions, some of which (such as the Separates, Freewills, and black congregations) were inherently American. Baptist identity in the colonies was not so much a matter of a particular view of the atonement or the practice of believer's baptism as it was a united front against religious persecution. By the time of the American Revolution, Baptists in New England and Virginia alike were in the vanguard of the movement for separation of church and state. As Baptists in America came of age (around 1800), they, like their English predecessors, directed their energies to evangelism, expansion, and world mission.

The nineteenth century for Baptists in America was a period of organizational and structural growth and intense controversy; the latter usually focused upon the predominate social reform movements. World mission demanded consistent financial support, and Baptists responded with strengthened associational life, state conventions, and finally a national convention that met every three years to promote international, domestic, and educational efforts. At the same time, debates over slavery, secret societies, centralized organization, the missionary movement, and the use of confessions of faith served to divide the Baptist phalanx but not to diminish the Baptist identity. By the end of the Civil War, Baptists of all persuasions numerically outdistanced all other Protestant groups.

Unlike other Protestant communions, which were split over the slave controversy and which later reunited, Baptists, North and South, developed in separate directions. Southern Baptists labored hard to forge an organizational identity while Baptists in the North through independent societies were challenged to respond to a rapidly changing cultural and intellectual milieu. At the conclusion of World War I, Northern Baptists had tightened their national organizational identity and developed permanent structures for social concerns, ecumenical relations, and theological debate. (With no prejudice other than spatial limitations, the editors' choice of source selections in this volume will highlight primarily Northern Baptist life and thought after 1880.)

Finally, American Baptists in the twentieth century have faced repeated challenges in their organizational life, their theological pluralism, and their ecumenical relationships. Unsettling cultural patterns, an economic depression, competition with other Baptist groups, and the de-Christianization of American society in the Northeast have together produced a profound impact upon American Baptist life since 1920. Yet, through division and reorganization, American Baptists have redoubled their efforts in evangelism, global missions, human rights, stewardship, and a keener understanding of the purposes of the local church.

Beyond and within the organizational/structural evolution of Baptist life in England and America, one can identify a uniquely Baptist polity and theology. Early in the seventeenth century, English Baptists developed a view of the gathered church, signified by believer's baptism, which clearly set Baptists apart from other Nonconformists. In colonial America, Baptists generated a strong associational life and missionary thrust; later in the nineteenth century, that associational life led to more centralized conventions and church-related institutions for most Baptists. Finally, in modern America, the majority of American Baptist congregations assumed a positive role in the larger Christian community.

Although Baptist theology is often hard to distinguish from Reformed thought in the early period and evangelical Protestantism (liberal and conservative) in the last century, Baptist writers and educators have made lasting contributions to English and American theology. In England, Thomas Grantham developed a connectional ecclesiology for General Baptists, and John Bunyan profoundly influenced the open Communion movement. In America, Isaac Backus and John Leland championed religious liberty while Morgan Edwards urged a more universal view of the Baptist "church." Local pastors from Maine to Kentucky defended a theology of evangelism that in the first decade of the nineteenth century produced the foreign and home missions movements. Similarly, following the Civil War, William Newton Clarke, Augustus H. Strong, and Walter Rauschenbusch were among the first

American theologians to respond to changing intellectual climates and the greater needs of American social life. In the twentieth century, Baptist theologians have been heavily influenced by major currents of religious thought and life, all the while operating with a relentless commitment to a theology of the local church.

Suggestions for Further Study

Investigations of Baptist historical themes and biography must begin with the basic reference tools that pull together over four hundred years of literature and archives. In addition to the general bibliographies of Christian church history since the Reformation, one should consult the catalogs of the American Baptist Historical Society; the Angus Library, Regents Park College; and the Boyce Library, Southern Baptist Theological Seminary for subject listings, recent monographs, and finding aids. Two major bibliographic works are essential in listing and locating the published literature: W. T. Whitley, *A Baptist Bibliography 1526-1776,* 2 vols. (London: Kingsgate Press, 1916) for English Baptist works; and Edward C. Starr, *A Baptist Bibliography,* 25 vols. (Rochester: American Baptist Historical Society, 1947-1976) which includes Whitley and McIntyre, plus American and international Baptist imprints to 1975. The various published catalogs of Dr. Williams's Library and the Bodleian Library at Oxford University are most helpful. The American Baptist Historical Society is conducting a national Baptist Archives and Records Survey on church records and archival material, the findings of which are published in a series of regional guides.

Students should also be aware of historiographical trends in Baptist studies. There were several early attempts to create a sense of historicity for "antipaedobaptists," most of which are found in works like Henry Denne's *Antichrist Unmasked in Three Treatises* (London: Stationers, 1646) and Henry Danvers's *A Treatise of Baptism* (London: Francis Smith, 1674) in the era prior to 1700. Thomas Crosby was the first to complete a comprehensive history of English Baptists (four volumes; London: 1738-1740), although he is not credited with originality. Apparently Crosby relied heavily upon Benjamin Stinton, his pastor and chief mentor, in gathering historical materials and in organizing his interpretations. Although Crosby defends an unbroken tradition for believer's baptism, he stops short of any theory of successive "Baptist" congregations, and he rejects any connection with Continental Anabaptists.

The "successionist" idea was introduced in Robert Robinson's *Ecclesiastical Researches* (Cambridge: Francis Hudson, 1792) and followed in the nineteenth century by G. H. Orchard's *A Concise History of Foreign Baptists* (Nashville: Graves, 1865). In America, both David Benedict, *A General History of the Baptist Denomination in America*

19

and *Other Parts of the World* (Boston: Lincoln and Edmands, 1820, 1848) and Thomas Armitage, *A History of the Baptists* (New York: Bryan, Taylor, 1888) followed a modified successionist model and were popular well into the twentieth century.

A new school of American interpretation evolved in the mid-eighteenth century in the work of Morgan Edwards, usually identified as *Materials Toward a History of Baptists in America* . . . (various states and editions) and Isaac Backus, *A History of New England, with Particular References to the Denomination of Christians Called Baptists* (Boston: 1777-1796). Edwards and Backus were little concerned with antiquity; their focus was upon the roots of Baptist churches in the American colonies and the evolution of associational life. Much of their writing is based upon original manuscripts and printed records. Champlin Burrage, *The Early English Dissenters in Light of Recent Research 1550-1641,* 2 vols. (Cambridge: University Press, 1912), challenged the successionist theory, as did Henry Vedder, *A Short History of the Baptists* (Valley Forge: Judson Press, 1907), and W. T. Whitley, *A History of British Baptists* (London: Kingsgate Press, 1912). Burrage argued that the Anabaptist movement had little or no bearing upon English Separatism before 1612, while Vedder traced modern Baptist identity only from the English Particular Baptist congregations about 1641 and Whitley made a sharp distinction between Continental Anabaptists and the first English General Baptists.

The contemporary debate focuses upon three approaches. Winthrop S. Hudson, *Baptist Convictions* (Valley Forge: Judson Press, 1963), denies that Baptists were Anabaptists, basing his argument upon the silence of any historical evidence. William R. Estep, *The Anabaptist Story* (Nashville: Broadman Press, 1963), posits a pronounced affinity of English Separatists for Anabaptist ideas. And Barrington R. White, *The English Separatist Tradition* (London: Oxford University Press, 1971), authoritatively locates the roots of both General and Particular Baptists in the English Separatist tradition.

Baptist periodicals that focus especially on historical disciplines are a rich treasury of ideas and contemporary scholarship. *The Chronicle,* published by the American Baptist Historical Society 1938-1957, contains two valuable essays, both entitled "Themes for Research in Baptist History" (early Baptist history: July, 1953; modern Baptist history: January, 1954). ABHS also published *Foundations* (1958-1982) which produced historiographical articles in April, 1963, and October, 1969 (the latter on Baptists in Northwest America). A current journal, *American Baptist Quarterly,* contains an update agenda for Baptist studies in its inaugural issue, October, 1982. The British Baptist Historical Society has published the *Baptist Quarterly* since 1908, and virtually all major topics of interest to British and British Empire Baptist studies are mentioned therein. Southern Baptists in America produce *The Review and Expositor* (Southern Seminary, since 1904), the *Quarterly Review* (Sunday School Board, since 1941), and *Baptist History and Heritage* (Historical Commission, since 1965). Of particular interest in *Baptist History and Heritage* are "Baptist Literature" (August, 1965, and July, 1966), "Baptist Historical and Theological Journals" (October, 1966), "Baptist Historical Writing in America" (July, 1967), and "Current Issues in Baptist Life: Historical Views" (April, 1981). Finally, although not specifically Baptist, the *Journal of Church and State,* published at Baylor University, features excellent material on social and political themes of interest to Baptists.

Researchers will also find helpful a number of general, ready-reference books that provide brief factual and biographical data. William Cathcart, *The Baptist Encyclopedia* (Philadelphia: Everts, 1881) and Clifton J. Allen, editor, *Encyclopedia of Southern Baptists,* 4 vols. (Nashville: Broadman Press, 1958-1982) are standard texts; G. A. Burgess and J. T. Ward, *Free Baptist Cyclopedia* (Boston: Stocking, 1889) and Ethel L. Williams, *Biographical Directory of Negro Ministers* (New York: Scarecrow Press, 1965) are less well known but most helpful. On geographical matters, consult Edwin S. Gaustad, *Historical Atlas of Religion in America* (New York: Harper & Row, Publishers, Inc., 1962) and William H. Brackney, *A Guide to American Baptist Mission and Historical Sites* (Valley Forge: Judson Printing, 1982).

Section I
The English Baptist Heritage
1600–1800

> The English Baptists, tho' they are unhappily disunited, and distinguished by the title of *Generals* and *Particulars;* yet it is the only point, I know of, wherein they differ from the *primitive* churches.
>
> Thomas Crosby, 1740

The emergence of the English Baptists during the first quarter of the seventeenth century was no historical accident or quirk. Rather, their origins can be traced to both indigenous and foreign sources, to both remote and recent roots. A long tradition of dissent existed in England, best represented by the late medieval Lollards, who questioned some of the basic theological doctrines of the Catholic Church in England and persisted as a historical force well into the sixteenth century. Recent research has established corelationships between these heretical dissenters and the radicals of the English Reformation. Subsequently, during the Elizabethan era a radical ecclesiology emerged—illustrated in Robert Browne and his followers, the Brownists—that rejected the concept of a national church and advocated that congregations of believers be accountable to Christ alone as the head of the church. Around 1600 when John Smyth and his coreligionists espoused these principles, they were forced to flee into exile, fearing for their lives. While exiled in Holland, these English people came into close contact with the Dutch Anabaptists (Mennonites), whose radical theology and sociopolitical views were anathema to most Europeans, Catholic and Protestant alike. The Mennonite influence, though imprecise and latent in nature, helped to reinforce and reshape the identity of that English Separatist congregation. Thus, the resultant fusion of these three religious elements—two indigenous and one foreign—helps to explain the explosive variety and diversity that characterized the Baptist movement during the Puritan Revolution and after.

Varieties of
English Baptists

The Baptist heritage is rich in its diversity. Just as the Reformation on the Continent produced a variegated spectrum of Protestants during the sixteenth century, so the Puritan movement in England gave birth to a multitude of sects in the seventeenth century. While many of these new religious groups proved to be ephemeral in nature, the Baptists, the Independents, and the Quakers developed permanent institutions on both sides of the Atlantic. Lacking the external coercion of a national church and lacking the cohesion of common ancestry, the English Baptist churches developed along different and multifarious lines. The selections that follow illustrate the diversity that existed within the English Baptist tradition.

Though inspired by John Calvin and adhering to his view of God's sovereignty, the English Baptists differed on such matters as predestination, sin, grace, and free will. The General Baptists, following the leadership of John Smyth and his successor Thomas Helwys, subscribed to those Arminian interpretations, which viewed God's grace as broad or general, hence the label. Others, however, became known as Particular Baptists, having adopted a limited view of the atonement, a view that ultimately came to predominate among Baptists in England. Still another branch of the movement held to Sabbatarian principles and took the name "Seventh Day Baptized Believers," in contrast to the other two groups. In all three cases the first generation of Baptists was organized according to local congregations; only later did associational clusters and regional groups emerge.

1. John Smyth, the Se-Baptist

John Smyth (d. 1612), a student of Francis Johnson at Cambridge and onetime lecturer in Lincoln, became pastor of the Separatist congregation in Gainsborough about 1606.

25

When threatened by the harsh policies of James I (1603–1625), Smyth and his congregation left England for the Netherlands. In Amsterdam they rejected amalgamation with other English Separatists and established ties with the Dutch Anabaptists (Mennonites) of Waterland. Eventually, after Smyth baptized himself (hence the term "Se-Baptist") and his congregation, they applied for membership in that church. Their application included the following twenty articles, penned in 1610 by Smyth, who died shortly thereafter. *Source:* The Latin original entitled "Corde Credimus . . ." is found in the Mennonite Archives, Amsterdam and reprinted in William T. Whitley, ed., *The Works of John Smyth, Fellow of Christ's College 1594–8* (Cambridge: University Press, 1915), 2, pp. 682-684. The English version follows with some corrections of the text as found in William L. Lumpkin, *Baptist Confessions of Faith* (Valley Forge: Judson Press, 1959), pp. 100-101.

1. That there is one God, the best, the highest, and most glorious Creator and Preserver of all; who is Father, Son, and Holy Spirit.

2. That God has created and redeemed the human race to his own image, and has ordained all men (no one being reprobated) to life.

3. That God imposes no necessity of sinning on any one; but man freely, by Satanic instigation, departs from God.

4. That the law of life was originally placed by God in the keeping of the law; then, by reason of the weakness of the flesh, was, by the good pleasure of God, through the redemption of Christ, changed into justification of faith; on which account no one ought justly to blame God, but rather, with his inmost heart, to revere, adore, and praise his mercy, that God should have rendered that possible to man, by his grace, which before, since man had fallen, was impossible by nature.

5. That there is no sin of origin, but all sin is actual and voluntary, viz., a word, a deed, or a design against the law of God; and therefore, infants are without sin.

6. That Jesus Christ is true God and true man; viz., the Son of God taking to himself, in addition, the true and pure nature of a man, out of a true rational soul, and existing in a true human body.

7. That Jesus Christ, as pertaining to the flesh, was conceived by the Holy Spirit in the womb of the Virgin Mary, afterwards was born, circumcised, baptized, tempted; also that he hungered, thirsted, ate, drank, increased both in stature and in knowledge; he was wearied, he slept, at last was crucified, dead, buried, he rose again, ascended into heaven; and that to himself as only King, Priest, and Prophet of the church, all power both in heaven and earth is given.

8. That the grace of God, through the finished redemption of Christ,

was to be prepared and offered to all without distinction, and that not feignedly but in good faith, partly by things made, which declare the invisible things of God, and partly by the preaching of the Gospel.

9. That men, of the grace of God through the redemption of Christ, are able (the Holy Spirit, by grace, being before unto them *grace prevenient*) to repent, to believe, to turn to God, and to attain to eternal life; so on the other hand, they are able themselves to resist the Holy Spirit, to depart from God, and to perish for ever.

10. That the justification of man before the Divine tribunal (which is both the throne of justice and of mercy), consists partly of the imputation of the righteousness of Christ apprehended by faith, and partly of inherent righteousness, in the holy themselves, by the operation of the Holy Spirit, which is called regeneration or sanctification; since any one is righteous, who doeth righteousness.

11. That faith, destitute of good works, is vain; but true and living faith is distinguished by good works.

12. That the church of Christ is a company of the faithful; baptized after confession of sin and of faith, endowed with the power of Christ.

13. That the church of Christ has power delegated to themselves of announcing the word, administering the sacraments, appointing ministers, disclaiming them, and also excommunicating; but the last appeal is to the brethren or body of the church.

14. That baptism is the external sign of the remission of sins, of dying and of being made alive, and therefore does not belong to infants.

15. That the Lord's Supper is the external sign of the communion of Christ, and of the faithful amongst themselves by faith and love.

16. That the ministers of the church are, not only bishops ("Episcopos"), to whom the power is given of dispensing both the word and the sacraments, but also deacons, men and widows, who attend to the affairs of the poor and sick brethren.

17. That brethren who persevere in sins known to themselves after the third admonition, are to be excluded from the fellowship of the saints by excommunication.

18. That those who are excommunicated are not to be avoided in what pertains to worldly business.

19. That the dead (the living being instantly changed) will rise again with the same bodies; not the substance but the qualities being changed.

20. That after the resurrection, all will be borne to the tribunal of

Christ, the Judge, to be judged according to their works; the pious, after sentence of absolution, will enjoy eternal life with Christ in heaven; the wicked, condemned, will be punished with eternal torments in hell with the devil and his angels.

2. Thomas Helwys on Sin and Free Will

An offshoot of Smyth's congregation, preferring to retain its separate identity, followed the leadership of Thomas Helwys (c. 1556–1616) and formulated its own confession of faith and published it in 1611. Shortly thereafter Helwys returned to England and established in London a General Baptist congregation. His appeal to the English authorities for toleration was rejected, and he died in Newgate prison about 1616. The following passage from a tract written by Helwys argues for universal redemption for infants in contrast to the prevailing Calvinistic position of original sin and condemnation. *Source:* Thomas Helwys, *A Short and Plaine Proofe, by the Word and Workes of God that God's Decree is not the cause of Anye Mans Sinne or Condemnation; and that All men are Redeemed by Christ; as also that no infants are Condemned* (London: n.p.), pp. 8, 21.

_____

When Adam was thus falle, & had off his owne Freewil first forsaken God, did God yet leave him? No: such was the mercie of God (everlasting glorie & praise bee given to his name) as he wou'd not yet leave Adam, but gives him Freely off his owne grace, deliverance by the promised seed Gen. 3.15. And as the Apostle hath shewed Rom. 5.12-21. That by Adams sinne the fault came on al to condemnation, so doth he in the same Chapter and verses equally shewe with equal like words & reasons, yea with the selff same words & reasons: that as by the offence off one (that was Adam) the Fault came on al to condemnation: Even so by the justifying of one (that is Christ Jesus) the benifit abounded towards al men to the justification of life. That as sinne reigned unto death, even so might grace also reigne by righteousness unto Eternal life by Jesus Christ. How hath the Lord by the unspeakeable evidence off his truth, proved to mens consciences that wil beleeve his word, that he did not leave & forsake Adam, nor for his sinne any mankind under that condemnation which by Adams offence went over al. But by grace in Christ, hath Freed Adam, & in him al man-kind from that sinne off Adam.

To make it yet more plaine, that as Adam was Freed From that sinne so al man-kind was Freed. . . .

And whereas the Holy Ghost Roman, 5.14, 15. Speaking of Infants, saith.

That death reigned also over them that sinned not after the like manner of thee transgression of Adam/the Grace off God/and gift by grace/ which is by one man Christ Jesus hath abounded much more to the. Hereby also is further confirmed that al infāts are freed by the universall redemption off Christ from that condemnation, which you (by your opinion off perticuler redemption) would cast upon the most of them, as is also before shewed.

3. Formation of a Particular Baptist Congregation in London

In 1616 Henry Jacob (1563–1624) established in London a "gathered church" from which evolved several Independent and Baptist congregations prior to 1642. About 1633 John Spilsbury (1593–c. 1668) broke away from Jacob's mixed communion, had himself rebaptized, and organized the first Particular Baptist congregation. William Kiffin (1616–1701) joined the Spilsbury church five years later and was also rebaptized. During the Civil Wars (1642–1648), Kiffin became one of the leading polemicists for the Particular Baptists. The following account of the church, an *aide-mémoire*, is attributed to Kiffin, although the only extant version is a copy made in 1712. *Source:* Benjamin Stinton, "A Repository of Diverse Historical Matters Relating to the English Anti-pedobaptists, Collected from Original Papers or Faithful Extracts," 1712. Unpublished manuscript, Angus Library, Regents Park College, Oxford.

Henry Jacob a Preacher, an Eminant man for Learning, haveing of others, often and many ways, sought for Reformation and showed the necessity thereof in regard of ye Church of England's so far wantonness from ye Apostolical Churches etc. in his Assertion dedicated to King James and he made an offer of Disputation therein . . .

He Haveing had much confozence about those things here; after that in ye low Countries he had conversed and discoursed muchwith Mr. Jno. Robinson late Pastor to ye Church in Leyden and with others about them: and returning to England, In London he held many several meetings with the most Famous Men for Godliness and Learning (viz) Mr. Throgwarton, Mr. Travers, Mr. Wing, Mr. Rich Mansell, Mr. Jno Dod . . . those with others haveing seriously weighed all things and circumstance Mr. Jacob and Some Others sought ye Lord about them, in fasting and Prayer together: at last it was concluded by ye most of them, that it was a very warrantable and commendable Way to set upon that course here as well as in Holland or elsewhere, whatsoever troubles should ensue. H. Jacob was willing to adventure himself for this King-dom of Christ's sake; ye rest encouraged him.

The Church Anno 1616 was gathered . . . well informed saints haveing appointed a Day to seek ye face of ye Lord in fasting and Prayer, wherein that perticular of their Union together as a Church was mainly commended to ye Lord: in ye ending of the Day they were United, thus, those who minded this present Union and so joyning togeather joyned both hands each with the other Brother and stood in a Ringwise: their intent being declared H. Jacob and each of ye Rest made some confession or Profession of their Faith and Repentance, some were longer some were briefer. Then they convenanted togeather to walk in all Gods Ways, as he had revealed or should make Known to them . . . After this Hen. Jacob was chosen and ordained Pastor to that Church, and many Saints were joyned to them.

Sundry of ye Church, whereof Mr. Jacob and Mr. John Lathrop had been pastors, being dissatisfied with ye churches owning of English Parishes to be true Churches desired dismission, and joyned togeather among themselves, as Mr. Henry Parker, Mr. Tho. Shepard, Mr. Samuel Eaton, Mark Lukar and others with whom joyned Mr. Wm. Kiffin.

1638 Mr. Tho. Wilson, Mr. Pen and H. Pen and 3 more being convinced that Baptism was not for infants but professed Believers joyned to Mr. Jo: Spilsbury ye churches Favour being desired therein.

1640 3d Mo. The Church became two by mutuall consent just half being with Mr. Barebane and ye other half with Mr. Jessy, Mr. Richard Blunt with him being convinced of Baptism that also it ought to be by dipping ye body into ye water, resembling Burial and rising again 2 Cor: 2:12 Rom. 6.4 had *sober* Conference about it in ye Church and them with some of ye forenamed who also were so convinced: And after Prayer and Conference about their so enjoyning it; now having *then* to so practised in England to professed Believers and hearing what some in ye Nether Lands had so practised they agreed and sent over Mr. Rich Blunt (who understood Dutch) and Letters of Commendation, who was kindly accepted there and Returned with Letters from them.
. . .

Those persons [which] were persuaded baptism should be by dipping ye body had mett in two companies and did intend to meet after this . . . And those (not by any formal Words or Covenant, which Word *was scrupled* by some of them, but by mutual desires and agreement each testified: Those two Companies did set apart one to Baptize the rest, So it was solemnly performed by them. Mr. Blunt Baptized Mr.

Blacklock [who] was a Teacher amongst them, and Mr. Blunt being Baptized, he and Mr. Blacklock Baptized ye rest of their friends that were so minded, and many being added to them they increased much.

4. The Particular Baptist Ideal

In the decade from 1633 to 1643 the Particular Baptist congregations increased sevenfold. Despite this growth, they were not tolerated by the Presbyterians and Independents who opposed their participation in the Westminster Assembly of Divines (1643–1648). In fact, Baptist minister Hanserd Knollys (1599–1691) was imprisoned by the House of Commons in the summer of 1644 for preaching openly against infant baptism. Shortly after his incarceration, representatives of the seven Particular Baptist congregations met and issued in October the confession that is excerpted below. Signees included Kiffin and Spilsbury. This declaration became a model for subsequent Particular Baptist creeds. Each local congregation, styled "a company of visible saints, called and separated from the world," practiced believer's baptism by immersion. A 1646 reissue of the *Confession* included the signature of Hanserd Knollys. *Source: The Commonly (though falsely) Called Anabaptists* (London: n.p., 1644).

III

That God hath decreed in himselfe from everlasting touching all things, effectually to work and dispose them according to the counsell of his owne will, to the glory of his Name; in which decree appeareth his wisdome, constancy, truth, and faithfulnesse; Wisdome, is that whereby he contrives all things; Constancy is that whereby the decree of God remaines alwyes immutable; Truth is that whereby he declares that alone which he hath decreed and though his sayings may seeme to sound sometimes another thing, yet the sense of them doth alwayes agree with the decree; Faithfulnesse is that whereby he effects that he hath decreed, as he hath decreed. And touching his creature man, God had in Christ before the foundation of the world, according to the good pleasure of his will, foreordained some men to eternall life through Jesus Christ, to the praise and glory of his grace, leaving the rest in their sinne to their just condemnation, to the praise of his Justice.

IV

In the beginning God made all things very good, created man after his own Image and likenesse, filling him with all perfection of all naturall excellency and uprightnesse free from all sinne. But long he abode not in this honour, but by the subtiltie of the Serpent, which Satan used as his instrument, himselfe with his Angels having sinned before, and not kept their first estate, but left their owne habitation;

first *Eve*, then *Adam* being seduced did wittingly and willingly fall into disobedience and transgression of the Commandement of their great Creator, for the which death came upon all, and reigned over all, so that all since the Fall are conceived in sinne, and brought forth in iniquitie, and so by nature children of wrath, and servants of sinne, subjects of death, and all other calamities due to sinne in this world and for ever, being considered in the state of nature, without relation to Christ.

5. Seventh Day Baptists

It is difficult to pinpoint the origins of the Seventh Day Baptists, but Francis Bampfield (1615–1684) was among the earliest to establish a separate congregation. Bampfield, a graduate of Wadham College, Oxford, remained an Anglican and Royalist throughout the Puritan Revolution. However, in 1662 he was ejected from his living for not taking the Oath of Allegiance and imprisoned in Dorchester for nine years. He became a convert to Baptist views while in prison, seemingly, and upon his release secured a license to preach. In 1676 he organized a Seventh Day church in his London residence and moved it to a nearby hall five years later. However, during the reign of James II (1685–1688) he was again jailed and died in Newgate prison. No doubt the publication of Sabbatarian views, like those in the following selection, explain his unpopularity. *Source:* Francis Bampfield, *Septima Dies, Dies Desirabilis, Sabbatum Jehovae. The Seventh Day Sabbath, the Desirable Day* (London: n.p., 1677), p. 9.

Six days thou shalt labour, but the seventh-day is the Sabbath: In it thou shalt not do any work: For six days Jehovah made Heaven and Earth, the Sea, and all that in them is, and rested the seventh-day: Wherefore Jehovah blessed that day, that Sabbath, the blessing is gone forth for this Seventh-day-Sabbath irreversibly from the Mouth of Jehovah Mashiach himself: it has his Applaud and approve for its due estimation and deserved renown, its noble majestickness and Royal imperialness. How many are the Prerogatives and Priviledges which he hath Conferred upon it! Christ is the Seventh-daies-benedictor and benefactor. This is the day which he hath Dedicated to the Instituted worship and service of Jehovah Aelohim; a day greatly to be desired and delighted in by his Children, Friends and Servants, as a day of holy rest, and of Heavenly joy; a day of sweet converse between him and his Saints; A day that calleth upon them for a singing-shouting-triumphing-rejoycing-frame!

and therefore there is a peculiar Psalm fitted for this purpose, to this end: Thus is the Crown of special Benediction put upon the head of the Seventh-day, and no other foregoing day of the week is to share with it in this princely honour. Isaiah, that evangelical Prophecier and Preacher, has from Jehovah Pronounced those Blessed even to admiration, (O the happy Progresses, O the happy goings on of such!) that do keep this Sabbath, and not prophane it! They shall enjoy many a covenant-favour! O how choice Spiritual blessings are there that do visit the Hearts of Holy observers of this Seventh-day-Sabbath! under the New-Testament Administration, O what a Blessed day did Christ make it to be unto some, whose sick bodies he healed, whose sinful Souls he pardoned, whose sadned Spirits he comforted; unto whom his Gracious words were converting and Restoring, teaching and enlightning, quickning and strengthning, whom he met in Sabbath ordinances, and gave them the Blessing of this separated day! and how many a Soul had cause to bless the LORD forever, who so prospered Pauls labours on the Seventh-day-Sabbath, for blessing, for good to them! Christ taught daily in the Temple, and Paul was often in the Synagogues on the foregoing daies of the Week, and much good was done thereby, but the whole Scripture doth take peculiar notice of this, That, the Seventh-day as the weekly Sabbath-day, carried away the Sabbath-blessings, which no other day in the week did, though the Lord do bless his People every day, yet not with Sabbath-blessings, but only on the seventh-day.

William Kiffin

Andrew Fuller

Hanserd Knollys

John Gill

The Quest for Identity

As in the Reformation Era, the sacraments—their meaning and administration—were focal points of concern for early English Baptists. For so-called Anabaptists in England, baptism was the chief concern: who should be baptized? by what means? in living or still waters? No uniformity of practice or theology could be achieved except when people agreed to a confessional statement. Such creeds or confessions came to be highly significant milestones in the evolution and clarification of Baptist identity.

Other ordinances or rites also came under the careful scrutiny of Baptist writers. Among these were the Lord's Supper (closed versus open Communion), the agape meal, and the ancient practice of the laying on of hands. As the confessional statements and church records indicate, English Baptist practices varied widely.

Finally, in order to perpetuate their principles and identity, Baptist congregations required knowledgeable and trained clergy. English universities were closed to Nonconformists; thus other means were necessary. When in the later seventeenth century the Bristol Baptists established an academy, another component of denominational identity emerged: a learned clergy with Baptistic sentiments.

1. Believer's Baptism—The First Step

In 1610 John Smyth and his English followers in Waterland, after considerable discussion with the liberal Mennonite community there, agreed to accept the Dutch Confessions of 1580, which contained the Mennonites' advanced views on baptism, war, oaths, and civil government. A shortened version of that confession was drawn up, translated, and submitted to Smyth's congregation. The *Short Confession* (1610), signed by John Smyth and thirty-nine men and women, served as the basis for the General Baptist

BAPTIST LIFE AND THOUGHT: 1600-1980

congregations when they returned to England. This selection shows that baptism and the Lord's Supper were symbolic rites administered only to consenting adults and not to "unspeaking children." *Source:* The original English manuscript is found in the Mennonite Archives in Amsterdam; the text used here was translated by Muller, the Mennonite archivist, for Benjamin Evans, *The Early English Baptists,* 2 vols. (London: J. Heaton, 1862), 1, p. 250.

28. There are two sacraments appointed by Christ, in his holy church, the administration whereof he hath assigned to the ministry of teaching, namely, the Holy Baptism and the Holy Supper. These are outward visible handlings and tokens, setting before our eyes, on God's side, the inward spiritual handling which God, through Christ, by the co-operation of the Holy Ghost, setteth forth in the justification in the penitent faithful soul; and which, on our behalf, witnesseth our religion, experience, faith, and obedience, through the obtaining of a good conscience to the service of God.

29. The Holy Baptism is given unto these in the name of the Father, the Son, and the Holy Ghost, which hear, believe, and with penitent heart receive the doctrines of the Holy Gospel. For such hath the Lord Jesus commanded to be baptized, and no unspeaking children.

30. The whole dealing in the outward visible baptism of water, setteth before the eyes, witnesseth and signifyeth, the Lord Jesus doth inwardly baptize the repentant, faithful man, in the laver of regeneration and renewing by the Holy Ghost, washing the soul from all pollution and sin, by the virtue and merit of his bloodshed; and by the power and working of the Holy Ghost, the true, heavenly, spiritual, living Water, cleanseth the inward evil of the soul, and maketh it heavenly, spiritual, and living, in true righteousness or goodness. Therefore, the baptism of water leadeth us to Christ, to his holy office in glory and majesty; and admonisheth us not to hang only upon the outward, but with holy prayer to mount upward, and to beg of Christ the good thing signified.

31. The Holy Supper, according to the institution of Christ, is to be administered to the baptized; as the Lord Jesus hath commanded that whatsoever he hath appointed should be taught to be observed.

32. The whole dealing in the outward visible supper, setteth before the eye, witnesseth and signifyeth, that Christ's body was broken upon the cross, and his holy blood spilt for the remission of our sins. That the being glorified in his heavenly Being, is the alive-making bread, meat, and drink of our souls; it setteth before our eyes Christ's office

and ministry in glory and majesty, by holding his spiritual supper, which the believing soul, feeding and * the soul with spiritual food: it teacheth us by the outward handling to mount upwards with the heart in holy prayer, to beg at Christ's hands the true signified food; and it admonisheth us of thankfulness to God, and of verity and love one with another.

2. Immersion—The Technique of Baptism

At first, Baptist congregations probably utilized several modes of baptism: sprinkling, pouring, dipping, and plunging. However, more study and discussion of the subject led most to hold that immersion was the New Testament practice and as such signified the death, burial, and resurrection of Christ. The London Confession of 1644 defines the practice. *Source: The Confession of Faith* (London: 1644).

XXXIX.

That Baptisme is an Ordinance of the new Testament, given by Christ, to be dispensed onely upon persons professing faith, or that are Disciples, or taught, who upon a profession of faith, ought to be baptized.

XL.

The way and manner of the dispensing of this Ordinance the Scripture holds out to be dipping or plunging the whole body under water: it being a signe, must answer the thing signified, which are these: first, the washing the whole soule in the bloud of Christ: Secondly, that interest the Saints have in the death, buriall, and resurrection; thirdly, together with a confirmation of our faith, that as certainly as the body is buried under water, and riseth againe, so certainly shall the bodies of the Saints be raised by the power of Christ, in the day of the resurrection, to reigne with Christ.

3. The River or the Baptistry?

The next question to consider in the theology and practice of baptism was whether to administer the rite in running or "living" waters, as John had baptized Jesus, or to construct baptismal pools for the convenience of candidates who had physical difficulties or did not wish to be baptized in inclement weather conditions. Selection A illustrates the outdoor tradition; Selection B describes an elaborate, regional baptistry in an eighteenth century meetinghouse. *Sources:* A. Records of the Broadmead Baptist Church, Bristol, Book I. The text follows the transcription of Roger Hayden, ed., *The Records of a Church of Christ in Bristol 1640–1687* (Bristol: The Record Society, 1974), pp. 126,

138. B. Thomas Crosby, *The History of the English Baptists,* 4 vols. (London: John
Robinson, 1738-1740), 4, pp. 166-167.

[A. Baptisms in Bristol]
ANNO 1668. Upon ye 15th of ye 12 month, 1668, Aged Mr. TEATH-
ER was propounded to ye church, spoken with ye 2d of first month
following, and afterwards *Baptized* in ye *River Froome,* though above
80 years of age, and Joyned Member to this Church. . . .
BR. NATHANEEL SNEED, and S. SNEED, his wife, and S. RACH-
EL CLARK their Servant, were Proposed to ye Congregation, as their
desire to Joyne, upon ye 5 day, ye 3 mo. 1672; and on ye 7th day
following, being ye Churches monthly day, they made their declaration
before ye Congregation of their Conversion or worke of God upon their
soules; with which ye Church being Satisfied, they were BAPTIZED
upon ye 10th day of ye 3d Month, 1672. Soe that then we saw (and
had experience of), A WHOLE HOUSEHOLD was baptized at one
time together; namely, himselfe, his wife, and Maid, which was all ye
family. Soe that it may be said (according to ye Judgment of Charity,
they having declared their Conversion, their faith, and repentance), as
it was said of ye JAYLOR, Acts xvi. 34, *He believed in God with all
his house.* So that here is a liveing president, that a man and all his (or
a whole) *Household* may be Baptized, and have no Child in it; *as many
more may be,* if ye Lord please to Change them, and grace them with
Faith, Repentance, and desires of ye Ordinance, as these Did, According
to ye practice of Christ and ye Apostles.

[B. The Baptistry at Barbican]
. . . [Barbican] was fixed upon as the most convenient place; the
meeting-house being very large, and a large empty space behind it, fit
to be turned into convenient rooms for the minister, and persons to be
baptized, to dress and undress in. The persons who took upon themselves
the management of this affair, and to defray the charges of it, were
Tho. and John Hollis, esqs; both Baptists, tho' members of an independent congregation.
This Baptisterion, or cistern, is fixed just before the pulpit, the sides
and bottom of which are made with good polished stone, and round
the top is put a kirb of marble, about a foot wide; and round it, at about
a foot or two distance, is set up an iron rail, of handsome cypher work;

under the pulpit are the stairs that lead down into it, and at the top of these are two folding doors, which open into the three rooms behind the meeting-house, which are large, and handsomely wainscotted. Under one of these rooms there is a well, sunk down to the spring of water; at the top of this there is a leaden pump fixed, from which a pipe goes into the bason, near the top of it, by which it is filled with water; at the bottom of the bason there is a brass plug, from whence there goes another pipe into the said well, to empty it again.

The charge of making this Baptisterion, and repairing the meeting-house, to make it fit for this use, amounted to more than six hundred pounds; and all that were to have liberty to use it, had license granted them. . . .

4. The Continuing Distinctive

Infant baptism, practiced by most other Protestant groups and Roman Catholics, continued to be a point of attack for English Baptists, long after their seventeenth century identification with believer's baptism by immersion. John Gill (1697–1751), a strict Calvinist and pastor at Great Eastcheap for twenty-five years, lectured widely on Baptist principles and penned a number of classic treatises. His pungent prose, laced with anti-papal asides, is here illustrated. *Source:* John Gill, *Infant Baptism a Part and Pillar of Popery* (London: n.p., 1766), pp. 51-52.

Now, infant baptism, with all the ceremonies attending it, for which also apostolical tradition is pretended, makes a very considerable figure in Popish pageantry. Romanists administer the rite with circumstances of great pomp and show; such as the consecration of the water; the presence of sponsors, who answer the interrogatories, and make the renunciation, in the name of the child; exorcisms, exsufflations, crossings, the use of salt, spittle, and oil. Before the baptism, the water is consecrated with much solemn parade. First, the priest makes an exorcism; breathing three times into the water in the figure of a cross, and saying, "I adjure thee, O creature of water!" Then he divides the water after the manner of a cross, and makes three or four crossings. Next, he takes a horn of oil, and pours it three times upon the water in the form of a cross, and makes a prayer, that the font may be sanctified, and the Eternal Trinity be present; saying, "Descend from heaven, and sanctify this water, and give grace and virtue, that he who is baptized according to the command of Thy Christ, may be crucified, and die, and be buried, and rise again, with Him."

5. The Lord's Supper—Closed Versus Open Communion

Early Baptists also struggled with the meaning of the Lord's Supper, some holding it to be a means of grace while others adopted the Zwinglian position that it is a symbolic ordinance. Many Baptist congregations in rural England had closed Communion, restricting the Lord's Supper to those believers in the local church; others were more inclusive. *An Orthodox Creed* (1678–1679) illustrates the belief in closed Communion (Selection A). In contrast, some London churches permitted non-Baptists to participate in the ordinance. John Bunyan (1628–1688), a Baptist minister in Bedford, advocated open Communion and denounced those who would exclude other Christians from the Lord's Supper (Selection B). *Sources:* A. *An Orthodox Creed: as A Protestant Confession of Faith; Being an Essay to Unite, and Confirm All True Protestants in the Fundamental Articles of the Christian Religion, Against the Errors and Heresies of the Church of Rome* (London: n.p., 1679). B. John Bunyan, *Differences in Judgement About Water-Baptism, No Bar to Communion* (London: John Wilkins, 1673), pp. 3-4.

[A. Closed Communion]
XXXIII. Article
Of the end and right Administration of the Lord's Supper.

The Supper of the Lord Jesus, was instituted by him the same Night wherein he was betrayed; To be observed in his Church, to the end of the World, for the perpetual Remembrance, and shewing forth the Sacrifice of himself in his Death, and for the Confirmation of the Faithful Believers in all the Benefits of his Death and Resurrection, and Spiritual Nourishment and growth in him; sealing unto them their continuance in the Covenant of Grace, and to be a Band and Pledg of Communion with him, and an Obligation of Obedience to Christ, both passively and actively, as also of our Communion and Union each with other, in the participation of this holy Sacrament. And the outward Elements of Bread and Wine, after they are set apart by the Hand of the Minister, from common Use, and Blessed, or Consecrated, by the Word of God and Prayer, the Bread being broken, and Wine poured forth, signifie to the Faithful, the Body and Blood of Christ, or holdeth forth Christ, and him Crucified; and the Minister distributing the Bread and Wine to the Communicants, who are to take, or receive, both the Bread and Wine at the Hands of the Minister, applying it by Faith, with Thanksgiving to God the Father, for so great a Benefit; and no Unbaptized, Unbelieving, or open Prophane, or wicked Heretical Persons, ought to be admitted to this Ordinance to prophane it.

[B.] Baptism No Bar to Communion

Be intreated to believe me, I had not set pen to paper about this Controversie, had we been let alone at quiet in our Christian Communion. But being assaulted for more than sixteen years; wherein the Brethren of the Baptized-way (as they had their opportunity) have fought to break us in pieces, merely because we are not in their way all baptized first; I could not, I durst not, forbear to do a little, if it might be, to settle the Brethren, and to arm them against the attempts, which also of late they begin to revive upon us. That I deny the Ordinance of Baptism, or that I have placed one piece of an Argument against it, (though they feign it) is quite without colour of truth. All I say, is, That the Church of Christ hath not Warrant to keep out of their Communion the Christian that is discovered to be a visible Saint by the Word, the Christian that walketh according to his Light with God. . . .

I find not (as I told you in my first) that Baptism is a sign to any, but the Person that is baptized. The Church hath her satisfaction of the Person, from better proof, Col. 2.12, Rom. 6.1, 2, 3, 4. I Cor. 15.29. Acts 2.38. & 22.16. I Pet. 3.21.

I told you also, that Baptism makes thee no Member of the Church, neither doth it make thee a visible Saint; it giveth thee, therefore, neither right to, nor being of membership at all.

6. Celebration of the Lord's Supper

Local congregations differed greatly in the administration of holy Communion as they did with baptism. In some cases, the agape meal or love feast (a community supper) preceded the Lord's Supper of bread and wine. One group, reported by the contemporary, D'Asigny, ate a prescribed meal first. In most churches it was the pastoral responsibility to distribute the elements, although in the absence of clergy, deacons could officiate. *Sources:* A. Records of the Broadmead Baptist Church (Hayden Transcript), Book I. B. Edward B. Underhill, ed., *Records of the Churches of Christ Gathered at Fenstanton, Warboys, and Hexham 1644–1720* (London: Haddon Brothers, 1854), p. 37. C. Marius D'Asigny, *Mystery of Anabaptism Unmasked* (London: S. Butler, 1709), p. 227.

[A. Broadmead]

In this year, 1670, our Pastor being deceased, ye Church did not break bread, (until we had another Pastor,) yett kept up our monthly day of Prayer, as we used to doe before breaking of bread. And ye Church, though they had no Pastor, yett they did notwithstanding deale with Members that walked Irregular in their conversations; and they cast out some from amongst them, and Received in others to be members with them. Thus, having Ruling Elders by them they carried on and managed ye *Church-Power,* and kept up all their meetings duly, only forbore *Breaking of Bread,* that holy Ordinance, till they had a Pastor, whose proper worke it is to Administer ye same.

[B. Fenstanton]

On the 1st day of the eleventh month, there was a general meeting holden at Cambridge, where the elders and brethren being assembled, was taken into consideration the difference between brother Gray, an elder, and the congregation: viz. about breaking of bread after supper. And for the finding out of a way for the reconciliation of that difference, much debate there was: but at length, after much discourse and consideration of the example of Christ, Luke xxii. 19, 20, and the words of the apostle Paul, 1 Cor. ii. 24,25, it was generally concluded from the rule of scripture, that we ought always to break bread after supper, and it was likewise ordered that breaking of bread shall be practised in that manner, viz. after supper, throughout the congregations. It was also concluded, that brother Gray had done amiss in proceeding so rashly as to reprove and labour to excommunicate some for the observing of it, and accordingly a letter was drawn up and sent by the hands of Thomas Pratt and Thomas Waller, to blame and reprove him for his temerity, and to desire him to yield unto that which the congregation had agreed upon from the rules of scripture.

[C. Whitechapel]

"Seventhly, Legs of Mutton Baptists, so named, because at the celebration of the Lord's Supper, as they pretend, they sit down at table, and feast themselves with legs of mutton and other meats at the time of breaking the bread, and distributing the wine." [D'Asigny] adds, however, "I can hear but of one congregation of them, in Lambert Street, near Whitechapel."

7. Laying on of Hands

Several congregations, especially General Baptists, took literally the advice of the epistle to Hebrews in prescribing the ordinance of laying on of hands as a sign of the coming of the Holy Spirit to individual Christians. Thomas Grantham (1634–1692), the able polemicist of the General Baptists and pastor at Norwich, Yarmouth and Kings Lynn, defended the practice; John Gosnold (1625–1678), a Cambridge graduate who founded a Baptist church at St. Paul's Alley, London, during the first Civil War (1642–1646), attacked the rite. *Sources:* A. Thomas Grantham, *The Fourth Principle of Christ's Doctrine Vindicated: Being a Brief Answer to Mr. H. Danvers* (London: n.p., n.d.), p. 33. B. John Gosnold, *A Discourse Concerning Laying On Of Hands* (London: M. Fabian, 1701), p. 33.

[A. Thomas Grantham]

To conclude, as we ought not to be Ignorant of the gifts of the Spirit so neither of the meanes ordain'd of God to obtain these gifts; The primative Churches herein our best guides as the word directs, and 'tis well known (and I think granted on all hands) that they used the holy Ordinance of Solemn Prayer and Imposition of hands, for obtaining the promised Spirit, at least with respect to these gifts. Now be it so (though I say for the graces also, 2 Tim. I.6.7.) then seeing these gifts are promised to us as well as unto them, and are attainable, and in part attained by many, what should hinder the Churches but that now they should tread in this path with Faith and full assurance that a Blessing is in it? As in holy Baptism we are placed (as it were) among those whose sins are washed away in the Blood of the Lamb. So in this holy Ordinance of Prayer, and Imposition of Hands, we are in a solemn manner ushered into the Promise of the Holy Spirit. And as the pardon of our sins signified in Baptism, doth not prevent, but better capacitate us to Pray daily, *Forgive us our Trespasses.* So the Prayer of Gods Ministers, with the Imposition of Hands,, doth put us into a better capacity to seek daily for the gifts and graces of the Spirit, because now solemnly admitted to the gracious obtaining of the Promise, in that very way wherein the primative Saints were admitted thereunto, Acts 8. 15,17. Acts 19, 2.6. 2 Tim. 1. 6,7. Heb. 6. 1,2.

Who, when they were come down, Prayed for them that they might receive the Holy Ghost, then laid they their hands on them, and they received the Holy Ghost.

Wherefore, I put thee in remembrance, that thou stir up the Gift of God which is in thee, by the putting on of my hands.

[B. John Gosnold]

Certainly this hath been a received Principle, we have of late years taken up and must continue to go by, if Christs Disciples; viz. That we must introduce nothing into the Worship of Christ, but what we have an express Word for, from that great Prophet in his New Testament.

See Acts 3. 22, 23. For this very cause we have all along separated from the Bishops, and the Church of *England;* and shall we now return again? God forbid.

Now that which hath not one word of Institution, or Command for it in all the New Testament, is no Ordinance of Christ, but Will-worship, and Superstition. (Superstition signifying something more than appointed.) But this laying on of Hands, on all baptized Persons, hath not one word of Institution, or Command for it in all the New Testament. Therefore, it is no Ordinance of Christ, but Will-worship and Superstition.

8. Foundations of Ministerial Education

One of the large obstacles that Baptists faced (along with other Nonconformists) was provision of adequate ministers for the congregations. At first, ministers in the Independent tradition simply converted to Baptist principles; in later generations, there was no consistent or recognized process for training candidates. Church leaders came to realize that Baptists needed a distinct educational identity and provided endowments for the education of pastors. The first such trust was Edward Terrell's (1634–1684) bequest to the Broadmead Church in 1679. The terms of his legacy, quoted below, influenced all of early English and American Baptist educational efforts. *Source: The Bristol Charities, Faithfully Copied from the Report of the Commissioners for Inquiry, Concerning Charities in England and Wales* (Bristol: T. J. Manchee, 1831), p. 275.

. . . all the residue of the yearly rents and profits of all the said hereditaments and premises (except aforesaid), should be for the use and subsistence of a holy learned man, well skilled in the tongues, to wit, Greek and Hebrew, and should profess and practice the truth of believers' baptism, as a pastor or teacher to the congregation aforesaid, and so to another after his death, successively, for ever; and that if it should happen that if any of the young students for the ministry, under the Baptist denomination, should be so poor, that himself, or any of his relations during such study, should be unable to maintain him in food, that such young student, or his assigns, should have the sum of 10 £ paid to him for his maintenance for one year, out of the rents and profits of the said premises, and so from that 10 £ yearly rent for that use, 10 £ more for another student the second year, and so on to the third and forth years. . . .

9. Bristol Baptist Academy

In the next century as the vision of Edward Terrell became Bristol Academy, the Bristol Education Society was formed in 1770. Often an intense opposition to formal education made it difficult to cultivate support, but the Bristol group persevered. To their credit, many English, Welsh, and American Baptist clergymen received a high quality, classical education at the Academy. *Source: An Account of the Bristol Education Society Began Anno 1770* (Bristol: W. Pine, 1770), pp. x-xi.

The importance of a liberal education, more especially to candidates for the Christian ministry, is so exceedingly obvious that we might almost think it impossible that any moderately intelligent person should not be convinced of it. Yet there are, it is well known, some very worthy people, who, from a mistaken view of things, not only call in question the importance of such an education, but even seem to imagine it is rather prejudicial than useful. . . .

It has been suggested, by some, that *learning* is designed to perfect the work of the Spirit of God. But this is meer slander. The only question is, are we to expect miracles, as in the apostolic age, to qualify us for the work of the ministry; or are we to use ordinary means? That we are not to expect miracles all will allow, and if not, then surely we are to use ordinary means. An so far is this from interfering with the work of the Spirit, that it appears to be the only way in which we may reasonably expect his continued influences: and it seems to be rather tempting the Spirit of God, to expect that in an extraordinary, which we are authorized to expect only in an ordinary way. We have already observed that no man can be an acceptable minister of the gospel if he be not a converted man, and furnished with those ministerial gifts or talents, which God alone can communicate; but then is he not to endeavor, in the use of proper means, to improve these talents? . . .

The plan of instruction, at present pursued in this seminary, is as follows.

The students are instructed as far as their capacities and the time allowed them may admit of it, in the following branches of useful knowledge.

I. The English grammar, and the learned languages, so as to enable them to examine any passage of scripture in the original.

II. Logic, to assist them in the exercise of their reasoning powers, and to direct them to the best method and order in the arrangement of their thoughts.

III. Oratory, to acquaint them with the various powers of language and pronunciation, and to enable them to express their thoughts in the most suitable language, and to deliver them in the most striking and acceptable manner.

IV. The elements of geography, astronomy, and natural philosophy in general, to enlarge and elevate their conceptions of the works of God, and his great and glorious persections.

V. Moral Philosophy, the evidences of Christianity, Jewish antiquities, chronology, Ecclesiastical History, and a system of divinity, to improve their morals, establish their faith, and enable them to instruct others by doctrine and example.

Baptist Polity—The Life
of the Congregation

The early Baptist churches emerged in seventeenth-century England as autonomous units. Each church had an ordained leader (minister, pastor, or teacher) and deacons elected by the members. Some churches also had elders while others appointed messengers to organize new churches or minister to those churches lacking a leader. Each church disciplined its own members, using a variety of practices, and each congregation kept its own records of membership and discipline.

Congregational autonomy also resulted in a variety of worship patterns. Gradually the Particular Baptists began to form loosely organized regional and urban associations so as to put forth a common confession; soon the General Baptists followed suit. Eventually all but the Seventh Day Baptists followed this trend. With the formation of regional and national associations came more uniformity of polity, offices, praxis, and creed.

1. Congregational Autonomy

Thomas Helwys (1556–1616), author of what is probably the earliest English Baptist confession of faith, borrowed much from his association with John Smyth, English Separatism, and the Dutch Mennonite community. The confession, written in 1611, strongly asserts the congregational autonomy of the believers' church traditions and thus became a vivid expression for the first Baptist church on English soil, founded at Spitalfields in 1612. *Source: A Declaration of Faith of English People Remaining at Amsterdam in Holland* (Amsterdam: n.p., 1611).

10.

That the church off CHRIST is a company off faithful people I Cor.

1.2. Eph. I.I. seperated frō the world by the word & Spirit off GOD. 2 Cor. 6, 17. being knit unto the LORD & one unto another, by Baptisme. I Cor. 12.13. upon their owne confessiō of the faith. Act. 8.37. and sinnes. Mat. 3.6.

11.

That though in respect off CHRIST, the Church bee one, Ephes. 4.4. yet it consisteth off divers particuler congregacions, even so manie as there shallbee in the World, every off which congregacion, though they be but two or three, have CHRIST given them, with all the meanes off their salvacion. Mat. 18.20. Roman, 8.32. I. Corin. 3.22. Are the Bodie off CHRIST I. Cor. 12.27. and a whole Church I. Cor. 14.23. And therefore may, and ought, when they are come together, to Pray, Prophecie, breake bread, and administer in all the holy ordinances, although as yet they have no Officers, or that their Officers should bee in Prison, sick, or by anie other meanes hindered from the Church. I: Pet. 4.10 & 2.5.

12.

That as one congregacion hath CHRIST, so hath all, 2. Cor. 10.7. And that the Word off GOD cometh not out from anie one, neither to anie one congregacion in particular. I. Cor. 14.36. But unto everie particuler Church, as it doth unto al the world. Coll. 1.5.6. And therefore no church ought to challeng anie prerogative over anie other.

13.

That everie Church is to receive in all their members by Baptisme upon the Confession off their faith and sinnes wrought by the preaching off the Gospel, according to the primitive Institucion. Mat. 28.19. And practice, Act. 2.41. And therefore Churches constituted after anie other manner, or off anie other persons are not according to CHRISTS Testament.

2. The Catholic Church—Visible and Invisible

At the same time that English Baptists stressed the autonomy of local congregations, most were also aware of the broader, believer's church universal. Baptists had much in common with other Nonconformists, especially in times of intensified persecution, and often the Baptist community responded to political and social difficulties in concert with other Protestant groups. *An Orthodox Creed* (1678-79), from which the following excerpt was taken, represented an attempt of both Particular and General Baptists to agree with each other and thus broaden their support with other Nonconformists. *Source: An Orthodox Creed* (London: n.p., 1679), pp. 40-41.

XXIX. ARTICLE
Of the Invisible Catholick Church of Christ.

There is one holy Catholick church, consisting of, or made up of the whole number of the Elect; that have been, are, or shall be gathered, in one Body under Christ, the only Head thereof. Which Church is gathered by Special Grace, and the Powerful and Internal Work of the Spirit; and are effectually united unto Christ their Head, and can never fall away.

XXX. ARTICLE
Of the Catholick Church as Visible.

Nevertheless, we believe the Visible Church of Christ on Earth, is made up of several distinct Congregations, which make up that one Catholick Church, or Mystical Body of Christ. And the Marks by which She is known to be the true Spouse of Christ, are these, viz. Where the Word of God is rightly Preached, and the Sacraments truly Administered, according to Christ's Institution, and the Practice of the Primitive Church: having Discipline and Government duly Executed, by Ministers or Pastours of God's Appointing, and the Church's Election, that is a true constituted Church: to which Church [and not elsewhere] all Persons that seek for Eternal life, should gladly joyn themselves. And although there may be many Errors in such a Visible Church or Congregations, they being not Infallible, yet those Errors being not Fundamental, and the Church in the *major,* or Governing part, being not Guilty, she is not thereby unchurched; nevertheless She ought to detect those Errors, and to Reform, according to God's holy Word, and from which Visible Church or Congregations, no Man ought by any pretence whatever, schismatically to separate.

3. Clandestine Conventicles (1669)

Although the Baptists had open meetings in churches or halls during the Puritan Revolution (1640–1660), after the return of Charles II they were forced underground by harsh parliamentary enactments. The following selection, dating from 1669, demonstrates how the Baptists of a rural Midland county continued to meet in their homes. The clerical returns, though biased against the Baptists, also reveal much about the socioeconomic status of the persecuted. *Source:* Quoted in William T. Whitley, ed., *The Church Books of Ford or Cuddington* (Chardon: Kingsgate Press, 1912), pp. viii–ix.

Drayton Beauchamp. At the house of Robert Clarke, husbandman; inconsiderable in number; heads and teachers, Steven Dagnall of Aylesbury, and William Emerton of "Awbry Monke."

Bledlow. Twenty met in the house of Edward Stevens, taught by John Sullins, a maker of lace; these were Seventh-day Baptists: tenn others, mostly silly women, met in the house of Daniel Baldwin, fuller.

Dinton. Twenty or thirty very indigent people met at the house or yard of William Bate, labourer; Clement Hunt of Upton was their teacher.

Bierton. Thirty inconsiderable people met in the house of Anthony Darvall, maltster; taught by him, Thomas Monk and Steven Dagnal[l].

Horton (near Cheddington?). Fifty mean antipadeo-baptists at the house of John Lane, taught by Thomas Hall, maltster, and Edmond Beard, shoemaker; all three excommunicated.

Ivinghoe. At the house of George Catherall, a person of good estate, taught by Thomas Monk and [Nehemiah] Neyle of Friesdan.

Wingrave. Middle and meaner sort of people, taught by Stephen Dagnall and William Smart.

Wycombe magne "a holy towne." Numbers very great, and the persons very insolent; met at the house of Richard Harding, baker; taught by mechanics.

4. Public Meetings in London

In London, Baptists were also compelled by the repressive acts of the Cavalier Parliament to meet clandestinely. However, because the Great Fire of London in 1666 destroyed many churches and because the blame was fixed upon the Roman Catholics, many Londoners turned to the Nonconformist meeting places, and these in turn became open and remained so for several years, as the following selection relates. The effects of this liberty were geographically far-reaching. *Source:* Records of the Broadmead Baptist Church (Hayden Transcript), Book I.

On ye 3d day of ye 7th Month, 1666, began that dreadful fire of London (ye *Metropolis* of England), and consumed ye greatest parte of that Citty, By ye wicked hands of that blood thirsty people called *Papist,* (as afterwards it was discovered) By which means, for want of Publique places called Churches, they being burnte down, ye People mett in Great Aboundance to hear our friends, called Nonconformist; and soe their *Meetings* became very Publique, and have remained soe Ever since in *London,* about these 10 years. And because ye Separates in London had liberty many partes of this Nation were Influenced therby, that we had alsoe liberty for about four years after in some good Measure, through ye Lord's goodnesse in fulfilling ye Scriptures and promises to us.

5. Elements of Divine Worship

John Smyth, the Se-Baptist, influenced several generations of Baptists in England and America, particularly in the areas of church government and worship. Smyth was guided by the principles of simplicity and spontaneity, and he viewed worship as an act of spiritual communion in the presence of God. The following selection illustrates his understanding of the purpose of Divine worship. *Source:* John Smyth, *Differences of the Churches of the Separation* (n.p., 1608), pp. 20-21.

To conclude: as it followeth not the seeing prayers were read in the old testament as prayers, therfor wee may read prayers now: for prayers no more doth it follow that though in the old testament they read Psalmes & prophecies, we may doe so now: namely, in the tyme of worship, or as parts, or helps of Spiritual worship, properly so called.

Therfor as the auncient brethren of the Seperation have taken all books from before the eye in tyme of prayer, so doe wee take all bookes from the eye in tyme of prophesying & singing; & that by the same reason they being al equally excellent parts of Spiritual worship, for God is asmuch honoured inprophesying & Psalmes, as in praying & they all of them remayne in the triumphant Church in heaven: even as they were all practised by Adam in Paradise before his fal: & therfor are properly moral, & Spiritual worship.

6. Congregational Singing

Congregational autonomy in matters of worship sometimes produced conflicts in practice. Well into the eighteenth century many English Baptists were unsure about singing. Among the General Baptists, the General Assembly discouraged the Warbleton Congregation from continuing the practice. At the same time, the noted Particular Baptist, John Gill, defended singing as a gospel ordinance for both men and women believers. *Sources:* A. Records of the General Assembly of General Baptists, Book I, p. 18. B. John Gill, *A Discourse on Singing of Psalms as a Part of Divine Worship* (London: n.p., 1734), pp. 18-23.

[A. Discouragement of Singing]

There are some Churches among the General Baptists, that are fallen into ye way of Singing, Psalms of David, or other Mens Composures with tuneable Notes, & a mixed Multitude; wch way of Singing appears to us wholly unwarrantable from the Word of God; Now Brethren, you as we are informed do admit of such to become as Members with you; by wch., whether you approve of their Way of Singing, or whether you disapprove, & use any Means to bring them off from it, or whether you look on it as a Thing indifferent, we cannot tell, but think one End of your assembling together is to watch against Innovations, wch. do easily find a Way into the Churches of Christ; and wn. one if admitted it makes Way for another, till at last we know not where to have an end. Therefore we desire, Brethren, that God will give you Wisdom to act in all such Cases as may equally tend to ye maintaining of Truth & the Preserving of Peace; that you may appear to be for the Defence of the Gospel of our Lord & Saviour Jesus Christ, to the Glory of God the Father.

[B. Singing as a Gospel Ordinance]

To consider the subject matter of singing, or what that is which is to be sung. The direction of the Apostle *Paul* in this case, is certainly to be regarded, who, in two distinct epistles, exhorts to the singing of *psalms, hymns,* and *Spiritual songs*; and what these are, it will be proper to enquire. . . .

1. By psalms, is meant the book of *psalms,* composed by *David, Asaph, Heman,* and others, under the inspiration of the Spirit of God; which is the only sense in which this word is used throughout the whole New Testament. . . .

2. By *hymns,* we are to understand, not such as are composed by good men, without the inspiration of the Spirit of God. I observe indeed, from ancient writers, and from ecclesiastical history, that such compositions were made use of very early, even from the times of the Apostles; and I deny not but that they may now be useful; tho' a great deal of care should be taken that they be agreeable to the sacred writings, and the analogy of faith, and that they be expressed, as much as can be, in scripture language; yet, after all, I must confess, that I cannot but judge them, in a good measure, unnecessary, since we are so well provided with a book of psalms and scriptural songs, indited by the Spirit of God, and suitable on all occasions. . . .

3. By *spiritual songs,* may be meant the same psalms of *David, Asaph,* &cc. the titles of some of which, are, *songs,* as sometimes a *psalm* and *song,* a *song* and *psalm,* a *song of degrees,* and the like; together with all other scriptural songs, written by men inspired by God, and are called *spiritual,* because the author of them is the Spirit of God, the writers of them men moved and acted by the same Spirit;

and subject matter of them spiritual, designed for spiritual edification, and opposed to all profane, loose and wanton songs.

7. Offices in the Greater Church Life

With other Independents, Baptists rejected episcopacy and grounded their leadership firmly in the local congregation. With Christ as the head of the church, each congregation elected a pastor, deacons, and, in some cases, ruling elders. As congregations grew in numbers and needs became more complex, regional assemblies approved messengers or traveling pastors. General Baptists (a more connectional group) appear to have developed the office of messenger more extensively than Particular Baptists, although both branches were careful to clarify and limit the functions of messengers. There is no record of women serving as messengers or pastors; however, they frequently served as deaconesses.

Sources: A. *An Orthodox Creed: Or, A Protestant Confession of Faith* (London: n.p., 1674), pp. 42-44. B. "A Book Containing a Record of The Acts of a Congregation of Christ in and About Bedford" (1671), p. 51. Records of the Bunyan Meeting, Bedford. C. Thomas Grantham, *The Successors of the Apostles or A Discourse of the Office of Messengers* (London: n.p., 1674), pp. 3, 17-18. D. Records of the Broadmead Baptist Church (Hayden Transcript), Book I.

[A. Of Officers in the Church of Christ]

The Visible Church of Christ, being compleatly Gathered and Organized, according to the Mind of Christ, consists of Officers and Members; and the Officers (appointed by Christ) to be chosen by his Church, for the peculiar Administration of Ordinances, and Execution of the power and Duty Christ hath injoyned them to the end of the World; Are these three, (viz.) *Bishops (k), (or Messengers), and Elders (l), (or Pastours), and Deacons (m), (or Overseers of the Poor): and the Way appointed by Christ, for the calling of any Person fitted and gifted by the Holy Ghost, unto the Office of Bishop, or Messenger, in the Churches is, (viz.) That he be chosen thereunto by the common suffrage of the Church (n), and solemnly set apart by Fasting and Prayer, with Imposition of Hands, by the Bishops of the same Function, ordinarily; and those Bishops so Ordained, have the Government of those Churches that had Suffrage in their Election (o), and no other ordinarily; as also to (o) preach the Word, or Gospel, to the World, (or Unbelievers) (p). And the particular Church; and he may not ministerially act in any other church before he be sent (r), neither ought his Power, or Office of his Bishop (*), God being a God of Order (s), having ordained things most harmoniously tending every way to Unity 11. The Deacons are in like manner to be chosen by Election and

Ordination, and are in their particular Congregations, to receive the charity and free Benevolence of the People (t): and the Bishops and Elders so Chosen, and Ordained, to the Work of God (u), ought to be enabled and capacitated thereunto, by a sufficient and honourable Maintenance (w) of the People that chose them, answerable to the dignity of their Places* and charge committed to them, without which they cannot discharge their Duty (As they ought to do) in studying to divide the Word of God aright, as St. Paul adviseth *Timothy,* and also to give themselves wholly to it (x); and this Maintenance is to be given out of the Labours, Profits, and Estates of the People, by Equality, and proportionable to their Ability, in Liberality, God having reserved a Portion for all his Labourers, out of all the Members worldly Goods, and Possessions.

[B. Selection of John Bunyan as Pastor]
At a full assembly of The Church at Bedford The 20th of the 10th month. After much seeking God by prayer, and sober conference formerly had, the Congregation did at this meeting with joyus consent (signified by Solemn lifting up of their hands) call forth and appoint our bro. John Bunyan to the pastoral office, or eldership; And he accepting there of gave up himself to serve Christ and his church in that charge. . . .

[C. The Office of Messenger]
. . . God hath given to his Church, a Ministry of Messengers or Apostles (though much inferior) yet truly to succeed the first Apostles, in such things as were ordinary and fixed to that office; as first,

1. In respect of Lawfull Power or Authority to preach the Gospell in all places, at all times, to all persons, as occasion and opportunity by God's providence shall be given them Mark 16,15; Math. 28. 19,20.

2. Unwearied dilligence in Teaching and Strengthening both Pastors and Churches (chiefly those which are but newly settled in the faith) in all the Councell of God; And by labouring to protect that which is lacking concerning the faith of any Churches, Act 20.31; Act 19.1 to the 6; 2 Cor. 11.28. 2 Pet. 1.12,13,14,15 Tit. 1.5.

3. In being set for a defence of the Gospell, or Doctrine once delivered, against false Apostles, or such as would introduce false Doctrines; Phil. 1.16,17. 1 Tim. 1.3 and also to strengthen the bands

of Particular Pastours against Usurpers, or such as despise the Ministers of Christ. 3 Ep. John. 5. I Tim 1.17 Gal 4.17,18.

. . . We give them no more Superintendency then *Timothy* and *Titus* had, whose care was for the churches indifferently, so that their preheminence was only a degree of honor (not of power) in being greater Servants than others. . . . And when we say the Messengers are umfixed, in respect of particular societies, our meaning is not thereby to deny, but that for the more convenient management of the great affairs of the gospel, they may divide themselves into diverse parts, and accordingly be called Messengers of such Countries, as with whom they most frequently converse of the gospel. Gal. 2.9.

[D. Women Officers]

Upon ye 2d of ye 5th Month, Ano 1673, by reason of ye age, and then sicknesse, of Brother Simpson, near unto death, not capable to perform ye Deacon's work, and by reason of ye decease of Sister West, ye widdow or Deaconnesse of ye Church, they tooke into Consideration to Elect two other. Wereupon ye said day at our Pastor's house, it being a day of Prayer, ye Congregation Chose Brother Mr. John Ford to be a Deacon, and Sister Murry to be a Widdow or Deaconnesse to ye Church. Thus, being Elected, and sett aparte by Prayer, they are Recommended to ye worke upon Tryall.

8. Preaching Without Ordination

Little is known about Edmund Chillenden (flourished 1656) except that he served in the parliamentary army as lieutenant and then captain, that he participated in the Putney Debates of 1647, and that he favored a nonprofessional ministry, as the following demonstrates. Many early Baptists agreed with Chillenden that a calling and an opportunity constituted the sole requisites of a gospel minister. *Source:* Edmund Chillenden, *Preaching Without Ordination* (London: George Wittington, 1647), pp. 2-3.

You cannot be ignorant, but this is the mayne designe of the Divell to hinder the propagation of the Gospel by preaching, because he knowes by the power thereof, Christs Kingdome is advanced and inlarged, and I am very confident that the maine reason that hath impeded and obstructed the Parliaments just proceedings, and that the people in many parts of this Kingdome are so ill-affected, is because they have not had the Lord Jesus Christ held forth to them in the preaching of the Gospel, for I have observed in my travills, since God called me into this Army, that in many of the Counties of England, there is not one Parish of tenn that hath one of your ordained men that is able to preach Christ, these things generally I have taken notice of, that where any of them are, they are either Drunkards, uncleane persons, dumb Idoles, or at the best cruel Malignants that have ever been opposite to the glory of God, the Parliaments just proceedings, so that the Proverb in the Prophet is made true; like Priest, like people.

9. The Ordained Ministry

It would appear that most congregations desired an ecclesiatically recognized, if not educated, ministry. By 1660 ordination was an accepted and widespread practice among both General and Particular churches. Predictably, the question of ministerial support arose in regional discussions; the Abingdon Association (Particular) offered advice. *Sources:* A. Edward B. Underhill, ed., *Records of the Church of Christ at Warboys* (London: Haddon Brothers, 1854), p. 272. B. "A Brief Confession or Declaration of Faith." Copy in Angus Library, Regents Park College, Oxford. C. Records of the Abingdon Association, 11 January 1656. Angus Library, Regents Park College, Oxford.

[A. Warboys, 1655]

Some added to the church. A choice of elders and deacons was made by the brethren here. Two elders were chosen, viz.: William Dunn and Thomas Chapman; and two deacons were chosen, viz.: Richard Hawkins and John Stokley. And these elders and deacons were ordained by laying on of hands, by John Denn and Edmond Mayle, elders and overseers of Stanton, who were appointed to do it by a council at Cambridge. John Kitson, who differed from the church, was again reconciled unto them. The order of lovefeast agreed upon, to be before the Lord's supper; because the ancient churches did practise it, and for unity with other churches near to us.

[B. General Baptist Confession, 1660]

That such who first orderly comes into, and are brought up in the School of Christs Church, and waiting there, comes to degrees of Christianity, rightly qualified, and considerably gifted by Gods Spirit; Ought to exercise their gifts not only in the Church but also (as occasion serves) to preach to the World (they being approved of by the Church so to do) Acts II: 22,23,24. Acts II. 19,20. and that among such some are to be chosen by the Church, and ordained by Fasting, Prayer, and Laying on of Hands, for the work of the Ministry, Acts 13. 2,3. Acts

1. 23. Such so ordained, (and abiding faithful in their work) we own as Ministers of the Gospel; but all such who come not first to repent of their sins, believe on the Lord Jesus, and so "Baptized" in his name for the remission of Sins, but are only brought up in the Schools of humane learning, to the attaining humane arts, and variety of languages, with many vain curiosities of speech, I Cor. I, 19, 21. 2.1,4,5. seeking rather the gain of large revenues, then the gain of souls to God: such (we say) we utterly deny, being such as have need rather to be taught themselves, than fit to teach others. Rom. 2.21.

[C. Ministerial Support, 1656]

iii. The true ministers of Jesus Christ are to be supported, as touching their outward subsistence, not by tithes, nor by any inforced maintenance but, as they shall be found worthy and as it shall be found [nee]dfull and convenient and the saints shall be enabled thereunto, [by] the voluntarie contribution of those that are instructed by them, Gal. 6.6.

10. Congregational Discipline

The extant minute books of congregational meetings are replete with cases of discipline. Most of the censors were male, it is interesting to note, while most of the censured were females. Three degrees of discipline prevailed: (1) admonition; (2) censure; and (3) excommunication. Clergy and laity alike were involved in disciplinary procedures. *Sources:* A. William T. Whitley, ed., *The Church Book of Cuddington or Ford* (London: Kingsgate Press, 1912), p. 8. B. Edward B. Underhill, ed., *Records of the Church of Christ at Caxton Pastures and Fenstantan* (London: Haddon Brothers, 1854), p. 8. C. Records of the Bunyan Meeting, Bedford, 1669, p. 28.

[A. Admonition and Censure]
Att the Church meeting held at Kimblewick June 4th 1690.

It is hereat agreed that sister Wildman (Under dealings & Church Censures for former sins of a very bad nature) uppon her great greife & Repentance & open Confession made and appearing to the Church be Restored againe & Received into Christian Communion.

That Rose Stevens (being formerly Charged for severall Grievious sins & haveing had many Admonishions for her appearance to Answer the same or make prove of her Repentance under them) by reason that the same have been manifestly proved against her & that notwithstanding she remains obstinate & impenitent that shee be therefore Excommunicate.

That bro: John Wade be admonished to forbeare partakeing at the table of ye Lord untill the Church hath satisfaccon for some things objected agt him & therefore that he & brother Greene be summoned to be at the next Church meeting by Br: Clarke & br: Jo: Goodchild That Bro: J:o:ny have Admonition tendered him touching some Disorders & be therefore summoned to the next Church meeting & yt b: Ransome & br Delafield pforme the same.

[B. Excommunication]

On the 19th day of the eleventh month (meeting at Fenystanton), John Ofley, and Elizabeth Ofley his wife, of Fenystanton, were excommunicated, 1 Tim. i. 19, (being formerly admonished and reproved according to the rules of scripture), for these ensuing reasons, viz.: – 1st, For forsaking the assembly of the saints; 2ndly, For denying all the ordinances of the Lord, as prayer, preaching, baptism, breaking of bread, &c., adding, moreover, that they were grown to perfection, and they would not follow the example of the apostles, who, as they said, were imperfect creatures; 3rdly, For slighting of the scriptures; 4thly, For saying that all things are God yea, that they are gods; 5thly, For saying that God is the author of all actions, and that the creature is but a mere passive creature; 6thly, For saying that there is no sin; 7thly, For despising and contemning the admonitions of the church; all of which things they did maintain with stubbornness.

John Denne
Edmand Maile
Thomas Coxe

[C. Discipline of Deacons]

The church also having taken notice of the utter neglect of Bro. Covonton and Bro. Wallis in the executing of The Office of a Deacon, where unto they had formerly been appointed; did judge them unworthy of that honourable imployment, and divest them of all authority and trust of that nature committed to them formerly.

11. Associational Life

In 1644 the Baptist congregations of London combined to promulgate a common confession. During the Protectorate of Oliver Cromwell (1653–1658) many congregations gathered together in regional associations and larger organizations known as General

Assemblies. The General Baptists held their first Assembly in 1654, the Particular Baptists in 1689. Associational participation promoted a sense of connectedness and offered congregations the advantage of conciliar advice on a variety of subjects. After 1700, interest in the Assemblies waned, and countywide associations evolved as the principal structures beyond the local churches. The selections that follow depict the range of interests of associational life. *Sources:* A. William T. Whitley, ed., *Minutes of the General Assembly of General Baptist Churches in England* (1698), (London: Kingsgate Press, 1909), p. 15. B. *Minutes of the General Assembly of Particular Baptists* (1689), Book I, p. 12. Angus Library, Regents Park College, Oxford. C. *Circular Letters and Breviates of the Midland Association for 1795, 1797,* pp. 14, 7.

[A. General Assembly of General Baptists, 1698]

Att a Genll. Assembly of Messengers Elders and Brethren mett together in the 15th Day of the 4th month Anno 1698.

An Address from the Western Association being read and the particulars therein being largely & Deliberately Debated.

It is Agreed by this Assembly that all the Churches of our Comunion do carefully keep and observe the Agreemt made the 14th of May Anno 1668 touching mixt marriage and for any to pceed therefrom is Disorderly.

It is Agreed that a Gifted Disciple as such may not Exercise his Gift in the Ministry of the Word abroad out of the Church whereof he is a Member without he be sent by the Church (Except in Cases of Journeying abroad) And we do desire and Advice all the Churches of Christ that relates to be very Carefull therein and not to permit thereof.

It is Agreed that the Members of the Churches of our Comunion may not joyn in the worship of God with those that are not And we do Advise all Members of the Severall Churches of our Comunion to keep themselves pure in the Seperacon and if any shall transgress therein wee advise the Churches unto whom they belong Carefully and Speedily to Admonish them of the Evill and danger that do attend it.

We do Judge it very Expediant for preventing of Scandall and Reproach that when there is a Marriage Intended between any Members of our Churches That publick notice thereof be given in the Church Meeting sometime before it be Solempnized.

These Questions being put whether Sound Doctrine or Erra viz: Whether the father or Distinct or Seperate from the Word and the Holy Host is the Most High God.

That our Lord Jesus Christ is a God only by Deputation as Magistrates and Judges are.

That the Body of our Lord Jesus Christ Consisting of flesh blood and bones is not of the same substances as ours (to Wit) Mankind.

In Answer thereunto

The Assembly being called over It is by all the Members thereof declared that the Sd 3 prticulars last above Mentioned and each one of them to be Error.

[B. General Assembly of Particular Baptists, 1689]

[In 1689, the assembly resolved to create a fund to maintain and support a regular ministry. Editor]

1. To communicate thereof to those churches that are not able to maintain their own ministry; and that their ministers may be encouraged wholly to devote themselves to the great work of preaching the gospel.

2. To send ministers that are ordained, or at least solemnly called, to preach both in city and country, where the gospel hath, or hath not yet been preached, and to visit the churches; and these to be chosen out of the churches in London, or the country, which ministers are to be approved of, and sent forth by two churches at the least; but more if it may be.

3. To assist those members that shall be found in any of the aforesaid churches that are disposed for study, have an inviting gift, and are found in fundamentals, in attaining to the knowledge and understanding of the languages, *Latin, Greek,* and *Hebrew* . . . [also]

Whether it be not expedient for churches that live near together, and consist of small numbers, and are not able to maintain their own ministry, to join together, for the better and more comfortable support of their ministry, and better edification of one another? Which was unanimously agreed to, and concluded in the affirmative.

[C. Midland Association, 1795]

Resolved That the Mission Society, formed by our brethren at Kettering, is worthy the encouragment of all our sister Churches, and that its support be particularly recommended to the Churches of this Association.

That *Monday* the 6th of *July,* be observed as a day of fasting and prayer, on account of the distresses of our country, and the circumstances of religion among us.

[1797]

Agreed, that in future the Pastor of the Church where the Association is held, be confirmed as Moderator for that year.

A question was proposed, Whether the title of *Reverend,* applied indiscriminately to preachers of the gospel of whatever age, talents, or reputation, be consistent in itself; or whether the application of that title to any man on account of his ministerial character, be warranted by the New Testament?

After a free discussion, the brethren present individually replied in the *negative*; and the ministers agreed from this time to renounce it in their intercourse with each other.

This was followed by another query—Do the precepts of the gospel enjoin, or the nature of the ministerial office require the observance of a peculiar and *distinctive habit,* either as to colour or form?

This also was with equal unanimity answered in the negative. . . .

Agreed that the institution of SUNDAY SCHOOLS appears to this association as a happy mean, which Providence has put into our hands, of discussing religious knowledge and happiness among the poor; and which it is the duty of the respective congregations to adopt, since much good may be accomplished thereby at a trivial expence.

John Bunyan Meetinghouse, built 1707

*William Carey Home, 1789-1793,
Leicester, England*

Piety and the Christian Life

The early English Baptists were biblicists: they looked to the Bible as the final and only authoritative guide to faith and practice. They rejected tradition, the primacy of Rome, and Anglican inventions; they also down-played the teachings of the church fathers. Instead, they looked back to the primitive church for inspiration: the life of Christ, John the Baptist, the Gospels and the Pauline Epistles, and the Apostolic Era. In their view the New Testament said nothing about an episcopal hierarchy with its center in Rome, nothing about institutionalized asceticism, and nothing about church councils or canon law. Rather, in the New Testament they found a sense of Christian community, the example of Jesus Christ, and Pauline dogma. These became their models for both individual and social behavior.

1. Holy Scripture: Guide to Faith and Practice

The authority of Scripture was noted everywhere in Baptist life. Theological and ecclesiastical pronouncements were made with supportive biblical texts; functions and ordinances were carried out according to primitive and apostolic examples; and the individual Christian life was predicated upon New Testament precepts. Selection A illustrates the recognized confessional preeminence of Scripture while B illustrates the use of the Bible in identifying "visible believers." *Sources:* A. *A Confession of Faith Put Forth by the Elders and Brethren of Many Congregations of Christians (Baptized upon Profession of Their Faith) in Freedom and the Country* (London: Benjamin Harris, 1677). B. Records of the Abingdon Association, 11 January 1656. Angus Library, Regents Park College, Oxford.

[A. The London Confession, 1677]

Chap. I

Of the Holy Scriptures

The Holy Scripture is the only sufficient, certain, and infallible (a) rule of all saving Knowledge, Faith, and Obedience; Although the (b) light of Nature, and the works of Creation and Providence do so far manifest the goodness, wisdom and power of God, as to leave men unexcusable; yet are they not sufficient to give that knowledge of God and His will, which is necessary unto Salvation. (c) Therefore it pleased the Lord at sundry times, and in divers manners, to reveal himself, and to declare that His will unto his Church; and afterward for the better preserving, and propagating of the Truth, and for the more sure Establishment and Comfort of the Church against the corruption of the flesh, and the malice of Satan, and of the World, to commit the same wholly unto (d) writing; which maketh the Holy Scriptures to be most necessary, those former ways of Gods revealing his will unto his people being now ceased.

[B. The Marks of a Believer]

. . . a visible believer may be manifestly discerned and known by these two things: his profession or confession of Christ and his practise or conversation; and the agreement betweene both these and their sutablenes to the rules of Scripture in these things following chiefly:

His love to all saints, I Jn. 3.14, Jn. 13.35, Heb. 6.9ff.

His universall obedience to God's commands according to the measure of light received, Ps. 119.6, Jn. 15.14.

His readinesse to lay downe all that he hath for Jesus Christ rather then to sin against him, Rev. 12.11, Acts 15.26, Mat. 10.38f., compared with Lk. 14.26 and 33.

His experimentall declaration of the worke of regeneration and of the worke of faith with power, Jer. 51.10, Ro. 10.9f., Ps. 145.6f., 10f., 66.16.

By these distinguishing characters appearing in visible effects as occasion and opportunitie is offered the children of God may be and are visibly manifested and differenced from others.

2. Women in the Churches

The role of women in the early Baptist churches tended to be passive and submissive to male leadership. The membership rolls reveal large numbers of women in the early congregations (sometimes over 50 percent), and some churches elected female deacons.

Although the records show men serving as pastors, elders, messengers, and teachers, they often depict women as the victims of reproof, especially in mixed marriages. Yet some remarkable women emerge from the male-dominated milieu, as the following selections from church records and Thomas Grantham's *Fourth Principle* illustrate. *Sources:* A. Records of the Broadmead Church (Hayden Transcript), Book I. B. *Ibid.* C. Grantham, *The Fourth Principle*, p. 34.

[A. The Piety of Mrs. Kelly]

Now at this, Mr. Kelly being some years deceased, his Widdow persevered in godlinesse; and it might be said of her as of Ruth iii, 11 *(all the Citty did know her to be a vertuous woman)*. She was like a hee-goat before ye flock; for in those dayes, Mrs. Kelly was very famous for Piety and reformation, well knowne to all, bearing a liveing testimony against ye Supersititions and traditions of those dayes, and she would not observe their invented times and feasts, called Holy days. Att which time she kept a Grocer's shop in High-street, between ye Guilders Inn and ye High Crosse, where she would keep open her shop on ye time they called Christmas day, and sit sewing in her shop, as a witnesse for God in ye midst of ye Citty, in ye face of ye Sun, and in ye sight of all men; even in those very dayes of Darknesse, when, as it were, all sortes of People had a reverence of that particular day above all others. And as ye Apostle saith, I Cor. viii. 7, *There was not in every man that knowledge for some, with conscience of the Idoll unto this hour eat it as things offered unto an Idoll, and their Conscience being weak is defiled.* But this gracious Woman (afterwards called Mrs. Hazzard), like a *Deborah* she arose, with strength of holy Resolution in her soul from God, even a Mother in Israell. And soe she proved, because she was ye first woman in this Citty of Bristoll that practized that truth of ye Lord (which was then hated and Odious), namely, *Separation.*

Now ye way that ye Lord tooke to bring her, with some others of ye Professors in this Citty, to Separate from ye World, was this. After thay had (as before rehearsed), been awakened and mett first together to Repeat sermon-notes, then they kept many dayes of Prayer together, as a company of Good people.

[B. The Conversion of Francis, a Blackamore]

And while they thus walked with Mr. Ingello their Teacher, by ye goodness of God they had one *Memorable* member added unto them;

namely, *a Blackymore maide, named Francis,* a servant to one that lived upon ye Back of Bristoll, which thing is somewhat rare in our dayes and Nation, to have an Ethyopian or Blackmore, to be truly Convinced of Sin, and of their lost state without ye Redeemer, and to be truly Converted to ye Lord Jesus Christ, as she was; which, by her profession or declaration at ye time of her reception, together with her Sincere Conversation, she gave greate ground for charity to believe she was truly brought over to Christ; for this poor *Aethiopian's* soule savoured much of God, and she walked very humble and blamelesse in her Conversation to her end. And when she was upon her death-bed, she sent a Remarkable Exhortation unto ye whole Church with whom she walked, as her last request unto them; which argued her holy, child-like fear of ye Lord, and how precious ye Lord was to her soule, as was observed by ye manner of her Expressing it which was this;—one of ye Sisters of ye Congregation coming to visit her in her Sicknesse, she solemnly tooke her leave of her, as to this world, and prayed ye Sister to remember her to ye whole Congregation, and tell them that she did begg every soule, To take heed that they did lett ye *glory of God to be dear unto them.*

[C. Women Officers]

For my part, I am fully satisfied there is sufficient ground in holy Scripture for *Womens* coming to the Table of the Lord, and for the Ordination of Church Officers by Prayer and Laying on of Hands; And I do solemnly profess, to dislike any Principle or practice in Religion, which cannot fairly be demonstrated by the evidence of Holy Scripture; But, yet this I must needs say, That there is as clear (if not clearer) grounds for the Fourth Principle as we hold it, as there is for either of the other points, specially the latter. For first, Womens receiving at the Lords Table, it is gathered by a rational deduction from the Holy Scripture as appears by Mr. D [anvers] wherein he hath done well as others in the same case hath done before him; yet should any man use his own Weapons against him, which he uses against his Brethern, they might worst him because of his inconsistency, though his cause be good.

3. Christian Marriage

Nearly all the Baptist confessions advocated the institution of marriage and disapproved of incestuous, bigamous, and consanguineous unions. Many creeds condemned interfaith or mixed marriages. "It is the duty of Christians to marry in the Lord," according to the *Orthodox Creed* of 1679, "and therefore those that profess the true religion, ought not to marry with infidels, or idolators, nor prophane wicked persons in their life, nor yet with any that maintain damnable heresies." Despite this admonition, the minute books are filled with discipline cases involving mixed marriages. The following selection, dating from 1744, is in the form of a letter written by the chairman of the General Assembly to a local congregation that had appealed a difficult case to the national body. *Source:* Clerk of the General Assembly of the General Baptists in England to the Church of Christ at Bessels Green, 16 May 1744, in Whitley, *Minutes of the General Assembly,* 2, p. 71.

To the Church of Xt Meeting on Bessels Green. Salutation. Beloved in the Lord.

Your case not having been referred to any Sister Churches, nor to any Association, could not come regularly before the Assembly.

I was, at the same time, desired to sattisfie you, that was the cause of its ommission, and not any want of tender respect or Care for your good estate; and also to give you my private thoughts on the affair mentioned in your Letter, which I desire to do with equal humility and Freedom. It is agreed on all hands, that *Mix'd Marriages* are not only inexpedient but dangerous, and some times lead to very bad consequences, and, as Such, are to be prevented as much as may be, by all seasonable advice, watchfulness and Caution. The only difficulty is; how the Church ought to deal with those Members who, after all, marry out of our Fellowship? And here, I must acknowledge there may be circumstances full of aggravation; as when, for instance, a person, thro mere worldly interest, shall marry out of the Church, when there are in it, at the same time, those who, on all other accounts, are equally, if not more deserving. But to make it a general rule, to suspend from Comunion all, without exception; is what I could never find defensible by the Word of God, or the primitive practice. . . .

The severity contended for, especially as to some persons, is a very great hardship. Marriage has its rise and expedients from our nature and constitution. 'Tis Honourable in all: 'Tis better to marry than to be in pain. Now, since among us in this nation the women are not permitted to Look out for themselves; and when they have no offers from among the men of their own Comunity, what must they do? Must they, on pain of Excommunication, refuse every sober, virtuous, Christian-like person merely because he has not happened to be baptized by immersion or profession of faith? Is this consistent with Xitian charity and forbearance?

4. Christian Virtues and Duties

Creedal statements and church covenants were often quite explicit about Christian conduct. Eighteen Particular Baptist churches issued in 1656 the Somerset Creed, which drew specifically upon New Testament language and practices. Violations of the prescribed code could mean admonition and censure. Most likely, the Creed is the work of Thomas Collier, a lay preacher in the West of England. *Source: A Confession of the Faith of Several Churches of Christ, In the County of Somerset and of Some Churches in the Countries Near Adjacent* (London: n.p., 1656).

XXV.

That we believe some of those commandements further to be as followeth.

1. Constancy in prayer, Col. II. 23, 24.
2. Breaking of bread, I Cor. II. 23, 24.
3. Giving of thanks, Ephes. 5. 20.
4. Watching over one another, Heb. 12.15.
5. Caring one for another, I Cor. 12. 25, by visiting one another especially in sickness and temptations. Mat. 25.36.
6. Exhorting one another, Heb. 3.13.
7. Discovering to each other and bearing one another's burdens, Gal. 6.2.
8. Loving one another, Hebrewes 13.1.
9. Reproving when need is one another, Mat. 18.15.
10. Submitting one to another in the Lord, I Pet. 5.5
11. Administering one to another according to the gift received, whether it be in Spirituals, or Temporals, I Pet. 4.10.
12. The Offender to seek reconciliation, as well as the Offended, Mat. 5.23, 24.
13. Love our Enemies and persecutors, and pray for them, Mat. 5.44.
14. Every one to work if he be able, and none to be idle, 2 Thes. 3.10, 11, 12.
15. The women in the church to learn in silence, in all subjection I. Tim. 2.11; I Corinthians 14.37.
16. Private admonition to a brother offending another, and if not prevailing to take one or two more, if he hear not Them; then to tell it

to the Church, and if he hear not them; to be accounted as an heathen and publican, Mat. 18.15.

17. Publick rebuke to publick offenders, I Tim. 5.30. . . .

5. Bunyan on the Holy Life

John Bunyan (1628–1688), the son of a Bedford tinker, became a Baptist preacher and writer during the Restoration era. Though best known for his autobiographical prose (*Pilgrim's Progress* and *Grace Abounding*), he also penned devotional prose for the Baptist laity. Several of his works, including the following selection, were written in prison. The call to a devout life is a recurring theme in Bunyan's works. *Source:* John Bunyan, *A Holy Life, The Beauty of Christianity or An Exhortation to Christians to be Holy* (London: Benj. Alsop, 1684), p. x.

Thus then we must learn to love one another. He that keepeth Gods Commandment, doth to his brother what is right, for that is Gods Commandment. He that keeps Gods Commandments doth to his Brother even as he would be done unto himself, for that is Gods Commandment. He that keeps Gods Commandment shutteth not up his bowels of Compassion from him; for the contrary is his Commandment. Further, He that keepeth Gods Commandment sheweth his Brother what he must do to honour the Christ that he professeth, aright: Therefore he that keeps the Commandment, loves his brother, Yea the keeping of the Commandment is loving the Brethren.

But if all love which we pretend to have one to another, were tryed by this one Text, how much of that that we call so would be found to be nothing less? Preposterous are our Spirits in all things, nor can they be guided right but by the word and spirit of God: the which the good Lord grant unto us plentifully, that we may do that which is well pleasing in his sight through Jesus Christ our Lord. Yea and that there may, by them, be wrought sound repentance in us for all that hath been done by us amiss, lest he give Jacob to the spoil, and Israel to the Robbers; for that they have sinned against him by not walking in his ways, and by not being obedient to his Law.

Let me add, lest God doth not only punish us in the sight, and by the hand of the wicked; but imbolden them to say, it was God that set them on, yea lest they make those sins of ours, which we have not repented of, not only there bye-word against us to after generations, but the argument one to another of their justification for all the evil that they shall be suffered to do unto us: saying, when men shall ask them wherefore hath the Lord done thus unto this Land? What meaneth the heat of this great anger? even because they have forsaken the covenant of the Lord God of their Fathers, and walked not in his ways.

Baptists and the State

The Elizabethan religious settlement represented a compromise devised by prominent lay and clerical leaders who served the Queen. All Englishmen were expected to affirm the Anglican faith and attend their parish churches. Those who refused to conform to the tenets of the Established Church, especially those who criticized church doctrine and practice from the pulpit or in print, were penalized in various ways: fines, ostracism, exile, imprisonment, and even death for extremists. Small wonder that Presbyterian Thomas Cartwright and Separatist Francis Johnson (John Smyth's mentor and friend) emigrated to the Continent with their families and congregations. The Sectaries Act of 1593 prohibited private religious meetings and established stiff penalties for violators, especially Nonconformist leaders. King James I (1603–1625) made it crystal clear during the early months of his reign that he would uphold the Act of Uniformity (1562) and enforce the Sectaries Act. That Nonconformists believed and feared the English sovereign became evident in their increased migration to Holland and America.

Although the Puritan Revolution (1640–1660) offered a measure of relief from severe persecution and a large measure of toleration, the Restoration of Charles II brought renewed conformity with the Conventicle Act and the Five Mile Act, which prohibited religious meetings within five miles of an urban center. The renewed persecution meant imprisonment for Baptist ministers like Bunyan and secret meetings for most congregations. Only after the Glorious Revolution, which brought to the English throne a Dutch Calvinist, did the Baptists enjoy the blessings of toleration. Even then toleration did not give them equality of status. The Church of England remained a privileged institution,

while the Baptists along with Presbyterians and Quakers stood outside
the mainstream of English politics and society.

1. Political Obedience

Often, at the expense of imprisonment and fines, Baptists recognized civil authority.
The Standard Confession adopted by the General Assembly of General Baptists in March,
1660, shortly before the return of Charles II, illustrates this submission to the secular
powers. *Source:* "A Brief Confession or Declaration of Faith." Copy in Angus Library,
Regents Park College, Oxford.

We believe that there ought to be civil Magistrates in all Nations,
"for the punishment of evil doers, and for the praise of them that do
well," I Pet. 2.14. And that all wicked lewdness, and fleshly filthiness,
contrary to just and wholesome (Civil) Laws, ought to be punished
according to the nature of the offences; and this without respect of any
Persons, Religion, or profession whatsoever; and that we and all men
are obliged by Gospel rules, to be subject to the higher Powers, to obey
Magistrates, Tit. 3.1. "and to submit to every Ordinance of man, for
the Lords sake," as saith Peter 2.13. But in case the Civil Powers do,
or shall at any time impose things about matters of Religion, which we
through conscience to God cannot actually obey, then we with Peter
also do say, that we ought (in such cases) to obey God rather than men;
Acts 5.29. and accordingly do hereby declare our whole, and holy
intent and purpose, that (through the help of grace) we will not yield,
nor (in such cases) in the least actually obey them, yet humbly purposing
(in the Lords strength) patiently to suffer whatsoever shall be inflicted
upon us, for our conscionable forbearance.

2. Persecution

The passage of several acts in the Cavalier Parliament (1660–1679) led to renewed
persecution. The legislation was enforced by bishops, sheriffs, and town constables.
Some churches constructed an escape door behind the pulpit for use when such officials
arrived at a session. Selection A shows how the Baptists in Bristol reacted to the
Restoration and the Five Mile Act. Selection B is an account of a Seventh Day Baptist
minister's brushes with the law. Selection C, an appeal by John Bunyan's second wife
for her husband's release from prison, dates from 1661 when Bunyan was arrested and
imprisoned in the Bedford jail for preaching without a license. The dramatic dialogue,
which most scholars feel Bunyan wrote himself, was located in 1740 and published in
post-eighteenth century limited editions of his works. *Sources:* A. Records of the Broadmead Baptist Church (Hayden Transcript), Book I. B. Henry Black, ed., *The Last Legacy*

or the Autobiography and Religious Profession of Joseph Davis, Jr. (London: Mill Yard, 1869), passim. C. *A Relation of the Imprisonment of Mr. John Bunyan, Minister of the Gospel at Bedford, in November 1660* (London: James Buckland, 1745), pp. 11-12.

[A. Secret Meetings in Bristol]

AN°. 1660-But upon ye 29th day of ye 3d month, An°. 1660, when King *Charles* II was brought from his Exile againe into ye *Nation* and to ye Crown, Then Sathan stirred up adversaryes against us, and our *Trouble* or *Persecution* began. And then our friends of ye Presbyterian party were turned out of their Publique Places as well as we. Then those who had preached against us for meeting in Private houses, they were faine to meet in Private houses as we had, and did doe. For then, when our Pastor, or Teacher, Mr. Ewins, was turned out of those Publique places called Nicolas and Christchurch, (then) we first mett every Lord's day at our Pastour's house in ye Castle, and there we continued a long time; but being straitened for roome, we took a large Place or Hall, towards ye end of Broadmead, called ye Fryars, which formerly had been some Chapell; and there we Continued, holding forth ye Gospell of God's Free grace by our Lord Jesus Christ.

And in ye 10 month 1660, Orders come that all above 16 years of age must take ye *Oaths of Allegiance and Supremacy*; which many scrupled to doe, because of ye *Extensiveness* of some words in ye Oath of Allegiance; as the words *Whatsoever* and *otherwise*. Whereupon ye *Brethren* only of our and Brother Hynam's congregation mett together, and discoursed our Judgements, and searched ye Scriptures, concerning our dutie and subjection to Magistrates; in which we all agreed, Concerning *Civill* matters they ought to be reverenced and obeyed . . .

In ye ninth month, 1665, there came a troope of horse to this Citty as reported on purpose to Suppresse ye Meetings; and they were very abusive to those Meetings they found.

In ye 11th month, 1665, by reason of ye Decease of one of ye Deacons, namely, Brother Spurgeon, ye Church choose Brother Wm. Dickason to be a Deacon, assistant with Bro. Simpson and Br. Tho. Rieves.

In this year 1665, we had many disturbances, and divers Imprissoned; but ye Lord helped us through it.

An°. 1666- In ye Beginning of this year, 1666, this Citty of Bristoll was visited with that Judgement of ye Lord, ye Plague, which struck Terror in ye Magistrates; and through ye moderation of Aldm. John

Willoughby, then Mayor, who began a stop to Persecution, by which means ye Lord ordained us much peace, that many this year, were added to ye Church. And there appeared seemingly, a spirit of life *Entering* into ye people not of ye Church, more unanimously resolved for *Meetings* separate from ye worship of ye world, than in some few years past had been. And ye Lord dealt very mercifull and gracious with ye Citty, that ye Plague abated and stopt; being not soe greate as feared and threatened. *Laus Deo*.

[B. Prison Experiences of Joseph Davis]

About the time the king entered London, I was illegally seized by the county-troops, and carried a prisoner seven miles from my habitation and calling, to Burford, and there detained two days, being oftentimes tempted to drink the King's health; but out of conscience I as often refused so vain an action, though it began to be very much the custom of the time.

My second imprisonment was after Venner's unlawful insurrection; when the militia of the county Horse and Foot, . . . came on the seventh day in the evening to our town, and Mr. Hoard, one of the captains of the county-troops, came to my shop, asking my name and demanding arms, rudely made me prisoner for nothing; . . . my house was rifled by his soldiers, who took away my goods feloniously . . . when Lord Lieutenant Faulkland came . . . he tendered me the oath of allegiance, which I did not refuse, and then demanding the good behaviour, the breach of which they interpreted would be going to any separate assembly, for the sake of religious worship. This arbitrary demand I refused indeed and was . . . on Monday sent to Oxford Castle, with others of my honest neighbours, until the Lent Assizes, when no matter being alleged against us, we were privately released by the Lord Lieutenant.

In January the year following, one Worge, a constable, as he said, had verbal order from the Lord Faulkland, to take me up again, and carry me to Oxford, which he did accordingly; and with such a guard, as if I had been a criminal, though without any warrant of commitment, and delivered me a prisoner to the gaoler, where I was detained till the Lent Assizes, and then obtained to be called.

The judge would know what I was committed for; and after I had opened the case to him he replied, "I must not interfere with the Lord

Lieutenant's power"; and so I was remanded back to prison until the Summer Assizes . . . but then, having a more just judge . . . he released me; the Lord Faulkland, my adversary, having before this, been summoned by death, to the great tribunal.

The next spring I was committed to prison by Sir Thomas Pennison, Deputy Lieutenant . . . where I remained about two years, and appearing in Court, where he was present, I told him before the Judge of the Sessions, that the English Laws were tender of men's liberty, and did not countenance the keeping them always, no, for so long in prison, although legal occasion had been given for the "Behaviour" to be required; whereas I had broken no law, nor was charged with the breach of any by my commitment . . . and they, whispering together, maliciously tendered the Oath of Allegiance. I answered them, I had taken it already . . . but however in a few sessions they praemunired me, which in severity is the loss of all my goods and chattels, and inprisonment during the King's pleasure. A frightful sentence, had not my God restrained the execution.

But now the proud waves went over my soul; for my dear wife, who, having had the encumbrance of my shop, and three children lying upon her hands. . . . fell into a deep consumption, of which she languished about two years, which much heightened my afflictions. During which time her affections carried her sometimes beyond her ability, to come and see me, when she was so weak I was forced to carry her upstairs in my arms. But when she was near her end, by means of the aforesaid Sir Thomas Pennison's Lady's midwife, he ordered me to so much liberty in the year 1665, that I had the opportunity to see her last end, and dispose of my house and shop-goods, and put my children out to nurse. After which I returned to prison again as ordered. . . .

[C. Elizabeth Bunyan Pleads for Her Husband's Freedom]
The first time my wife went, she presented it to Judge Hale, who very mildly received it at her hand, telling her that he would do her and me the best good he could; but he feared, he said, he could do none. The next day, again, lest they should; through the multitude of business, forget me, we did throw another petition into the coach to Judge Twisdon; who, when he had seen it, snapt her up and angrily told her that I was a convicted person, and could not be released, unless I would promise to preach no more, etc.

Well, after this, she yet again presented another to Judge Hale, as he sat on the bench, who, as it seemed, was willing to give her audience.

The place where she went to them was to the Swan Chamber, where the two judges, and many justices and gentry of the country, were in company together. She then, coming into the chamber with abashed face, and a trembling heart, began her errand to them in this manner:—

Woman. My Lord (directing herself to Judge Hale), I make bold to come once again to your Lordship, to know what may be done with my husband.

Judge Hale. To whom he said, Woman, I told thee before, I could do thee no good; because they have taken that for a conviction which thy husband spoke at the sessions; and unless there be something done to undo that, I can do thee no good.

Woman. My Lord, said she, he is kept unlawfully in prison; they clapped him up before there was any proclamation against the meetings; the indictment also is false. Besides, they never asked him whether he was guilty or no; neither did he confess the indictment . . .

Twis. What, will your husband leave preaching? If he will do so, then send for him.

Wom. My Lord, said she, he dares not leave preaching, as long as he can speak.

Twis. See here, what should we talk any more about such a fellow? Must he do what he lists? He is a breaker of the peace.

Wom. She told him again, that he desired to live peaceably, and to follow his calling, that his family might be maintained; and, moreover, said, My Lord, I have four small children that cannot help themselves, of which one is blind, and have nothing to live upon, but the charity of good people.

Hale. Hast thou four children? said Judge Hale; thou art but a young woman to have four children.

Wom. My Lord, said she, I am but mother-in-law to them, having not been married to him yet full two years. Indeed, I was with child when my husband was first apprehended; but being young, and unaccustomed to such things, said she, I being smayed at the news, fell into labour, and so continued for eight days, and then was delivered, but my child died.

Hale. Whereat, he looking very soberly on the matter, said, 'Alas, poor woman!'. . .

Twis. But Judge Twisdon told her, that she made poverty her cloak; and said, moreover, that he understood I was maintained better by running up and down a preaching, than by following my calling.

Hale. What is his calling? said Judge Hale.

Answer. Then some of the company that stood by said, 'A tinker, my Lord.'

Wom. Yes, said she, and because he is a tinker, and a poor man, therefore he is despised, and cannot have justice . . . He preacheth nothing but the Word of God, said she.

Twis. He preach the Word of God! said Twisdon; and withal she thought he would have struck her; he runneth up and down, and doth harm.

Woman. No, my Lord, said she, it is not so; God hath owned him, and done much good by him.

Twis. God! said he; his doctrine is the doctrine of the devil.

Wom. My Lord, said she, when the righteous Judge shall appear, it will be known that his doctrine is not the doctrine of the devil.

3. Ministerial Recognition Under Charles II

Following the restoration of King Charles II in 1660, many ministers and congregations were able to conduct their affairs in public without fear of persecution. Indeed, some ministers received printed licenses to "teach" religion from place to place. As the following license for Andrew Gifford (1642–1721) illustrates, the Crown chose to confuse Baptists with Presbyterians. On the original document, Gifford, who was pastor of the Broadmead church, substituted "Baptist" for "Presbyterian." *Source:* "Andrew Gifford Remains." Manuscript book, Archives, Bristol Baptist College.

CHARLES by the Grace of God, King of England, Scotland, France, and Ireland, Defender of the Faith etc. To all Mayers, Bayliffs, Constables, and other Our Officers and Ministers, Civil and Military, whom it may concern, Greetings. In pursuance of our Declaration of the 15th of March, 167 1/2. We do hereby permit and license Andrew Gifford of our City of Bristol of the Persuasion commonly called Presbyterian (Baptist) to be a Teacher, and to teach in any place licenced and allowed by Us according to Our said Declaration. Given at Our Court at Whitehall, the 5th day of September in the 24th year of Our Reign, 1672.

By His Majesties Command
Arlington

4. Liberty of Conscience

The Baptists were among the first Protestants to plead for liberty of conscience. Little is known about the author of Selection A, Leonard Busher (flourished 1614), except that he was a member of Thomas Helwys' congregation and a "citizen of London." His *Religions Peace,* from which this is extracted, was directed to King James I; it was printed in 1614 and reissued in 1646. Richard Overton (flourished 1646) the author of Selection B, became a member of a Baptist congregation in Holland before returning to England in the 1630s. *Sources:* A. Leonard Busher, *Religions Peace: Or A Plea for Liberty of Conscience* (London: John Sweetling, 1646) in Edward B. Underhill, ed., *Tracts in Liberty of Conscience and Persecution 1614-1661* (London: J. Haddon, 1846), pp. 41-42, 52. B. Richard Overton, *An Appeale from the regenerate Representative Body the Commons of England assembled at Westminster* (London: n.p., 1647), pp. 25-26. C. *An Orthodox Creed.*

[A. Busher on Freedom of Conscience]

. . . persecution for difference in religion is a monstrous and cruel beast, that destroyeth both prince and people, hindereth the gospel of Christ, and scattereth his disciples that witness and profess his name. But permission of conscience in difference of religion, saveth both prince and people; for it is a meek and gentle lamb, which not only furthereth and advanceth the gospel, but also fostereth and cherisheth those that profess it, as may be seen by the permission of the Princess Elizabeth, and others that were permitted and fostered in Dutchland at that time.

Also permission of conscience is a great and sure band and benefit to the king and state, as may likewise be seen in the same Princess Elizabeth; who, if she had not been permitted, but had suffered death, as the bloody bishops earnestly desired, then had not the kingdom been so surely, nor yet so purely, kept and preserved for his majesty and his royal issue, as now it is. The Lord be praised therefore. . . .

Therefore permission of conscience, and liberty of the gospel, in our land of Great Britain, will mightily further the advancement of the apostolic faith, and chiefly their books, whereout sufficient matter will be drawn for the convincing of every particular religion which is against the religion established by Christ and his apostles: who by all means lawful, sought the conversion and salvation both of Jews and Gentiles. And they are inconstant and faithless men, or at least every ignorant, that think error will overcome and prevail against the truth.

For the abolishing of such thoughts, I desire such men to consider the mighty victory and prevailing of the truth, in the time of Christ and his apostles; which, notwithstanding resisted and disputed against by the most part of the priests and learned men, both of Jews and Gentiles, yet overcame and prevailed against all the errors of the high priests and great learned men, both of the Jews and Gentiles. And the apostle saith, *We cannot do any thing against the truth, but for the truth.*

[B. Overton on God and Caesar]

And as for matters of conscience or opinion about *Religion* or Worship, with which humane society, cohabitation and safety may freely subsist and stand together, that doth not fall under the power of the Magisteriall sword, either for introduction and settlement, or for *extirpation* and subversion; for the limits of Magistracy extend no further then humanity, or humane subsistance, not to spirituality, or spirituall being; and no further, then its owne nature extends, no further may its compulsive power be stretched; And this is the true distinction for matter of subjection, betwixt God and *Caesar,* and what is Gods wee must in the first place give unto God, and what is *Caesars,* in the second place, freely and readily we must give unto *Caesar*; the inward man is Gods prerogative, the outward man is mans prerogative; God is the immediate Lord over the inward, and mediately over the outward, but man is onely Lord over the outward, and though immediate thereover, yet but by Deputation or Commission from him who is thus both over the one and the other: And God who onely knoweth the heart, and searcheth the reines, hath reserved the governation thereof to himself as his own prerogative, and the onely means which he useth in this kinde of Government, that by his Ministers must be dispensed, is onely by the word, not by the sword. . . .

[C. *An Orthodox Creed*]
XLVI ARTICLE
Of Liberty Of Conscience

The Lord Jesus Christ, who is King of Kings, and Lord of All by Purchase, and is Judge of Quick and Dead, is only Lord of Conscience, having a peculiar right so to be: He having died for that very end, to take away the Guilt, and to destroy the filth of Sin; that keeps the Consciences of all Men in Thraldom, and Bondage, till they are set free by his special Grace. And therefore he would not have the Consciences of Men in Bondage to, or imposed upon, by any Usurpation,

Tyranny, or command whatsoever, contrary to his revealed Will in his Word, which is the only Rule he hath left, for the Consciences óf all Men to be ruled, and regulated, and guided by, through the assistance of his Spirit. And therfore the obedience to any Command, and Decree, that is not revealed in, or consonant to his Word, in the holy Oracles of Scripture, is a betraying of the Liberty of Conscience. And the requiring of an implicite Faith, and an absolute blind Obedience, destroys Liberty of Conscience, and Reason also, it being repugnant to both. And that no pretended good and whatsoever, by any Man, can make that Action, Obedience, or Practice, lawful and good, that is not grounded in, or upon the Authority of holy Scripture, or right Reason agreeable thereunto.

The Wider World

Faced with persecution and threat of extinction, the early Baptist congregations looked inward rather than outward. Individual believers and families met clandestinely in their homes from the days of John Smyth through the beginning of the first Civil War (1642). With the relaxation of persecution during the Civil Wars and the Interregnum, Baptists possessed the freedom to organize openly, to unite with their churches, and to evangelize. Though eventually the Restoration brought renewed persecution, the Glorious Revolution (1688) and the Act of Toleration (1689) gave the Baptists a freedom they had never enjoyed. They met this challenge of freedom through various ways and means. Baptists became more concerned with English society as a whole rather than their own communions, and they looked at the wider world of the British Empire, the trans-Atlantic colonies, and the slaves of Africa.

1. Social Concerns

Stuart England was plagued with chronic unemployment, poor harvests, civil strife, and agrarian unrest, all of which made poverty endemic. The early Baptists responded to these socioeconomic ills through diaconal ministries. That this social concern had a biblical root is reflected in the creedal statement of the General Assembly in 1660 (Selection A). Similarly, during the last quarter of the eighteenth century several English Baptist preachers, echoing the Quakers, denounced the evils of slavery and the slave trade. The petition in Selection B was drafted by Mr. Robinson, a Cambridge Baptist leader, and presented to the House of Commons in 1788. *Sources:* A. ''A Brief Confession or Declaration of Faith.'' Copy in Angus Library, Regents Park College, Oxford. B. Quoted in Joseph Ivimey, *A History of the English Baptists,* 4 vols. (London: Burditt, 1811-1830), 4, pp. 49-50.

[A. Poverty]

That the poor Saints belonging to the Church of Christ, are to be
sufficiently provided for by the Churches, that they neither want food
or rayment, and this by a free and voluntary contribution, (and not of
necessity, or by the constraint or power of the Magistrate) 2 Cor. 9.7.
I Cor. 8. 11,12. and this through the free and voluntary help of the
Deacons, (called Overseers of the poor), being faithful men, chosen by
the Church, and ordained by Prayer and Laying on of Hands, to that
Work, Acts 6. 1, 2, 3, 4, 5, 6. So that there is no need in the Church
of Christ, of a Magisterial compulsion in this case, as there is among
others, who being constituted in a fleshly and generational way, are
necessitated to make use of a carnal sword, to compel even a small,
mean, and short Maintenance for their poor; when as many other
Members of their Churches can and do part with great and large Sums
of Money, to maintain their vain fashions, Gold, Pearls, and costly
Array, which is expresly contrary to the Word of God, I Tim 2.9, 10.
I Pet. 3.3. Alas, "what will such do when God riseth up, and when
he visiteth, what will they answer him?" Job. 31.14 . . . .

[B. Slavery and the Slave Trade]

To the honourable the Commons of Great Britain in parliament
assembled.

The humble petition of the gentry, clergy, freeholders and others in
the county of Cambridge, sheweth,

That your petitioners, understanding that the slave trade is likely to
become a subject of parliamentary investigation, cannot help expressing
their most earnest desire of a change in the present system of African
trade.

Your petitioners are aware, that Britain derives innumerable benefits
from her plantations, and that the plantations depend upon the labours
of negroes; but they are not convinced that a slave trade is necessary
to a supply of labourers. They abhor slavery in every form, and that
kind most of all which renders cruelty necessary to the safety of the
slaveholders.

Your petitioners humbly represent, that a slave trade is neither just,
nor safe, nor, in the present case, productive; for it obstructs other
branches of traffic, which promise far greater national advantages.

Nor can your petitioners help observing with sorrow, that a slave trade is a dishonour to humanity, a disgrace to our national character, utterly inconsistent with the sound policy of commercial states, and a perpetual scandal to the profession of Christianity.

Your petitioners, therefore, humbly pray this honourable house to take the premises into consideration, and to grant such relief as they in their great wisdom shall see fit.

And your petitioners, as in duty bound, shall ever pray.

2. Baptists and Other Protestants

During the Puritan Revolution (1640–1660) many English Protestants gravitated to the radical sects. Some Independents became Baptists; some Baptists became Quakers; some Quakers became Fifth Monarchists—all of which gave rise to rivalries and bitterness. Selection A illustrates Particular Baptist antipathy to clergy and lay relations with the Church of England. The opposition of the General Baptists to the Fifth Monarchists, a sect which believed the Second Coming was imminent, is shown in Selection B. During the Restoration, however, several of the Protestant churches united to defend themselves against the repressive religious policies of Charles II. This situation manifested itself in Bristol (Selection C). *Sources:* A. Records of the Abingdon Association, 30 October 1656. Angus Library, Regents Park College. B. *The Humble Representation and Vindication of Many of the Messengers, Elders, and Brethren Belonging to Several of the Baptized Churches in this Nation* (London: R: I., 1654), p. 3. C. Records of the Broadmead Baptist Church (Hayden Transcript), Book I.

[A. The National Church]

It is not lawfull for saints to joyne with the national church assemblyes or the nationall church ministers (viz. those that preach and pray as men authorised to act as ministers of the nationall church commonly called the Church of England, as namely, parsons, vicars, curates and parish lecturers) in any part of their nationall worship, or so to heare the said national church ministers' in their preachings or ministeriall exhortations whether in their churches, so-called, or at burialls or in any other like way, as in any appearance to countenance the same or to seeke edification thereby, the nationall church worship and the nationall church ministrie being antichristian and Babilonish. Consider 2 Cor. 6.17 with Rev. 18.4.

[B. Baptists and Fifth Monarchists]

Nor do they know any ground for the saints, as such, to expect that the Rule and Government of the World should be put into their hands, untill that day in which the Lord Jesus shall visibly descend from Heaven in power and great glory, when indeed they verily believe, that according to the Scriptures, the Kingdoms of this World shall become the Kingdoms of the Lord and of his Christ, and that then the Kingdom, and Dominion, and the greatness of the Kingdom under the whole heaven shall be given to the people of the Lord.

[C. An Early Union of Protestants]

Ye King makeing warr with ye Dutch, his Majesty graunted Liberty (to all ye Dissenters in ye Nation, to enjoy their meetings quiet,) by a Declaration for lycences to be given them that would seeke for them. At which time these four Congregations, each of us, had gott out Lycences for our places and Pastours. Whereupon we stood out against ye Bishop, ye Mayor, and Hellier, by law.

Thus ye Lord's Permissive providence caused these four Churches, (two Baptized, one Presbyterian, and one Independent congregation,) that were begun to be troubled, to Joyne together and *unite* (in councell and charge,) as poore sheep driven together by Wolves; And Resolved to Endeavour what they could to defend themselves by Law against those vile Persecutors, that were risen up against their peaceable and quiett Meetings, Resolving to destroy us. In order thereunto, these four churches chose *Two men* of each congregation to Act for ye whole; and those Eight men tooke care of ye matters of Law, to follow it. And as often as occasion required, these Eight men, deputed for ye Congregations, mett together to advize, consider, and manage Matters of our generall concerne, for ye four congregations, in their legall defence.

3. Trans-Atlantic Ties

Trans-Atlantic ties between English and American Baptist congregations existed long before the American Revolution. As early as 1702 the General Assembly records demonstrate connections between the General Baptists and colonists in the Carolinas (Selection A). Similarly, the Baptists of Pennsylvania appealed to the Baptist ministers of London for more preachers, as evidenced in Mr. Abel Morgan's letter of August 12, 1744, penned in Philadelphia (Selection B). During the American Revolution many English, especially those connected with nonconforming churches, sided with the American colonists against their mother country. Selection C, an excerpt of a 1784 letter from Reverend John Rippon, shows the affinity of the English and American Baptists. *Sources:* A. General Association Book, p. 32; also in Whitley, *Minutes of the General Assembly,* p. 75. B. Quoted in Ivimey, *A History of the English Baptists,* 3, p. 117. C. John Rippon to James Manning, 1 May 1784. James Manning Papers, John Hay Library, Brown University.

[A. Financial Assistance for the Carolina Baptists]

Whereas our Brethren of the Baptist perswation and of the Generall Faith who haue their aboad in Carolina haue desierd us to Supply them wth a Ministry or with books, we being not able at present to doe the former haue collected ye Sum of Seuen pounds twelve Shillings wch wth wt can be farther obtain'd we haue put into the hands of our Bro S Keeling to Supply ym wth ye latter. & yt ye sd Bror Keeling doe wright a letter to them in the name of this Assembly.

[B. Pennsylvania Baptists Appeal for Help]

We are now nine churches, having, for the better assisting one the other, four general meetings; 1. At Welch Tract, which all the Pennsylvanian Churches resort to in May. 2. At Cohansy, for conveniency of those parts, where Philadelphia assists. 3. At Middleton, where also Philadelphia assists. 4. At Philadelphia, in the month of September, to which all do resort, and where most of the public matters are settled, by messengers from each particular church.

In these churches there are about five hundred members, but who are greatly scattered on this main land. Our ministers are necessitated to labour with their hands. We hope, if it please God to supply us with more help, we shall be more churches in a little time. Most churches administer the sacrament once a month. These ministers are all sound in the faith; and we practise most things like the British churches.

[C. John Rippon to James Manning]

Grange Road, Southwark, May 1, 1784.

Reverend and Dear Sir:

I have long wished for an opportunity of introducing myself to you, and to several other brethren on your side of the Atlantic. And as God in his wisdom has now put an end to the late bloody and unrighteous war, and opened a free communication between this country and America, I take the liberty, by the hands of your neighbor Mr. Chase (who speaks in the highest terms of you, Messrs. Stillman Gano, etc.) of soliciting such a Christian correspondence as your wisdom may suggest, and your large connections and many avocations may permit. . . .

I believe all our Baptist ministers in town, except two, and most of our brethren in the country, were on the side of the Americans in the late dispute. But sorry, very sorry were we to hear that the college was

a hospital, and the meeting-houses were forsaken and occupied for civil
or martial purposes. We wept when the thirsty plains drank the blood
of your departed heroes, and the shout of a king was amongst us when
your well-fought battles were crowned with victory. And to this hour
we believe that the independence of America will for a while secure
the liberty of this country; but that if the continent had been reduced,
Britain would not long have been free.

4. From Strict to Evangelical Calvinism

Andrew Fuller (1754–1815) represents the turning point in English Baptist theology
from the stagnation of the early eighteenth century Particular Baptist position to a moderate
and warm evangelical emphasis. Although lacking formal education, he was in touch
with all the major currents of thought in his day: the Wesleyan Revival and the writings
of Robert Hall (1728–1791) and John Ryland, who in 1785 advised Fuller that "there
was scarcely anything worth the name of religion left upon the earth." With William
Carey, Fuller became a passionate advocate of evangelism and missions, the practical
outworking of his theology. Below are two excerpts from his most outstanding tracts.
Sources: A. Andrew Fuller, *The Gospel of Christ Worthy of All Acceptation; or The
Obligations of Men Fully To Credit Whatever God Makes Known Etc.* (Northampton: T.
Dicey, 1785), p. 146. B. Andrew Fuller, *A Defense of a Treatise Entitled The Gospel
Worthy of All Acceptation* (Northampton: T. Dicey, 1787), pp. 24, 37, 38.

[A. The Work of The Ministry]

The work of the christian ministry, it has been said, is to *preach the
gospel,* or to hold up the free grace of God through Jesus Christ, as
the only way of a sinner's salvation. This is doubtless true; and if this
be not the leading theme of our ministrations, we had better be any
thing than preachers. *Wo unto us, if we preach not the gospel!* The
minister who, under a pretence of pressing the practice of religion,
neglects its all important principles, labours in the fire. He may enforce
duty till duty freezes upon his lips; neither his auditors nor himself will
greatly regard it. But on the other hand, if by *preaching the gospel* be
meant the insisting solely upon the blessings and privileges of religion,
to the neglect of exhortations, calls, and warnings; it is sufficient to
say that such was not the practice of Christ and his apostles. It will not
be denied that they preached the gospel: yet they warned, admonished,
and intreated sinners to *repent and believe; to believe while they had
the light; to labour not for the meat that perisheth, but for that which
endureth unto everlasting life; to repent and be converted, that their
sins might be blotted out; to come to the marriage-supper, for that all*

things were ready: in fine, *to be reconciled unto God.*

[B. The Gospel An Embassy of Peace]

True faith *includes a spiritual* understanding of the glory of the gospel, but it includes *something more.* It does not appear to me to have its seat barely in the understanding, but in the whole soul. It is the whole soul's yielding up its own false notions and dependencies and, falling in with God's way of salvation by Jesus Christ. By a spiritual discernment of the glory of the gospel, we *see the Son,* and by the whole soul's concurring with it, we *believe in him.* It is with the *heart* man believeth unto righteousness. If it is said the heart here is not opposed to the understanding, but to the *mouth,* with which confession is made unto salvation—I answer, this is true; but then neither is it used, I apprehend, for the understanding, to the exclusion of the affections; but for the whole soul in distinction from the mouth, by which our faith is openly professed. . . .

That the gospel is an *embassy of peace,* addressed to sinners indefinitely, and that any sinner whatever has a warrant to apply to the saviour, and a promise of acceptance on his application, is evident from the whole current of scripture. To oppose Arminianism by the denial of this well-known truth must be an unsuccessful attempt. Instead of destroying, it is the most effectual method to establish it. No Arminian, so long as he has a bible in his hand, can ever be persuaded that the language of scripture exhortations to repentance and faith in Christ, is not indefinite. If then his system is acknowledged to stand or fall with the universality of such exhortations, he will not desire a greater concession. He is well satisfied of this, that if general invitations speak the language of Arminianism, the bible must be written upon Arminian principles. Such a concession, therefore, tends to confirm him in his sentiments; and I believe such a way of speaking and writing amongst the Calvinists has been more than a little advantageous to the Arminian cause.

God gathers his elect out of mankind by a gospel equally addressed to one man as to another. No one, on his first application to Christ, comes to him considering himself as an elect person, or as having any peculiar privilege belonging to him above the rest of mankind; but every such person applies to Christ merely as a poor, guilty, self-ruined sinner;

and if the gospel did not speak an indefinite language, to sinners as such considered, he could have no hope.

5. Roots of Foreign Missions

In the English Midlands, Andrew Fuller's moderate Calvinism (see pages 86-87) and stress upon individual responsibility had perhaps its most far-reaching impact upon the least likely of persons. William Carey (1761–1834), a humble cobbler in Northampton, converted to Baptist principles in 1783 and thereafter entered the pastorate in Moulton. At the 1791 meeting of the Northampton Association, Carey joined Fuller in making a plea for missionary endeavor, and the two men became the chief advocates of a "Baptist Society for Propagating the Gospel among the Heathens" (formed October 2, 1792). Carey's simple philosophy—"Pray, plan, pay"—was more explicitly defined in his classic *Enquiry*, which is here excerpted. *Source:* William Carey, *An Enquiry Into the Obligations of Christians to Use Means for the Conversion of the Heathens* (Leicester: Ann Ireland, 1792), pp. 13, 75-77.

It has been objected that there are multitudes in our own nation, and within our immediate spheres of action, who are as ignorant as the South-Sea savages, and that therefore we have work enough at home, without going into other countries. That there are thousands in our own land as far from God as possible, I readily grant, and that this ought to excite us to ten-fold diligence in our work, and in attempts to spread divine knowledge amongst them is a certain fact; but that it ought to supercede all attempts to spread the gospel in foreign parts seems to want proof. Our own countrymen have the means of grace, and may attend on the word preached if they chuse it. They have the means of knowing the truth, and faithful ministers are placed in almost every part of the land, whose spheres of action might be much extended if their congregations were but more hearty and active in the cause: but with them the case is widely different, who have no Bible, no written language, (which many of them have not) no ministers, no good civil government, nor any of those advantages which we have. Pity therefore, humanity, and much more Christianity, call loudly for every possible exertion to introduce the gospel amongst them. . . .

The Missionaries must be men of great piety, prudence, courage, and forbearance; of undoubted orthodoxy in their sentiments, and must enter with all their hearts into the spirit of their mission; they must be willing to leave all the comforts of life behind them, and to encounter all the hardships of a torrid, or a frigid climate, an uncomfortable manner of living, and every other inconvenience that can attend this undertaking. Clothing, a few knives, powder and shot, fishing tackle, and the articles of husbandry above-mentioned, must be provided for them; and when arrived at the place of their destination, their first business must be to gain some acquaintance with the language of the natives, (for which purpose two would be better than one,) and by all lawful means to endeavour to cultivate a friendship with them, and as soon as possible let them know the errand for which they were sent. They must endeavour to convince them that it was their good alone, which induced them to forsake their friends, and all the comforts of their native country. They must be very careful not to resent injuries which may be offered to them, nor to think highly of themselves, so as to despise the poor heathens, and by those means lay a foundation for their resentment, or rejection of the gospel. They must take every opportunity of doing them good, and labouring, and travelling, night and day, they must instruct, exhort, and rebuke, with all long suffering, and anxious desire for them, and, above all, must be instant in prayer for the effusion of the Holy Spirit upon the people of their charge. Let but missionaries of the above description engage in the work, and we shall see that it is not impracticable.

Suggestions for Further Study

Since English Baptist life cannot be divorced from the larger context of Nonconformity and Separatism, one should begin with general studies of those traditions. See, for instance, Evelyn D. Bebb, *Nonconformity and Social and Economic Life 1660-1800* (Philadelphia: Porcupine Press Inc., 1980); Geoffrey F. Nuttall, *The Beginnings of Nonconformity* (London: J. Clark, 1964); and Barrington R. White, *The English Separatist Tradition* (London: Oxford University, 1971). The outstanding texts specifically about Baptists are A. C. Underwood, *A History of the English Baptists* (London: Kingsgate Press, 1947); T. M. Bassett, *The Welsh Baptists* (Swansea: Ilston House, 1981); and George Yuille, editor, *History of the Baptists in Scotland* (Glasgow: Baptist Union, 1927). Underwood masters a good deal of contemporary literature in a very succinct presentation. Also relevant in more specialized treatments are Louise F. Brown, *The Political Activities of the Baptists and Fifth Monarchy Men in England During the Interregnum* (Washington: American Historical Association, 1912); Champlin Burrage, *The Early English Dissenters in Light of Recent Research 1550–1641*, 2 vols. (Cambridge: University Press, 1912); and Caroline F. Richardson, *English Preachers and Preaching 1640–1670* (New York: Macmillan Inc., 1928). For the role of women in the Baptist tradition, see A. S. Clement, *Great Baptist Women* (London: Carey Kingsgate, 1955).

The regional and associational Baptist histories provide background on the larger life of the Baptist community. The most worthwhile examples from the literature are Ashley J. Klaiber, *The Story of Suffolk Baptists* (London: Kingsgate Press, 1932); Jerom Murch, *A History of the Presbyterian and General Baptist Churches in the West of England* (London: R. Hunter, 1835); Earnest A. Payne, *The Baptists of Berkshire* (London: Carey Kingsgate, 1951); H. Wheeler Robinson, *et. al.*, *Baptists in Yorkshire* (London: Kingsgate, 1912); and W. T. Whitley, *The Baptists of London 1612-1928* (London: Kingsgate Press, 1928). Similarly, for background on the local church, see John T. Godfrey and James Ward, *The History of Friar Lane Baptist Church, Nottingham* (London: Simpkin, Marshall, *et. al*, 1903); and Frederick Overend, *History of the Ebenezer Baptist Church, Bacup* (London: Kingsgate, 1912). While the focus of S. F. Paul, *History of the Gospel Standard Baptists*, 5 vols. (Brighton, 1951), is on the strict Baptist movement, the book also includes information about the history of local chapels.

For information on Baptist missions, two works are relevant. The older work by F. A. Cox, *History of the Baptist Missionary Society of England 1792-1842* (Boston: Damrell, 1843) is a useful general survey to accompany E. Daniel Potts, *British Baptist Missionaries in India 1793-1837* (Cambridge: University Press, 1967). S. Pearce Carey, *William Carey* (Valley Forge: Judson Press, 1923) is still standard; however, Mary Drewery, *William Carey: A Biography* (Grand Rapids: The Zondervan Corp., 1979) is currently available.

Books on education in the British Baptist tradition include Norman S. Moon, *Education for Ministry: Bristol Baptist College 1679-1979* (Bristol: The College, 1979) and John Rippon, *A Brief Essay Towards an History of the Baptist Academy at Bristol* (London: Dilly and Button, 1796). Other readable works are Robert E. Cooper, *From Stepney to St. Giles: The Story of Regents Park College 1810-1960* (London: Carey Kingsgate, 1960); and D. Mervyn Himbury, *The South Wales Baptist College 1807-1951* (Cardiff: J. D. Lewis, 1957).

The best clue to early Baptist theology and polity is found in Horton Davies, *Worship and Theology in England*. From Cranmer to Hooker, 1534-1603, vol. 1 (Princeton: Princeton University Press, 1970). As Roger Hayden has observed, "doctrine and polity [were] fluid," so one must consider the individual church and associational confessions of faith. William L. Lumpkin, *Baptist Confessions of Faith* (Valley Forge: Judson Press, 1959) is handy for this purpose if its use is supplemented by published church records. For information on the General Baptists, see Thomas Grantham, *Christianismus Primitivus or the Ancient Christian Religion* (London: Francis Smith, 1678). For information on the Particular Baptists, read the First London Confession (1644), the Somerset Confession (1656), and the Second London Confession (1677). Winthrop S. Hudson, editor, *Baptist Concepts of the Church* (Valley Forge: Judson Press, 1959) provides approaches to John Gill and Andrew Fuller. H. Wheeler Robinson, *The Life and Faith of the Baptists* (London: Kingsgate, 1946) is an excellent summary of the thought and style of British Baptists. The first widely used hymnal was John Rippon, *Hymns: Original and Selected* (London: Duckworth, n.d.). Finally, Ralph F. Chambers, *The Strict Baptist Chapels of England*, 5 vols. (Stanley Hunt, 1952) illustrates some of the structures of Baptist life, according to theological and liturgical realities.

A rich source of biographical information for the seventeenth century is the introductory material in Roger Hayden, editor, *The Records of a Church of Christ in Bristol, 1640-1687* (Bristol: The Record Society, 1974). There are some very readable and reliable biographies, such as John Brown, *John Bunyan: His Life, Times, and Work* (New York: Houghton Mifflin Co., 1885); Gilbert Laws, *Andrew Fuller: Pastor, Theologian, Ropeholder* (London: Carey Press, 1942); Henry M. Dexter, *The True Story of John Smyth The Se-Baptist* (Boston: Lee and Shepard, 1881); and John Rippon, *A Brief Memoir of the Life and Writings of John Gill* (London: John Bennett, 1838). Published editions of the works of major Baptist writers include *The Complete Works of Andrew Fuller with a Memoir of His Life*, 2 vols. (Boston: Lincoln and Edmands, 1833); *The Works of Robert Hall with a Brief Memoir* (New York: Carvill, 1830); and William T. Whitley, editor, *The Works of John Smyth, Fellow of Christ's College 1594-98*, 2 vols. (Cambridge: University Press, 1915). For a complete list of the many editions of Bunyan's works, consult Frank M. Harrison, *A Bibliography of the Works of John Bunyan* (London: Oxford University Press, 1932).

British Baptist historians and archivists have provided scholars with many editions of printed, primary source materials. In most cases the transcriptions follow original texts critically and carefully. Those that should be perused for national and regional bodies are William T. Whitley, editor, *Minutes of the General Assembly of the General Baptist Churches in England with Kindred Records 1654-1811*, 2 vols. (London: Baptist Historical Society, 1909–1910), and Barrington R. White, editor, *Associational Records of the Particular Baptists of England, Wales, and Ireland to 1660* (London: Baptist Historical Society, 1974). The latter is in multiple booklet form with excellent critical apparatus. For information on local congregations, see Edward B. Underhill, editor, *Records of the Churches of Christ Gathered at Fenstanton, Warboys, and Hexham 1644-1720* (London: Haddon Brothers, 1854); and *Records of a Church of Christ Meeting in Broadmead, Bristol 1640-1687* (London: J. Haddon, 1847). Roger Hayden, editor, *The Records of a Church of Christ in Bristol, 1640-1687* (Bristol: The Record Society, 1974) has updated the earlier edition and added much explanatory notation. Hayden's prefatory material is vital for understanding the political, social, and general religious contexts. An increasingly rare item is William T. Whitley, editor, *The Church Books of Ford or Cuddington, and Amersham in the County of Bucks* (London: Kingsgate, 1912). A facsimile edition of Bunyan's church records is reproduced in G. B. Harrison, editor, *The Church Book of Bunyan Meeting 1650-1821* (London: 1928). Whenever possible, the printed transcriptions were compared to original editions to achieve the accuracy of text in this volume.

For those who wish to consult the original sources themselves, visits to several centers are essential. The most extensive collection of published literature and church and associational records is in the Angus Library, Regents Park College, Oxford. Nearby is the Bodleian Library of Oxford University which, for Baptist items, complements the Angus. In the London area are the British Museum, Dr. Williams's Library, small but relevant archives at Baptist Church House, and the headquarters of the Baptist Missionary Society. The Mennonite Archives in Amsterdam contain original copies of the Separatist confessions and related materials, and the Library of Bristol Baptist College has many manuscripts relating to education and the leadership of the Bristol Church. Finally, the Samuel Colgate Library of the American Baptist Historical Society in Rochester, New York, possesses the largest amount of published English Baptist literature (some are rare editions), associational records, proceedings of the Baptist Missionary Society, published church records, and a number of manuscript collections relating to eighteenth century Anglo-American Baptist affairs. The lone periodical, Rippon's *Annual Register,* may be found in most British collections and ABHS.

Section II
Baptists in Colonial America
1630–1812

> But as the Baptists hold all religion to be personal,
> between God and individuals, and that all church power
> is in each particular church, it is impossible for them
> ever to form any great body, that can be dangerous to
> any civil government.
>
> Isaac Backus, 1795

During most of the colonial period the Baptists in the British colonies of North America were a small, scattered, and persecuted group. In the royal colonies they were dissenters from the Church of England; in the New England colonies they were dissenters from the Congregational establishment. Only in Rhode Island did they exist in sufficient numbers to have any political influence, although they freely practiced their faith in New Jersey and Pennsylvania. As dissenters they first had to struggle simply for the right to form congregations, and in Massachusetts in the early seventeenth century they were whipped, imprisoned, and banished. By the end of that century they had obtained toleration, but they were still taxed to support the established churches. For several decades they struggled for exemption from these religious taxes, and when they finally won this privilege, they moved to advocate total separation of church and state with religious liberty for all. It was not a fight easily won. In Virginia their ministers were denied licenses to preach until the eve of the Revolution, and when they preached nonetheless, they were hounded by mobs and imprisoned by sheriffs. Even after the

95

Revolution, the Baptists in New England had to struggle against the remnants of the Congregational establishment until 1833.

The turning point in colonial Baptist history was the First Great Awakening—the religious revival that swept through the British colonies from 1730 to 1760. The religious enthusiasm generated in this revival produced thousands of come-outers from the established churches and made the Baptists the fastest growing American denomination in the latter half of the eighteenth century. As they grew, they established ties with the Baptists in England, formed intercolonial associations of Baptist churches, actively lobbied for religious liberty, and in 1764 established the first Baptist college in North America in Warren, Rhode Island.

In the course of their development the Baptists quarreled often among themselves over the proper forms of worship, polity, and theological doctrine. Insisting upon adherence to the purest form of primitive Christianity, the colonial Baptists as a group were continually dividing into subgroups, but their adherence to a congregational polity allowed them to grow in diversity and during adversity. Although they resented the infringement of their religious liberty by the authorities in the colonies, most of them sprang ardently to the support of the patriot cause after 1776. After 1787 as they grew in numbers and respectability, they engaged in the many religious and philanthropic enterprises that voluntarism encouraged in the new nation: home and foreign missions, education and tract societies, Sabbath schools, and antislavery activity. Though predominantly Calvinistic in theology, they shared the general optimism of Americans that the United States had a special destiny to fulfill in the redemption of humanity. Their democratic polity appealed to an independent, republican people and was particularly adapted to the needs of a mobile society. Essentially a church of the disinherited, the uneducated, and the poor, the Baptists also appealed to Afro-Americans and frontier dwellers. As the nineteenth century began, a second Great Awakening rapidly made the Baptists the largest single denomination in the new nation, rivaled only by the Methodists. Colonial Baptists embodied both America's pietistic Protestantism and its faith in government of, by, and for the people. That was the secret of their popularity.

Varieties of Baptist Expression in Colonial America

The New World became a haven for the Baptists, as it was for other oppressed religious groups, and Baptists of all kinds settled in various parts of British North America. In America, as in England, the Baptists were divided in many ways. The most basic division was between the Arminian and Calvinist wings, described at that time as the General and the Particular. The former held that Christ died to make salvation available to all people (General atonement); the latter held that Christ died only for the elect (Particular atonement). Until the mid-eighteenth century the General Baptists were more numerous in New England and the Southern colonies than the Particular Baptists, while the Particular Baptists probably were in the majority in the Middle Colonies, especially around Philadelphia and southern New Jersey where they organized the first Calvinistic association in 1707. However, the General Baptists in New England had organized an association as early as 1670.

Another important source of division among the American Baptists in these early years concerned the laying on or imposition of hands upon all believers after baptism as a prerequisite for church membership. In New England the General Baptists all held this doctrine and were known as the Six Principle Baptists because "laying on of hands" was one of the six articles of faith and practice described in Hebrews 6:1-2. Those churches that did not require this rite (usually Calvinistic) were often called Five Principle Baptists.

The first Baptist church in America, founded in Providence, Rhode Island, by Roger Williams (c. 1603-1683) and Ezekial Holliman (?–1659) in 1638 or 1639, was a Five Principle Calvinistic church, but in 1652 it split over the laying on of hands issue. Similar divisions occurred among other Baptists in regard to other aspects of worship, ritual, and polity, including whether to worship on the first or seventh day and whether to hold open (or mixed) Communion with persons who favored infant baptism. After 1750 the dominant form of the Baptist persuasion, however, was Five Principle, first day, closed Communion, and Calvinistic.

1. Six Principle Baptists

While in New England and much of the South most Six Principle Baptists were Arminians, some Calvinistic Baptists, especially the Welsh and German, also practiced laying on of hands. John Comer (1704–1734) described one of the Six Principle General Baptist churches in Newport, Rhode Island, as "one owning the Doctrine of General Redemption." In his diary, Comer recorded a statement of its doctrines, as shown in Selection A. But a Calvinistic Baptist church from Wales, whose members settled in Pencader, Newcastle County, Pennsylvania, in 1701, also held similar views about the imposition of hands. *Sources:* A. Diary of John Comer, 18 April 1730. Manuscript Collections, Rhode Island Historical Society. B. "Minutes of the Welsh Tract Baptist Meeting." *Papers of the Historical Society of Delaware,* 1904, pp. 7-10.

[A. Newport Baptist Doctrines, 1706–1707]

By faith and practice with us, we mean and intend those that are dipped into water with a verbal demonstration of their faith and repentance, yielding obedience to all the rest of the ordinances of our Lord Jesus Christ, as laying on of hands with a real faith in the Resurrection of the dead and the Eternal Judgment; as also keeping their holy union and fellowship in Breaking of Bread and Prayer; as will be better seen and is set forth more at large in a printed sheet or declaration of faith and practice of the Baptized churches, falsely called Anabaptist, in London and other places in England; which sheet is signed by certain Elders and Brethren of said churches to the number of 73 and printed in the year 1691.

[B. The Welsh Tract Church]

In the year 1701, some of us (who were members of churches of Jesus Christ in the countys of Pembroke and Caermarthen, South Wales in Great Britain, professing believers baptism; laying-on-of-hands, elections; and final perseverence in grace) were moved and encouraged in our own minds to come to these parts, viz.: Pennsylvania. . . . After landing, we were received in a loving manner (on account of the gospel)

by the congregation meeting in Philadelphia and Pennepek who held
the same faith with us (excepting the ordinance of Laying-on-of-hands
on every particular member) with whom we wished much to hold
communion at the Lords-table: but we could not be in fellowship with
them in the Lords-supper; because they bore not testimony for God
touching the fore-mentioned ordinance.

The Philadelphia Baptist Association, founded in 1707, agreed that Communion between Five Principle and Six Principle Calvinistic Baptist churches was permissible. But
the dispute continued throughout the eighteenth century, and when the Reverend Samuel
Jones (1735–1814) published a tract in 1805 calling for the abrogation of this open
Communion practice, the Reverend David Jones (1736–1820) of Burlington, New Jersey,
rose to defend it. *Source:* David Jones, *A True History of the Laying On of Hands*
(Burlington, N.J.: 1805), pp. 1-7, 22.

I am sorry that there is occasion again to appear publicly in defence
of a gospel ordinance which hath been practised from the apostles'
days, till, since the reformation it has been laid aside by some of
Calvin's pretended disciples; for he himself has written in defence of
laying on of hands, as will appear in this History. . . . It might have
been expected that Dr. Jones, in composing his *Brief History of Laying
on of Hands,* would have given some texts of scripture to support his
sentiments, and thereby convince us of our mistake. . . . The first
passage I shall notice, is Acts vi. 6. which says *when they had prayed
they laid their hands on them.* . . . The Rev. Doctor has been pleased
to say, that laying on of hands 'was practised for the purpose of
conveying miraculous gifts, and only by the apostles, who had that
power.' . . . In the above passage, we read of seven persons who had
hands laid on them; but not one word is said about miraculous gifts
being conveyed, or any other gifts. . . . The next passage demanding
our attention is Acts viii. 14, 15, 17. . . . 'Now when the apostles
which were at Jerusalem heard that Samaria had received the word of
God, they sent unto them Peter and John: who, when they were come
down, prayed for them. . . . Then laid their hands on them' . . . whether
the [Philadelphia] association had, or had not authority to vote laying
on of hands no bar to communion, they thought it the wisest measure
to quiet the churches at that time, and the best method to prevent a
schism in our churches.

2. Five Principle Calvinistic Baptists

Apart from Roger Williams, the chief early exponents of Five Principle Calvinism were John Clarke (1609–1676) of Newport, Rhode Island; Obadiah Holmes (1607–1682) of Seekonk, Massachusetts; and Thomas Goold (?–1675) of Charlestown, Massachusetts. Clarke founded the first Baptist church of Newport sometime between 1641 and 1644; Holmes was an early member and later pastor of that church after the Puritans broke up his church in Seekonk; Goold adopted Baptist views in 1655 when he was deacon of the Puritan church in Charlestown and later formed the first Baptist church in Boston. Clarke left the following statement of his Calvinistic position. *Source:* Isaac Backus, *History of New England with Particular Reference to the Denomination of Christians Called Baptists* (Boston: Edward Draper, 1777), 1, pp. 255-256.

The decree of God is that whereby he hath from eternity set down with himself what shall come to pass in time, Eph. i.11. All things, with their causes, effects, circumstances, and manner of being, are decreed by God. Acts ii. 23. Him being delivered by the determinate counsel and foreknowledge of God, &c. Acts iv. 28. . . . The special decree of God concerning angels and men is called predestination. Rom. viii. 30. . . . Election is the decree of God, of his free love, grace and mercy, choosing some men to faith, holiness, and eternal life, for the praise of his glorious mercy. I Thess. i, 4. . . . The cause which moved the Lord to elect them who were chosen was none other but his mere good will and pleasure. Luke xiii. 32. . . . The sending of Christ, faith, holiness and eternal life, are the effects of his love. . . . Sin is the effect of man's free will, and condemnation is an effect of justice inflicted upon man for sin and disobedience. A man in this life may be sure of his election. 2 Peter i. 10. I Thess. 1. 4. Yea, of his eternal happiness, but not of his eternal reprobation. . . .

3. Seventh Day Baptists

Searching for the original basis of church order in the New Testament, some Baptists concluded that there was no warrant for worshiping on the first day of the week. This led to a dispute in the First Baptist Church of Newport in the years 1665 to 1671. This dispute ended in a schism led by Stephen Mumford, Samuel Hubbard, and William Hiscox. Mumford had adopted Seventh Day views in England; Hubbard came to accept them after leaving the Puritan church in Connecticut. Calvinistic in theology, the Seventh Day Baptists formed other churches in Rhode Island and, after 1701, in New Jersey and Pennsylvania. *Source:* Records of the First Baptist Church, Newport, Rhode Island, 1671, typescript, pp. 1-5. Archives, Seventh Day Baptist Historical Society.

Several of ye Church . . . having been in the practice of observing the 7th day as a Sabbath to the Lord for Several Years Sam'l Hubbard began the 1st of April, 1665. Roger Baster, the 15 of Ap. 1665. Will'm Hiscox 28 Ap. 1666. Rachel Langworthy, 15 day of January 1666. Tacey Hubbard, March the 11th 1664-5 but Still kept their places in the Church. . . . and as to the 7th day Sabbath, they [the first-day believers] asserted . . . that what was written on tables of Stone was done away as the old Covenant with which the Gentiles had nothing to do and that now we were to Hearken to the Law written in the heart. . . . Since now we were under the New Covenant. . . . a Sister of the Church uttered these words with much concern That it is a Sad thing that in Such a time as this when the hand of God is Stretched out over us by takeing away many by Death, yet Instead of Calling Sinners to Repentance the whole time for many Days together was Spent in preaching against one another, as if that were the great work of the Day. . . . hereupon for a few weeks there was a forebearance. So that they went on in Church fellowship and Communion with them. . . . there was much Discourse . . . with Mr. Wilds (one of them that laid down the observation of the 7th day) about his denying of the law to whome he replied Who Denies it; upon which Mr. Tory Said I do. . . . What Said Mr. Hiscox must we be forced to Walk by your legs and See by your Eyes. . . . At that Meeting Everything Appeared Dark as though there was no likelyhood of accomodation to be One Church; Hereupon Mr. Hiscox Desired to propose. . . . that Since there was an Apparent Difference between them and if they could not go on as formerly he in behalf of the rest desired the Church Seriously to Consider whither it would not be more for the glory of god and both their Comfort to let them have their liberty to walk by themselves. . . .

4. Open (or Mixed) Communion Baptists

Not all the early Baptists insisted on the separation of church and state or upon separating from those who practiced infant baptism. Elder John Myles (c. 1621–1685), who had founded a Baptist church in Illston, Wales, in 1649 accepted the Cromwellian connection between church and state. After the restoration of the king, Myles and one of his deacons, Thomas Proud, fled to Plymouth Colony where they established a church in Rehoboth in 1662 that practiced open Communion with those who wanted their children baptized or who refused to be rebaptized by immersion. However, the authorities in Plymouth forced them to move further west to the unsettled area of the colony where they and some pedobaptists formed the town of Swansea in 1667. Myles became, in effect, the established minister of that town, and although he accepted no religious taxes, he not only admitted pedobaptists into his church but also acquiesced in the town's policy of excluding "erroneous" heretics from settling in the town. *Source:* Diary of John Comer. Manuscript Collections, Rhode Island Historical Society, p. 61.

The church of Christ [in Swansea] here gathered . . . in the carrying on of a township according to the grant give us by the Honorable Court [of Plymouth] [agree] to the non-admission of erroneous persons [into the town] . . . such as hold damnable heresies, inconsistent with the faith of the gospel; as, to deny the Trinity or any person therein; the deity or sinless humanity of Christ, or the union of both natures in him, or his full satisfaction to the divine justice of all his elect, by his active and passive obedience, or his resurrection, ascension into heaven, intercession, or his second coming personally to judgment; or else to deny the truth or divine authority of the Scriptures; or the resurrection of the dead, or to maintain any merit of works, consubstantiation, transubstantiation, giving divine adoration to any creature or any other anti-Christian doctrines. . . . We desire that it be also understood that this is not understood of any holding opinion different from others in any disputable point yet in controversy among the godly learned, the Belief thereof not being essentially necessary to salvation; such as paedobaptism or anti-paedobaptism, church discipline or the like but that the minister or ministers of the said town may take their liberty to baptize infants or grown persons as the Lord shall persuade their Consciences, and So also the Inhabitants to take their Liberty to Baptism or to forbeare.

5. The Separate Baptists

The Separate Baptists as a group developed during the First Great Awakening in New England between 1740 and 1760. They began as Separate or radical "New Lights," persons who left the established Puritan churches because they believed in congregational autonomy, church membership limited to those experiencing conversion, and separation of church and state. In the early 1750s roughly 125 Separate churches were scattered throughout New England, many of them practicing open Communion with persons who rejected infant baptism as part of their revolt against what they considered the corruptions of the Puritan establishment. In 1754 a general conference of Separate churches voted against further open Communion. Those Separates who opposed infant baptism thereupon formed Baptist churches which, because of their origin, were called "Separate Baptists" or "New Light Baptists." Led by Isaac Backus (1724–1806), Ebenezer Hinds (1719–1812), and Ebenezer Moulton (1704–1783), and later joined by Baptists from the Philadelphia Association (James Manning, John Davis, Hezekiah Smith, Samuel Stillman), the Separate Baptists in New England practiced an intense form of evangelical Calvinism and engaged in extensive itinerant evangelism. They revitalized many older Calvinistic Baptist churches and soon outnumbered the General Baptists and Seventh Day Baptists combined. By the time of the Revolution, they were the major dissenting group in New England and led the fight for separation of church and state. Their evangelists also spread this new form of evangelical Calvinism to the Southern colonies, creating a new sense of intercolonial Baptist unity. By the time of the Revolution, the adjectives "Separate" and "New Light" had been dropped in New England although they were used in the South until 1788 when the Separate Baptists united with the Particular Baptists there. The Articles of Faith of the First Baptist Church of Middleboro, Massachusetts, drawn up by Isaac Backus in 1756, are typical of the sentiments of this closed Communion, evangelical Calvinist group of Baptists. *Source:* "The confession of faith of the Church of Christ in Titicut," 16 January, 1756. Isaac Backus Papers, Andover Newton Theological School.

We believe that there is one only Liveing and true God, Who is a Spirit, Infinite, Eternal and Unchangeable in his being, Wisdom, Power, Holiness, Justice, Goodness and Truth.

That there are three Persons in the God-head. . . . That the holy Scriptures of the old and new testament is the word of God, wherein he hath given us a perfect rule of faith and practice.

That God for his own glory, hath fore-ordained Whatsoever Comes to Pass. . . . That man being thus Dead, his recovery is Wholey in and from God. . . . That God of his mear good pleasure from all Eternity hath Chosen a number in Christ Jesus to Eternal salvation. . . . That We are of the number that Christ hath Purchased with his Blood. . . . That true Believers by vertue of their union to Christ have sencabel fellowship one with another . . . That the first Day of the week, comonly Caled The Lords day, is the Christian Sabbath. . . . We Believe that a visable Church is a number of true Believers by mutual acquaintance and Communion volentarily and understandingly Covenanting and Embodying Together for the Carrying on the Worship and service of God. That there are two Sacriments of the new Testament: viz. Baptism and the Lords Supper. That true Believers and their infant seed and None but such have a right to the ordinance of Baptism, Acts 1:37 and 2:38.39. . . . The door of the Church should be Carefully Kept at all times against all Such as Canot Give Scriptural Evidence of their union to Christ by faith. . . .

That a Church thus gathered, hath Power to Chuse and ordain those officers that Christ Hath Apointed in his Church: Such as Bishops or

Elders or Deacons, and by the same power to depose such officers as Evidently apear to walk Conterary to the Gospel: and also to Disapline their members: But yet In such Cases it is Convenience to advise with neighbouring Churches of the Same Constitution. . . .

That the minister hath a right to a temporal maintainance from the People, and that it Should be done by free Contribution . . . That the Deacons office work is to take care of the poor and of the Churches treasure to distrebute to the Support of the Pastor, the propegation of Religion, and to minister at the Lords table. . . .

6. Free-Will Baptists

By the end of the eighteenth century the Arminian principles of free will and general atonement had made considerable impact upon Calvinists of all denominations in England and America. Many Calvinistic Baptists were attracted to these doctrines (associated with Wesleyan Methodism and with the more general optimism and faith in human nature representative of Enlightenment philosophy). A major Baptist schism occurred in the years 1778 to 1780 when Benjamin Randal (1749–1808), a popular evangelist converted by George Whitefield in 1770, began to preach that Christ died for all people and that "whosoever will may be saved." Excommunicated for this Arminian heresy in 1780, Randal formed a group of churches into the Free-Will Baptist Connexion in eastern New Hampshire and southern Maine. Ardent evangelists spread this movement throughout New England and for a generation it rivaled the popularity of the Calvinistic (Separate) Baptists. Though not formally united with the Free-will Baptists, the General Baptists of Virginia and the Carolinas shared many of their views. Benjamin Randal's disciple and biographer provides a good description of Randal's departure from the Calvinistic ranks. *Source:* John Buzzell, *The Life Of Elder Benjamin Randal* (Limerick, N.H.: Hobbs, Woodman & Co., 1827), pp. 75-76.

Mr. Randal says, 'As the doctrine of Calvin had not been in dispute among us, I had not considered whether I believed it or not. But as the Lord had shewed me an universal atonement, and fulness enough in Christ for all men—the appearance of grace to all men—that the call of the gospel was to all, and that God was not willing that any should perish—that same love constrained me to go forth and call upon all men to come to Christ and be saved.' Mr. Randal was, at that time, [1778] a regular member of Berwick [Maine] [Baptist] church, and for anything that he knew, in good standing. He went on preaching from place to place, as he thought he was led by the Spirit. The reformation increased, converts were multiplied, and love and harmony prevailed among the brethren. But alas! the scene soon changed and trials succeeded. Mr. Randal soon found himself in a place too strait for him. He was one day very unexpectedly called upon by one of his old brethren in the ministry in a public assembly, to tell why he did not preach election as Mr. Calvin held it. Mr. Randal replied, 'Because I do not believe it.' Upon hearing this, the minister fell into dispute with him, and the longer they conversed on the subject, the more they differed; and finally, a complete separation was the result.

7. The German Tunkers (Dunkers or Dunkards)

The Baptist movement in Europe also contributed to the variety of Baptist persuasions in the New World. Persecuted by both Catholic and Lutheran rulers, many European Baptists sought refuge in the Middle Colonies in the early eighteenth century. Among them were the Tunkers from Schwartzenau, Germany. Twenty families came to Lancaster, Pennsylvania, in 1719 under their ministers John Naas and Alexander Mack. German-speaking and Arminian, they practiced a number of rituals not usually followed by Baptists in England and America: foot-washing, the kiss of peace (or kiss of charity), the love feast, anointing with oil, and trine immersion (in which the candidate for baptism kneels in shallow water and is immersed by the minister's bending the candidate's head forward). A disagreement in 1730 over seventh or first day worship split the Tunkers. The Seventh Day Tunkers formed a communal society at Ephrata, Pennsylvania, under Johann Conrad Beissel (1690–1768). The contemporary Baptist historian, Elder Morgan Edwards of Philadelphia, provided one of the first accounts of the Tunkers. *Source:* Morgan Edwards, *Materials Towards A History of the American Baptists in XII Volumes* (Philadelphia: Joseph Crukshank and Isaac Collins, 1770), 1, pp. 66-67.

It is very hard to give a true account of the principles of these Tunkers as they have not published any system or creed. . . . They are *general baptists* in the sense which that phrase bears in Greatbritain; but not *Arians* nor *Socinians,* as most of their brethren in Holland are. General redemption they certainly hold; and, withall, general salvation; which tenets though wrong are consistent. They use great plainness of language and dress, like the Quakers; and like them will neither swear or fight. They will not go to law; nor take interest for the money they lend. They commonly wear their beards; and keep the first day sabbath, except one congregation. They have the Lord's supper with its ancient attendents of *love-feasts, washing feet, kiss of charity,* and *right hand of fellowship.* They anoint the sick with oil for recovery; and use the *trine immersion,* with *laying on of hands* and prayer, even while the person baptized is in the water. . . . every brother is allowed to stand up in the congregation to speak in a way of exhortation and expounding;

and when by these means they find a man eminent for *knowledge* and *aptness* to teach, they choose him to be a minister, and ordain him with imposition of hands, attended with fasting and prayer and giving the right hand of fellowship. They also have *deacons;* and ancient widows for *deaconnesses;* and *exhorters;* who are licensed to use their gifts statedly. They pay not their ministers unless it be in a way of presents. . . .

8. Black Baptist Churches

Because the congregational autonomy of the Baptists provided great freedom for faith and worship, many African slaves and former slaves preferred to attend and join Baptist churches when free to do so. Historians have found traces of African religious practice in the singing, preaching, and general temper of black Christian churches. Furthermore, black Christians emphasized themes in Jewish and Christian history and in theology which seemed to them particularly relevant to their oppressed status in the New World (the Babylonian captivity, the Exodus of the chosen people from slavery in Egypt, freedom in Christ, the Second Coming of the Messiah to begin a new day of liberty for all believers). Whether slave or free and whether in the North or the South, black Americans were given Communion after the white church members.

The first black Baptist church was formed by George Leile about 1778 in Georgia, but he fled to Jamaica after the Revolution. One of his converts, Andrew Bryan, continued the church in Savannah, Georgia, where, despite persecution from whites, the church continued to grow. The first African Baptist church in New England was formed in Boston in 1809 by Thomas Paul, later missionary to Haiti. Leile's account of his early ministry in Kingston, Jamaica, written in 1791 for the English Baptist, John Rippon, reveals the popularity and difficulties of early black Baptists in a slaveholding community. Andrew Bryan's letter to Isaac Backus recounts the trying circumstances in Savannah following the 1792 slave rebellion in Haiti. *Sources:* A. David Benedict, *A General History of the Baptist Denomination in America,* 2 vols. (Boston: Lincoln and Edmands, 1813), 1, pp. 196-197. B. Andrew Bryan to Isaac Backus, 27 January 1795. Isaac Backus Papers, Andover Newton Theological School.

[A. George Leile's Account]

I cannot justly tell what is my age, as I have no account of the time of my birth; but I suppose I am about 40 years old (in 1791.) I have a wife and four children. My wife was baptized by me in Savannah, and I have every satisfaction in life from her. . . . My occupation is a farmer, but as the seasons, in this part of the country, are uncertain, I also keep a team of horses and waggons, for the carrying goods . . . I have a few books, some good old authors and sermons, and one large Bible that was given me by a gentleman. A good many of our members can read, and all are desirous to learn . . . I agree to election, re-demption, the fall of Adam, regeneration, and perseverance, knowing the promise is to all who endure, in grace, faith, and good works, to the end, shall be saved.

There is no Baptist church in this country [Jamaica] but ours. We have purchased a piece of land at the east end of Kingston, containing three acres, for the sum of £155, currency, and on it have begun a meeting-house, 57 feet in length by 37 in breadth. We have raised the brick wall eight feet high from the foundation, and intend to have a gallery. Several gentlemen, members of the House of Assembly, and other gentlemen, have subscribed toward the building, about £40. . . . The chief part of our congregation are *slaves,* and their owners allow them, in common, but three or four bits [5 to 20 pence] per week for allowance to feed themselves; and out of so small a sum we cannot expect any thing that can be of service from them; if we did, it would soon bring a scandal upon religion; and the free [Black] people in our society are but poor, but they are willing, both free and slaves, to do what they can. . . . And, Rev. Sir, we think the Lord has put it in the power of the Baptist societies in England to help and assist us.

[B. A Letter from Andrew Bryan]

We request you and Gods people will pray for us; we are distressed and persicuted, but hope to trust in the Lord; we have built a place of worship, but have not had the opportunity of enjoying it much; since it was built, we have been prohibited from preaching in it for four months at one time and two months at another. Brother, pray for us; that the Lord would grant us Grace to walk in his fear and give us favour in the eyes of those that rule over us. We shall be happy to hear from you and our Brethren at the Northword, we are distitute of the Gospel here in a great measure; there are a few of our white Brethren visit from above [the North], but very few. . . . should be glad if some of the ministering B[rethren] would visit us.

First African Baptist Church of Savannah, Georgia, 1794

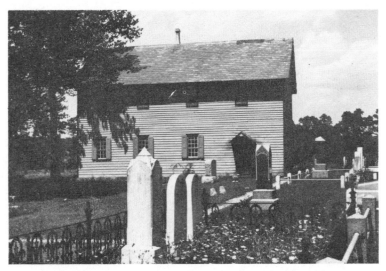

Old Yellow Meetinghouse, Imlaystown, New Jersey, 1766

Evolution of a
Baptist Identity in America

As they sought to purify the beliefs, rituals, and church order of Christianity, Baptists suffered continued persecution in the New World as they did in the Old. Neither the Puritan establishments in New England nor the Anglican establishments in the South would grant them liberty of worship. Weak and unsure of themselves, the early Baptists had to overcome years of prejudice stemming back to the Peasant's Revolt of 1522 and the Munsterite Rebellion of 1535–1536, both of which were blamed upon the Baptists (or Anabaptists, as their enemies continued to label them in America). In part, their own sense of a separate Christian identity in America derived from their efforts to distinguish themselves from these early continental "Anabaptists" (regarding pacifism, the taking of oaths, the validity of magistrates, polygamy, and so on). In spite of their efforts, Baptists continued to be considered undesirable elements in the towns of Massachusetts and Virginia until the Revolution and even later. A Congregational deacon in Warwick, Massachusetts, said in 1774 he would "rather court a negro than a girl that had been to such [Baptist] meetings." In other places, ministers and respectable citizens led mobs against Baptist meetings through the 1780s.

At first the Baptists in the Puritan and Anglican colonies sought only toleration, the right to worship as they pleased; not until the 1740s did they launch a concerted effort for religious equality and the separation of church and state. The Baptists tried to persuade their neighbors and their legislators to grant them exemption from religious taxes to support the established church. Occasionally they appealed overseas to the King in Council for justice, and as a result, they were considered in the 1760s

110 BAPTIST LIFE AND THOUGHT: 1600-1980

to be opponents of the movement for colonial independence. In Virginia, Baptist ministers were mobbed and jailed in the years 1763 to 1775 because they refused to ask the civil authorities for a license to preach.

1. Controversies with the Colonial Establishment

A good indication of the prevailing view of "Anabaptists" among English settlers in the New World is vividly stated in the Law of 1644 banishing all Baptists from the Massachusetts Bay Colony. *Source: The Book of the General Laws and Libertyes Concerning the Inhabitants of the Massachusetts* (Cambridge: Samuel Green, 1648), p. 1.

Forasmuch as experience hath plentifully and often proved that since the first arising of the Anabaptists about a hundred years since, they have been the incendiaries of the commonwealths and the infectors of persons in main matters of religion and the troublers of churches in all places where they have been, and that they who have held the baptizing of infants unlawful have usually held other errors or heresies together therewith though they have (as hereticks use to do) concealed the same till they spied out a fit advantage and opportunity to vent them, by way of questions or scruple; and whereas divers of this kind have, since our coming into New England, appeared amongst ourselves, some whereof (as others before them) denied the ordinance of magistracy, and the lawfulness of making warr, and others the lawfulness of magistrates and their inspection into any breach of the first tables; which opinions, if they should be connived at by us, are like to be increased amongst us, and so must necessarily bring guilt upon us, infection and trouble to the churches, and hazard to the whole commonwealth; it is ordered and agreed that if any person or persons within this jurisdiction shall either openly condemne or oppose the baptizing of infants or go about secretly to seduce others from the approbation or use thereof, or shall purposely depart the congregation at the ministration of the ordinance or shall deny the ordinance of the magistracy or their lawful right and authority to make warr or to punish the outward breaches of the first table, and shall appear to the Court willfully and obstinately to continue therein after due time and means of conviction, every such person or persons shall be sentenced to banishment.

When John Clarke, Obadiah Holmes, and John Crandall entered Massachusetts Bay from Rhode Island in 1651 to baptize a man named William Witter in the town of Lynn, they were arrested and sentenced to fines or whippings. Holmes, refusing to pay his fine, received thirty-nine lashes with a three-corded whip. During his trial, Clarke defended the Baptists against the common stereotype held of them. *Source:* John Clarke, *Ill Newes from New England or A Narrative of New England's Persecution* (London: H. Hills, 1652), pp. 31, 36-37.

We being by virtue hereof committed to prison upon the 5th day sevennight after were brought to our tryall; in the forenoon we were examined, in the afternoon, without producing either accuser, witness, jury, law of God, or man, we were Sentenced; in our examination the Governor upbraided us with the name of Anabaptists; To whom I answered, I disown the name, I am neither an Anabaptist, nor a Pedobaptist, nor a Catabaptist; he told me in hast[e] I was all; I told him he could not prove us to be either of them; He said, yes, you have Rebaptized. I denyed it saying, I have Baptized many, but I never Rebaptized any; then said he, you deny the former Baptism, and make all our worship a nullity; I told him he said it; moreover I said unto them (for therefore do I conceive I was brought before them to be a testimony against them) If the Testimony which I hold forth be true, and according to the mind of God, which I undoubtedly affirm it is, then it concernes you to look to your standing. . . . I Testifie that Baptism, or dipping in Water, is one of the Commandements of this Lord Jesus Christ, and that a visible believer, or Disciple of Christ Jesus . . . is the only person that is to be Baptized, or dipped with that visible Baptism. . . . I testifie that no such believer, or Servant of Christ Jesus hath any liberty, much less Authority, from his Lord, to smite his fellow servant, nor yet with outward force, or arme of flesh, to constrain, or restrain his Conscience, no nor yet his outward man for Conscience sake, or worship of his God, where injury is not offered to the person, name or estate of others, every man being such as shall appear before the judgment seat of Christ, and must give an account of himself to God, and therefore ought to be fully perswaded in his own mind, for what he undertakes, because he that doubteth is damned if he eat, and so also if he act, because he doth not eat or act in Faith, and what is not of Faith is Sin.

Fifteen years later in 1665 when Thomas Goold and others from the Puritan church in Charlestown separated from the congregation (or were excommunicated from it for not allowing their children to be baptized), they formed their own church on Baptist principles and were soon thereafter banished by the General Assembly. John Russell, who succeeded Goold as elder of the Boston church (the Puritans, through fear of the king's displeasure, tolerated the Baptists in Boston) published a tract in 1680, defending his members from charges of being ''turbulent,'' heretical, anti-intellectual, and disturbers of the peace. *Source:* John Russell, *Some Considerable Passages Concerning the First Gathering and Further Progress of A Church of Christ in Gospel Order in Boston in New England Commonly (though Falsely) Called By the Name of Anabaptists* (London: n.p., 1680), pp. 9-14.

Another thing laid to our charge is, That we are disorderly persons, and walk disorderly. Ans. This is also a mistake: for our practice, and walking, is according to, and agreeable with the Orders of the Lord Jesus Christ, therefore orderly: for we walk in Church-fellowship together; and continue in the Apostles Doctrine, Fellowship, breaking Bread, and Prayer, Act 2. and that on the first day of the week, by Persons elected, and ordained to Office, for the Administration of the holy Ordinances of Christ.

Another thing we are charged with is, That we are disturbers of the Publick Peace. Ans. We have never yet been found making any disturbance, by raising any Tumults, or causing any Sedition, either in church or Commonwealth. . . . Indeed after the way that is called Heresie, so worship we the God of our Fathers, believing all things which are written in the Law, and the Prophets. . . . we peaceably follow our lawful Imployments, disturbing no Man, being desirous to have peace with all Men.

We are charged to be underminers of the Churches. This is also a great mistake: we never designed . . . any such thing, but heartily desire and daily pray for the well-being, flourishing, and Prosperity of all the Churches of Christ, that the Lord would more and more appear among them, to revive the life and power of Godliness in them . . . to reform whatever is amiss among them . . . the utmost Tendency our Principles, and practices can have with respect to their Churches, is but to reduce them to a nearer conformity to the will of Christ. . . .

We are charged to be Enemies to Civil Government. Ans. We know no reason why we should be charged with this. . . . It is directly against our Principles, and contrary to what we asserted in a Confession of Faith, that we formerly gave into the Court, as also to that Confession of Faith lately put forth by our Brethren in Old England, which Confession we own in every particular. . . . In paying all due demands whatsoever; not being desirous to withhold from Caesar at any time, any of his dues. . . . divers of us did with some others, freely offer ourselves for the service of the Countrey against the Indians, even in the time of their [persecution]; Among whom was William Turner, whom they pleased to make a Captain [in King Phillip's War]. . . . In this fight did good captain Turner lose his Life [at what is now called Turner's Falls]. . . .

And here we cannot but take some notice of a Book lately put forth by Mr. [Increase] Mather, entitled *the Divine Right of Infant Baptism* (sooner said than proved). . . . one main design of the Author of it . . . was (whatever is pretended) to render us as odious as he could. . . . He chargeth us with the Sin of Jeroboam in making of the lowest of the people Priests. We easily understand what he meaneth in this; our Evil in this respect, is our calling to office those that have not bin bred up in Colleges, and taught in other Tongues [Greek and Latin] . . . but it is not because we are against Learning; for we do esteem it and honor it in its place . . . But we do not think that the Spirit of God is locked up within the narrow limits of Colledge-Learning. . . .

Although the established (Congregationalist) order of Massachusetts and Connecticut exempted *bona fide* Baptists, Quakers, and Episcopalians from religious taxes after 1728, it put the power of exemption within such a narrow compass and in the hands of justices of the peace who were so highly prejudiced against them that many Baptists were either forced to pay taxes to support Congregational churches or forced to go to jail or to have their goods sold at auction by the sheriff in order to pay the tax. This "persecution for conscience' sake" continued throughout most of the eighteenth century in both Puritan and Anglican colonies. It finally pushed Baptists into demanding total separation of church and state. In 1749 and 1750 the Baptists in Massachusetts undertook a petition to the King in Council knowing that the king had the power to "disallow" laws of the colony. *Source:* Isaac Backus Papers, Andover Newton Theological School.

Inasmuch as the Cause and Interest of Our Lord Jesus Christ, & the precious truths of his Gospel & the duty of Believers consequent thereupon cheerfully to submit themselves unto a Strict Obedience to all the Institutions of our ascended Saviour, as the same are held forth & maintained by that part of his Church & People called Baptists; . . . To the Intent therefore that the present Situation of our Ecclesiastical Affairs in this distant Land . . . may be laid open & made as extensively known to Our brethren in England as conveniently may be, in order to obtain their Prayers Advice & Assistance . . . And inasmuch as it is well known to be the Settled Opinion of many of Our brethren both in

Town & Country, for us conjunctly to appoint some meet Person of
Our denomination to Embark home for England & there as Our agent
& representative personally fully & particularly to set forth the respective
circumstances & present Situation of the Baptist Churches . . . &
moreover that it is highly Requisite & expedient by all means to have
the advice & assistance of Our said Brethren at home to cooperate with
Our said agent, in Our most humble supplications to the King & in
laying before his Majesty in Council the Illegal & Oppressive measures
which for many years past have been carried on, & still to this very
day are coercively extended against our Brethren . . . in open Violation
also to the Act of Toleration & Royal Indulgence granted to his Majestys
Protestant dissenters, and quite contrary to the Tenor & true intent &
meaning of the Government at home, namely that One denomination
of Dissenters [Congregationalists] in this Province should Usurp to
themselves the absurd authority, to assess rate & lay their Taxations
upon the Necks of their fellow dissenters, & if for matters purely
Ecclesiastical, & thereby forceably to Compel them . . . to support &
maintain a set of dissenting Teachers whose public worship they, the
said Baptists, do not attend . . . We have had Our Estates plundered
& the bodies of Our said brethren committed to Gaol. . . .

2. Struggle for Religious Freedom

The result of the Baptists' petitions to the king and of their continual efforts to oppose
religious taxes was to increase the opposition of established churches and lawmakers, as
well as their neighbors, to the Baptist cause. As the colonists, after 1765, moved rapidly
toward the war for independence, the Baptists were charged with being loyal to the king,
siding against their own countrymen. This charge was given some substance when the
Baptists refused to join a "Christian Union" of colonial denominations to oppose plans
by the Archbishop of Canterbury to send an Anglican bishop to America. The following
anonymous letter was attributed to Elder Morgan Edwards of Philadelphia. *Source:
Philadelphia Chronicle,* 20 November 1770.

The Fraternity [Presbyterians and Congregationalists] last year [1769]
have sent Letters to Baptist Ministers in New England, requesting their
aid against the Church of England. But truly it is the Interest of the
Baptists that the Church of England should multiply in Massachusetts
& Connecticut, so far as to form a Balance of Ecclesiastical power
there, as in other colonies. And as for Bishops they are welcome here:
their coming thither is an Object worthy of Petitions: we cannot be

worse off; we may be better; they are Gentlemen at least and have some Generosity for Vanquished enemies. But the New-England People (of a certain denomination) are supercilious in Power, and Mean in Conquest. I will Venture to say that all the Bishops in Old England have not done the Baptists there so much harm for eighty years past, as the Presbyterians have done this year to the Baptists of New England.

Ezra Stiles (1727–1795), one of the leading Congregationalists in New England, and later president of Yale, made repeated references to the Tory inclinations of Edwards and other leading Baptists in his diary in these years. *Source:* F. B. Dexter, ed., *The Literary Diary of Ezra Stiles,* 3 vols. (New York: Charles Scribner's Sons, 1901), 1, p. 78; 2, p. 23.

Nov. 26, 1769: This Afternoon in a Conversation with Mr. C ____ of P _____, he told me it was certain that Ld. Hillsborough [one of the King's ministers] in Discourse with Revd. Morgan Edwards, the Baptist Min. in Philad'a, when in London. Aug't 1769, had encouraged & promoted the complaints of the persecution of the Baptists by the Presbyterians [i.e., Congregationalists] in N. Engld., & directed him to collect & procure all Baptists Complaints, and send them home to Engd. & they should be favorably heard, with Assurance of Redress. And this was a Scheme of the Ministry to set the Baptists against the Congregationists, & prevent the former from joyning the Latter in opposing an American Episcopate, under the notion that they should meet with more Liberty & less oppression under episcopal than presb. Government. . . .

July 16, 1776. Mr. Manning, Presid't of the Baptist College [in Rhode Island], is a Tory, affecting Neutrality. He never prayed for the [Continental] Congress or Success to our Army, till Gen. Washington returning from Boston last Spring being at Providence on Lordsday, he went to Mr. Mannings Meeting—then for the first time he prayed for the Congress & Army. But he & most of the Heads of the Baptists especially Ministers thro' the Continent are cool in this Cause, if not rather wishing the Kings side Victory. This is witnessed by the Baptist Congress at Phila. the fall before last to enter an Accusa[tion] of Massachusetts to the Gen. Congress [about religious persecution in New England]. But Mr. Manning has particul[ar]ly been against his Country in heart. . . . he said openly that there was not a Member of the Congress but might be bo[ugh]t. . . . he suggested that this was a Presbyterian

War—that the Congregationalists at the northward had prevailed upon
the Chhman [Anglicans] to the Southward to joyn them—& that it was
worth considering who (viz. Baptists) would be crushed between them
both, if they overcome. This is the heart of the bigotted Baptist Poli-
ticians.

The Baptists did in fact suffer as much, if not more, under the Anglican establishment
in the South, especially in Virginia, after 1760. A letter from a Baptist preacher, John
Waller, written in jail in Middlesex County, Virginia, in August, 1771, notes the persecution by the authorities of Baptists who said it was against their conscience to obtain
a license from "Caeser" to preach the gospel. *Source:* Quoted in James B. Taylor, *Lives
of Virginia Baptist Ministers* (Richmond: Yale & Wyatt, 1838), pp. 79-80.

At a meeting which was held at brother McCains in this county, last
Saturday, whilst brother William Webber was addressing the congregation, from James ii, 18, there came running towards him, in a most
furious rage, Captist James Montague, a magistrate of the county,
followed by the parson of the parish, and several others, who seemed
greatly exasperated. The magistrate, and another, took hold of brother
Webber, and dragging him from the stage, delivered him, with brethren
Wafford, Robert Ware, Richard Falkner, James Greenwood, and myself,
into custody, and commanded that we should be brought before him
for trial. Brother Wafford was severely scourged, and brother Henry
Street received one lash, from one of the persecutors, who was prevented
from proceeding to farther violence by his companions; to be short, I
may inform you that we were carried before the above mentioned
magistrate, who, with the parson and some others, carried us, one by
one, into a room, and examined our pockets and wallets for fire-arms,
&c. charging us with carrying on a mutiny against the authority of the
land. Finding none, we were asked if we had license to preach in this
county; and learning we had not, it was required of us to give bond
and security not to preach any more in the county, which we modestly
refused to do, whereupon, after dismissing brother Wafford, with a
charge to make his escape out of the county by twelve o'clock the next
day, on pain of imprisonment, and dismissing brother Falkner, the rest
of us were delivered to the sheriff, and sent to close jail, with a charge
not to allow us to walk in the air until court day. . . . The most dreadful
threatenings are raised in the neighboring counties against the Lord's
faithful and humble followers.

3. Problems with Other Religious Groups

As the movement gained steadily in numbers, influence, freedom, and respectability, Baptists became polemicists. No longer simply defending themselves against Puritans and Anglicans, they aggressively debated with other dissenting competitors, accusing them of perverting the gospel and maliciously leading naive souls astray. These attempts to distinguish themselves from other denominations and sects further helped them to define what it meant to be a Baptist in America. Beginning in the 1740s Baptist writers attacked a spate of sects including the New Side Presbyterians, the Sandemanians, the Shakers, the Society of the Universal Public Friend, and later in the 1780s the Universalists, Methodists, deists, and Unitarians. In part their vehement opposition to these groups derived from the fact that they had lost many of their members to them. When the Reverend Samuel Finley, a leader of the New Side Presbyterians in New Jersey, attacked the propriety and hazards of baptism by immersion, Elder Abel Morgan (1713–1785) responded in 1749. *Source:* Abel Morgan, *Anti-Paedo-Rantism or Mr. Samuel Finley's Charitable Plea for the Speechless Examined and Refuted* (Philadelphia: Benjamin Franklin, 1749), pp. 153, 155, 158.

Pray what does Mr. F. mean by his Insinuation that Dipping is dangerous, and prejudicial to People's Healths? unless he had given Instances of Persons whose Health had been injur'd by it; but this he has not, and I'm persuaded cannot: 'Tis nothing therefore but a mere Bugbear, to fright his Admirers from giving due Obedience to Jesus Christ, in this sacred Ordinance. . . . As to Mr. F's Suggestion, that Dipping is immodest and indecent; it must be only for want of better Argument; for if he has ever seen the Ordinance administered, he must acknowledge it was done with all Modesty and Decency becoming the Solemnity . . . What an odd way has Mr. F. got of representing Things! When did he ever hear any of us say that there were no Christians in other Denominations? Or how is it possible we should unchristian them, when according to our Principles, we do not administer Baptism to any, but to those, who in the Judgment of Charity, are look'd upon to be Christians? Does he think Infant-Baptism to be Essential to Christianity, when he talks at this Rate? That if we deny the one, we exclude the other. Does a Society unchristian all others with whom it cannot or doth not hold Community? If so, the Presbyterian Society unchristians all other Communities with whom it cannot, or does not hold Communion. 'Tis then high time for Mr. F. to look about him, and answer for himself.

Elder Valentine Rathbun (1723–?), having first fallen under the spell of the Shakers and then turned to the Baptists, concluded that "the spirit of witchcraft . . . leads this new scheme" and wrote to his fellow Baptists condemning not only Mother Ann Lee and the Shakers but also Jemima Wilkinson and The Society of the Universal Public Friend. The same year, 1781, Elder Isaac Backus in Massachusetts attacked the Universalists by comparing Elhanan Winchester's errors to those of James Relly. Winchester (1751–1797) formerly was a Baptist; Relly (1722–1778) was a prominent Universalist writer. *Sources:* A. Valentine Rathbun, *An Account of the Matter, Form, and Manner of a New and Strange Religion, Taught and Propagated by a Number of Europeans Living in a Place Called Nisqueunia in the State of New York* (Providence: Bennett Wheeler, 1781), p. 20. B. Isaac Backus, *The Doctrine of Universal Salvation Examined and Refuted* (Providence: John Carter, 1782), pp. 20, 21, 24.

[A. Rathbun Against Two Sects]

The great and glorious doctrines of the gospel are intended as a sacred barrier against bewitching error. . . . There never was a day that more loudly called for faithful watchmen, than the present time; while we see Satan transforming himself into an angel of light, and bringing forward his deep laid scheme, to undermine the glorious plan of redemption by Christ: And as he at first deceived the woman, and made use of her to delude the man [in Eden]; so he is playing his old prank over again, sending one woman from the state of New York [Ann Lee], and another from the State of Rhode Island (Jemima Wilkinson) who vie with each other, and are as dangerous to the heedless passenger, as Scylla and Charybdes are to the unskilful mariner.

[B. Backus on Universalism]

In March, 1781, we were surprized with a report, that Mr. Elhanan Winchester, who went from hence [Massachusetts] the autumn preceding, had fallen in with [Relly's and] Murray's doctine. . . . Relly builds upon an imaginary union with Jesus, but Winchester upon the benevolent nature of the Deity. Relly declares sin to be an infinite evil, deserving of infinite punishment; but Winchester treats it as a natural, and not a moral evil; as a calamity rather than a crime. Relly holds that salvation is already compleat in Christ, so as to exempt men from all future punishment; but Winchester denies the need of Christ's blood to appease any wrath in the Deity, and holds it as a medicine to purge away disorders in nature, which are so great as to require the sufferings of many ages before all will be removed. Relly rather takes it for granted that all men are in Christ, than attempting any fair proof of it; but

Winchester states plain arguments upon it, and answers objections. Relly's scheme did not permit him to speak of salvation for devils; but Winchester's points thereto. . . . One of the errors that this carried him [Winchester] into was to say, 'that the torments of the damned will have an end; and that as Christ has been crucified in this world to save mankind, he is to be crucified in the next to save the devils.' From this source came the doctrine of monkery, purgatory, prayers for the dead, and all the rest of the corruptions and tyrannies of Rome. . . . Truth says, 'The wrath of God is revealed from heaven against all ungodliness, and unrighteousness of men, who hold the truth in unrighteousness;' Rom. i, 18. Winchester says, 'Fury, wrath, or anger, can never dwell in the fountain of love, but are only to be found in fallen nature, separated from the life of God.'

How could any man talk at this rate, who pretended to regard the truth of scripture, if he was not involved in a great mist of darkness!

4. The Ordinances—Signs of the Faith

Together with most other Protestants, the Baptists emphasized as central to church membership and fellowship the two basic ordinances of baptism and the Lord's Supper. What made the Baptist persuasion different was its beliefs that only those old enough to make an oral profession of their faith (and their conversion experience) were eligible for baptism and that baptism itself should be by total immersion. Most Baptists believed in total immersion "in living waters," and a common place for baptisms was the shallow bank of a river or stream (although the First Baptist Church in Providence used the headwaters of Narragansett Bay). The Lord's Supper, usually held monthly or bimonthly (among those in good Christian fellowship), utilized a common Communion cup and fermented wine. Churches that had black members usually gave the cup first to white members. While some Baptists added the ordinance of the laying on of hands upon all believers as a requisite for church membership and some practiced foot washing, the kiss of charity, anointing with oil, and other rituals, the overwhelming majority of Baptists considered baptism and Communion the only ordinances clearly prescribed in the New Testament. The following selections demonstrate the variety of ordinance experiences among colonial Baptists. *Sources:* A. Morgan Edwards, *Materials Towards A History of the Baptists in Pennsylvania* (Philadelphia: Joseph Crukshank, 1770), 1, pp. 130-132. B. Minutes of the Lower Dublin Baptist Church (c. 1692), p. 3. Archives, American Baptist Historical Society. C. *Minutes of the Charleston (South Carolina) Baptist Association,* 1810, p. 3.

[A. Morgan Edwards, A Baptismal Scene]
In this river I have baptized many. My predecessor, Rev. J. Jones, &c. had done the same before me. Nay, a late clergyman of the church of England was wont to make this river his baptisterion. The part above

refered to is about a mile and a half out of Philadelphia; and is not only convenient for the celebration of baptism but most delightful for rural sceneries. Hither the townspeople in summer resort for recreation and entertainment. To this river hath Francis Hopkinson Esq. led his bards and literati to sweep their lyres and meditate on justice and religion. Round said spot are large oak, affording fine shade. Underfoot, is a green, variegated with wild flowers and aromatic herbs. Just by was lately erected a house for dressing and undressing, and for the use of the *proseuches* of the ancients. Act. xvi, 13: it is divided into two rooms by a hanging partition, and so contrived that when the partition is lifted up and the doors opened, and the folding shutter in the front let down, that it resembles an alcove, facing a prospect of land, wood, water, rocks, hills, boats, &c. In the midst of this spot is a large stone rising about three feet above ground, round which I have often seen the people (in imitation of Christ, Lu. iii, 21) kneel to pray after baptism had been administered. The top is made level by art, and steps hewn to ascend; on the top stands the minister to preach to the people who resort thither to see baptism performed; and a multitude of hearers he commonly has. I have once reckoned there 32 carriages, and have often seen present from 100 to 1000 people, all behaving much better than in some other places. With these exercises of religion and the delightfulness of the place many confess to have had such feelings as the disciples when they said, *Lord, it is good for us to be here! Let us here erect tabernacles!* By way of conclusion to this appendix I will add the hymn that is wont to be sung in this place upon the occasions before named, with some additions to accomodate it to Helmsley-tune; if it be sung to the old tune the additions [in crotchets] must be omitted, and two verses put together.

Schuylkill Hymn

Jesus master O discover
Pleasure in us, now we stand
On this bank of Schuylkill river,
To obey thy great command,
[Pleasure in us, pleasure in us, pleasure in us, Who obey thy great command]

Make this stream, like Jordan, blessed.
Leprous Naamans enter in.
Rise, saith Jesus, *be baptized,*

And you wash away your sin.
[Be baptized, be baptized, be baptized, And you wash away your sin]

> Here the world and flesh and devil
> We do solemnly renounce;
> Here we vow to cease from evil;
> And a life to God announce.

[Cease from evil, cease from evil, cease from evil, And a life to God announce.

> Of our vows this stone's a token
> *Stone of witness* bear record
> 'Gainst us, if our vows be broken
> Or if we forsake the Lord.

[Solemn vowing, solemn vowing, solemn vowing, Stone of witness bear record.]

> Help us, thou baptized Jesus!
> What we vowed to fulfil.
> Of our fears of failing ease us.
> Form and mould us to thy will.

[Help us Jesus, help us Jesus, help us Jesus, What we vowed to fulfil]

> Hence we go our way rejoicing
> Conscious of our pleasing God,
> Foll'wing Jesus still proposing
> In the paths his feet have trod.

[Go rejoicing, go rejoicing, go rejoicing, Conscious of our pleasing God]

[B. The Lord's Supper]

The usual Customs oberved by Elias Keach at the Celebration of the Lords Supper was to deliver the bread and the Cup to the Deacon, and the Deacon delivered it unto the Communicants. Also he usually Concluded with singing of A hymn of praise Composed for that purpose, and then with Committing us to god by prayers.

The Deacon used to provide bread & wine for the Lords table with the money which was gathered as there was occasion at the time of Communion.

[C. Foot Washing]

Query: from the church at Little Pedee—'Is the washing of feet, mentioned in the 13th chapter of John, to be considered an ordinance of the Gospel?

Answer: We are induced to think it is not: at least, not to be ranked with baptism and the Lord's supper, as a church ordinance. For a variety of reasons it appears to us that the thing signified, rather than the bodily act is enjoined by the Redeemer; but should any think it their duty to perform that act as a religious rite, especially in a private manner, among friends, we think it may be done without just cause of offence to any.

5. Ties with England

Colonial America was a provincial society on the edge of a wilderness, and the Baptists were, throughout most of the colonial period, a struggling group of diverse and scattered congregations without leadership or institutional power.

On more than one occasion Americans turned to the Baptist theologians and scholars in England for arguments, tracts, apologia, and creedal statements to defend their faith against the learned attacks of other ministers. The leading English Baptists with whom they corresponded in the eighteenth century were John Rippon, John Gill, John Stennett, John Ryland, Benjamin Wallin, John Keith, and Isaac Woodman, many of whom favored the colonies in their war for independence. Typical of the kinds of assistance Baptists in America sought from their English brethren can be found in this letter from the Philadelphia Association "To the board of Particular Baptist Ministers in London," in May, 1762. *Source:* Abraham Dunn Gillette, ed., *Minutes of the Philadelphia Baptist Association 1707-1807* (Philadelphia: American Baptist Publication Society, 1851), p. 84.

We greet you well: and as a part of that community in the British dominians [called Baptists] . . . we offer you our acquaintance and solicit a share of your public care and friendship. Our numbers in these parts multiply, for when we had the pleasure of writing you in 1734, there were but nine churches in our Association, yet now there are twenty-eight, all owning the Confession of faith put forth in London in 1689. Some of the churches are now destitute [of pastors], but we have a prospect of supplies, partly by means of a Baptist academy lately set up [in Hopewell, New Jersey]. This infant seminary of learning is yet weak, having no more than 24 pounds a year towards its support. Should it be in your power to favor this school in any way, we presume you will be pleased to know how. A few books proper for such a school, or a small apparatus or some pieces of apparatus are more immediately wanted, and not to be had easily in these parts. We have also of late, endeavored to form a library at Philadelphia for the use of our brethren in the ministry who are not able to purchase books. This design also wants the assistance of our brethren in England.

An extensive correspondence took place between James Manning (1738–1791), the first president of the Baptist College of Rhode Island, and various ministers in England. He not only solicited books and funds for the college but also sought advice on whom the college might honor in England with honorary degrees at each commencement. He also kept the English brethren informed of the revivals and the persecutions of the Baptists and solicited their help against the latter. Typical is an exchange with the Reverend John Ryland in London in 1772. *Sources:* A. James Manning to John Ryland, 19 May 1772. James Manning Papers, John Hay Library, Brown University. B. John Ryland to James Manning, 9 February 1773. *Ibid.*

[A. Manning to Ryland, May 19, 1772]

On the 5th ult. I received your letter, as I judged from the contents, for it had neither your name nor any date to it. The contents gave me very great pleasure on various accounts,—as a testimony of your regard for me, the college, and the cause of religion in general, and especially for the zeal you discover in promoting the Baptist interest. The list of names you sent me [for honorary degrees] shall be laid before the Faculty next September, and without doubt they will receive the honors of the college. We shall also be obliged to you for your proposed favor of sending us some names every year, and such, too, as are worthy of honor. I saw a paragraph in a letter to Rev. Isaac Backus from Rev. Benjamin Wallin, of London, in which he intimated we had conferred degrees on some on your side of the water who would not do us honor. I shall therefore rely on you to pay particular regard to the literary qualifications of those whom you recommend, in order that our enemies may not have it in their power to reproach us on this head. . . . The present of the volume of poems will be very acceptable. Please give my cordial love to the author, of whom I shall be mindful amongst others who deserve the honors of the college. . . . I shall make free to draw on you again the 1st of June, by Mr. [Morgan] Edwards' instruction, and continue to do so yearly until you forbid me. What think you of an application to England, by some suitable person in order to augment our little and insufficient fund [for the college], as Mr. Edwards made but a partial application [for money when he was in England]; or would a well-concerted scheme of a lottery to raise £1000 or £2000 sterling meet with encouragement by the sale of tickets in England? Some method must be adopted unless some generous, able benefactors should arise to assist us. . . .

[B. John Ryland's reply, February 9, 1773]

I have enclosed a few hints for your notice and consideration. If they are of any service to you, or to the cause of religion and to your college of learning, I shall be glad. . . . In January, 1772, I sent a box of twenty-five books . . . to Rhode Island College, but have heard nothing. . . . For me to ask any of those gentlemen I nominated in my letter, whether he would please to accept of a degree from your college, would spoil all the honor and delicacy of conferring it. Its coming *unsought,* yea, *unthought* of, constitutes its chief excellence and acceptableness to men of fine feelings. . . . By your withholding these honors from the men I so well knew to deserve them, and not one would have refused them, you have done your college damage in its temporal interests. My design was to serve you by attaching men of grace, learning, property, and influence to you. . . . As to raising money by a lottery, I dislike it from the bottom of my heart. 'Tis a scheme dishonorable to the supreme Head of all worlds and of the true church. . . . Let the devil's children have them all to themselves.

Institutional Characteristics
of a Denomination

From despised, persecuted, hole-in-the-corner dissenters within the established church-state colonies of New England and the South, the Baptists slowly grew in organization and respect until by 1776 they assumed the rank of one of the most important denominations in the new nation. In the process they exchanged some of their original fervor and egalitarianism for a more formal sense of ecclesiastical structure and order. More important, the Baptists wished to band together in associations to muster their strength to fight for religious liberty and to maintain the doctrinal purity of their churches. At the same time, they wished to expand their activities and number of members, to ordain evangelists, to raise funds to educate ministers, to found academies and a college, to start a missionary society, and to publish their own periodicals.

The development of Baptist leadership and ecclesiastical organizations caused internal dissension. Some felt that the denomination was losing its piety to worldliness; others feared that a learned ministry might not be a spirit-filled ministry; and some worried over the strategy of seeking civil incorporation from the state for their religious societies. As Baptists grew in wealth, especially in urban communities, they wished to have dignified meetinghouses with cushioned pews and ornate candelabras and to have their ministers dress as fashionably as other ministers, display college learning, speaking Latin and Greek, and be able to defend the faith in published sermons and tracts. By 1812 the Baptists had ceased to be a small despised sect and were rapidly becoming the largest denomination in the United States.

1. Church Covenants—Compacts of Congregations

Theologically and organizationally, church identity often commenced with the creation of a covenant. It was a frequent pattern for those who wished to form a Baptist congregation to meet together, to agree upon a set of principles that would guide their common life, and to create specific vows of membership. Those signing the covenant originally would thus constitute a church, and those wishing to join the congregation at a later date would usually be required to affirm the terms of the covenant as a means of church discipline upon all members. Most early church records begin with a covenant and the covenants vary among congregations. In an attempt to offer a standard form of covenant, Samuel Jones (1735–1814) wrote the following model that was included in the first Baptist church manual printed in America. *Source:* Samuel Jones, *A Treatise of Church Discipline and a Directory, Done by Appointment of the Philadelphia Baptist Association* (Philadelphia: S. C. Ustick, 1798), pp. 9-10.

THE CHURCH COVENANT

We, whose names are under written, being desirous to be constituted a church of Jesus Christ, in this place, and having all due knowledge of one another in point of a work of grace on our hearts, religious principles, and moral characters, and being desirous of enjoying the privileges that appertain to the people of God in a church relation, do, in the name of the Lord Jesus, voluntarily and freely give ourselves up to the Lord, and to one another, according to his word, to be one body under one head, jointly to exist and act by the bands and rules of the gospel, and do promise and engage to do all things, by divine assistance, in our different capacities and relations that the Lord has commanded us, and requires of us: particularly to deny ourselves, take up our cross, follow Christ, keep the faith, assemble ourselves together, love the brethren, submit one to another in the Lord, care one for another, bear one another's burdens, endeavour to keep the unity of the spirit in the bond of peace, and, finally, to honour, obey, and maintain them that may have the rule over us in the Lord. This is the Covenant we solemnly enter into, in the fear of God, humbly imploring the Divine assistance and blessing that we may be built up and established to the glory of God, the advancement of the Redeemer's interest, and the comfort and edification of our own souls, through the infinite riches of free grace, which is in Jesus Christ our Lord: and now, to the only wise God, Father, Son, and Holy Spirit, be worship, honour, power, glory, dominion, and obedience rendered, now and ever more, Amen.

2. Church Offices, Titles, and Functions

Baptists held firmly to the autonomy of each congregation and church to choose its ministers and other officers. But the precise means of calling persons to offices and acceptable definitions of the offices were more difficult to achieve. Throughout the colonial era in America, different churches and associations wrestled with the problems of licensing preachers, ordaining ministers, and choosing ruling elders and deacons. Some worried over whether it was proper for a licensed preacher to baptize; some thought only ordained ministers could preach or teach the gospel publicly. One of the thornier questions involved ordaining gifted persons as "evangelists," traveling preachers able to perform baptisms and serve Communion. After the First Great Awakening, it was clear that traveling preachers "promised much advantage to the Baptist interest" by spreading Baptist principles, and by the 1770s associations in the various colonies were ordaining evangelists who were free to preach and administer the ordinances anywhere. The following excerpts from minutes of the Philadelphia Association provide illustrations of these efforts to define the titles and functions and to grant recognition of Baptist church officers in the eighteenth century. It is worth noting that while Baptists eschewed the terms "reverend" and "minister" prior to 1776 (because the titles were associated with the established churches), thereafter they began to abandon the humble title of "elder" and assume the same right as other denominations to call their pastors "reverend ministers." *Source:* Gillette, *Minutes of the Philadelphia Baptist Association,* pp. 38, 56, 86, 50, 29, 119, 130.

[Ministers]
[1738]

Query. Whether a person, ordained by laying on hands, for a ruling elder, who should afterwards be called by the church, by reason of his gifts, to the word and doctrine, must be again ordained by imposition of hands? Resolved in the affirmative.

[1747]

. . . it is the duty of the churches to call and prove their candidates for the ministry, whom we judge ought to wait with self denying meekness, humbleness, and lowliness of mind to a further approbation from the churches of their ordination and investiture into the sacred functions, and not urge or hasten it themselves, contrary to the mind and judgment of the church which gave them a call to exercise their gifts.

[1762]

. . . Certificates of the ordination and good morals of Rev. David Thomas and Rev. David Sutton, were drawn up by Rev. Samuel Jones and Isaac Jones, Esq., and the city seal affixed thereto by the Recorder, Benjamin Chew, Esq., for which he took no fees.

Here follows a copy thereof:

CERTIFICATE

"The ministers and messengers of the several Baptist congregations in Pennsylvania and adjacent provinces, met in annual Association at the city of Philadelphia, October 12, 1762.

"To all Christian people, to whom these presents may come, send greeting.

"This certifies that the bearer hereof, Rev. David Thomas, late of Chester county, in the province of Pennsylvania, but now residing and dwelling in Farquair county, in the province of Virginia, was, (after due examination, whereby he appeared to have a competent share of learning and other prerequisites to the sacred office,) admitted into holy orders, according to the known and approved rites of the Baptist church, whereby he is authorized to preach the gospel, and adminster the ordinances thereof. And also certifies, that at all times, before and after his ordination, (for any thing known, heard, or believed to the contrary,) he lived a holy and unblemished life. And we do hereby recommend him as such to the notice, esteem, and regard of all Christians where he now does, or hereafter may, reside.

"Signed by order of the Association, October 13, 1762, by their moderator,

"Morgan Edwards, A.M."

[Teachers]
1746

. . . Seeing men are called teachers, as Paul and Barnabas are in Acts xiii. 1, and did undoubtedly teach profitably in the church of Antioch before and without ordination, what reason can be given why there may not be in churches *men of useful gifts,* and profitable to teach all the days of their life without ordination? It is very probable that the Apostle Paul, seeing he occupied such a station himself a long time, speaks of such *gifted brethren,* Ephes. iv. 11, by the name of teachers. Seeing they are mentioned besides the pastors, or that such useful men may be the helps the same apostle mentions, 1 Cor. xii. 28, for helps cannot be more useful in any thing than in teaching. Our churches have had such teachers very frequently, as we might instance in many of them by name, if need were as well as the church of Antioch.

Here it will be proper to consider what time of trial or probation is, or ought to be taken, in proving church officers in general. We must note that the Holy Ghost hath no where limited or bounded the time that a church is to take for the trial of any of her officers; and therefore every particular church is at liberty to use her discretion in this matter; the call, choice, and ordination of her own officers being a special privilege that Christ hath given to his church under the gospel dispensation. Since the Lord Jesus Christ hath left these important affairs to his church, and intrusted her to apply his directions, according to her circumstances, by the rules of prudence and discretion; therefore it must be an intrenchment upon her liberty and privilege, for any to use means to force or constrain a church, either to put a person on trial or to hasten his ordination; both of which ought to be the free, joyful, and unconstrained acts of a church. . . .

[Ruling Elders or Deacons]
[1728]

Query from Hopewell: What course to take in choosing a ruling elder in the church? We answer, that a church wanting ruling elders or deacons, as in other cases, should set a day apart, and by fasting and prayer, seek the guidance and direction of God, and then unanimously pitch upon one or more of their brethren to act upon trial in the office of ruling elder or deacon; and our judgment is, that persons called upon trial in the said offices, may act by authority of the church, with as full power as if completely qualified; but not so teaching elders or ministers of the word and ordinances. . . .

[1746]

Query: Whether it is regular for any to use the office of deacon, or to exercise the office of a ruling elder in a church, without ordination?

Solution. As touching ruling elders or deacons; if there had been no other rule but mere parity of reason, it would appear necessary to have a proof of the persons delegated to those offices by a trial in the office itself; for experience teacheth that some very regular members cannot become useful officers when tried, and if persons, likely to bear the ministerial function, may be found unfit for the office when tried, though sound in the faith, and of approved conversation, so may well minded and well respected persons be found, when tried, to be unfit for inferior offices. If it be objected that we have a precedent for choosing and ordaining deacons, without any proof or trial, it may be sufficient to answer, that the precedent in Acts vi. is very proper to inform us of the nature and property of the deacon's office; but cannot reasonably be pleaded to be imitable in future times, in that particular, in debate;

because, 1, that was an extraordinary time, and done by extraordinary persons; and therefore not imitable in ordinary times nor ordinary persons, unless we could bring extraordinary times and persons to be alike, which we cannot. 2. Because the Holy Ghost, since that precedent, hath given us a positive rule to direct the church in ordinary times, which we are bound to follow, 1 Tim. iii. 10; from which the church in after ages ought not to deviate. . . .

[Evangelists]
[1771]

A motion being made in the Association, relative to the appointment of an Evangelist, it was universally agreed that such an appointment promised much advantage to the Baptist interests. Five ministers were put in nomination for the office, viz: Rev. Messrs. John Gano, Benjamin Miller, Samuel Jones, David Jones, Morgan Edwards. The choice fell on the last, which he accepted on the conditions then specified.

[1773]

. . . The usefulness of a traveling minister on this continent appearing more manifest by trials, and Brother Morgan Edwards declining the office, it was agreed that Brother John Gano be a messenger of the churches for this year; and that the treasurer do pay him the interest of the Association fund, to help defraying his expenses.

3. The Associational Principle at Work

At first the covenant and articles of each individual, autonomous, Baptist congregation provided the only form of organization known to the denomination, but after 1707 the major sources of institutional order, unity, growth, and oversight of the denominations lay in the associations. A "Circular Letter" in the Shaftsbury Association minutes of 1791 indicates the continuing effort to protect the autonomy of local churches by spelling out the respective rights of churches and associations. *Source: Minutes of The Shaftsbury Association* (1791), pp. 7-14.

In our minutes of last year we expressed our intention, of explaining the third article of the plan of this association; which particularly relates to its power. In order to throw light on this subject and discover the distinctions really existing between the power of churches and that of an association; it is necessary to attend primarily to the scripture account of the nature, business, power and government of a gospel church. . . . The church is said to be the pillar and ground of the truth, I Tim. iii.

15. . . . It must then be the prerogative of the church to say, who shall be received as members. . . . if it is the church's province to say who shall be admitted, it is hers also to say who shall be continued as visible members . . . and to exclude such from her fellowship, as are transgressors of divine rule. . . . Furthermore the rule given to deal with those guilty of private offences, must issue in telling it to the church, as the proper board of trial; from which there is no appeal to any higher place of trial, on earth. . . . It is also the church's province, to try, prove, and judge of those who profess to be ministers of Christ; and receive or reject them according as they appear to be true or false. . . . As to the office of bishop or the gospel ministry, they have a special commission from Christ, to go forth and teach and baptize. . . . But if by their consent they are appointed as pastors of particular churches, then they are said to have the rule over them, and the church is to be in subjection to them. . . .

We come now to speak of an association, by which we mean no more, than a number of churches in sister relation, mutually agreeing to meet by their delegates, at stated seasons, for free conference on those matters that concern the general good of the churches: that we might be mutual helpers to each other.. . . In which conference any church has a right to propose any question that relates to doctrine or discipline, provided that such questions are always so circumstanced, that the solution of them will not interfere with the government of particular churches . . . in case any church or churches shall apostatise from the faith and become corrupt, . . . it is the duty of this association . . . to inform the churches in general, that we consider those churches who have fallen, no longer in our fellowship. It is the duty of this association to give information of apostates, and corrupt men in the ministry; that the churches may not be imposed upon by them. . . . Finally brethren we consider ourselves, to have no power as an association to determine any cases of discipline in the churches; but we are only to give our advice and opinion in those points, and intelligence to such matters as come within the limits of a free christian conference.

4. A Plan for a General Union

By the time of the American Revolution, Baptist organizational life was rapidly expanding. The Philadelphia Association had become the hub of a network of associations from Rhode Island to the Carolinas, and several of its strong leaders helped to shape church life in a broad geographic area. One of those leaders, Morgan Edwards, in 1770 proposed a union of churches into associations, which would be coordinated by the central Philadelphia organization. Although 104 associations were formed between 1775 and 1815, the plan for a general union was ahead of its time, in part because of fiercely autonomous attitudes in New England and regional sentiments in the South. Edwards' plan is revealed below. *Source:* Morgan Edwards, *Materials . . . in Pennsylvania,* 1, pp. i-iv.

By the said union is meant, an union of individuals into churches so that no baptized believers abide loose and scattered (like the stones of the sanctuary in the book of Lamentation) as is now the case in some places; also, an union of those churches (and of other churches which have hitherto stood by themselves) into associations in proper vicinities, which associations may be multiplied so as to have one in every province; and likewise, an union of those associations (like that of Ketokton and Warren) to the associations of Philadelphia, which, from its situation, must ever be central to the whole—By the forementioned means of intercourse are to be understood, letters and messengers from the churches to their respective associations, and from those associations to their common center; and from the center back to the associations, and thence to the churches, and so to individuals. These means will not only be useful for receiving and returning intelligence, mutual advice, help &c but also for "knitting together" the several parts of the visible baptist church on the continent, as the parts of the natural body are by "joints and bands. Gal. ii. 19. This project is not a new one, but was begun in the year 1765 when the churches to the west of Philadelphia formed themselves into an association at Ketokton in Virginia; and was furthered in 1767 when the churches to the east of Philadelphia did the same at Warren in Rhodeisland government, both adopting the philadelphian plan and engaging to use the means of union and intercourse before described. The thing is practicable, as appears by five years trial; and withal, most beneficial, as might be proved by variety of examples. What remains is only to perfect what has been begun. In order to which the following things have been judged requisite.

    1. That the association of Philadelphia be embodied by charter; and that one person from every provincial association be made a member of that enchartered body

    2. That an able preacher be appointed to visit all the churches in the character and office of an EVANGELIST; and a sufficient fund raised to

defray his expences. Such a fund was set on foot in Philadelphia in 1766, and is increasing every year.

3. That the nature of associations among the Baptists be made public. Something of the kind was attempted in 1769 under the title of THE SENTIMENTS AND PLAN OF THE WARREN ASSOCIATION: wherein it is shown that they are only ADVISORY COUNCILS, disclaiming all jurisdiction and power and every thing else which may clash with the rights of particular churches or those of private judgment; and herein they differ from all assemblies of the kind known by the same or other names.

4. That all the baptist churches from Nova Scotia to Georgia be made sufficiently known one to another; for it hath been found by experience that a want of this kind of knowledge hath much retarded the proposed design. . . .

5. Lastly, that the terms of the proposed union should be so general as not to preclude any baptist church of fair character, though differing from others in unessential points of faith or order. Practising believer's-baptism is our denominating article.

5. An Educational Institution

A major source of institutional strength for the denomination came with the decision in 1764 to obtain a charter from Rhode Island to establish a four-year college, equivalent to Harvard, Yale, New Jersey, or William and Mary, for the purpose of providing bachelor of arts and master of arts degrees under the aegis of a corporation, trustees, and college president dominated by members of their own persuasion. *Source: Acts and Resolves at the General Assembly of the Governor and Company of the English Colony of Rhode Island and Providence Plantations October 1747–October 1800,* 18 vols. (Providence: J. J. Bongartz, 1908-25), 5, p. 110.

An Act for the Establishment of a College or University
within this Colony, February, 1764

Whereas institutions for liberal education are highly beneficial to society, by forming the rising generation to virtue, knowledge, and useful literature; and thus preserving in the community a succession of men duly qualified for discharging the offices of life with usefulness and reputation; they have therefore justly merited and received the attention and encouragement of every wise and well-regulated-state: And whereas a public school or seminary, erected for that purpose within this Colony, to which the youth may freely resort for education in the vernacular and learned languages, and in the liberal arts and sciences, would be for the general advantage and honour of the government, . . . Now, therefore, know ye, That, being willing to encourage and patronize such an honourable and useful institution, we the said Governor and Company, in General Assembly convened, Do, for ourselves and our successors . . . enact, grant, constitute, ordain and declare that [those named] and their successors, shall be forever hereafter one body corporate . . . known in law by the name of Trustees and Fellows of the College or University in the English Colony of Rhode-Island and Providence Plantations. . . . And that the number of the Trustees shall and may be thirty-six of which twenty-two shall be forever elected of the denomination called Baptists or Antipaedobaptists.

6. Voluntary Associations and Incorporation

Colonial laws in support of the established churches made it difficult or impossible for Baptist churches to protect their financial and property interests or to collect membership assessments and tithes that were agreed to voluntarily. Incorporation as a voluntary society provided an effective vehicle to meet both needs, and local churches often followed this pattern for these reasons. Incorporation also became a means of establishing societies and associations to achieve benevolent purposes, as in the case of the Warren Baptist Association's creation of an Education Society in 1791 to raise money to train young men for the ministry.

In 1774 James Manning and thirty-eight members of the First Baptist Church in Providence, Rhode Island, petitioned the colonial government to incorporate the "Charitable Baptist Society," which would essentially conduct the legal and business affairs of the congregation. One of the first projects of the corporation was to raise support in order to erect a suitable meetinghouse (which became a landmark of Baptist achievement). The delineation between "church" and "society" became an important pattern for congregations in the Northeast as "spiritual" affairs began to be administered separately from "temporal" matters. *Source:* Records of the Charitable Baptist Society, (1774), 1, pp. 4, 12. Archives, Rhode Island Historical Society.

By the Honourable the Governor and Company of the English Colony of Rhode Island and Providence Plantations in New England in America, in General Assembly convened at Newport within and for the said Colony, on the Third Wednesday in May in the year of our LORD one Thousand Seven Hundred & Seventy four and Fourteenth of the Reign of His most Sacred Majesty George the third by the Grace of God. King of Great Britain and so forth.

To All Whom these Presents shall come,
Greeting

Whereas sundry Persons belonging to the Congregation assembling for the Publik Worship of Almighty God, with the Christian Church called Baptist or Antipedobaptist in the Town of Providence being the oldest Christian Church in the State or Colony and professing to believe that Water Baptism ought to be administered by Immersion only and that professed Believers in Jesus Christ and no others are proper Subjects of the Same have petitioned this Assembly to grant them a Charter of Incorporation, with the privileges and powers herein after mentioned. . . . [These persons] and their Successors shall be forever hereafter, One Body corporate and Politick, in Fact and Name, with perpetual succession, to be known in the Law, as the name of the Charitable Baptist Society in the Town of Providence in the Colony of Rhode Island and Providence Plantations.

And the said Charitable Society is hereby empowered to take, receive and hold any voluntary Subscriptions, contributions, Legacies & Donations of any sum or Sums of Money, or of any Real or personal Estate: Also to have, take, possess, purchase, acquire, or other (wise) receive and hold Lands, Tennements, _____, goods, chattles, or other Estates, of all which they shall and may stand sacred, notwithstanding any misnomer of this Corporation, and by whatever name or however imperfectly, the same shall be described in Donations, Legacies, Assignments and Grants, provided the true intent and meaning of the assigner or Benefactor be evident. Also the said Charitable Society, is hereby empowered to take hold and stand seized of all estates aforesaid, solely to and for the use and Benefit of the said Baptist or Antipedobaptist Church and Congregation, and their Successors forever, and the same to use occupy and improve towards the support of Pastors, relief of the Poor, in Schooling their Children or otherwise, or any other Religious uses in said Church and Congregation according to the will of the Donors, and to the purpose, Trusts and uses to which they shall be siezed thereof, or the same shall be designed. . . .

To many Baptists, legal incorporation as a religious society seemed to be a breach of the important principle of separation of church and state. Many associations adopted positions similar to the following by the Shaftsbury (Vermont) Association, which discouraged in most circumstances any form of incorporation. In view of the nonbinding nature of such resolutions, many congregations chose to ignore such advice. *Source: Minutes of the Shaftsbury Association,* 1803, p. 10.

We view it derogatory to the dignity of Zion's King, and undervaluing his ample code of laws, for Christian churches to apply to civil authority to be incorporated as bodies politic, for the purposes of regulating their ecclesiastical concerns, or forcing their members to support their preachers; or even for the sake of getting exemption from religious oppression [the courts having refused to recognize the existence of unincorporated churches in Massachusetts]: believing religion (in all its branches) to be no object of civil government, nor any wise under its controul. It may, nevertheless, be proper in some of the states, for Churches to avail themselves of the act of incorporation, for the sole purpose of holding social property.

7. Baptists Join the Mainstream of American Protestantism

With a growing emphasis upon a learned clergy and growing access to the surplus wealth of prosperous Baptists, the denomination, particularly in the cities, began to seek the accoutrements of respectability. A young Baptist minister, who later left the Baptists because he found them too worldly, recalled his entry into the Baptist ministry in urban Massachusetts in the 1790s. *Source:* Elias Smith, *The Life, Conversion, Preaching, Travels, and Sufferings of Elias Smith* (Portsmouth: Beck and Foster, 1816), pp. 104-105, 224-225, 278-279, 282-283.

As I had been brought up in the woods, everything in such a great town as Springfield attracted my attention; particularly things under the name of religion. . . . The first thing that drew my attention was the meeting-house, which was adorned beyond what I had ever seen in the log meeting-houses in Vermont. It was solemn to me, as I was told it was the house of God. The next thing I noticed was the dress of the people, particularly the young men, who were in costly array, compared to my clothing. The third object which set me to staring was the minister, who made such an appearance as I have never before seen. In the first place, he had a long, black, outside garment on with a broad belt of the same round his waist. The sleeves I then thought were as wide as the meal bags used in Vermont. . . . Next he had something fastened under his chin, which then appeared to me like what the children in Connecticut used to wear, when they were cutting teeth, called a bibb. . . . In addition to this, he had on his head, what Dr. [Thomas] Baldwin [of Boston] used to call a folio wig. This was very large, white and powdered; or as I then thought, covered over with flour. From all this pompous appearance, I supposed much divinity and good matter was contained in the head, the wig contained. . . . When he read his psalm, it was in a cold, dull, lifeless manner. When he prayed, his prayer was as long as a Pharisee's prayer. . . . [Later, in Boston] the Doctor [Baldwin] came, and we all went to meeting together. As soon as I entered the door, the chandelier took my attention, and on ascending the pulpit stairs, the damask curtains, cushing [cushions], and silver candlestsicks set me to gazing. . . . [After being chosen minister in Woburn, near Boston] The ministers in Boston said, 'You must be installed.' This I was entirely ignorant of, as no such thing was mentioned in the bible. . . . When we came out of the counsel chamber, and formed a procession to walk in baptist clerical order to the meeting-house, we looked as much like the cardinals coming out of the conclave after electing a pope. . . . After performing, this man-made, anti-Christian ceremony [of installation], . . . we all returned to the council chamber. . . . While at Woburn . . . I became quite too respectable for a minister of Christ. They dressed me in black, from head to foot; and on some occasions a part of my dress was silk, with a large, three-cornered hat and a cloak of the best. I built an house there; kept an horse and carriage, and lived in ease as other salary men do. . . . I once told Mr. Baldwin, we [Baptists] were going back to the place from whence we came out. His reply was 'We wish to make our denomination respectable. . . .'

Benjamin Randall

Isaac Backus

Andrew C. Marshall

Adoniram Judson

Social Ethics and
Christian Life-Style

Being devoutly committed to the transcendent standards of biblical principles, most Baptists tried to avoid worldliness. Still they had to make ethical decisions regarding certain social, political, and economic practices upon which the Bible provided only ambiguous guidance. So long as they were an oppressed and downtrodden group, they could measure their private code of conduct by contrast with the worldly corruptions of their persecutors. Where the members of the establishment in church and state were haughty, proud, censorious, cruel, materialistic, ambitious, and harshly competitive, the Baptists held up as their standards of conduct a spirit of loving community, egalitarianism, philanthropy, mercy, fair-dealing, sharing, and self-abnegation. Where the dominant social class used political power to suppress religious dissent, Baptists called for religious liberty and equality in preaching God's Word. Where the well-to-do upper class seemed vain, profligate, and lacking piety, Baptists held up high standards for their members of humility, simplicity, and family prayer.

However, in social ethics Baptists found themselves participants in political and economic issues in which they could not distinguish themselves from their neighbors. They, too, owned black slaves and condoned slavery; they, too, confined women to a narrow inferior sphere in church and state; they, too, worried over British interference in the colonial economy. And they shared the regional attitudes of their neighbors toward other parts of the colonies—New England Baptists found it easier to denounce slavery, for example, than Southern Baptists; eastern, urban Baptists found it easier than western, rural Baptists to denounce Shay's Rebellion and the Whiskey Rebellion. While most

Baptists deplored partisan political factions, the vast majority voted for
Jefferson's party out of respect for Jefferson's commitment to religious
liberty and low taxes. While they, as individuals, deplored gambling,
most Baptists thought lotteries to raise money for their churches or
college were justifiable. Even those white Baptists who opposed slavery
as an institution doubted the intellectual equality of blacks and Indians
with whites and consented to their economic, social, and religious
segregation as second-class citizens. Ethnocentric prejudice generally
prevailed over transcendent Christian ideals among white Baptists as it
did among other white, Protestant, English-speaking Christians.

1. The Question of Revolt Against England

The Baptists were ardent supporters of the right of revolution, and many Baptists
served as chaplains in Washington's army. A petition to the political leaders of Virginia
in 1775, from the "Virginia Baptists now Associated in Cumberland," explains their
patriotism despite the persecution they had suffered under the established church in that
state since 1760. *Source:* Colonial State Papers (petitions). Virginia State Library, Richmond, Virginia.

Alarmed at the shocking Oppression which in a British Cloud hangs
over our American Continent, we, as a Society and part of the distressed
State [of Virginia], have in our Association consider'd what part might
be most prudent for the Baptists to act in the present unhappy Contest.
After we had determined 'that in some Cases it was lawful to go to
War, and also for us to make a Military resistance against Great Britain,
in regard of their unjust Invasion, and tyrannical Oppression of, and
repeated Hostilities against America,' our people were all left to act at
Discretion with respect to inlisting, without falling under the Censure
of our Community. And as some have inlisted, and many more [are]
likely to do so, who will have earnest Desires for their Ministers to
preach to them during the Campaign, we therefore deligate and appoint
our well-loved Brethren in the Ministry, Elijah Craig, Lewis Craig,
Jeremiah Walker and John Williams, to present this address and to
petition you that they may have free Liberty to preach to the Troops at
Convenient Times . . . and as we are conscious of their strong attachment to American Liberty, as well as their soundness in the principles
of the Christian Religion, and great usefulness in the Work of the
Ministry, we are willing they may come under your Examination in
any Matters you may think requisite.

2. The New Nation

The most important political issue for early Baptists in America was disestablishment. Nine of the thirteen colonies had at one time or another some form of tax-supported or favored church. It was the Baptists in Danbury, Connecticut, who had to fight until 1818 against the Congregationalist establishment in that state and elicited from Jefferson in 1804 the famous statement urging Americans to maintain "a wall of separation" between church and state. Typical of many efforts of the Baptists to oppose the bill supported by Patrick Henry and George Washington favoring a "general Assessment tax" in Virginia, which would require every citizen to pay taxes for the support of the church of his choice, was one from the General Committee of the Baptists in Virginia (formed in 1783). *Source:* Minutes of the General Committee of the Baptists in Virginia, 13 August 1785. Quoted in Robert B. Semple, *A History of the Rise and Progress of the Baptists in Virginia* (Richmond: John O'Lynch, 1810), p. 71.

Resolved, that it be recommended to those counties which have not yet prepared petitions to be presented to the General Assembly against the engrossed bill for a general assessment for the support of teachers of the Christian religion, to proceed thereon as soon as possible; that it is believed to be repugnant to the spirit of the gospel for the Legislature thus to proceed in matters of religion; that no human laws ought to be established for this purpose, but that every person ought to be left free to respect to matters of religion; that the Holy Author of our religion needs no such compulsive measures for the promotion of his cause; that the gospel wants not the feeble arm of man for its support; that it has made and will again through divine power make its way against all opposition; and that should the Legislature assume the right of taxing people for the support of the gospel, it will be destructive to religious liberty.

In 1780 Massachusetts adopted a new constitution that permitted the majority of voters in each township to levy taxes for the support of the town minister and meetinghouse. Because Congregationalists constituted a majority in every town, the Baptists of Massachusetts protested this clause. However, not until 1833 did Massachusetts vote to put an end to the privileged position of Congregationalism. *Source:* Isaac Backus (for Warren Association) to The rulers and ihabitants [sic] of the Commonwealth of Massachusetts, [September] 1781. Isaac Backus Papers, Andover Newton Theological School.

The compilers of our new [state] Constitution of Government say, in their address to the people, "Religion must at all times be a matter between God and individuals," which will remain in immutable verity

as long as Christianity endures; and no man is permitted to have a seat
in our Legislature till he solemnly declares, 'I believe the Christian
religion and have a firm persuasion of its truth.' . . . As religion must
always be a matter between God and individuals, no man can be made
a member of a truly religious society by force or without his own
consent, neither can any corporation [i.e., township] that is not a
religious society have a just right to govern in religious affairs. Since
the name Christian is derived from Christ, it must be essential to a
Christian society that it be constituted and governed by the laws of
Christ; and the choice, work, and support of his ministers are some of
the weightiest concerns of such a society; and obedience to his laws
therein is of infinite importance to all. But the drawing of a local [town
or parish] line around a certain number of inhabitants, and empowering
the majority of them to covenant for the rest with soul guides, and to
compel the minority to fulfil such contracts, is an invasion of the
essential rights of Christians, and if any are still resolved to promote
such invasions, they will doubtless have their names and actions transmitted to posterity as enemies to Christian liberty and to the welfare of
their country.

Baptists did not, as ministers or churches, campaign for political parties, but John
Leland delivered a mammoth cheese to President Jefferson as a token of esteem from
his hometown of Cheshire, Massachusetts (a town that voted for Jefferson), and Isaac
Backus recorded in his diary in 1802 that he supported Jefferson not only because he
favored religious liberty but also because he would balance the national budget. *Source:*
Diary of Isaac Backus, 31 December 1802. Isaac Backus Papers, Andover Newton
Theological School.

The favours of Providence towards us have been wonderful. The
earth has been made so fruitful, that bread and meat are as plentiful
through our land as was ever known therein. And though our government
was so managed that our national debt had been increasing ever since
the war, and very fast under the administration of Mr. Adams, yet in
two years since Mr. Jefferson was president, the debt has been lessened
about ten millions of dollars, and they are going to extinguish it wholly.

One of the more peculiar positions taken by the Baptists after adoption of the Constitution was their decision in 1791 to petition Congress to license the publication of Bibles
in order to prevent some sect or deists from printing Bibles with mistranslations, inter-

polations, or omissions that might mislead simple folk. They seemed to forget that giving the state the power to license (or not to license) publications of the Bible was to raise the possibility of seriously limiting the spread of God's Word. *Source: Minutes of the Shaftsbury Baptist Association,* 1791, p. 6.

Agreeable to a motion from the Warren Association on the utility of a united address to our congress, earnestly praying, that they would take such measures, as the constitution may permit, that no edition of the Bible, or its translations, be published in America without its being carefully inspected, and certified to be free from errors: voted that brother Blood, brother Hull, and brother Gano, be appointed a committee in behalf of this association, to prepare and transmit a petition to congress on this subject.

3. Slavery and Human Freedom

Baptists were never easy over the institution of slavery and, in the South as well as the North, bore their witness against it. But while the Northern states managed to abolish slavery between 1776 and 1800, the Southern states could not. The General Committee of the United Baptist Churches of Virginia, led by John Leland, did adopt an anti-slavery statement in 1789; however, three years later, the Strawberry Association of Virginia repudiated the action of the General Committee, saying, "We advise them not to interfere in it." Consequently, in 1793 the General Committee rescinded its position, voting "that the subject be dismissed from this committee, as believing it belongs to the legislative body" and not to the church. (Leland had left Virginia for New England in 1791.) While the Virginia Baptists were debating emancipation of slaves, the Charleston, South Carolina, Association moved in another direction to vote that slave members of Baptist churches need not follow Christian forms of marriages. *Sources:* A. Quoted in Semple, *A History,* p. 79. B. *Minutes of the Charleston Baptist Association,* 1788, p.2.

[A. Antislavery in Virginia]

Resolved, that slavery is a violent deprivation of the rights of nature, and inconsistent with a republican government, and [we] therefore recommend it to our brethren, to make use of every legal measure to extirpate this horrid evil from the land; and pray Almighty God that our honorable legislature may have it in their power to proclaim the great Jubilee, consistent with the principles of good policy.

[B. Marriage in the Slave Community]

Query: Have not negroes, who are members of churches, as great a right to marry, if agreeable to their owners, as to the ordinances of

God's House; and may not their living together in the neglect of marriage when it can be procured, be termed fornication: if so, have they a right to communion?

Answer: Slaves not being entitled to the privileges of freemen by the laws of the land; and the ceremony of marriage being circumstantial, we do not think the customary mode with us essential: but if they cohabit without entering into obligations to each other, according to the usual mode among negroes, it is fornication; therefore they are to be admitted or debarred communion accordingly.

Baptist churches in the North found it somewhat easier than those in the South to take a clear and simple stand. A Baptist pastor of Ashfield, Massachusetts, wrote a strong statement denouncing slavery in 1773; similarly, the entire congregation in Clifton Park, New York, passed an antislavery resolution in 1794. *Sources:* A. Ebenezer Smith to Isaac Backus, 16 October 1773. Isaac Backus Papers, Andover Newton Theological School. B. Articles of Faith, Records of the Clifton Park, New York, Baptist Church, 1794. Archives, American Baptist Historical Society.

[A. Ebenezer Smith to Isaac Backus]

One thing that I verily believe ought to be Razed out of the Church of Christ—and that is makeing slaves of the poor Negroes. We complain of Bondage [to the established authorities], and shall we at the same time keep our fellow men in bondage—tho I know of but few in our churches that have Negroe slaves, yet the thing is alowed and not Witnessed against as I think it ought to be.

[B. The Clifton Park, New York, Statement]

We believe that all mankind are born Equally free and that none has a Right to Enslave or hold them in Bondage, let their Colour be what it may and we have no fellowship with such unfruteful works of Darkness.

In the West, as might be expected, proslavery and antislavery views often conflicted. Baptists were found on both sides of the issue as the following selections about Kentucky Baptist life illustrate. In 1802 the North Baptist Association was ready to expel from ministerial fellowship any preacher who advocated abolition of slavery. Contrariwise, David Barrow, one of several Virginians in Kentucky who formed a group called "The Emancipators" in 1802, replied to this expulsion in the earliest-known antislavery pamphlet in the West. *Sources:* A. *Minutes of the North District Baptist Association* (Kentucky), 1802, p. 3. B. David Barrow, *Involuntary, Unmerited, Perpetual, Absolute,*

Hereditary Slavery Examined, on the Principles of Nature, Reason, Justice, Policy and Scripture (Lexington: D. C. Bradford, 1808), pp. 30-31, 40-41.

[A. The North District Association]

Brethren Robert Elkin, Moses Bledsoe, James Quessenberry, James Haggard, and Leonard Turly reported, That, agreeable to the provision made last association for the trial of ministers, they had been dealing with brother David Barrow, for preaching the doctrine of emancipation, to the hurt and injury of the feelings of the brotherhood. And the association, after considering the foregoing report, and hearing what brother Barrow had to say in justification of his conduct on that subject, and brother Barrow manifesting no disposition to alter his mode of preaching as to the aforesaid doctrine, on that subject, and brother Barrow manifesting no disposition they proceeded to expel him from his seat in this association, and appointed brethren [named] . . . to deal with brother Barrow at the church at Mount Sterling at their next monthly meeting.

[B. David Barrow's Response]

The No. District Association of Baptists, will have to acknowledge their wrong, for 'expelling the author, from his seat in the Association for preaching the doctrine of Emancipation.' For if Hagar, Bilhah, and Zilpah, Abraham's and Jacob's wives, were in the same state that slaves among us are, then certainly, the patriarchs must have Emancipated the children had by them, or they would according to our laws, have been the property of their other brothers: which was not the case. . . . We have an infallible rule. Rom. xiii: 10. 'Love worketh no ill to his neighbour: therefore love is the fulfilling of the law.' But unmerited, involuntary, perpetual, absolute, hereditary slavery works the greatest ill to our neighbour, because it deprives him of every thing, that is near and dear to a rational creature in this world. . . . And this is not all, for he and his, are . . . subjugated to almost every kind of abuse, drudgery, dirtiness, brought up in worse that Gothic ignorance, &c. . . . If holding a fellow creature in such a state, and treating him in such a manner, (when it is in my power to do otherwise) be to 'Love him as myself,' and to 'do to him as I would he should do to me;' then I must confess, I neither understand our Saviour, his prophets or apostles.

4. Attitudes Toward Women

There was less division among Baptists about denying equal rights to women than there was over denying equal rights to black slaves. Most Baptists agreed that women were not to be ordained, not to vote in church affairs, not to have any role in politics. On rare occasions a woman might speak in church, but these occasions were to be the exception, not the rule, and even then women should "make a brother a mouth to ask leave to speak." *Source:* Gillette, *Minutes of the Philadelphia Baptist Association, 1746,* p. 53.

Query: Whether women may or ought to have their votes in the church, in such matters as the church shall agree to be decided by votes?
Solution: As that in 1 Cor. xiv. 34, 35, and other parallel texts, are urged against their votes, as a rule, and ought, therefore, to be maturely considered.

If then the silence enjoined on women be taken as absolute, as that they must keep entire silence in all respects whatever; yet, notwithstanding, it is to be hoped they may have, as members of the body of the church, liberty to give a mute voice, by standing or lifting up of the hands, or the contrary, to signify their assent or dissent to the thing proposed, and so augment the number on the one or both sides of the question. But, with the consent of authors and casuists, such absolute silence in all respects cannot be intended; for if so, how shall a woman make a confession of her faith to the satisfaction of the whole church? or how shall the church judge whether a woman be in the faith or no? How shall a woman offended, after regular private proceeding with an offending member, tell the church, as she is bound to do, if the offender be obstinate, according to the rule, Matt. xviii, 17? How shall a woman do, if she be an evidence to a matter of fact? Shall the church grope in the dark for want of her evidence to clear the doubt? Surely not. Again, how shall a woman defend herself if wrongfully accused, if she must not speak? This is a privilege of all human creatures by the laws of nature, not abrogated by the law of God.

Therefore, there must be times and ways in and by which women, as members of the body, may discharge their conscience and duty towards God and man, as in the cases above said and the like. And a woman may, at least, make a brother a mouth to ask leave to speak, if not ask it herself; and a time of hearing is to be allowed, for that is not inconsistent with the silence and subjection enjoined on them by the law of God and nature, yet ought not they to open the floodgate of speech in an imperious, tumultuous, masterly manner. Hence the silence, with subjection, enjoined on all women in the church of God, is such a silence as excludes all women whomsoever from all degrees of teaching, ruling, governing, dictating, and leading in the church of God; yet may their voice be taken as above said. But if a woman's vote be singular, her reasons ought to be called for, heard, and maturely considered, without contempt.

5. The Christian Life-Style

The Christian life-style of Baptists involved male supremacy in the family and appropriate Christian behavior in wives and children. The minutes of Baptist associations are filled with warnings against the sins of card playing, gambling, dancing, swearing, and indulging in luxury. They are also strong in their opposition to fornication, adultery, and intemperance. Some churches disciplined women for gossiping, backbiting, quarreling, and talebearing. Civil suits, price gouging, and the use of inflated paper money were all discouraged. Some associations bore witness against the sin of dueling, and it was considered "covetousness" for church members to fail to do their share toward supporting their minister or repairing their meetinghouse. Regular family prayer and strict Sabbath observance were fundamental to the Christian life, and a Baptist could be censured or excommunicated for failing to attend church regularly. *Sources:* A. *Minutes of the Warren Baptist Association,* 1785, pp. 6-7. B. *Minutes of the Goshen (Virginia) Baptist Association,* 1800, pp. 10-11. C. *Minutes of the Mattapony (Virginia) Baptist Association, 1801,* pp. 12-14. D. *Minutes of the Charleston Baptist Association,* 1788, p. 13. E. *Ibid.,* 1804, p. 2.

[A. The Christian Family]
Every head of a family should represent the Great Parent of the universe, who provides for his numerous dependents, and most reasonably expects subjection to his authority. . . . The oracles of God, enjoin it on parents to bring up their children in the nature and admonition of the Lord. . . . Let us not neglect the religious education of those for whose souls we must given an account to God. The propriety of attending to these obligations is also apparent from our expectations being placed on the rising generation, for future usefulness in the church and state. . . . The good of the civil community should likewise induce us to attend to this practice. Mankind, by being restrained in the early stages of life, are more easily led into subjection to government.

[B. Moral Values for Children]
As soon as children are capable of receiving ideas and reflecting on

the nature of things, endeavor to inspire their minds with reverent notions of the Divine Being. . . . Carry them at suitable times to hear the words of God. . . . Inculcate on their minds the duty and privilege of prayer: and as example should always aid precept, pray with them, and for them, in the family, in a stated manner. . . . Prevent, if possible, prevent your children from following the abominable practices of cards, dice, horse-racing, cock-fighting and all such sinful soul-destroying pursuits.

[C. Intoxication and Its Consequences]

Drunkenness is a sin, which in the New Testament is expressly declared, to be a bar to the kingdom of God. . . . Quarreling, fighting, profanity, and even something like brutality, are the almost certain consequences of habitual drunkenness. . . . Bad company—there is not perhaps a vice in the world which is oftener contracted by bad company, than that of drunkenness. . . . Intemperance is frequently produced by the habit of drinking at first, small, but unnecessary quantities of Spirituous Liquor. . . . Those who have often endeavored to avert this evil, and have been still frequently overcome, cannot do better than to enter into a determination through divine aid, never to taste a drop of anything that can intoxicate, except in time of communion.

[D. Christian Marriage]

The importance of marriage to human life makes it a subject of parental concern; and while our children are cautioned to avoid connection, in that intimate union, with the vicious, the profane, the indolent and the despicable, it may not be amiss to point out the peculiar advantage of being united with those of the same sentiments in religion.

[E. Abolition of Dueling]

Resolved unanimously, That this Association will unite, with their fellow citizens, in the petition to the Legislature of this State, for an act to abolish the bloody practice of duelling, and that the Moderator and Clerk sign said petition, officially, in behalf of the whole body.

Evangelism, Expansion, and Missions

Until the Baptist movement achieved a measure of stability and toleration, it was too busy defending itself from persecution to have much time or energy for aggressive evangelism. But by 1750, with the upsurge of a new optimism and piety resulting from the tremendous growth in their numbers during the First Great Awakening, a new zeal for evangelistic work prevailed. Baptists felt the same urge as other major denominations to build churches in the Southwest, the old Northwest, and Nova Scotia. Associations began to ordain evangelists, and churches licensed gifted young men to go out and preach wherever they could find an audience. Association minutes contained annual statistics to let the Baptists and the world see how God was helping their cause to prosper. By 1812 Baptists in America at last saw themselves as a transatlantic and intercolonial denomination of major significance in Protestantism.

When a Second Great Awakening broke out after 1795 simultaneously in the Southern colonies, New England, and trans-Appalachia, the Baptists were ready to take advantage of it with a home mission movement. And when the English Baptists sent William Carey to India, the Baptists in America were quick to raise their horizons to include a global vision. As the nineteenth century dawned, Baptists fully shared the view that the United States had a manifest destiny to lead the world to the millennium, and they expected the Baptists to be at the forefront.

1. Baptists and Revivals of Religion

When the First Great Awakening began in 1735, it released the initial impulse for itinerant evangelism among the Baptists. Isaac Backus, who averaged over 1200 miles of itinerant evangelism a year throughout New England for most of his life, described

149

his call to the ministry and earliest preaching trips in the years 1746 and 1747. *Source:*
"Some brief account of My Travels & experiences." Isaac Backus Papers, Andover
Newton Theological School.

On Saturday the 27 of Sept. 1746 the Lord Caled me forth to Preach
the Gospel and the next day, Sept. 28, I Preached from the 53 Psalm.
then I went with Brother Hide to Preston Stonington & westerly where
we saw much of gods Power both in Conviction and Consolation &
returned again oct. 8 and oct. 10 the Lord caled brother John fuller out
of Spiritual Darkness & deadness and the next week we went to Colch-
ester & lyme together where the Lord apeared to Comfort his Children
and for the Conversion of one Soul. after that we went to Stoningtown
and westerly where we had Some Sharp trials But blessed deliverances
afterwards we went to Lyme again and Decem'r. 7 he was Chosen their
Pastor there after this I went again to westerly where I saw much of
the glory of the lord Especialy in the naraganset Indians who apeared
great numbers of them wonderfully in the image of god & speaking
forth his Praises which did ravish my Soul. after this I traveled in Sundry
Places Round about there labouring in the Strength of the lord with
renewed Confermations from him all glory be to his name on Jany. 6,
1747 Brother hide & I went to Stonington & westerly where the Lord
apeared very gloriously. from thence we went through volintown down
to Providence atelbury Rehoboth and W. Rentham where the lord gave
me Some Clearer views of divine things than Ever before to his name
be the Praise he also did apear wonderfully for the Quickning & bringing
forth his Saints there. . . . May 24 [1749] I set away & 2 brethren with
me Early this morning, & got to attelborough before noon Where a
number of brethren from various parts of the government met together
& agreed to send a Petition to the General Court to be freed from paying
Rates to Support a worship that we Can't join with. We drew Copys
of the petition & sent around into various parts of the Province; & it
fell to my Lot to carry one to the Cape.

Daniel Marshall and Shubal Stearns, two Separate Baptist itinerants from Connecticut
decided to carry the gospel to the southern colonies in 1754. Marshall's preaching led
to the formation of forty-three Separate Baptist churches in Virginia and North Carolina
over the next seventeen years. Stearns was equally successful in these states. It is reported
that Martha Stearns Marshall, Daniel's wife and Shubal's sister, was once jailed for
preaching in Windsor, Connecticut, and that she was extremely helpful to both men in

exhorting and leading in prayer at public meetings throughout their careers. *Source:* Semple, *A History*, pp. 3-4, 374-375.

The doctrine of Mr. Stearns and his party was consequently quite strange. To be born again, appeared to them as absurd as it did to the Jewish doctor, when he asked, if he must enter the second time into his mother's womb and be born again. . . . But their manner of preaching was, if possible, much more novel than their doctrines. The Separates in N. England had acquired a very warm and pathetic address, accompanied by strong gestures and a singular tone of voice. Being often deeply affected themselves while preaching, correspondent affections were felt by their pious hearers, which were frequently expressed by tears, trembling, screams, shouts and acclamations. All these they brought with them into their new habitation. The people were greatly astonished having never seen things in this wise before. Many mocked, but the power of God attending them, many also trembled. In process of time some of the natives became converts, and bowed obedience to the Redeemer's sceptre. These, uniting their labours with the chosen band, a powerful and extensive work broke out. From 16, Sandy Creek Church soon swelled to 606 members; so mightily grew the work of God!

Daniel Marshall, tho' not possessed of great talents, was indefatigable in his endeavours. He sallied out into the adjacent neighbourhoods, and planted the Redeemer's standard in many of the strong holds of Satan. . . .

In fact, it should not be concealed that his extraordinary success in the ministry, is ascribable in no small degree, to Mrs. Marshall's unwearied, and zealous co-operation. Without the shadow of a usurped authority over the other sex, Mrs. Marshall, being a lady of good sense, singular piety, and surprising elocution, has, in countless instances, melted a whole concourse into tears, by her prayers and exhortations!

Another cause to which Mr. Marshall's distinguished utility is attributable, in a great measure, was his bold and independent method of procedure. With a soul expanded by contemplations on august objects, a boundless ambition directed to a correspondent prize, and the world completely under his feet, he was capable of the most difficult and arduous enterprizes; and could be dismayed by no dangers. Superior to local attachments, he went from place to place, instructing, exhorting, and praying for individuals, families, and congregations; whether at a muster, a race, a public market, the open field, an army, or a house of worship; wherever he was able to command attention.

Such conduct was, indeed, and may still, by many, be considered irregular; and little less than as favouring of insanity. But if he acted in some of these instances as if he were beside himself, it was for the sake of precious souls: and the fruits of his astonishing exertions have abundantly shown that he was constrained by the love of Christ.

Black Baptist preachers were equally important in spreading the gospel. David George, born a slave in Essex County, Virginia, provided an account of his work in Nova Scotia and Sierra Leone (after fleeing Virginia with the British Army in 1779) for John Rippon's *Annual Register* in 1792. *Source:* John Rippon, *The Baptist Annual Register for 1790–1793* (London: n.p., 1793), pp. 476-478, 482-483.

I continued preaching at Silver Bluff [General], till the church, constituted with eight, encreased to thirty or more, and till the British came to the city Savannah and took it [in 1779]. My Master was an Antiloyalist; and being afraid, he now retired from home and left the Slaves behind. . . . When the English were going to evacuate Charlestown, they advised me to go to Halifax, in Nova Scotia, and gave the few Black people . . . their passage for nothing . . . I got leave to go to Shelburne, [Nova Scotia]. . . . I found the White people were against me. I began to sing the first night, in the woods, at a camp, for there were no houses then built; they were just clearing and preparing to erect a town. The Black people came [from] far and near, it was so new to them. I kept on so every night in the week, and appointed a meeting for the first Lord's-day, in a valley between two hills, close by the river; and a great number of White and Black people came, and I was so overjoyed with having an opportunity once more of preaching the word of God. . . . We had a meeting now every evening, and those poor creatures who had never heard the gospel before, listened to me very attentively; but the White people, the justices, and all, were in an uproar, and said that I might go out into the woods, for I should not stay there. I ought to except one White man, who knew me at Savannah, and who said I should have his lot to live upon as long as I would, and build a house if I pleased. I then cut down poles, stripped bark, and made a smart hut, and the people came flocking to the preaching every evening. . . . The next fall, Agent (afterwards Governor) Clarkson came to Halifax, about settling the new colony at Sierra Leone. . . .

Our passage from Halifax to Sierra Leone was seven weeks. . . . I preached the first Lord's day, it was a blessed time, under a sail, and so I did for several weeks after. We then erected a hovel for a Meeting-house, which is made of posts put into the ground, and poles over our heads, which are covered with grass. While I was preaching under the sails, sister Patty Webb and Lucy Lawrence were converted, and they, with old sister Peggy, brother Bill Taylor, and brother Sampson Hay-wood, three who were awakened before they came this voyage, have since been baptized in the river.

After 1795 the second great religious awakening proved of even greater benefit to Baptist growth than the first. Associated in the popular mind with camp meetings on the frontiers, this awakening had, by 1830, made the Baptists the largest denomination in America. David Benedict, writing in 1811, reported on recent Baptist increases. *Source:* David Benedict, *A General History of the Baptist Denomination in America and Other Parts of the World,* 2 vols. (Boston: Lincoln and Edmands, 1813), 1, pp. 251-256.

From 1799 to 1803, there were, in most parts of the United States, remarkable out-pourings of the Divine Spirit, among different denominations; multitudes became the subjects of religious concern, and were made to rejoice in the salvation of God. . . . This great revival in Kentucky began in Boone County on the Ohio River, and in its progress extended up the Ohio, Licking, and Kentucky Rivers, branching out into the settlements adjoining them. It spread fast in different directions, and in a short time almost every part of the States was affected by its influence. It was computed that about ten thousand were baptized and added to the Baptist churches in the course of two or three years. This great work progressed among the Baptists in a much more regular manner than people abroad have generally supposed. They were indeed zealously affected, and much engaged. Many of their ministers baptized in a number of neighbouring churches from two to four hundred each. . . . Those camp-meetings, those great parades, and sacramental seasons, those extraordinary exercises of falling down, rolling, shouting, jerking, dancing, barking &c. were but little known among the Baptists in Kentucky, nor encouraged by them. . . . Generally speaking, they were among the Presbyterians and Methodists. . . . A Baptist minister by the name of Mr. Connico, was once preaching where one of the jerkers began his emotions. The preacher made a pause, and with a loud and solemn tone, said, 'In the name of the Lord, I command all unclean spirits to leave this place.' The jerker immediately became still, and the report was spread abroad, that Mr. Connico cast out devils.

2. Organization for Mission—The Domestic Scene

As revivals on the frontier opened new opportunities for preaching and church development, the home missions movement emerged. At first, associations licensed or ordained new young ministers or encouraged experienced pastors to set aside part of the year "to travel and preach in distant parts." Later, as the need grew, permanent missionary organizations were chartered to raise funds, appoint missionaries, and supervise the work. The first of these among Baptists was the Boston Female Society for Missionary Purposes, established in 1800. Whether through associations or voluntary societies, domestic missions usually consisted of travelling evangelists, pastoral supply to destitute churches, and work among Indian tribes.

The transition from associational domestic missions to organized missionary societies is seen in the problems encountered among New York City Baptists. In response to directions taken at the 1795 New York Association meeting, Elkanah Holmes (1741–1844), of the Staten Island church, commenced a missionary endeavor on the Niagara frontier. But the burden of his support was too great for the Association, and it applied to the New York Missionary Society (Congregational and Presbyterian) for assistance in 1800. This irenic arrangement lasted until 1812 when the Baptists withdrew over the issue of infant baptism and formed the New York Baptist Missionary Society. *Sources:* A. *Minutes of the New York Baptist Association* 1795, 1797, pp. 3, 4. B. *The New York Missionary Magazine and Repository of Religious Intelligence,* 1 (November, 1800), p. 292.

[A. Minutes of the New York Association]
[1795]
2. We advise the Churches in this Association, to give encouragement to their Ministers to travel and labour in the Gospel, among Congregations which are destitute, as often as may be consistent; and those who are favoured with their instructions, are requested according to their abilities, to contribute to their support; and we wish them not to omit affording assistance to travelling preachers, who visit destitute Congregations. . . .

[1797]
3. Resumed the consideration of the Letters from our Indian Brethren. Reflecting on the cordial reception they gave Brother Holmes, the affection with which they received his ministrations, and their desire to enjoy more such assistance; also his inclination to travel and preach the Gospel in the western parts of this State, and amongst the Indians, as Providence shall open the door for his usefulness; and the Church

of Staten-Island, to which he belongs, giving their full approbation to his intentions: Resolved, We feel ourselves called upon by this combination of favorable events to encourage him in this laudable work, to pray for his success, and recommend him to the benevolent and pious assistance of our Brethren and at the churches thro which he may pass.

[B. A Request for Assistance, 22 May 1800]

To the Directors of the New-York Missionary Society, for the Promulgation of the Gospel among the Indians.

Gentlemen,

Whereas the above-mentioned Association hath, for some years past, held a correspondence with some of the Indian tribes on our northwestern frontiers, in which sundry talks and tokens of friendship have reciprocally passed: and whereas it appears by the Indian letters (some of which we lay before you), that they are solicitous that our brother, the Rev. Elkanah Holmes, should again visit them, and preach the gospel among them; and he having manifested a willingness to leave his family in this city, and again to explore the western wilds, and, if practicable, even far beyond the limits of any of his former travels; it was therefore moved in the said Association, that he be again requested and encouraged to go foreward: the whole were unanimous in their wishes, that his former and future labours might be abundantly blessed among the poor Indians, and that, if practicable, he would again visit them; but our having no funds for the support of a Missionary, or, if need be, for the assistance of his family in his absence, was a forbidding circumstance: they, however (without the most distant idea of encouraging any project that should seem to be counter to, or separate from the benevolent designs of the Missionary Society in this city), appointed us a Committee to pursue such measures as to us might seem proper, in order, if practicable, to carry the design into effect, under exciting circumstances.

We, therefore, considering that a door hath thus been opened, and that the poor Indians have so far placed confidence in Mr. Holmes, and wishing that every log, and brier, and stone, might, if possible, be removed from his path to their fire-places; and being confident that your views in the Missionary business are not confined to any particular denominations of Christians, we are induced and encouraged to solicit your pecuniary aid, so far as to enable him to perform a tour of five or six months of this season in the western wilderness. . . .

3. First Baptist Mission Society in America

With the formation of benevolent organizations for missionary purposes in other denominations, women took the lead among Baptists. Mary Webb (1779–1861) of Boston, pioneer of the "Mother Society," delivered an address before the Society in 1812 in which she identified the importance of the work. *Source:* "Address of the Female Society, in Boston, to the Female Friends of Zion," *Massachusetts Baptist Missionary Magazine* 3 (December, 1811), pp. 156-157.

———————————

Though destined by the Parent of nature to fill more retired stations in life than our brethren, we are nevertheless permitted to repair to a throne of grace, (and even to unite in a social manner) to plead for the salvation of sinners and the prosperity of Zion. It affords us much pleasure, to hear from time to time of the constitution of Female Societies in various parts of the United States, for the purposes of prayer and of aiding missionary exertions. And the Lord, we trust, has condescended to use these Institutions as a means of extending the triumphs of the cross. The members of the 'Boston Female Society for Missionary purposes,' believing that a more extensive and particular knowledge and acquaintance with these societies of a similar nature would be promotive of the divine glory and their mutual edification, beg leave to address them through this medium. Engaged as we professedly are, dear Sisters, in the cause of God, and the pleasing work of endeavouring to advance the spread of the gospel. . . . We likewise think it desirable, (as far as may be convenient) that we should all hold our meetings on the same day. The idea that many of our dear Sisters, in different places, were met at the same time, and engaged in the same delightful employment of praying down blessings on mankind, would tend to strengthen our faith, increase our union, animate our hopes, and cheer our prospects. . . . And though we wish ever to preserve our place as females, we cannot view it inconsistent with that modesty and shame-facedness enjoined by the Apostle, thus openly to come out on the Lord's side. We have the approbation of *good* men of different denominations; we believe that angels smile on our endeavors to communicate the knowledge of salvation to those souls at whose repentance they rejoice. God himself has disposed us to the work, and is engaged in our defense; and if He 'be for us, who can be against us?'

4. English Influences and Concern for Foreign Missions

English Baptists preceded by a decade their American counterparts in organizing for world mission (see pages 88-89). The Baptist Missionary Society in Kettering (later London) in 1792, sent its first appointee William Carey (1761–1834) to Serampore in 1793 (see page 88). News of the Carey mission was shared regularly through English periodicals and letters sent to prominent Baptist ministers in America, such as Isaac Backus, James Manning, and Samuel Stillman. The first American missionary group to address specifically the need for a global strategy was the Massachusetts Baptist Missionary Society, formed at Boston in 1802 by two Baptist ministers, Samuel Stillman (1733–1807) and Thomas Baldwin (1753–1825). The English Baptist influences, illustrated below, were undeniable. *Sources:* A. Minutes of the Massachusetts Baptist Missionary Society, 26 May 1802, p. 1. Archives, Andover Newton Theological School. B. William Carey to Thomas Waterman, 16 October 1805, quoted in *Massachusetts Baptist Missionary Magazine* 1 (May, 1806) pp. 195-196.

[A. Organization in Massachusetts]
To our CHRISTIAN BRETHREN united with us in the faith and order of the Gospel, we send,
GREETING.
DEARLY BELOVED,
Wishing grace, mercy and peace to abound, through the knowledge of our Lord and Saviour, Jesus Christ.

Being deeply impressed with the important obligations we are under, as professing Christians, not only to pray for the prosperity of Zion, but to use our best endeavours to promote, and spread far and wide, the knowledge of our Divine Immanuel; and reflecting seriously upon the affecting situation of many of our dear fellow-men, who, from local, and other circumstances, are deprived of the means of Christian knowledge and consolation, which we enjoy from a preached gospel; feel our hearts go out towards them, in ardent desires for their salvation.

Under these impressions, and animated by the laudable exertions which many of our Christian friends, of different denominations, on both sides of the Atlantic are making, to extend the empire of truth and promote the salvation of dying men, we propose the forming of a Missionary Society, for the purposes hereafter mentioned. And, in order to make our intention more explicit, we submit to your consideration the following

CONSTITUTION.

Article I. THIS Society shall be distinguished and known by the name of The MASSACHUSETTS BAPTIST MISSIONARY SOCIETY.

Art. II. The Society shall be composed of such members only, as shall subscribe and pay at least One Dollar annually to its funds.

Art. III. The members, at their first meeting, and at their annual meeting ever after, shall by ballot appoint twelve Trustees, eight whereof shall be ministers, or professing brethren, of the Baptist denomination: the other four may be chosen from the members at large; who shall conduct the business of the Society in the manner hereafter described.

Art. IV. The object of this Society shall be, to furnish occasional preaching, and to promote the knowledge of evangelic truth in the new settlements within these United States; or farther, if circumstances should render it proper.

Art. V. The Trustees shall have power to apply the funds of the Society, according to their discretion, in all cases in which they shall not be limited by special directions of the Society.

Art. VI. They shall have power to appoint and dismiss Missionaries, to pay them, and generally to transact all the business necessary for the accomplishment of the important object of the Society. . . .

[B. William Carey's Response]

Dear Brother,

Yesterday I received your favour of Dec. 1, 1804, by the Asia, with three numbers of the Massachusetts Baptist Missionary Magazine, and the other pamphlets. For these friendly communications accept my best thanks.

It gives me real pleasure to hear of the attempts made in America to spread abroad the name of our Lord Jesus Christ; and among the institutions which are designed for the encouragement of these attempts, I consider the Massachusetts Baptist Missionary Society as one of the first; and the Magazine connected therewith as a very useful means of spreading religious intelligence, and seconding the intentions of the Society. It will give me pleasure to be able at any time to contribute to its promotion. . . .

5. Facing a New Era

As the new century dawned and as the United States began its tremendous expansion amidst freedom and prosperity, it is hardly surprising that the Baptists should feel euphoric over how far they had come and how far, under the new outpourings of spiritual blessings, they would yet go. Isaac Backus, a venerable historian of the denomination, published his fourth and final volume in 1804. He had begun his career during the First Awakening and was now witnessing the second. Though he regretted that the former Puritan states had not yet rid themselves of the last vestiges of Puritan establishments, he nonetheless concluded his history with a paean to "The Latter Day Glory," implying that the United States was "the New Israel" and that its republican, Christian form of government, under Baptist leadership, would inaugurate the millennium. *Source:* Isaac Backus, *Church History of New England* (Philadelphia: Baptist Tract Depository, 1839), pp. 239-246.

And since a door is now opened in our land for a clear deliverance from these evils [an established church system], can any man be free of guilt if he tries to shut it? This consideration is enforced by late experience; for the man [John Adams] who was the chief magistrate of these United States for four years, was very fond of such partiality. But a man was elected into that office in 1801, who is for equal liberty to all the nation. And if the Holy Scriptures are well regarded, we shall be the happiest people upon earth. . . . We may see that the support of religious ministers in Israel, as well as the poor, was to be done voluntarily, as each man would desire the blessing of God. . . . The nation of Israel was advanced above all other nations, when they obeyed the will of God. . . . And many nations shall come and say, Come, let us go up to the mountain of the Lord . . . and he will teach us of his ways and we will walk in his paths . . . and they shall beat their swords into ploughshares, and their spears into pruning hooks. . . . Now it is most certain that this prophecy hath never yet been fulfilled, but it will as surely come to pass hereafter as ever the promise did of Christ's being born of a virgin. . . . Real Christians are the best subjects of civil government in the world, while they obey God rather than man. . . . The apostles explained the prophets, and finished writing the book of God; and heaven and earth will rejoice to see his truth and justice glorified.

First Baptist Church, Charleston, South Carolina, 1887

West Union Baptist Church, Oregon, 1853

Suggestions for Further Study

Still the best overall multiregional survey of Baptists in the colonial period is Robert G. Torbet, *A History of the Baptists,* 3rd. ed. (Valley Forge: Judson Press, 1963). Additionally, William G. McLoughlin's *New England Dissent 1630–1833* (Cambridge, Mass.: Harvard University Press, 1971) is unsurpassed in its analysis of political and social issues and Baptist relations with the established churches in New England, and David Benedict's *General History of the Baptist Denomination in America* (New York: Lewis Colby, 1848) continues to be the best source of information on organizational developments and schisms of the colonial and early national periods. Thus far, Albert J. Raboteau's *Slave Religion: The Invisible Institution in the Antebellum South* (New York: Oxford University Press Inc., 1978) is the most contemporary statement of black Baptist life in the early period, and Leon McBeth, *Women in Baptist Life* (Nashville: Broadman Press, 1979) is the lone treatment of a very important subject.

Special studies of great value that have direct bearing upon Baptist life and thought in this era include Clarence C. Goen's *Revivalism and Separatism in New England 1740–1800* (New Haven: Yale University Press, 1962), which identifies the transition from New Light Congregationalism to Baptist identity, and Robert Torbet's *A Social History of the Philadelphia Baptist Association 1707–1940* (Philadelphia: Westbrook Co., 1944), which analyzes the original Regular Baptist association against its cultural background. Stuart Ivison, *The Baptists in Upper and Lower Canada Before 1820* (Toronto: University of Toronto Press, 1956) describes early Canadian Baptist heritage in this period while Norman H. Maring, *Baptists in New Jersey: A Study in Transition* (Valley Forge: Judson Press, 1964) has become the model for United States regional Baptist studies and contains much useful information on the Middle Colonies. Good, comprehensive studies of Baptist life in the colonial South and, later, the trans-Appalachian West have yet to be written. Whenever available, the original histories of Morgan Edwards (1770), Isaac Backus (1804), and Robert Semple (1810) supply very worthwhile background.

For diverse Baptist traditions, see Norman A. Baxter, *History of Freewill Baptists: A Study in New England Separatism* (Rochester: American Baptist Historical Society, 1957); *Seventh Day Baptists in Europe and America* (Providence: Smith and Parmenter, 1827); John B. Rogers, *The Rogerenes: Some Hitherto Unpublished Annals Belonging to the*

Colonial History of Connecticut (Boston: Stanhope Press, 1904); and Martin G. Brumbaugh, *A History of German Baptist Brethren in Europe and America* (Mt. Morris: Brethren Pub. Co., 1899).

Partially offsetting the need for more regional studies in early Baptist life are the many published primary sources. Abraham D. Gillette's edition of the *Minutes of the Philadelphia Baptist Association 1707–1807* (Otisville, Mich.: Baptist Book Trust, 1976) is again in print and William G. McLoughlin's *Isaac Backus on Church, State, and Calvinism: Pamphlets 1754–1789*, 2 vols. (Cambridge, Mass.: The Belknap Press, 1968) is also available. Published memoirs are a valuable resource and the best of these for the period are: C. Edwin Barrows, ed., *The Diary of John Comer* (Philadelphia: ABPS, 1892); Deidamia Brown, *Memoir of Rev. Lemuel Covell* (Brandon, Vt.: Telegraph Office, 1839); John Gano, *Biographical Memoirs of the Late Rev. John Gano of Frankfort, Kentucky* (New York: Southwick and HardeCastle, 1806); Edwin S. Gaustad, *Baptist Piety: The Last Will and Testimony of Obadiah Holmes* (Grand Rapids: Wm. B. Eerdmans Publishing Co., 1978); Reuben A. Guild, *Life, Times, and Correspondence of James Manning* (Boston: Gould and Lincoln, 1864); Samuel W. Lynd, ed., *Memoir of William Staughton D.D.* (Boston: Lincoln and Edmands, 1834); George E. Levy, ed., *The Diary of Joseph Dimmock* (Wolfville, N.S.: Lancelot Press, 1979), William G. McLoughlin, ed., *The Diary of Isaac Backus*, 3 vols. (Providence: Brown University Press, 1980); William R. Millar, ed., "The Diary of Job Seamans," *Foundations*, 25 (January, 1982); Ruth W. Sherman, ed., *Peleg Burrough's Journal* (Providence: R.I. Geneological Society, 1981). Yet to be published in book form and easily overlooked are John D. Broome, "The Journal of Hezekiah Smith" (Th.D. Dissertation, New Orleans Baptist Theological Seminary, 1965) and Horatio G. Jones, "Diary of Samuel Jones" (Typescript, American Baptist Historical Society).

Biographies of major figures range from hagiographa to critical analyses. At times, appendices contain data not found elsewhere, thus the importance of the genre in the colonial period. See especially Henry S. Burrage, "Some Added Facts Concerning Rev. William Screven," *Proceedings of the Maine Historical Society 1894;* L. Butterfield, *Elder John Leland, Jeffersonian Itinerant* (Worcester: American Antiquarian Soc., 1953); Jeremiah Chaplin, *Life of Henry Dunster: First President of Harvard College* (Boston: J. R. Osgood, 1872). Of all the Williams studies note especially Cyclone Covey, *The Gentle Radical: A Biography of Roger Williams* (New York: Macmillan Inc., 1966); Reuben A. Guild, *Chaplin Smith and the Baptists* (Philadelphia: ABPS, 1885); Henry M. King, *Rev. John Myles and Founding of the First Baptist Church in Massachusetts* (Providence: Preston and Rounds, 1905). For information on the many Virginia persecutions see Lewis P. Little, *Imprisoned Preachers and Religious Liberty in Virginia* (Lynchburg: J. P. Bell, 1938); Thomas R. McKibbens, Jr., and Kenneth L. Smith, *The Life and Works of Morgan Edwards* (New York: Arno Press Inc., 1980); William G. McLoughlin, *Isaac Backus and the American Pietistic Tradition* (Boston: Little, Brown & Co., 1967); Wilbur Nelson, *The Hero of Aquidneck: A Life of Dr. John Clarke* (New York: Fleming H. Revell Co., 1983); Elias Smith, *The Life, Conversion, Preaching, Travels and Sufferings of Elias Smith*, ed. Edwin S. Gaustad (New York: Arno Press Inc., 1979); Joseph R. Sweeny, "Elhanan Winchester and the Universal Baptists" (Ph.D.

Dissertation, University of Pennsylvania, 1969); Albert L. Vail, *Mary Webb and the Mother Society* (Philadelphia: ABPS, 1914); and Frederick Wiley, *Life and Influence of Rev. Benjamin Randall* (Philadelphia: ABPS, 1915). Not yet published is a fine work by George T. Rogers, "A Biography of David Jones 1736-1820" (Ph.D. Dissertation, University of Colorado, 1976); a popularized version, *Bibles and Battle Drums,* was published by Judson Press in 1976.

Similarly, histories of local churches must not be neglected, and good examples exist for most of the major colonial congregations. These are: Robert A. Baker and Paul J. Craven, *Adventure in Faith: History of the First Baptist Church, Charleston, S.C. 1682-1982* (Nashville: Broadman Press, 1982); William W. Keen, *The Bicentennial of the Founding of the First Baptist Church Philadelphia* (Philadelphia: ABPS, 1899); Henry M. King, *The Mother Church: History of the First Baptist Church in Providence* (Philadelphia: ABPS, 1896); James Simms, *The First Colored Baptist Church in North America* (Philadelphia: J. B. Lippincott Co., 1888); and Nathan A. Wood, *History of the First Baptist Church of Boston* (Philadelphia: ABPS, 1899).

American Baptist theology and polity were in their formative stages during the colonial period, and there was much dependence upon English Baptist literature. The *Confession of Faith Put Forth by the Elders and Brethren of Many Congregations of Christians* (Philadelphia: Ben. Franklin, 1743) became the model expression of both theology and polity among Regular Calvinistic Baptists in the late eighteenth century. (It was, of course, the slightly modified London Confession of 1689.) Other and earlier confessions of faith are to be found in the records of individual congregations, especially Swansea, Massachusetts; Boston, Massachusetts; Newport, Rhode Island; and Welsh Tract, Pennsylvania. In 1781 Benjamin Randal wrote an Arminianized set of principles for Freewill Baptists, which may be found in the New Durham, New Hampshire, yearly meeting minutes (unpublished; microcopy is available at ABHS). As printed associational minutes became more common at the time of the Revolution, such items served as sources of theological and organizational debate: see especially the Warren (Rhode Island), Philadelphia, New York City, Kehukee (North Carolina), and Sandy Creek (North Carolina) minutes. The first "manual" was Samuel Jones, *A Treatise on Church Discipline* (Philadelphia: S.C. Ustick, 1798; also published by Charleston, S.C., Association, 1805). Of great relevance to American clergymen were the works of English Baptists Andrew Fuller, John Gill, and Robert Hall. The first hymnal to achieve popular usage beyond a single congregation was John Rippon's *A Selection of Hymns from the Best Authors* (London: n.p., 1787).

On early Baptist educational developments two unpublished essays are most helpful. William T. Vandever, "An Educational History of the English and American Baptists in the Seventeenth and Eighteenth Centuries" (Ph.D. dissertation, University of Pennsylvania, 1974) traces the connections between Rhode Island and the Bristol, England, Baptists, and Dean H. Ashton, "Hopewell Academy and the Lives of Outstanding Graduates" (Typescript, ABHS, 1974) tells the story of American Baptists' first educational institution. The published reports of the Philadelphia, Warren, and Charleston Baptist Associations also shed light on the regional efforts of Baptists to finance ministerial education.

Primary source materials for the colonial period become more accessible as the larger repositories provide guides to their collections and microfilm editions of selected materials. The major repositories are the Charles Merrill Department of Rare Books and Special Collections, Franklin Trask Library, Andover Newton Theological School, the Archives and Libraries of the American Baptist Historical Society, and the John Hay Library of Brown University. Specific collections of personal papers relevant to the era are Andover Newton Theological School: Isaac Backus Papers, Hezekiah Smith Papers; American Baptist Historical Society: Philadelphia Baptist Association Papers, Morgan Edwards Papers, David Jones Papers, Peleg Burrough's journal, and John Rylands correspondence; Brown University: College of Rhode Island Records, James Manning Papers, Thomas Ustick Papers; Furman University: Richard Furman Papers. Important organizational records, including churches, may be located at Andover Newton (New England parishes) and ABHS (Middle Colonies and printed matter from the South). Several local churches retain original materials with microcopy available through ABHS (First Baptist Boston, Newton Centre, Massachusetts; First Baptist, Philadelphia, Pennsylvania; Middletown, New Jersey). ABHS also has the most extensive set of printed association and institutional records. Seventh Day Baptist records and papers are preserved at the Newport (Rhode Island) Historical Society, and the Rhode Island Historical Society administers a good collection of General Six Principle Baptist parish records and the diary of John Comer.

Baptist periodical literature is quite scant until 1800. The available resources are as follows: *New York Missionary Magazine* 1796–1801; *Georgia Analytical Repository* 1802–1803; and *Massachusetts Baptist Missionary Magazine* 1802–1816. However, there is much useful information in John Asplund's *Annual Register of the Baptist Denomination in North America* 1790–1795, and John Rippon's *Baptist Annual Register* 1790–1797; the latter was printed in London but filled with American data.

Section III
Missions, Organization, and Controversy 1812–1877

Since the commencement of the Christian dispensation, never did people of our sentiments find a country so suited to their principles and pursuits, where they could operate with such entire freedom, and such surprising effect . . . How often I have grieved and astonished that so many of them would spend so much of their time in carping about little matters and in distressing each other with their sectional or provincial jealousies and altercations.

David Benedict, 1848

The national period of Baptist life in America is characterized by organization, extension, conflict, and schism, all in the midst of numerical growth and slowly maturing denominational consciousness. The major catalyst to national organization was the unexpected conversion of pedobaptist missionaries, already on the field, to the Baptist position of believer's baptism by immersion. These missionaries turned to the Baptists for support as missionaries and thrust the Baptists into organizing for foreign missions work. This organizing led, in turn, to a widening interest in domestic missions, education, publication, and various other interrelated denominational enterprises. Numerical growth and geographical spread brought a widening pluralism and clashes over doctrine, church order, and the proper way to confront moral issues in American society.

The dispute over slavery became irreconcilable in the denomination, as it did in the nation at large, and ultimately divided the Baptists (as well as Methodists and Presbyterians) along sectional lines. After supporting their respective sides in the Civil War, Baptists in the North and in the South remained apart. Each section pursued a separate course of development according to its own understanding and interests while independent black Baptist organizations came into their own. Notwithstanding such persistent lines of division, common Baptist convictions continued to nourish basic affinities, to maintain Baptist identity, and to provide opportunities for fellowship and cooperation at many levels.

Organizing for Mission

Adoniram Judson (1778–1850) and his bride, Ann Hasseltine Judson (1789–1826), appointed by the American Board of Commissioners for Foreign Missions (a Congregationalist-Presbyterian society), set out for India in 1812. Expecting to contact William Carey and the English Baptist missionaries in Calcutta first, they sought to prepare themselves for this encounter by studying the meaning of baptism in the Greek New Testament. To the consternation of their companions, they became persuaded of the correctness of believer's baptism by immersion and shortly after their arrival requested baptism at the hands of Carey. Luther Rice (1783–1836), arriving soon afterward on another ship, was equally agitated by the baptismal question, made his own independent study, and, after resolving his doubts, also sought baptism by immersion.

The young missionaries could not honorably continue to accept support from the pedobaptist body that had sent them, but Baptists in America had no foreign missionary organization to which they could turn. They, therefore, severed their connections with the American Board of Commissioners, and Rice returned to the United States to organize the Baptists. The result of his wide-ranging labors was the General Missionary Convention, formed at Philadelphia in 1814.

The Convention's work soon expanded to embrace education and domestic missions, which led to considerable controversy over whether Baptists should have an inclusive body for all denominational enterprises or form a separate society for each cause. Advocates of the latter method eventually prevailed at the national level, but the state conventions that began to organize after 1820 were generally of the more inclusive type.

1. American Missionaries Turn Baptist

On September 1, 1812 Judson wrote to the corresponding secretary of the American Board of Commissioners, Noah Worcester, describing his new conviction and resigning his appointment under the board. The same day he wrote to Lucius Bolles, pastor of the First Baptist Church of Salem, Massachusetts, urging "the formation of a society among the Baptists in America for the support of foreign missions." Selection A details Judson's thoughts. Also on September 1 Joshua Marshman, one of the British Baptist missionaries, sent a similar appeal (Selection B) to Thomas Baldwin, pastor of the Second Baptist Church in Boston. *Sources:* A. *Massachusetts Baptist Missionary Magazine* (March, 1813), p. 238. B. *Ibid.,* pp. 269-270.

[A. Judson's Conversion to Baptist Principles]

Within a few months, I have experienced an entire change of sentiments on the subject of Baptism. My doubts concerning the correctness of my former system of belief, commenced during my passage from America to this country; and after many painful trials, which none can know, but those who are taught to relinquish a system in which they had been educated, I settled down in the full persuasion that the immersion of a professing believer in Christ is the only Christian baptism.

Mrs. Judson is united with me in this persuasion. We have signified our views and wishes to the Baptist missionaries at Serampore, and expect to be baptized in this city next Lord's day.

A separation from my missionary brethren, and a dissolution of my connection with the Board of Commissioners, seem to be necessary consequences. The missionaries at Serampore are exerted to the utmost of their ability, in managing and supporting their extensive and complicated mission.

Under these circumstances, I look to you. Alone, in this foreign, heathen land, I make my appeal to those whom, with their permission, I will call *my Baptist brethren* in the United States. . . .

[B. Joshua Marshman's Appeal]

A note which brother Judson sent to brother Carey last Saturday; has occasioned such reflection among us. In it he declares his belief that Believers' Baptism alone is the doctrine of the Scriptures, and requests to be baptized in the name of the Lord Jesus. . . .

This change then, which I believe few who knew brother Judson will impute to whim, or to any thing beside sincere conviction, seems to point out something relative to the duty of our Baptist brethren with you, as it relates to the cause of Missionaries. It can scarcely be expected that the Board of Commissioners will support a Baptist missionary, who cannot of course comply with their instructions, and baptize *whole households* on the parents' faith; and it is certain that the young man ought not to be left to perish for want, merely because he loved the truth more than father or mother; nor be compelled to give up missionary work, for want of support therein; Now, . . . it seems as though Providence itself were raising up this young man, that you might at least partake of the zeal of our Congregational missionary brethren around you. I would with them that you should share in the glorious work, by supporting him. After God has thus given you a Missionary of your own nation, faith, and order, without the help or knowledge of man, let me entreat you, and Dr. Messer, and brethren Bolles and Moriarty humbly to accept the gift.

2. American Baptists Respond

Luther Rice, having been baptized on November 1, 1812, returned to America early the next year. News of his conversion and that of the Judsons had spread rapidly among Baptists in America, and local foreign missionary societies had already formed in Salem, Boston, Philadelphia, and Richmond. The plan of a general missionary society linking together the various local societies came to Rice, he testified later in a letter to Judson, during his travels in the South in the fall of 1813. *Source:* James B. Taylor, *Memoir of Rev. Luther Rice: One of the First Missionaries to the East* (Baltimore: Armstrong & Berry, 1841), p. 146.

While passing from Richmond to Petersburg in the stage, an enlarged view of the business opened upon my contemplations. The plan which suggested itself to my mind, that of forming one principal society in each state, bearing the name of the state, and others in the same state, auxiliary to that; and by these large, or state societies, delegates be appointed to form one general society. The society in Richmond, in the outset, took the name of the state, as did one afterwards in North Carolina; but in no case, have auxiliaries been formed to these state societies. Recently, however, this same kind of system, in substance and effect, but differing in form and modification, begins to come into action. Several state conventions have been formed already, and more will probably be originated. To these, it is calculated, auxiliaries will be formed, and that associations will also become constituents; and that from these delegates, perhaps, ultimately, the delegates will be appointed to the general convention.

Baptist delegates gathered in Philadelphia in May, 1814, to organize the proposed foreign mission convention. After electing Richard Furman of Charleston, South Carolina, as president and Thomas Baldwin of Boston as secretary, the delegates adopted a constitution, which is excerpted in Selection A. The excitement that Luther Rice evoked on his first tour of the churches produced not only funds but volunteers for the missionary endeavor. In 1815 the Board of the General Missionary Convention appointed George H. Hough to serve in Burma, whence the Judsons had gone. The commissioning of Hough was the first commissioning for the Baptist foreign mission society. *Sources: A. Minutes of the General Missionary Convention, 21 May 1814. Archives, American Baptist Historical Society. B. First Annual Report of the Baptist Board of Foreign Missions for the United States,* 1815, p. 28.

[A. Constitution of the Board]

We the delegates from Missionary Societies, and other religious Bodies of the Baptist denomination, in various parts of the United States, met in Convention, in the City of Philadelphia, for the purpose of carrying into effect the benevolent Intentions of our Constituents, by organizing a plan for eliciting, combining, and directing the Energies of the whole Denomination in one sacred effort, for sending the glad tidings of Salvation to the Heathen, and to nations destitute of pure Gospel-light, DO AGREE to the following Rules or fundamental Principles, viz.

I. That this body shall be styled *"The General Missionary Convention of the Baptist Denomination in the United States of America for Foreign Missions."*

II. That *a triennial Convention* shall, hereafter, be held, consisting of Delegates, not exceeding two in number, from each of the several Missionary Societies, and other religious bodies of the Baptist Denomination, now existing, or which may hereafter be formed in the United States, and which shall each, regularly contribute to the general Missionary Fund, a sum, amounting, at least, to one hundred Dollars, per annum.

III. That for the necessary transaction and dispatch of business, during the recess of the said Convention, there shall be a Board of Twenty-one Commissioners, who shall be members of the said Societies, Churches, or other religious bodies aforesaid, triennially appointed, by the said Convention, by ballot, to be called the "Baptist Board of Foreign Missions for the United States:" seven of whom shall be a quorum for the transaction of all business; and which Board shall continue in office until successors be duly appointed; and shall have power to make and adopt by-laws for the government of the said Board, and for the furtherance of the general objects of the Institution.

IV. That it shall be the duty of this Board, to employ Missionaries, and, if necessary, to take measures for the improvement of their qualifications; to fix on the Field of their Labours, and the compensation to be allowed them for their services; to superintend their conduct, and dismiss them, should their services be disapproved; to publish accounts, from time to time, of the Board's Transactions, and an annual Address to the public; to call a special meeting of the Convention on any extraordinary occasion, and, in general, to conduct the executive part of the missionary concern.

V. That such persons only, as are in full communion with some regular Church of our Denomination, and who furnish satisfactory evidence of genuine Piety, good Talents, and fervent Zeal for the Redeemer's Cause, are to be employed as Missionaries. . . .

[B. The Commissioning of George Hough]
The setting apart of brother George H. Hough as a missionary to India beyond the Ganges.

The Board are persuaded that the circumstances attendant on the acceptance and employment of brother Hough will afford gratification, and create thankfulness to the Head of the church, who asks not in vain "whom shall I send, and who will go for us?" The language of the heart of brother Hough is, *"Here am I, send me."*

Mr. Hough is about 28 years of age, a native of Windsor, Vt., and member of the Baptist Church at Pawtucket, R.I.

In his letter soliciting the patronage of the Board, after some account of the religious exercises of his mind, he observes,—"with an impression that it was my duty to become a servant in the church, for Christ's sake, and having a special regard in my heart for the advancement of the Redeemer's Kingdom and the everlasting welfare of men, I obeyed, as well the call of duty as that of the church, and engaged with much weakness and trembling in the ministry of the word. Since the time I received the knowledge of the truth, I have had a disposition of mind towards a missionary life;—have felt a peculiar and strong desire for the fulfilment of those prophecies, which relate to the universal reign of Christ on earth, and have been, and still am, not only willing, but desirous of offering my body as a living sacrifice to God, that his gracious purposes might be accomplished in me and others. For about one year past, my impressions of duty relative to engaging in the India mission have been increasing. Having spent my early years in acquiring the art of printing, and it having been intimated that a new station would be sought by the American missionaries, where a printing establishment would be eminently useful towards accomplishing the object of the mission, I felt upon my mind a kind of double obligation to offer myself to the respected Board of Foreign Missions for their patronage and assistance; that they would allow me the happiness of making the sacrifices, encountering the trials, enduring the fatigues, and dying the death of a missionary.

"One persuasion has ever occupied my mind upon this subject, that if it were my duty, if God designed me to labour in that part of his vineyard, He himself would conduct me towards it by his Providence; and I cannot help observing, that every step which I have taken towards the present interview has been apparently to my mind providentially directed; and I think I could never have felt satisfied that I had done my duty, without presenting myself, as I now do, to this Board, and intreating that they would bestow on me the favour, which it is now in their power I hope consistently to grant, of living and dying their missionary in India.". . .

India was not the only focus of the Board of foreign missions. The appeal of "the dark continent" to English and American evangelicals had long been strong, and the founding of Freetown (in Sierra Leone) as a refuge for liberated slaves seemed to offer a providential opportunity. The Board approved of the formation of the American Colonization Society by a secular group in 1817—a venture which led to the establishing of Liberia—and began to contemplate a mission to west Africa. An opening came when a letter from William Crane, a member of the First Baptist Church of Richmond, Virginia, arrived in 1819. *Source: Fifth Annual Report of the Baptist Board of Foreign Missions,* 1819, pp. 261-262.

Richmond, March 28, 1819.

"You will probably recollect, that I introduced you to two of our coloured brethren in this place, who are accustomed to speak in public; one named Collin Teague, the other Lot Carey. Ever since the missionary subject has been so much agitated in this country, these two brethren, associated with many others, have been wishing they could, in some way, aid their unhappy kindred in Africa; and I suppose you have heard of their having formed a missionary society for this sole purpose. They are now determined to go themselves to Africa; and the only questions with them are, in what way will it be best for them to proceed? and what previous steps are requisite to be taken? They think it necessary to spend some time in study first. They both possess industry and abilities, such as, with the blessing of Providence, would soon make them rich. It is but two or three years since either of them enjoyed their freedom; and both have paid large sums for their families. They now possess but little, except a zealous wish to go and do what they can. Brother Lot has a wife, and several little children. He has a place a little below Richmond, that cost him $1500, but will probably not sell for more than $1000 at this time. Brother Collin has a wife, a son 14 years of age, and a daughter of 11, for whom he has paid $1300, and has scarcely any thing left. Both their wives are baptists; their children, amiable and docile, have been to school considerably; and I hope, if they go, will likewise be of service. Collin is a saddler and harness maker. He had no early education. The little that he has gained, has been by chance and peace-meal. He has judgment, and as much keenness of penetration as almost any man. He can read, though he is not a good reader, and can write so as to make out a letter. The little knowledge he has of figures, has been gained by common calculations in business. Lot was brought up on a farm; and for a number of years has been chief manager among the labourers in the largest tobacco ware house in this city. He has charge of receiving, marking and shipping tobacco; and the circumstance that he receives $700 a year wages may help you to form an estimate of the man. He reads better than Collin, and is in every respect a better scholar. They have been trying to preach about ten or eleven years, and are both about forty years of age. . . .

Their object is to carry the tidings of salvation to the benighted Africans. They wish to be where their colour will be no disparagement to their usefulness. I suppose the funds of our African Mission Society here, after their next meeting, on Monday after Easter, will probably amount to $600, which I believe the society will be willing to appropriate to the aid of their brethren should they go.''

3. The Convention's Work Enlarges

As originally organized, the General Missionary Convention was only a foreign mission society. At its second meeting in 1817 the Board, which had been acting vigorously in the triennial interim, recommended "that the powers of this Convention be extended so

as to embrace home missions and plans for the encouragement of (ministerial) education."
Accordingly, the constitution was amended to include the wider concerns, and in 1820
the focus of the Convention was enlarged to take in "other important objects relating to
the Redeemer's kingdom." With such authorization in 1817 the Board moved into the
field of domestic missions, designating John Mason Peck (1789–1858) and James E.
Welch (1789–1876) as missionaries to the Western Territory of the United States. As it
turned out, Peck also devoted a significant portion of his efforts to evangelizing among
blacks. His report of the conversion of an aged slave reveals something of the blacks'
response. *Sources:* A. Proceedings of the General Convention, 1817, p. 175. Archives,
American Baptist Historical Society. B. John M. Peck to the Editor, 7 December 1823,
American Baptist Magazine (March 1824) pp. 307-308.

[A. Instructions to Peck and Welch]

Arrived, as is the case with both of you, at years considerably
matured, your judgment and experience will often suggest to you, when
residents in the country whither you are going, ideas which the Board
may not immediately possess. They will be always happy to hear your
sentiments, and to concur in every plan which they shall judge calculated
to advance the common design. They, at present, request you to commence your missionary career at St. Louis, or in its vicinity. The board
feels the propriety and importance of your endeavouring to establish a
school or schools in that neighbourhood. . . . They wish you also to
collect such scattered brethren through districts of the country, as you
may be able, and encourage and assist their formation into regular
churches of Christ. It is not improbable that from such brethren and
churches, men of God may be found who will rejoice to become your
associates in the work before you. The Board is particularly desirous
that the Fox, the Osage, the Kanses, and other tribes of Indians, should
engage your peculiar zeal.

[B. John M. Peck to Massachusetts Baptist Missionary Society
7 December 1823]

Rev. and Dear Sir,

Last night was the time of our church meeting in St. Louis, for the
black members. By arrangements made some months since, I hold
special meetings for that branch of our church, as it is not convenient
for them to attend at the time the whites meet. Though very rainy, the
meeting was well attended. One old man related his experience as
follows; which I here repeat verbatim, as a specimen of the state of

religious feeling and sanctified knowledge in an old illiterate slave. It was not till all the members present had spoken of the state of their minds that he ventured forward, when he arose and addressed the members as follows: "I am an old man, and have lived a long time in this world; but lately I have had a great many calls to be religious, and must die soon. I live so long and do no good—no good done yet—Well, then the call say, I must pray God to have mercy—so I pray as well I could—but feel distress. I want to go meeting—but afraid to go—people see me. But I feel can't stay home. So the call said—must go meeting. I went to meeting, and set way back side of house. The man preach, and he preach right to me—I hang my head down, and try pray all the time I dare not look up—I feel so big a sinner. Then the preacher tell the mourners come forward and get pray for. Some come forward, but I stay back yet. I look down and think, Me poor sinner, and want prayer for mercy. Then I go forward and kneel down, and the preacher pray for me. I go home and lie down, and try to sleep—but no sleep—I feel so distress, and see me such a sinner. Try to pray for mercy. I don't know if I fall asleep but think I see a small light a great distance up. I try to go to it, and I feel though I rising up and feel light. It seems as if I hear beautiful singing and rejoicing. I lie till break-day—then I get up—look out. All look beautiful—thought I never see so fine a day—all praising God—then I begin to think he pardon my sin—I never did any good—all sin—Then I think how good God is—he hear my poor prayer—he pardon and save sinner. I feel he pardon me. The call say, praise God. Then I think, I can't half praise enough. Then I want to see the Christians. I felt as though I want to tell them how God pardon my sin—how my poor soul rejoice. I went around to see the Christians, and they rejoice with me. . . . Now I love sit and hear every word, and never get tired all the preacher say—only sorry when he stop. Never tire hearing about precious Savior. I know I did not love these things once. . . . But I love to serve God. I don't care about freedom in this world, not much matter, I only want free from sin. I then go home to happy place. I want to serve Jesus. He best massa in the world."

No interruption was made during the above recital. . . . I know there is nothing peculiar in the above relation, but it shows that religious influence is the same in its nature and effects in all conditions and classes of men. I have just closed a public meeting for the blacks, which I hold on Sabbath evenings when in the city. It was a solemn, joyful, and impressive season. . . .

J.M. Peck

Richard Furman and others had urged the cause of education from the beginning. Upon enlarging its scope, in 1820 the General Convention approved a plan for a college, and the following year Columbian College opened in Washington, D.C., with the Rev. William Staughton (1770–1829) of Philadelphia as president. *Source: Seventh Annual Report of the Board of Managers of the Baptist General Convention,* 1821, pp. 7-9.

The committee appointed by the Board to procure an incorporation of the Convention, endeavoured at the last session of Congress to fulfil the duty assigned them. They have with much labour succeeded in obtaining a charter, which completely covers the education concern. It imparts a full legal character to a *College* which shall embrace classical and a theological department; leaving room for arrangements which by the Trustees of the College have already been made, and which place the whole Institution, virtually and for ever, under the power of the Convention. . . .

It was gratifying in a high degree, to behold, on one of the most beautiful and commanding sites in the metropolis of the Union, a substantial brick edifice, of 117 feet in front by 47 in depth, completely covered in, a large part of the interior carpentry finished, and the whole promising in a short time to become a nursery of science and of ministerial talent, which shall diffuse its blessings not only around the district of Columbia, but through every section of the United States, and, by the agency of christian missionaries, to the uttermost parts of the earth. The Board could not but feel grateful for the indefatigable and self-denying exertions of their brother, the Rev. Mr. Rice; and could not but pray, that his useful life may be prolonged for years to come, and that his endeavors and resolutions, in the name of the Lord, by persevering appeals to the benevolence of the churches and the public, to extinguish every unsatisfied claim, may be crowned with the most entire success. . . .

The College is divided into a classic and a theological department. The duties of the latter, it is expected, will commence at Washington in September next; those of the former, with the beginning of the year 1822.

4. The General Convention Reverts to a Foreign Mission Society

The college soon fell on troubled times. Luther Rice, acting as agent for the trustees, was careless in handling the funds; and though an investigating committee cleared him of all charges of immoral conduct, it judged that he "is a very loose accountant, and that he has very imperfect talents for the disbursement of money." The financial troubles of the college convinced the leaders of the Convention that they should dissociate themselves from the school and restrict their efforts to foreign missions. The reasons for the Convention's retreat from a fully inclusive charter were amplified in an important journal. *Source: The American Baptist Magazine* (July, 1826), pp. 208-209.

In our last number we took occasion hastily to state the fact that the Constitution of the Convention had been so amended as to restrict its operations exclusively to Missionary business. The reasons for this amendment were then of necessity omitted, and this omission it is now our intention very briefly to supply. Some of the considerations which seemed to justify this measure at the meeting of the Convention, were, if we mistake not, the following:

1. There is no necessary connection between the Missionary and Education concerns of our denomination. Both are important, both are necessary; but this is no reason why both should be managed by the same men, or their funds cast into one common treasury.

2. It is difficult to conceive of any substantial benefit which could result to either from this connection. By the express letter and spirit of the Constitution of the Convention, its funds of every sort must be appropriated exclusively to that object for which they were designed by the donor. The mission has no control over the funds for education, nor has the education concern any control over the funds of the missions. Different agents require to be employed to promote their different objects, and different Boards engaged in their management—Boards in the present instance widely separated from each other. We see no reason therefore why they should be united.

3. Some reasons might easily be suggested why they had better be disunited. The feelings of our brethren in different portions of the United States in relation to these two objects are not entirely coincident. Some are more particularly favourable to missionary, and others to education exertions. The blending of these two concerns together must evidently injure the success of both of them in respect to all persons in both these classes. Either party would give more liberally towards his favourite

object if it stood alone, and totally disconnected with the other.

And again it is evident that complication of object in any case diminishes the prospect of success. A benevolent purpose is better sustained when it is managed by men who are singly devoted to its promotion. In the present imperfect state it is not to be expected that any number of men could be found who would devote equal attention to both education and missions, and at the same time give to each the full attention that it deserved. One or the other will almost of necessity be neglected, as the claims of its rival are more urgent, and being neglected by its constituted guardians, will lose its interest in the feelings of the publick.

4. The history of this connection in the present case has abundantly demonstrated the evil of connecting these charities together. It has proved that each has been of very serious injury to the other.

5. State Conventions Organize

In December, 1821, the Baptists of South Carolina were the first to form a fully organized state convention. Such regional bodies were instituted to promote missions and education. In 1826 the Hamilton Baptist Missionary Society (founded in 1808) merged with the Baptist Missionary Society of New York to form the State Convention. The following excerpt reveals the decision to unite. *Source:* Minutes of the Hamilton Baptist Missionary Society, 1825. Archives, American Baptist Historical Society.

At the meeting of the Board in August last, some Brethren attended who are connected with the New York Baptist state convention; and expressed a strong desire that a committee from the Board should meet the convention at Elbridge in October next; for the purpose of devising some expedient to form a (union) between the two bodies, thereby to unite the energies of the whole denomination, throughout the state, in carrying into effect the important design of domestic missions. Accordingly a committee was appointed, who in company with several members of the Board, and of the Society, met the convention. Upon which the convention appointed a committee to consult with them upon the great object in view. During the conference the committee of the Board did not for a moment lose sight of those plain and practical principles incorporated in the constitution of this Society; under which we have for seventeen years so happily, unitedly, and successfully rallied.—The committee saw no cause to abandon those principles; although they desired an increase of influence, and usefullness which union with their brethren was calculated to effect.—

After suitable deliberation: The committee of the convention, agreed to recommend to that body, the adoption of the constitution of this Society, with an alteration of the name of the Society and an increase of the number of Directors. This was with a view to unite the two bodies in order to increase the strength and missionary exertions of the Baptist denomination in the State.—The committee of the Board could see no reasonable objection to this measure and therefore agreed to recommend it to your attention. Accordingly a special meeting of the Society was called in November last: but on account of the inclemency of the weather, and badness of the roads, but few members attended.— However, matters were arranged at that time as far as was consistent in anticipation of a complete union at this time. . . .

An impartial view of the existing state of things in our degenerate world, will serve to convince us of the necessity of unremitting exertions to maintain the blessed cause of our glorious Redeemer:—For which cause a combination of strength, and a union of effort is highly requisite.—We find that in this state, there are more than thirty nine thousand church members of the Baptist denomination.— Let these be united in one body, and what a formidable Phalanx would be presented to the enemy. Would it not be desirable that measures should be adopted to produce such a union, that the whole strength of denomination may be brought on one point. . . .

And all that is now wanting to compleat an entire conquest, is, for the children of God in one consolidated mass to fall upon the flying ranks of the Philistines.—Let all those who profess to love the Lord consider the necessity of exerting all their energies, to accomplish a compleat union among the friends of Zion, and diffuse the light of the gospel among the destitute.—There is much work before us and many calls to renewed labors.

Although the idea of a national Baptist college failed, state organizations met the challenge with the establishment of "literary and theological institutions." The first one was started at Waterville, Maine, in 1813 and later became Colby College.

As this report shows, Ohio Baptists had bright hopes for a school that would serve the needs of the western part of the country. The Granville Institution later became Denison University. *Source: Annual Report of the Meeting of the Ohio Baptist Education Society and of the Trustees of the Granville Literary and Theological Institution,* 1832.

General Object and Plan.—Our object has been, and is, to build up a useful Institution—suited to the wants, and calculated to promote the welfare of a rapidly growing and free country, where virtuous intelligence, industry and enterprise are sure to meet a quick reward. It designs to embrace, agreeably to its appellation, two departments, Literary and Theological. In the literary department, we aim to establish such a course of instruction as will fit the youth of our country to be skillful instructors of our common schools, and for the ready and accurate transaction of business, whether in public or private life. It is our purpose to furnish the means of obtaining a thorough classical and English education, which shall not be inferior to what can be obtained in any institution, of whatever name, in the western country. The Theological department is designed specially for those young men, members of the Baptist denomination, whom their respective churches judge to be called to the ministry. This description of students will enjoy all the advantages of the Literary department; and in addition to these advantages, will have their attention directed to such studies and exercises as will serve to render their labours in their appropriate work more efficient and acceptable than otherwise they would be.

The large and excellent farm attached to the Institution, will not only be of essential utility to the boarding establishment, but will greatly facilitate the prosecution of the manual labor system, on the part of the students. It is our purpose to make such arrangements that those young men, who feel disposed, may spend a part of each day in profitable manual labor, which, without at all interfering with their progress in study, will serve the double purpose of preserving health and sustaining in part their current expenses.

Extension and Maturation

As the denomination matured and outgrew its self-consciousness, many projects took shape in education, publishing, and evangelism. While state education societies sponsored institutions for collegiate purposes, other benevolent groups created schools designed solely for clergy training. Sunday schools spread rapidly throughout the denomination, while the religious needs of the West pressed their claims on missionary-minded Baptists in the East. These concerns all required Bibles, periodicals, and other literature and led, naturally, to many publishing ventures. Since the General Missionary Convention after 1826 operated only as a foreign missionary society and no other organization emerged to embrace all denominational causes in one overarching enterprise, Baptists did much of their cooperative work through a nexus of single-purpose societies. The Home Mission Society, organized in 1832, assumed responsibility for evangelizing in the less developed areas of the nation and quickly established itself as a major instrument of Baptist witness. Meanwhile, revivals waxed and waned—though never dying out completely—as preaching, worship, and church architecture evidenced the transformation of Baptists in America from a fringe sect to a main-line, middle-class denomination.

1. Ministerial Education

Notwithstanding the General Missionary Convention's dissociation from educational concerns in 1826, many Baptists continued to give to education, and especially education for ministry, a high priority. As the church college movement spread, Massachusetts Baptists moved to establish a seminary that would remain a theological school. *Source: The American Baptist Magazine* (July, 1826), pp. 217-218.

CIRCULAR
RESPECTING THE NEWTON THEOLOGICAL INSTITUTION
Boston, June 1826

Dear Sir,

The undersigned, a Committee of the Trustees of the NEWTON THEOLOGICAL INSTITUTION, beg leave to submit to your consideration the following statements relative to the origin, present state, and prospects of the Seminary with which in the providence of God they are connected.

The origin of the Newton Theological Institution, may be dated from a numerous meeting of ministers, and private brethren, from various parts of New England, held in May, 1825, at the vestry of the First Baptist Church in this city. It was then resolved that the necessities of our denomination imperiously require the the establishment of a Theological Institution in the vicinity of Boston, and the gentlemen present pledged themselves to use every suitable exertion towards the promotion of such an object. Brethren from all parts of the State addressed the meeting, and each one seemed most deeply impressed with the importance of such an institution to the interests of piety among our churches. As there was at that time no other incorporated body to whom the management of the business could be immediately intrusted, it was left with the Executive Committee of the Massachusetts Baptist Education Society, to carry these resolves into effect.

The execution of this trust they assumed, and immediately took such measures as the providence of God seemed to direct, and the attainment of the object necessarily to require. The Rev. Irah Chase, A.M. late Professor of Languages and Biblical Criticism in the Columbian College, was appointed Professor of Biblical Theology. A site was purchased in the town of Newton about 7 miles from this city containing eighty-five acres on elevated ground, and commanding one of the most delightful prospects in this vicinity. Upon the land is a large mansion house, abundantly sufficient for the residence of a steward and twenty-five students, besides out houses and a large and profitable garden. This whole property was purchased for $4,250, the expense of which was defrayed by the distinguished liberality of a few individuals in this city, and its vicinity. Since the purchase it has been necessary however to commence a series of alterations and repairs to render the house more suitable for its present design. These will cost not much less than the

original price of the property, and will bring its net expense to about
$8,000. . . .

Whilst these arrangements were in progress, the Executive Committee
of the Baptist Education Society, were aware that it was not the expectation of their brethren, nor was it consistent with the best interests
of such a seminary, that its management should continue in their hands
longer than was absolutely necessary. They therefore took early measures towards obtaining an act of incorporation. This act was passed
February 21, 1826, by which the most distinguished benefactors to the
institution, and others deeply interested in its prosperity in this vicinity
and in New England, were incorporated by the name of the Trustees
of the Newton Theological Institution. Under their direction a course
of theological instruction commenced in December, 1825, by Professor
Chase, and several young men have already enjoyed its advantages.

2. The Sunday School Idea

Baptists were expanding their educational enterprise in another direction as well. The
Sunday school idea, generally credited to Robert Raikes (1735–1811), an English evangelical, spread rapidly throughout America in the early nineteenth century. In 1826 the
General Missionary Convention, notwithstanding its reversion that year to a single-purpose
society for foreign missions, recommended Sunday schools "to the patronage of the
Baptist community." Most associations and state conventions regularly heard reports
from Sunday school committees, but in 1839 the Hudson River Association adopted a
more far-reaching proposal calling for an American Baptist Sunday School Union.
Source: Minutes of the Hudson River Baptist Association, 1839, pp. 14-15.

The enlightened policy which prompted our brethren in the eastern
states, to organize "the New England Sabbath School Union," is worthy
of all praise. . . .

American Baptists are awaking from the slumber of ages, and your
Committee, believing that concentrated action is essential to efficiency,
recommend that a Special Committee be appointed to issue a Circular
addressed to the Baptist State Conventions, Associations, and Churches
throughout the land, inviting their attention to the importance of forming
an American Baptist Sunday School Union; contemplating also the
reprint of standard Baptist works now extant, and such other approved
books as may proceed from the pens of our brethren. And that the
churches be requested to authorize their delegates to the societies, which
will meet in New York in April, 1840, to act on their behalf in the
formation of such an institution.

As Baptists, we cannot but feel a deep interest in Sunday Schools. It is within the knowledge of your Committee, that the first Sunday School taught in the state of New York, and it is believed, in the United States, was under the management of two brethren, then members of the Baptist church in Mulberry-street, in the city of New York. Upon this Association therefore, it would seem to be particularly incumbent to promote by every proper means, the best interests of an institution, which may be said, in this country, to have originated among themselves. Your Committee are aware, that at an early period, attempts were made in Philadelphia, (and at a still earlier period, by a Baptist brother in Rhode Island) to instruct the ignorant on the Sabbath day; but the Sunday School in Division-street, (commenced prior to the benevolent efforts of the devoted Isabella Graham) was the first Sunday School established in the United States, upon *the voluntary plan* of Wm. Fox, a member of the Baptist-church; in England, whose praise in this department of Christian duty, will be celebrated when the fame of statesmen, poets, and orators, shall be merged in oblivion.

3. Publishing Ventures

The missionary movement could not survive, much less flourish, apart from adequate dissemination of news and appeals for contributions. While Baptist periodicals did not confine themselves to items of missionary intelligence, this was certainly one of their primary preoccupations. In 1823 Luther Rice outlined a brief history of Baptist periodicals to which must be added Henry Holcombe's *Georgia Analytical Repository* (1802) actually the first Baptist serial. *Source: The Latter Day Luminary* (November, 1823), pp. 348-350.

The first religious periodical work published by the Baptists in this country, was the *American Baptist Magazine,* established about twenty years ago by a few worthy brethren in Boston, Massachusetts. Foreign missions were then little thought of, though the church was using some efforts for supplying the destitute of this country with evangelical instruction. The work, therefore, for several years, contained the journals of domestic missionaries, religious communications, concise biographies of departed saints, accounts of revivals, constitution of churches, ordinations, and other miscellaneous matter; all generally well adapted to the taste of its readers, and calculated to effect the intended good. Its patronage has been very extensive. Though never sectarian, it has ever been decidedly Baptist; holding ever in view a distinct and marked design, that of maintaining inviolably the cause of truth against aggressions of errour in creed or practice, and of diffusing among those who walk in the truth, that spirit of general benevolence which knows no difference between heathen at home and heathen abroad. Its profits, which some years have been considerable, are devoted to the interest of missions. For several years, this work was a solitary light along a dark coast; but time has changed, and others have appeared to illumine our religious horizon, and to spread the light of heavenly truth in all directions.

The Western New-York Baptist Magazine was first issued several years ago, published by the Hamilton Baptist Missionary Society, and edited by a committee of the same. Its circulation has not been very extensive, though read, we learn, with considerable interest in the region round about where it is published. It contains missionary journals and letters, copied from other works of a kindred nature, reports of Mission and Education Societies, biographies, and other matter suited to a work of the kind. Its profits are sacred to the cause of Christian benevolence.

The *Latter Day Luminary* was commenced by a Committee of the Baptist Board of Foreign Missions, in Philadelphia, February, 1818. For the first four years it was published once in three months, embracing religious communications, the official intelligence of the Board, concerning both missions and education, memoirs of good men, and a mass of other interesting intelligence relative to the state of religion in our own and in other countries. In 1822 it was removed to Washington, and is now published monthly. Its profits are sacred to the cause of missions.

The *Christian Watchman,* a weekly paper, was established in Boston, in the beginning of the year 1820. This paper possesses a considerable share of interest. It receives intelligence from India, and religious publications from Europe, earlier than any other work of the kind published by the Baptists.

The *Religious Intelligencer,* a weekly paper published in Providence, Rhode Island, was commenced in May, 1820, by a young man, a Baptist, then associate editor of the Rhode Island American. After six months he relinquished it, and it was taken up by a Pedobaptist, who has recently given up the editorial office to a Baptist of good talents and liberal principles.

The *Columbian Star,* a weekly paper, commenced at the office of the Latter Day Luminary, in February, 1822. It is edited with ability, and is rapidly increasing in patronage. Its profits are devoted to the benefit of missions.

The *Christian Secretary,* a weekly paper, in quarto size, commenced on the same day with the Star, in Hartford, Connecticut. It is a neat little work, and worthy of support.

The *Baptist Monitor,* a weekly paper, was established at Bloomfield, Kentucky, in April the present year. About the same time commenced the *Waterville Intelligencer,* in Waterville, Maine. The characters of these papers have hardly become sufficiently fixed, to determine the degree of good they may probably effect. But from their localities, their present appearance, and extensive patronage, the assumption can be ventured, that they will be productive of much benefit to the church, by diffusing correct principles, and exciting the public mind to a consideration of the mighty work now advancing for the salvation of fallen man. Proposals have been issued for publishing two or three other papers of a kindred class. If founded on good principles, and well conducted, every brother ought to wish them success.

The Sunday school movement reinforced a need for simple religious tracts. In the excerpt below, Noah Davis, a Maryland Baptist minister, proposed in 1824 the establishment of a Baptist General Tract Society, a proposal that took only eleven days to bear fruit. In response to initiatives of the Hudson River Baptist Association, the Tract Society was expanded in 1840 to become the American Baptist Publication and Sunday School Society. *Source: Columbian Star,* 14 February 1824.

[Baptist General Tract Society]

It has been suggested to us, that it is desirable that a *Baptist General Tract Society* be established in this city. A friend, whose delight it is, to devise and execute plans for the advancement of religion, writes to us thus: "I have been thinking for some time how a Tract Society can be got up in Washington, which shall hold the same place among Baptists, that the American Tract Society does among Congregationalists. I now feel very much the necessity of having Tracts to scatter in the waste places. It is a plan of doing good, which is scarcely known among Baptists. No place is more suitable for such a Society than Washington. Resources would be principally obtained through auxiliaries, and the exertions of Agents. Many of our ministers might become life-members."

We leave this hint with our readers for the present, with the remark, that in our opinion, the distribution of Tracts is an object of sufficient importance to solicit the attention of every denomination of Christians. They are unobtrusive but most efficient *preachers of righteousness,* winning their way where a minister could not penetrate; telling and repeating their simple message, at those hours, too, when it may be most likely to reach the heart and the conscience. It is therefore worth while to take heed what doctrines they teach. Tracts are either essays on moral virtues, or statements of religious truth, or more frequently, narratives of individuals who have remarkably exemplified the effects of Christian principles. No objectionable sentiments may be advanced, but the tendency may nevertheless be, to sanction opinions and practices which we do not approve. Much may be *implied,* much be taken for granted, and certain processes be pointed out, and the whole assume a complexion very different from that which we should ourselves give it. We are not sufficiently familiar with Tracts to know how far these remarks are applicable to those, now in circulation—but we think it can do no harm to form a Society. Among other advantages, we can supervise the character of these messengers of religious truth, before we commission them to go forth, to enter into controversy with the consciences of men, and to beseech them, in Christ's stead, to be reconciled to God.

The Tract Society, so quick to organize, was slow in getting started and might have died except for vigorous support by faithful Baptist women. The following circular, sent ''to the females of some of the churches,'' shows the extent of women's participation during the early years. *Source: The American Baptist Magazine* (April, 1828), pp. 126-127.

Philadelphia, February, 1828
Dear Sisters,
We hope it will gratify you to be informed that the object of this epistle is to solicit you to contribute the sum necessary to constitute your pastor a Member or Director for life of the Baptist General Tract Society. This can be easily done, if one or two of you will use a little diligence in collecting donations from those who may be disposed to give for this purpose. By making your minister a life member or director, the Society will be increased in numbers and ability. You will give this demonstration of attachment to him and love of the cause of Christ,

which it is our single object to promote. He will be bound to the Society by an additional tie, and have the privilege of receiving half the amount contributed by you in Tracts. These he may put in circulation, and the Lord may graciously bless them to the everlasting good of many. All who are acquainted with the subject will acknowledge the great value of scriptural and well selected Tracts as an instrument of diffusing knowledge of the way of salvation. It is evidently the duty of Christians to make use of them for this purpose. We have engaged in the work, and we ask you to assist us, that we may have the means to publish an extensive variety and a large number of these advocates of truth. Our Society has never been able since its formation, from the want of sufficient funds, to meet the wishes of its friends. The present demand for Tracts is greater than at any previous time, and in order to meet it we are trying to raise by subscriptions and donations as soon as practicable one or two thousand dollars. From the commencement of the Society a principal portion of its income has been the life subscriptions paid by females for their ministers.

4. A Separate Organization for Home Missions

The General Convention's retreat from domestic missions in 1826 (see pages 177-178.) left several missionaries in the West without any certain means of support. The obvious solution in view of the way Baptist denominational life lay was in developing another single-purpose society. Foremost in the new venture was Jonathan Going of Massachusetts, who toured the West with John Mason Peck in 1831. Early the next year Peck wrote to Going of the urgent need for more missionaries (Selection A). Going laid Peck's concern, reinforced with his own, before the Massachusetts Baptist Missionary Society, which set in motion a series of events culminating in the formation of the American Baptist Home Mission Society in April, 1832. In Selection B the minutes of the first meeting of the society in New York City summarize its provenance and purpose. *Sources:* A. John Mason Peck to Jonathan Going, 10 January 1832. Manuscript Collections, Andover Newton Theological School. B. Minutes of the Board of Managers, 1832, ABHMS. Archives, American Baptist Historical Society.

[A. Peck's Appeal for Eastern Assistance]

You must make some extra exertions to send us an able man for *Jacksonville,* one who will hold his head even with the Paedos and the College folks. Bro. Jones pledges himself to Board a man, others will help, and betwixt Jacksonville and Jersey Prairie, it is thought a man may receive a support. This is a very important site and will decide the fate of the Baptists in Morgan County. If the right man can be put there, it is thought the *truth* will prevail in that quarter and the Anti-nomian influence kept down. A Church will be formed in Jacksonville soon as we know if a man can be had to put there. Have you no Newton students—or some New England pastor who has caught the emigrating fever? Send him out. . . . I have not strength or time to present my views on a general system of operations at this time, only I observe the project of a "Home Missionary Society"—That is very necessary—but means must be used to inform the people and arouse up the Baptists. Cannot you write a series of articles for the Watchman on the subject? *Try, Try, Try.* . . . Please write and let me know all your movements about a home mission society and prospects. You *MUST* devote yourself to the cause in the West—Now is the crisis—tomorrow will be too late.

[B. Origin of the Home Mission Society]

The spiritual destitution of many of the new states in the Union having been the subject of anxious consideration, to some individual members of the Baptist Denomination, in the vicinity of Boston, *one* of their number, [Going], was solicited by the others to make a missionary tour to the west. The result of the observations thus made, was presented to the Baptist Missionary Society of Massachusetts.

At a meeting of that body held in Boston, in the month of November last, it was resolved, in view of the spiritual wants of our country, that measures should be taken to arouse the Baptist community throughout the United States, to systematic and vigorous efforts in the cause of Domestic Missions. The field to be assumed included the whole of the United States, but more especially the Valley of the Mississippi. It was further resolved, that, for this purpose, a general Home Mission Society ought to be formed. At the same time, a resolution was adopted expressing it as the conviction of the meeting, that it was the duty of the Rev. Jonathan Going, of Worcester, Mass., to relinquish his pastoral charge, and to devote himself to the interests of the proposed Society.

As a deputation from the Baptist Missionary Society of Massachusetts, the Rev. Dr. Sharp, and the Rev. Dr. Bolles, of Boston, and the Rev. Jonathan Going, visited the city of New York, and held a conference with members of the Board of the New York Baptist Missionary Society, and others of the denomination, who regarded with interest the spiritual needs of our country. In this city, and also in Philadelphia, which was visited by a part of the deputation, the measures already taken and the further proceedings which were proposed, received the sanction of the friends of Missionary effort in our churches.

The degree of interest and favour, wherewith the design was met, together with other attendant circumstances, seemed clearly to indicate the will of Divine Providence, that the American Baptists should forthwith enter upon vigorous and united efforts, for the maintenance and enlargement of Domestic Missions.

To make arrangements for gaining with the utmost promptitude and clearness, the sentiments of the denomination throughout the United States, a Provisional Executive Committee was elected in the city of New York, and a Constitution Drafted for the proposed Society, subject, of course, to future revision. The Committee having been organized chose as officers, to act for the time in advancing the proposed object, the Rev. Jonathan Going as the Corresponding Secretary; William Colgate, Esq., of New York, as the Treasurer, and William R. Williams, of the same city as the Recording Secretary. A Committee were instructed at the same time, to issue a circular, stating the designs of the proposed institution, containing also the draft of a Constitution; and inviting the attendance of members of the denomination from all parts of the Union, at a Convention to be held in the Mulberry-street Baptist Meeting House, in the City of New York, on the 27th of April, 1832, for the purpose of giving to the Society a formal organization. The circular accordingly prepared was published in several of the newspapers conducted by members of the denomination.

On the day above mentioned, (the Baptist General Convention for Foreign Missions, which was in session in the same city at the time, adjourning to allow the attendance of its members upon this meeting,) there was a numerous attendance of ministers and other brethren at the place before designated; comprising individuals from fourteen of the States and one of the Territories of the Union.

5. Revivals

The technique of revivalism had long been a major means of spreading the Baptist message, multiplying converts, and enlarging churches. Although pastors often encouraged and sometimes experienced revivals in the ordinary course of their ministry, the number of professional revivalists increased after the Second Great Awakening. A typical exemplar was Jacob Knapp (1799–1874), whose services were widely sought. *Source:* Jacob Knapp, *Autobiography of Jacob Knapp* (New York: Sheldon, Co., 1868), pp. 150-153.

Near the close of the year 1843, I was invited by a little band of brethren and sisters in Washington, D.C., consisting of eleven persons,—eight women and three men,—who had formed themselves into a church, to hold a series of meetings with them. The only other Baptist church was a small, inefficient affair, exerting no moral power in the community.

This small company hired a hall, agreeing to pay one hundred dollars per month for the use of it, with the understanding that we were to vacate it two evenings in every week, on which nights it was engaged for holding balls.

This dance-hall proved to be well adapted to our purposes; the side-rooms served as for holding female, inquiry, young people's meetings. The Spirit of God soon began to move on the souls of men, and the hall itself seemed to be pervaded with the divine presence. We had to vacate it two nights for the service of the devil, but the balls proved miserable failures. One lady, who had paid three hundred dollars for a dress to wear on one of these occasions, said that she was never so wretched in all her life as on that night. The managers called on the proprietors, and told them that if they did not get Knapp out of the hall they would never hire it again. But our brethren had taken the precaution to secure, in writing, a lease for a given time, and in this case the children of light were wiser than the children of this world. We had got the start of the devil, and we kept in the advance. During the two evenings in which we were out of the hall, we were invited to occupy the Presbyterian Church, and did so. By this means we gained new recruits, and gathered increased strength to renew the battle on the devil's ground.

After I got well under way, I came out against the sin of slavery; denounced it as an institution of the devil; and advocated the equality and universality of human rights. Dr. Chapin called upon me, and tried to dissuade me from alluding to "the peculiar institution;" and informed me that if he had known I was going to preach against slavery, he would not have given me his influence; that it would not have been safe for himself, nor for the college, nor for the church. I replied that I could not help it; he must pursue such a course as he thought duty required, but that I should not, and could not, change my course. I was bound to preach up Christ, and preach down the devil.

Happily the work had, by this time, come to such a pitch, and gone on to such an extent, that the doctor did not dare to set his influence against it; nor would it have availed if he had, for it was not in the power of all the pro-slavery D.D.'s, nor all the devils in hell, to stop the mighty tide of salvation which was then sweeping through the city. . . . Several of the students in the college were brought under the power of the gospel; some of them are now ministers.

Our baptismal services were usually scenes of great interest. On one occasion I formed twenty men in a line on the banks of the Potomac, and locking arms, they walked with me abreast down into the water, the congregation on the shore singing as they went. On reaching suitable depth, I commenced baptizing them; and each one standing in the water till all had been "buried with Christ;" we then locked arms again, and returned to the shore amid the greetings of song from the congregation who had witnessed the scene. Among the spectators were members of Congress, and several foreign ministers; some were standing, some were sitting in their carriages, but all were deeply affected, and many of them to tears. . . .

I remained in Washington about seven weeks, preaching day and night. As the result of this meeting, movements were inaugurated before I left, for the erection of the Baptist Church on E Street. The number of persons brought into the church in consequence of this effort, including those gathered in by brother Sampson after I had gone, amounted to about two hundred.

6. Public Worship

Although Baptists had long prized spontaneity and informality in public worship, they were not averse to doing things "decently and in order." The earliest printed order of worship appeared in 1827. (See page 193.)

In 1843 the American Baptist Publication and Sunday School Society issued a new hymnal called *The Psalmist*. The Preface gave instructions on the nature of music in public worship. *Source: The Psalmist* (Philadelphia: ABPS,1843), pp. 7-8.

Worship must have its own forms of utterance. These forms can be neither didactic nor expository. Worship is not designed to communicate illumination to the intellect of him who offers it, nor information to the omniscient Being to whom it is offered. If it be confined to the understanding, or if it pass from the heart to the understanding, and thus become a merely intellectual exercise, it departs from its proper aim. Worship is prompted by emotion. Its first object is praise; after this,

ORDER OF EXERCISES,

At the Dedication of the *Baptist* New Meeting-House in New London, on Thursday, January 11, 1827.

1. Auditory Anthem---

Lift up your heads, O ye gates, and be ye lift up, ye everlasting doors, and the King of Glory shall come in.—Who is this King of Glory ? It is the Lord, strong and mighty in battle, and trial of the sword.——The earth is the Lord's, and all that therein is ; the compass of the world, and all that dwell therein. For he hath founded it upon the seas, and prepared it upon the floods.--Hallelujah !—Amen.

2. Invocation :

And reading a portion of Scripture.

3. Singing---

O come let us sing unto the Lord : let us heartily rejoice in the strength of our salvation: let us come before his presence with thanksgiving, and show ourselves glad in him with psalms. For the Lord is a great God, and a great King above all gods. In his hands are all the corners of the earth : and the strength of the hills is his also. The sea is his, and he made it: and his hands prepared the dry land.——O come let us worship, and fall down, and kneel before the Lord our Maker. For he is the Lord our God : and we are the people of his pasture, and the sheep of his hand.

4. Prayer.

5. Singing a Hymn.

1 Great Lord of angels, we adore
  The grace that builds thy courts below ;
  And through ten thousand suns of light,
  Stoops to regard what mortals do.
2 We bring the tribute of thy praise,
  And sing that condescending grace,
  Which to our notes will lend an ear,
  And call us, sinful mortals, near.
3 These walls, we to thy honour raise :
  Long may they echo with thy praise ;
  And thou, descending, fill the place
  With choicest tokens of thy grace.
4 Here let the great Redeemer reign,
  With all the glories of his train ;
  While Pow'r Divine his Word attends,
  To conquer foes, and cheer his friends.
5 And in the great decisive day,
  When God the nations shall survey,
  May it before the world appear,
  Thousands were born to glory here.

6. Sermon.

7. Consecrating Prayer.

8. Consecrating Anthem--

I was glad when they said unto me, We will go into the house of the Lord. Our feet shall stand in thy gates, O Jerusalem.—Jerusalem is built as a city that is at unity with itself : for thither go the tribes of the Lord—to testify unto Israel, and to give thanks unto the name of the Lord. For there is the seat of Judgment, even the seat of the house of David.—O pray for the peace of Jerusalem : Peace be wi hin thy walls, and plenteousness within thy palaces. For my brethren and companions' sakes, I will wish thee prosperity, and I will seek to do thee good.—— Amen. Hallelujah !—Amen.

9. Closing Prayer.

10. Closing Anthem.

1 Grateful notes and numbers bring,
  While Jehovah's praise we sing ;
  Holy, holy Lamb of God,
  Be thy glorious name ador'd.
2 Men on earth, and saints above,
  Sing the great Redeemer's love :
  Lord, thy mercies never fail—
  Hail! celestial goodness, hail!
3 Though unworthy, Lord, thine ear,
  Our humble hallelujahs hear :
  Fervent praise we hope to bring,
  When with saints we stand and sing.
4 Lead us to that blissful state,
  Where thou reign'st supremely great :
  Look with pity from thy throne ;
  Send thy Holy Spirit down.
5 While on earth ordain'd to stay,
  Guide our foot-steps in thy way ;
  Till we come to reign with thee,
  And thy glorious greatness see.
6 Then with angels we'll again
  Wake a louder, louder strain :
  There, in joyful songs of praise,
  We'll our grateful voices raise :
7 There, no tongue shall silent be ;
  There, all join sweet harmony ;
  That through heav'n's all-spacious round,
  Praise, O God, may ever sound.

11. Benediction.

GEORGE HOUGH, PRINTER, CONCORD.

the expression of emotions of penitence, joy, humility, hope, love, or dependence, in such a manner as to involve an acknowledgment of God, and thus to glorify him. It is the offspring of religious emotion. From whatever feeling it takes its rise, it tends towards God. If it begins in our own misery, it elevates the soul to the contemplation of the divine mercy. It is, in truth, the utterance of the spirit of man, aspiring upward to its Creator.

The nature of worship determines the proper mode of its expression. As it is an act of the heart, it should be expressed in the language of the heart. This is not cold, nor in the manner of common conversation, but fervent and impassioned. Acceptable worship is the fruit of deep and true emotion. The expression of worship should be in language suited to such emotion. Sacred harmony is the union of measured sounds with the words of worship. In order to be sung well, the words of worship must be expressive of the emotions which belong to worship; and any want of mutual adaptation is immediately felt by a sensitive mind. It is the want of adaptation of the words to the music, or of the music to the words, which often renders singing heavy. The words are either expository, or didactic, or in some other way prosaic. They are expressive of no emotion, or destitute of poetry, and therefore unsuited to be sung. Or, on the other hand, the leader, having no true poetic feeling, selects a tune which indicates an emotion of a character different from that which is indicated by the words of the hymn. The music and the words should breathe one spirit. Both should breathe the spirit of a fervent, humble, spiritual worshipper.

Beside lyrical excellence, there are other requisites of a good hymn. It should possess unity—treating of only one subject from the opening to the close. It should be a complete composition, having, however short it may be, a beginning, middle, and end. Every verse should add something to the preceding, making the sense, finally, complete, and raising the soul to the highest conception of the theme. The sentences should be brief. The sense should not extend from one verse into another. Parenthetic clauses should be avoided. The style should be simple, and the words, generally, short, and easy to be understood. The accent should be uniformly on the same syllables in each verse. A profusion of ornament should be avoided. A sounding epithet should never be used merely to furnish the requisite number of syllables. The whole spirit of the hymn should be lyrical. It should be adapted not only to be read, but to be sung.

It is hoped that this compilation will be successful in exemplifying many of these principles. The hymns of Dr. Watts take the lead, being more numerous than those of any other author. All his pieces are inserted which possess lyrical spirit, and are suited to the worship of a Christian assembly. The book contains, also, a large number of hymns of Beddome, Steele, Doddridge, and other standard writers, whose productions have become consecrated by use. Besides these, numerous hymn books, both ancient and modern, and many other books, together with various periodicals, American and foreign, have been carefully examined. From these sources many hymns have been selected, whose decided merit and high spiritual tone eminently adapt them to the purposes of worship
. . . .

The work is dedicated to Christ and the church. If it shall tend to the elevation of evangelical taste, the interest of worship, the diffusion of a more fervent piety, and the glory of God, their aims will be accomplished.

Along with heightened dignity in church music, preaching became more structured and polished. Early in the century, Baptists almost universally preferred extemporaneous preaching, but instruction in the seminaries tended to the more formal. A student notebook preserves the lectures of James Davis Knowles, professor of sacred rhetoric at Newton Theological Institution in the 1830s. *Source:* "Lectures on Sacred Rhetoric," from Unidentified Student Notebook, pp. 158-159. Manuscript Collections, Andover Newton Theological School.

Lecture II
Delivery—Articulation

Having treated of the principles of Sacred Rhetoric, with reference to written compositions we now proceed to the second branch of the subject—that to which the word Rhetoric in its etymological sense more properly applies,—spoken language. A convenient word to designate that branch of Sacred Rhetoric is Delivery. The ancient rhetoricians, called it *pronunciation* or action, meaning to include everything which pertains to spoken language. But these words have now a more restricted sense. By *pronunciation,* we mean the utterance of single words, and by action, the gestures which a speaker uses. It may be added, here, as an example of the changes which occur in the signification of the words, that the term *elocution,* which we now use to signify *speaking* or that act of speaking, was used by the ancient rhetoricians, to mean

style, diction, the clothing of ideas in words. These different, signifi-
cations must be born in mind [or] we shall be *liable* to misunderstand
the ancient writers. The famous reply of Demosthenes to the question,
what are the three chief responsibilities of an orator, has been misun-
derstood. His answer was, *action, action, action,* by which he meant
Delivery in its widest sense, including articulation, accent, emphasis,
intonation, gesture, and in short, whatever belongs to the art of speaking.
But many have understood him to mean by *action,* mere gesticulation,
and have accordingly quoted the authority of the great orator of Greece
for placing the chief merit of eloquence in mere motions of the body.

Church architecture varied widely from North to South, East to West, city to countryside, and revealed much about the people who worshiped in such places. Benedict gave
a wide-ranging description. *Source:* David Benedict, *Fifty Years Among the Baptists*
(New York: Sheldon Co., 1860), pp. 54-57.

In Boston, the houses occupied by Drs. Stillman and Baldwin, when
I first saw them, were commodious and in good repair, but they were
barn-fashioned buildings, destitute of any architectural style or attrac-
tion.

The house in which the late Dr. Sharp officiated more than forty
years, was dedicated in 1807. This building was then considered number
one, of the kind, among the Massachusetts Baptists.

The old church in Providence, Rhode Island, now an octogenarian
among church buildings, was, I think, the only one then existing in
this country, and perhaps in any other, for Baptists, which was planned
by scientific rules. A Baptist meeting house, of such broad dimensions,
with a steeple two hundred feet high, and all in so much architectural
taste, was a wonder to our people far and near. I myself was not a little
surprised, when I first saw this stately temple, at being informed that
it was the place of meeting for our plain, old-fashioned sort of people,
as I had resided mostly in a region of country where our people would
not suppose there could be found any Holy Ghost in such a house as
that, and where, moreover, they had been accustomed to associate
steeple houses with formalism, bigotry and intolerance. The American
Baptists then had no zeal for steeples—the cost of them was a hindrance,
if nothing else. . . .

In the whole of Connecticut, my native State, our people had no
good houses of worship anywhere. In Hartford was one of small dimensions, in New Haven none at all.

A similar account may be given of the entire State of New York, except one building in the city, belonging to the first church, then located in Gold street. This was a substantial stone edifice, then but lately erected. It bid fair to last for ages, and might have done so, but for the uptown fever among the people, who, under the ministry of the late Dr. Cone, reared their costly temple in that direction.

In Philadelphia, the famous rotunda, or round house, commonly called Dr. Staughton's church, in Sansom street, was an object of much attention in its early day, for its size, being ninety feet in diameter, for the singularity of its form, and for the large assemblies which the eloquence of its famous pastor collected there. Besides this, there were three good buildings of an ordinary form, for Baptist use, in this Quaker city, where, if I remember right, there were but two steeples on the church houses of any denomination. . . .

In Baltimore, was one church for Baptists of the first class for that age.

In Washington city there was then but one small house for Baptist use, which was of an unattractive appearance.

The same may be said of Richmond, Virginia. This edifice, after a number of additions, has fallen into the hands of the colored people, and is the resort of a very large church of our order.

Dr. Furman's church, the only one in Charleston, South Carolina, for the Baptists, was a good, commodious building. The same may be said of those in Beaufort and Savannah. . . .

In all new settlements in this country, log cabins are generally the first edition of dwellings for families, and also of sanctuaries for religious assemblies; and how many thousands of the best of meetings have been held, by multitudes of our people, in rude and unsightly structures of this kind, from the Canadas to the remotest parts of the South and West. In my early travels I saw enough of them to form some opinion of the inconveniences of new country life, and my complaint of the people in these countries and in the older regions, too, has often been, that they were too remiss in providing more comfortable and commodious houses for religious worship, and that they kept in old and desolate buildings in some cases, and in log cabins in others, long after their early family mansions had been exchanged for those of a far superior style.

Francis Wayland

James R. Graves

Jacob Knapp

Joanna P. Moore

Widening Pluralism:
Issues of Doctrine,
Church Order, and Society

As Baptists grew numerically and expanded organizationally, they also were becoming more diverse. This diversity in turn created tension and disputes over points of doctrine and polity, as well as the question of how to deal with society issues such as Freemasonry and slavery. At times various groups formed independent denominations, as in the cases of the Freewill Baptists, some of the immigrant converts, and—after emancipation—black Baptists. The most serious and lasting division in the main body occurred as part of the sectional conflict that was pulling the whole nation apart at midcentury. While most Baptists in America sought to maintain a distinct Baptist identity, vis-à-vis other Christians and the great mass of still unchurched Americans, many of them were at the same time sharpening the differences between themselves and other members of the Baptist family. Thus disputes became so alienating as to cause some groups to surrender the name of ''Baptist'' entirely.

1. Terms of Communion

The issue of whether Baptists should join with pedobaptists in the observance of the Lord's Supper produced not only a great deal of contention among Baptists but also made them the target of misunderstanding and criticism from fellow Christians of other denominations. The strict Baptist position (not always adhered to in practice) was: baptism is prerequisite to participating in Communion; and if baptism be defined exclusively as the immersion of a professed believer in water, then pedobaptists, sprinklers, and others must be regarded as unbaptized and thus ineligible for Communion. In Selection A the 1824 circular letter of the Hudson River Association defended the case for restricted Communion. However, the Free Communion Baptists, a group largely confined to the Northeast, was one of several sects to react against closed Communion. Their egalitarian, evangelistic principles (Selection B) soon found them discussing merger with the Freewill Baptists, but not until their case for totally open Communion was firmly established. The merger was consummated in 1841. *Sources:* A. *Minutes of the Hudson River Baptist Association,* 1824, pp. 10-16. B. Alvin D. Williams, *Memorials of the Free Communion Baptists* (Dover, N.H.: Freewill Press, 1873), pp. 40-41.

[A. Baptism Prerequisite to Communion]

Baptism, upon profession of faith in the Messiah, must remain an indispensable term of communion, until it can be proved that unbaptized persons were added to the churches planted by the apostles in different parts of the world. And this will appear yet more abundantly if we consider,—

The order which is uniformly observed in the New Testament, with reference to Baptism and the Lord's Supper. When the Great Head of the Church sent forth his ministering servants to build up his kingdom in our ruined world, he gave them a commission in the following words:—Go ye therefore and teach all nations, baptizing them in the name of the Father, and of the Son, and of the Holy Ghost,—teaching them to observe all things whatsoever I have commanded you. This language is lucid and definite. It directed them first to teach, or, as it is elsewhere expressed, to preach the Gospel to every creature. When the word preached was accompanied by an unction from the Holy One, men were made wise unto salvation; they were effectually taught; they were made disciples; and then, and not till then, were the apostles commanded to baptize them. After this, they were to instruct them to observe all things enjoined upon them by the Saviour; and among the all things, who dare deny to the Lord's supper a place? . . .

But it is plain that baptism must precede the communion, not only because the Lord Christ hath so decreed, but because this order is necessary in the very nature of things, if there be a reciprocal adaptation between the sign, and the thing signified by it. We must first be made alive, before we need bread to sustain life; and in like manner, the ordinance which shadows forth the washing of regeneration and the renewing of the Holy Ghost, must of necessity, go before that which holds out to us in a figure the bread which came down from heaven, whereof it a man eat, he shall live forever. . . .

We shall close this epistle by replying briefly to some of the most plausible objections which are constantly urged against the sentiments we have advanced.

First objection. "You lay too much stress upon baptism by making it an indispensable term of communion."

To this we reply;—We pay no greater regard to it, nor do we give it a higher place in our system, than the Lord Christ hath enjoined, or the Apostles and primitive Christians, by their example, have warranted. And here we may ask, why should more stress be laid upon the Lord's supper than upon baptism; and why should many professing Christians so earnestly advocate the observance of the former, while they pervert, or entirely neglect the latter? Were not both ordinances instituted by the same Lord, and do they not, therefore, come to us clothed with the same authority? . . .

A second objection, charges us with causing a separation between the children of the same Heavenly Father.

Suppose we grant that baptism is an insuperable barrier in the way of our communing, in church capacity, with unbaptized persons; does it necessarily result from this concession, that the blame righteously attaches itself to the skirts of our garments? Shall those who understand and keep the ordinances, in their nature, order, and design, as they were originally delivered to the churches, be condemned? and those who depart from them, and embrace "a figment of their own imagination," be justified? God forbid! We hesitate not to say, most explicitly, that baptism is a separating line, but it is one of the Lord's own making, and we endeavour constantly, both by preaching and example, to enlighten the minds of our Paedobaptist friends on the subject. We warn them of their error; we hold up to them the truth; we point them definitely to chapter and verse; and we exhort every believer among them, quite as often as they wish to hear us, to arise and be baptized and wash away their sins, (in a figure,) calling upon the name of the Lord. . . .

A third objection states, that it is the Lord's table, and therefore we have no right to hinder those who wish to approach it.

That it is the Lord's table, is the appropriate and sufficient answer to this objection. Were it ours, we might cheerfully admit to it the objector and his friends; but since it is confessedly the Lord's table, we dare welcome to it only such as He invites. . . .

A fourth objection is presented in this shape: We conscientiously believe ourselves to be baptized; you are not the judge; to our own master we stand or fall.

This objection brings us at once to the questions, What is Christian baptism? Is it sprinkling, or is it pouring? With the New Testament in our hands, we most confidently and unhesitatingly answer, neither. It is immersion in the name of the Father and of the Son and of the Holy Ghost. And here we cannot but say to our cavilling friend, when were you baptized? "In infancy." Are unconscious babes, or the unbelieving, unprofessing seeds of pious parents, proper subjects of baptism? Whether men will hear or whether they will forbear, upon the testimony of God we are obliged to answer, no.—These things were not so in the beginning; for it is written, Then they that gladly received the word were baptized; Acts 2. . . .

The last objection which our limits will allow us to notice, supposes that strict communion is inconsistent with brotherly love and christian forbearance.

By advertising to the distinction made in the commencement of this letter, between communion with God, our fellow-christians, and a particular church, this objection will be stripped of all its difficulties. It will there be seen that real believers may hold converse with the Deity, and love each other as brethren in the Lord, without walking together in church relationship. The Baptists differ from all others in their views of a Gospel Church, and the scriptural qualifications for admission to its privileges; but these views we believe to be coincident with the directions of the Saviour, and the example of Apostles and primitive christians, and having maintained them in the face of persecution, danger, and death, from the days of Paul to the present moment, we cannot abandon them, until convinced that we have hitherto misapprehended altogether the language of the New Testament. Nor can this course of conduct be righteously construed into a breach of brotherly love and Christian forbearance, until it can be proved that we ought to love men more than we love God, and that the charity which rejoiceth not in iniquity, but rejoiceth in the truth, requires us to disregard the commandments and dispense with the ordinances of our Lord and Saviour, Jesus Christ.

A fifth objection, viz. That the saints will all commune together in Heaven, and ought therefore to do so on earth, is thought to be a very strong one, but really we are not able to perceive its force. We rejoice and are exceeding glad in the anticipation of that perfect union and uninterrupted fellowship, which the general assembly and church of the first born, whose names are written in Heaven, shall, to all eternity, enjoy; but whatever may be the terms of communion in the world of glory, we are fully persuaded that while here, the revealed will of

Christ, and not what shall take place after death, should be the only man of our counsel. . . .

[B. The Free Communion Baptists]
Admitting Church Members

1. Every person presenting to church, fellowship and communion must be born again, agreeably to John 3: 3, 4, 5, and bring a satisfying witness to the church of his new birth; or have no external church privileges.

2. Every member in the church ought to give gospel fellowship (to any one) coming into church relation. . . .

3. We believe the church of Christ to be a spiritual school, into which we enter for Divine instruction and teaching. Therefore we testify that the door of this church is open night and day for all the children of the kingdom, of every denomination, to enter, and with this church have liberty of conscience in meats and drinks, or in respect of an holy day, or other circumstantial points, until the church shall be brought to see eye to eye, and all be of one mind—steadfastly believing the term of external communion is to become a new creature, or to have Christ within the hope of glory. And we do most truly and joyfully bid all such welcome to all the benefits and privileges of the new covenant within the pales of the church, viz: all such that can bring a satisfactory evidence that they have been born of God, and thereby initiated to all the church privileges, as aforesaid.

2. Freewill Baptists

Following a theological tradition that openly rejected traditional Calvinism, the Freewill Baptists were strengthened by growth on the New York frontier and in the Ohio Valley, and they created a national General Conference in 1827. After an 1841 merger with Free Communion Baptists (see pages 199-200), they were called Free Baptists. Several of the General Conference statements illustrate the character and activities of the denomination. *Source:* Minutes of the Freewill Baptist General Conference, 1828, 1831, 1837, 1853. Archives, American Baptist Historical Society.

ITINERANT MINISTRY

The Maine Western Y.M. proposed the following question,—Should we encourage an Itinerant Ministry?

This question was referred to the Committee on that subject, who reported as follows:

(1) That we think it expedient and very necessary that an Itinerant Ministry should be established throughout this connection.

(2) We recommend to the several Quarterly Meetings belonging to the same, to choose one preacher or more to travel and preach to the destitute churches within its limits.

(3) That funds be raised in each church or Q.M. by subscription, contribution, or otherwise, as they may judge best; and that said minister or ministers return to the Q.M. from which they received their appointment, an exact account of all, and of whom they have received.

(4) We advise the several members of this Conference to endeavor to carry these resolutions into effect in their several Q.M.'s.

WOMEN

Question 3d. Have females a right to be active in the concerns of the church and how far? Should they be active in receiving members, in church labors, or choosing officers, etc?

Ans. Females, in our opinion, have a right to be active in receiving members into the church, and rejecting them; but in this, and in all other respects in church government, they should be in subjection to the male members.

SLAVERY

18. The Committee to draft resolutions on Slavery, reported the following, which were accepted:

(1) Resolved, That Slavery is an unjust infringement on the dearest rights of the slave; an unwarrantable exercise of power on the part of the Master, a potent enemy to the happiness and morals of our slaveholding population; and, if continued, it must ultimately result in the ruin of our country.

(2) Resolved, That as Christians, patriots and philanthropists, we ought to exert our influence to induce all slaveholders to use their best exertions, in their respective States, to procure the abolition of Slavery.

(3) Resolved, That a candid discussion and mutual interchange of views, on the best method of abolishing Slavery, is loudly called for by the present crisis.

(4) Resolved, That it is the duty of Christians to frequently and fervently pray that, the evil of Slavery may be removed from our beloved country.

(5) Resolved, That we have abundant cause for gratitude to God that, as a denomination, we are generally united in our views on the distracting subject of Slavery.

PREACHING

Whereas, a question has been presented to this Conference requesting an opinion respecting the propriety of ministers using skeletons or notes, while preaching—therefore,

Resolved, That this Conference recommends to the ministry of the connection to avoid the use of skeletons, notes, or written discourses in preaching the gospel, as a general practice, believing that extemporaneous discourses are more scriptural, interesting and useful. Notwithstanding, we think that every minister should follow that method in his preaching which he conscientiously believes or finds by experience to be most conducive to his own spiritual interest and the advancement of the Redeemer's kingdom.

MORAL REFORM

1. Resolved, That the great prevalence of licentiousness and its consequent moral and physical evils, not only in our cities and large towns, but also in the country, calls loudly for the united and systematic efforts of all good citizens and Christians, to promote moral purity, especially that ministers should preach and otherwise insist on the strict observance of the seventh commandment.

2. That we recommend the formation of Societies in places where they do not exist, for the specific purpose of promoting Moral Reform—that males and females be organized in separate Societies, to secure the advantage of familiar and united efforts with their own sex, to caution the unwary and unsuspecting and reclaim the vicious from the paths of misery and death.

3. That all persons wishing to promote Moral Purity, should aim to correct a vitiated public sentiment, which, while it scarcely leaves to the vicious female the possibility of being reformed, allows her more guilty seducer to pass with but a slight recognition of his crimes and oft-repeated offences.

PEACE

The Committee on Peace reported the following resolutions:

(1) Resolved, That we regard the principles of universal peace and good will to men, to be in strict accordance with the gospel so eminently promulgated by Christ, and practically demonstrated by the Christian church in its primitive state.

(2) Resolved, That we hail with joy the brightening prospect when national differences will be amicably adjusted by arbitration or a Con-

gress of Nations, rather than by the strength of arms.

(3) Resolved, That we regard the enormous appropriations made by the respective governments of civilized Nations to support navies and standing armies, to be hostile to the reign of universal peace.

(4) Resolved, That the auspicious era foretold by prophets when hostilities should cease, the practice of war be abandoned, and its implements be converted to agricultural purposes, should be earnestly sought in prayer, and by the faithful use of all available means.

3. Campbellism

Alexander Campbell (1788–1866) was a Scotch-Irish Presbyterian who withdrew from his church and came to the United States in 1809. With his father, who had emigrated to America two years earlier, he formed an independent church in western Pennsylvania. Because they administered baptism by immersion, they were received into the Redstone Baptist Association in 1813, but sharp doctrinal differences between the church and the association led to much controversy and eventually to a separation in the 1820s. Campbell continued to attack Baptist beliefs and practices, and Campbellism became a long-lived object of Baptist polemics. In 1830 the Franklin (Kentucky) Association warned its member churches against Campbell's errors. *Source: Minutes of the Franklin Association of Baptists,* 1830, pp. 5-15.

To the Churches composing the Franklin Association.
Dear Brethren:

You will learn from our Minutes, the results of this called session of our association. Before Alexander Campbell visited Kentucky, you were in harmony and peace; you heard but the one gospel, and knew only the one Lord, one faith and one baptism. Your church constitutions were regarded, and their principles expounded and enforced, by those who occupied your pulpits. Thus you were respected by other denominations, as a religious community. Often were you favored with refreshing seasons from on high, and many of your neighbours and of your families were brought to a knowledge of the truth. How delightful were your morning and evening interviews, cheered by the songs, prayers, and exhortations of brethren, and by the presence of him who has promised, that where two or three are gathered together in his name, to be in the midst. Have not these happy days gone by? In place of preaching, you now may hear your church convenants ridiculed, your faith, as registered upon your church books, denounced, and yourselves traduced; while the more heedless and unstable, abjure the faith, and join the wicked, in scenes of strife, schism and tumult. The fell spirit of discord stalks in open day through families, neighborhoods and churches. If you would protect yourselves as churches, make no compromise with error; mark them who cause divisions; divest yourselves of the last vestige of Campbellism.

As an Association we shall esteem it our duty to drop correspondence with any and every Association, or Church, where this heresy is tolerated. Those who say they are not Campbellites, and yet countenance and circulate his little pamphlets, are insincere: they are to be avoided. When they say they are persecuted, because "they will not swallow the Philadelphia Confession of Faith," you are not to believe it; for no church has called one of them in question on that point, so far as we know. It is not so much their objection to this book, but rather our objections to their Confession of Faith, that makes the difference.

When they tell you that the Holy Spirit begins the work of salvation, that he carries it on, and that he perfects it, they may only mean that all this is done, by the words of the Holy Spirit, that is, by the Testament, read or heard, and not by the quickening energies of God's Spirit, directly. All supernatural, immediate influences are discarded by them, as mere physical operations. All that we have esteemed religion, the work of God's Grace in the soul, directly, is rejected. Mr. Campbell calls it a whim,—a metaphysical whim! And that you may know the full extent of our objections, we herewith send you several articles gathered from his Christian Baptist, and Millenial Harbinger, with a reference to the pamphlet and to the page, where you can read and judge, whether they are, or are not, the reformation tenets.

It may be said that these scraps are garbled from many volumes. Verily, they are but scraps; but each scrap embodies an opinion easily understood; so that this may, with some propriety, be called a Confession of Opinions. We are not obliged to re-publish his pamphlets. Were we, however, to do it, the nature and bearing of these opinions would not be changed.

THE THIRTY-NINE ARTICLES!!

or

A new edition of old errors, extracted from Alexander Campbell's Christian Baptist and Millenial Harbinger.

1. "That there has been no preaching of the gospel since the days of the apostles."

2. "That the people have been preached to from texts of scripture

until they have been literally preached out of their senses.''

3. ''That all the public speaking now necessary, is to undo what has already been done.''

4. ''That John Calvin taught as pure Deism as was ever taught by Voltaire or Thomas Paine; and that this Deism is taught in all the colleges in Christendom.''

5. ''That all the faith that men can have in Christ, is historical.''

6. ''That the words 'little children,' in the phrase, 'I write unto you, little children,' (in the epistle of John) are to be understood literally.'' (For the proof see his Millenial Harbinger, no. 3, p. 100, compared with p. 104-5.)

7. ''That faith is only a historical belief of facts stated in the Bible.''

8. ''That baptism, which is synonymous with immersion, and for which every such believer is a proper subject, actually washes away sin, and is regeneration.'' . . .

Brethren: Can you read this, and say or think that it is not, even now, high time to ''march out of Babylon?'' Doubtless you cannot hesitate. In February, 1825, Mr. Campbell denounced reformation. ''The very name, (he said,) has become as offensive as the term ''Revolution in France.'' He is now in a paroxism about Reformation. In all the extravagance of unbridled fanaticism, he fancies that he has already introduced the Millenium, as far as his tenets, have prevailed. The Millenium, he dreams, has bursted in, upon South Benson, Versailles, Clear Creek, David's Ford, and Shawnee Run. Who besides himself, and those who have sold their birth right—who have commuted their heads and hearts for reformation pottage, can indulge, in a conceit so silly and ridiculous. From such frenzy and quackery, and above all, from such a Millenium, may a kind Providence deliver us. Amen.

4. Antimission Baptists

The work of Luther Rice and other agents of the missionary and benevolent societies in soliciting funds for cooperative effort encountered stiff resistance in several quarters. Some opponents (among whom was Alexander Campbell) objected that missionary societies were unknown in the New Testament; others feared encroachment on the sources of their own limited support, and some were hyperpredestinarians who totally rejected all human instrumentality in the work of evangelism. The influence of Daniel Parker, author of the predestinarian theory of the ''two seeds,'' is described in a letter from David Hornaday. *Source:* David Hornaday to ''Mr. Editor,'' 4 April 1835. Archives, American Baptist Historical Society.

I have lived in this country twenty two years, near what was formerly called the "White Oak Springs" now Petersburgh Pike County & was baptised by Elder Isaac McCoy the 24th Feby 1818 a short time after he had received an appointment from the Baptist Board of Foreign missions. At this time there were perhaps not more churches in this country, say within sixty or seventy miles of Vincennes, than there are now associations. The Wabash Association was the only one in this part of the country & was in a peaceable & prosperous condition & corresponded with Long Run, Red River & Little River of Kentucky & Silver Creek of Indiana. This was an eventful period amongst the Baptists, the country was fast settling the Baptists more numerous & perhaps more respectable than any other denomination. About this time there was a Missionary Society formed near Vincennes called the Bruceville Missionary Society which was joined by some of the members of Maria Creek Church & about this time Daniel Parker came to this country & settled on the Wabash twenty five miles above Vincennes & about Ten miles from Maria Creek Church & commenced an unyielding opposition against missions. This began to produce some distress in the Wabash association. It was the first introduced as a "query"—is the principle and practice of the Baptist Board of foreign missions agreeable to Gospel order. This the association answered in the negative. It was then enquired what is to be done with those churches that suffer their members to belong to Missionary Societies. The Association recommended the Churches to bear one anothers burdens & so fulfill the Law of Christ. Notwithstanding this, Daniel Parker proceeded to take the Maria Church under dealings for suffering her members to support missions. The Association heard his complaints & went on (to) try Maria Creek Church for her supposed disorder & decided that she was not guilty of death or of bonds. The Association now considering herself at peace and having become very numerous, extending about One hundred & fifty miles up the Wabash from the mouth concluded to divide & Salem Association was formed. But Daniel Parker was not reconciled with what the Wabash Assoc. had done with Maria Creek Church & went on to try her again & finally accomplished his object. The Association again divided & Union association was formed. This left the Wabash Association with not more than three or four hundred members, and Parker proceeded to exclude Maria Creek Church for her missionary principles. This began to interupt the correspondence of

the Association. . . . We now had three or four years contention in all
these associations about the correspondence; Parker contended that
Union Association was in disorder, because Maria Creek Church was
riven of her body & she had been excluded for Missionary principles
& notwithstanding the Bruceville Society had been dissolved some
years before this Parker contended that the mission spirit was still alive
amongst them, & he frequently declared that he would kill the missionaries or they should kill him. The surrounding Associations generally refused to comply with his request that they should drop correspondence with Union Association. The Wabash Association stopped
correspondence with all that would not drop correspondence with Union.
. . . Parker now published his "two seeds." This produced a change
of circumstances amongst the Baptists in this country, for notwithstanding all the contention that had been amongst us, we do not think that
fellowship was ever destroyed until Parker published his *"two seeds."*
Locust Church of which he was a member took him under dealings for
holding and publishing heresy & excluded him for what he had published
in his "two seeds." Locust Church contained about this time forty five
members; Parker gained a party of nine members, went to the Wabash
association and gained a seat in preference to Locust Church which had
excluded him. Locust Church now joined Union Association. The fellowship of the Baptist Church was now fairly Broken. . . .

We now ask our brother Baptists of Ohio or Kentucky if an Association should say we agree that the Mormon Bible stand or fall on its
own merits would clear them of Mormonism, or should an association
say we agree that the doctrine of a Campbell stand or fall on its own
merits clear them of Campbellism. We know that if they will say we
agree that the Missionary principle stand on or fall on its own merits
& that Daniel Parker was excluded for heresy & act accordingly, the
contention would be at an end in this part of the country. . . .

As to their preachers and preaching we know no difference between
them and Parker only in talent; we personally know that whilst he stayed
here his preaching was admired more than the preaching of anyone
else, & we know that the churches of Salem Assoc. exclude their
members for joining a Temperance Society. The Assocs that correspond
with Wabash are Eel River, Little Wabash, Salem, Blue River, San-
gaman, Ocan, Vermillion, Sugar Creek. . . .

Thus eight associations correspond with Wabash. Two have dropt correspondence with Union on account of her Missionary principles & One to get clear of disputes. Thus Union has lost the correspondence of all the surrounding associations because she would not agree to kill Missionaries & received Locust Church that had excluded Daniel Parker from her body. We have now given you as true an account of the Baptists in this country as our information & circumstances would admit & which we respectfully submit to your consideration.

5. Freemasonry

Many denominations in antebellum America were exercised about whether to permit their members to belong to secret societies. Among the Baptists the controversy over Freemasonry was sharpest in New York State. A convention meeting in Livonia, New York, in August 1828 sharply condemned the Order. *Source: New York Baptist Register,* 31 October 1828.

In our opinion, the honour of God, and the peace and purity of the church require, that the church should purge itself from this relic of the dark ages, and withdraw from those who still adhere to the order.

Among the reasons which have led to this conclusion, may be mentioned the following:

1. The secrets and principles of the order are now revealed. We can no longer plead ignorance. Two years ago, Free Masonry was in the full tide of prosperity. The public knew nothing, or very little of its doing; and was criminally careless of its secret operations,—Its secrets were guarded by the most awful penalties, and supported by the names and authority of the great ones of the earth. The votaries of the order, with bare-faced temerity proclaimed, that "all the world in arms could not stop it; good or bad, we must have it as it was." But by the mysterious providence of God, its vile mechinations are now laid open to the public gaze; its secrets are revealed; and may all who love our Lord Jesus Christ join in one common prayer to God, that he would hasten its ruin, and rescue his children from its infatuation and thraldom.

2. It is now perfectly evident that its pretensions are false and hypocritical,—Its pretensions to such high antiquity, have no foundation in truth. It is evidently an offspring of the dark ages. The masonic fables of King Solomon, and of Grand Master Hiram, and his tragical death, are base fabrications; mere assumptions, invented to deceive and impose upon the credulity of mankind.—When the profane and disgusting ceremonies of raising, as it is called, to the third degree are

attended to, the candidate is gravely told that this place (the lodge-room) represents the Sanctum Sanctorum, or holy of holies, in the temple of God! and these fooleries a scene once transacted there! But is not all this a mere farce? . . .

3. The principles, obligations, and usages of the order, in our opinion, are wicked, and incompatible with the Christian religion. Masons always forswear themselves, when they swear to keep secrets and perform obligations not yet made known to them. Their obligations and penalties are unauthorized, and in their nature awful, and abhorrent to every principle of morality and religion.—The sacred oracles require us to deal justly, love mercy, and speak every man truth with his neighbour. Masonry requires, and under no less penalty than death, to conceal the truth, and cover each others crimes, not excepting the most flagrant violations of the laws of God and our country. . . .

When our brethren who belong to the order will come out and confess their wrong, and abandon the institution as wicked and anti-christian, and abjure its obligations as profane and unscriptural; then will we confirm our love to them, and endeavour to walk with them in the bond of the Gospel. But while they behold the sore troubles that afflict Zion in consequence of their connexion with this institution, and will not renounce it for the peace of Jerusalem; we must consider them disorderly walkers. We think that man cannot be a friend to Christ and his cause, who will not abandon it as foolish and sinful. Masons have it in their power, by this one act of duty, to heal an awful breach in Zion, and restore peace in the church. But if they will not thus seek the thing that makes for peace, but still adhere to this relic of darkness; they must be considered as those that cause divisions, and offences, contrary to the doctrine which we have learned, and however painful, we must avoid them.

6. Growing Ethnic Diversity

Baptists in Europe characteristically existed as a dissenting, or at least nonconforming, sect under the shadow of an established state church. At times persecuted, at other times barely tolerated, they rarely enjoyed the social acceptance and steady expansion that marked the denomination in America. In the 1830s the Board of the General Missionary Convention learned of an independent evangelist in Hamburg, Johann Gerhard Oncken (1800–1854), whose study of the Scriptures had convinced him of the correctness of believer's baptism. The Board requested Professor Barnas Sears of Hamilton, New York, then travelling in Europe, to investigate. Sears' letter and the action taken by the Board in response mark the beginning of the modern Baptist movement in Europe.

Source: *Proceedings of the Eighth Triennial Meeting of the Baptist General Convention,* 1835, pp. 26-27.

"I know not that there is any regular Baptist church in all the north of Germany. Of the Mennonites, I have nothing to say now; but aside from them, there are in Germany not a few individuals who are Baptists in sentiment. On my arrival at Hamburg, I called on Mr. Oncken, whom I found to be in all respects an interesting man. He is a German, a little more than thirty years of age, married in England, has two children is perfectly master of the English language, (which is spoken much in Hamburg,) and though not a man of liberal education, has a very strong, acute mind, has read much, is a man of much practical knowledge, and is very winning in his personal appearance and manners. From 1823 to 1828, he was a missionary of the Continental Society, and preached in Hamburg and vicinity, with very considerable success. Since that time, he has been agent of the Edinburgh Bible Society, and has more influence than any other man in selecting the publications of the Lower Saxony Tract Society. He has the confidence of Tholuck, Hahn, Hengstenberg, and many other distinguished individuals of the evangelical party, and has their co-operation in circulating Bibles and tracts. He has at length become so thoroughly a Baptist, that he cannot be satisfied without being a member of a Baptist church, and the second day after my arrival, he requested me to baptize him; but in consequence of his going to Poland as an agent of the Bible Society, to be absent two or three months, and also of a variety of circumstances connected with the formation of a church, it was deemed advisable to defer it until spring. Six or eight (Mrs. Oncken is one of the number) are wishing to receive the ordinance at the same time. The design at present is, that after his return, I, in connection with some other Baptist minister, if possible, (I know of no one nearer than Switzerland,) should go to Hamburg, administer the ordinance, form a church, and ordain Mr. Oncken pastor. . . . I have learned, that there are three other young men besides Mr. Oncken, who are Baptists, (though one, Mr. Lewis, is unbaptized,) and preachers, all employed as tract agents, laboring single handed, in different quarters of the country. They simply know each other's names. They need to be encouraged, and brought into a system of co-operation."

The Board immediately adopted measures to secure the services of Mr. Oncken, as a missionary, and they placed, in the mean while, at the disposal of Professor Sears, a moderate sum, to be expended, at his discretion, in promoting the cause of religion, in connection with the Baptist churches in Germany.

On the 22d April, 1834, Mr. Oncken and six other individuals were baptized by Professor Sears, and were the next day formed into a church of which Mr. Oncken was ordained as the Pastor.

Norwegian Baptist work in America began with Hans Valder (1813–1899), an 1842 convert to the Baptist church in Ottawa (now Leland), Illinois. After gaining additional converts from among his fellow Norwegians, Valder organized a church in his home and was ordained pastor—"the first ordained Norwegian Baptist minister not only in this country, but in the world, as the modern Baptist work in Norway was not begun before 1857." The little group in Ottawa could not be self-supporting, and Valder applied to the American Baptist Home Mission Society for assistance. *Source:* Quoted in Peder Stiansen, *History of the Norwegian Baptists in America* (Philadelphia: ABPS, 1939), pp. 23-25.

Indian Creek, Illinois March 7, 1848

Dear Brethren:

According to request from a number of my country-men, I will lay before you a brief statement of our destitute condition, and want of religious improvement; and perhaps it will be well here to state something in relation to my labor among my Country-men and trials, etc.

I was born and brought up in the Lutheran church of Norway, and taught to believe that in my infant baptism I was made an heir of heaven, regenerated or born again; and thus and in such a way my time was wasted until 1841, when through mercy I was converted to God, and learned my duty from His Word. I was baptized by Elder Harding, the 22nd of June, 1842. I felt it my duty to hold meetings and exhort my country-men to repentance. The church gave me license to preach, but my circumstances were such, that I could not devote so much of my time as was necessary in order to do some good, for I could not look for any support for my services, but to labor with my hands for living for my family, and preach when I could. We had some very interesting meetings; weekly prayer meetings were well attended, where we united in solemn devotion to God. It was a little Heaven to us.

In August, 1844, I was ordained to labor as an evangelist among the Norwegians. Long before this time some of the Norwegians and Americans too (that is, the guides of different orders), began to be alarmed lest the Baptist cause should prosper. Much of a party spirit was manifested. A Methodist preacher held meetings several times, and undertook to establish infant baptism and sprinkling from the Bible to the Norwegians, and a Presbyterian was the interpreter. The minds of my country-men were now aroused against me crying out, "Rebaptizer, rebaptizer," and on examining their Lutheran creed they found that Luther himself condemned Anabaptists: so they thought they had a good authority for abusing a poor Baptist and calling him a heretic.

I have had many trials and difficulties. All this must be overcome before any good can be done, and hitherto the Lord has been my helper, and I am yet willing to preach the gospel of glad tidings to Christ's enemy. I must say that those who once opposed me have broken their pledge. They open their houses for meetings, and are willing to lend a listening ear to the preached word, and a number, as you will see below, call upon me to preach to them, and are willing to aid towards my support, according to their ability. Some I trust, are converted to God, while others are almost persuaded to become Christians. In the month of January last, seven brethren and sisters united together by covenant to become a church, believing as we did, and do yet, that such a course is highly necessary for our prosperity and enjoyment in having the gospel preached in our own language, while many are unacquainted with English. As soon as this was laid before the church, and three members called for letters, a doubt was expressed by the church as to our stability, and as to the materials, etc. This wounded the feelings of some, while our opposers were glad to hear that the Baptist Church would hardly recognize a feeble band that is trying to become a co-worker for Christ. We are sensible that we cannot live and prosper there unless God will be with us and bless our feeble efforts, but we will trust in His promise.

I have told you about my labors and trials and prospects of success, and if the Baptist denomination can aid us a little in supporting a minister to labor among us, the cause of Christ may yet prosper, and sinners can be converted to God. We are in great want, and we feel our unworthiness. We have no claims upon you or any other; but the commission is, "Preach the gospel to every creature," so 20,000 Norwegians must not be neglected in a Christian land. . . .

Thirteen dollars is all that is expected of the Norwegians this year for my support. You know, brethren, that this is a greater sacrifice than

I am able to make. If the sum can be raised up to fifty dollars, I would enter upon the field, for I feel I cannot give them up. Brethren, please let me know if anything can be done for us, as soon as you can; if not, we must try some other source. The gospel we will and must have preached to us.

Yours in the Lord,
Hans Valder.

Native Americans held a long-standing claim on the evangelistic impulses of Baptists. Besides John M. Peck and James E. Welch (see page 174), a notable missionary to Native Americans was Isaac McCoy (1784–1846). He founded the Carey Mission in Michigan in 1822 and spent many years trying to persuade the United States Congress to set aside a special territory in the West where Indians could be colonized away from white influence. In 1842 he organized the American Indian Mission Association in Louisville, a venture that was taken over by the Board of Domestic Missions of the Southern Baptist Convention in 1855. The report of the Committee on New Territories of the AIMA illustrates something of that organization's philosophy. *Source: Proceedings of the Fifth Annual Meeting of the American Indian Mission Association,* 1847, pp. 7-8.

The Committee to whom was submitted the subject of a New Territory for exclusive Indian occupation west of the Rocky mountains, begs leave to report:

It is a question which no longer admits of debate, that the Indian in an uncultivated state can make little or no improvement in the arts and virtues of civilized life, nor reach a much higher stand of moral elevation, while surrounded by the white race; but on the contrary, sad experience has demonstrated the extraordinary fact, that his condition is rendered vastly more miserable. In proof of this we have only to refer to the small remnants of tribes still remaining within the borders of the several States; who, notwithstanding the persevering efforts of the benevolent to improve their condition, have been constantly descending the scale of morality, and with fearful rapidity decreasing in numbers.

Deeply impressed with this condition of the Indian tribes, the lamented McCoy conceived the idea of a remedy by giving them a territory from which the white race should be excluded, except in special cases, and over which the Indian should exercise exclusive territorial jurisdiction.

After persevering for ten years or more, in pressing this subject upon the attention of Congress, he enjoyed the pleasure of seeing his scheme in successful operation, and the result has more than realized his warmest anticipations, and convinced the most sceptical of its wisdom and feasibility.

By the recent rapid settlement of Oregon and California, the Indians within their borders have become subjected to the same pernicious influences which have operated so disastrously among the tribes east of the Mississippi; and while we are here consulting about their condition, the strife as to who shall possess and govern the soil is going on, nor will the question remain long undecided.

The tribes indigenous to the Rocky Mountains could not be removed to the territory already provided, even supposing it of sufficient extent for their reception and maintenance; the question then very naturally arises, ''shall these tribes be permitted to remain in a condition which will ensure a repetition of all the calamities which have befallen their unhappy brethren in the East? or shall we, like wise and christian men, resort to a well tested remedy, and avert, by its timely application, a doom so terrible?''

The white man, it is certain, will soon occupy the whole scope of the Rocky Mountains, and the Indians must move; and if some suitable provisions are not speedily made to give them ''a local habitation and a name'' somewhere, their destruction is inevitable. Much delay will effectually prevent the application of the remedy.

The country is now comparatively unoccupied by white inhabitants, and consequently a tract of suitable country can be easily selected for their occupancy; but wait a few years, and every suitable portion will have become the possession of civilized man, and when an attempt is made to carry into operation the plan here urged, the plea of ''pre-emption right'' will be an effectual bar to its progress.

In view of the above facts your committee would recommend the adoption of the following resolution:

Resolved, That we urgently request ministers, laymen and all well wishers of the Indians every where, to give this subject their special attention; and to use their influence with the members of Congress from their respective districts to secure their aid in the passage of a law establishing such a territory as referred to in this report; and also, that they aid in getting up petitions to the President of the United States and the two Houses of Congress in behalf of this object, and that the work be persevered in from year to year, until the end shall be fully accomplished.

7. Black Religion, Slave and Free

Most Baptist slaves worshiped with their masters in churches controlled by whites where they suffered all the indignities of inferior status. Narratives of former slaves recall the late antebellum period. *Source:* Norman R. Yetman, *Life Under the Peculiar Institution* (New York: Holt, Rinehart & Winston, 1970), pp. 266-267.

Us didn't have no separate church for colored folkses. De white folkses had a big Baptist church dey called Mill Stone Church, down at Goosepond, a good ways down de road from Marse Billie's plantation. It sure was a pretty sight to see, dat church, all painted white and set in a big oak grove. Colored folkses had dey place in de gallery. Dey weren't allowed to join de church on Sunday, but dey had regular Saturday afternoons for de slaves to come and confess dey faith, and join de church. Us didn't know dey was no other church but de Baptist. All de baptizin' was done on Sunday by de white preacher. First he would baptize de white folkses in de pool back of de church and den he would baptize de slaves in the same pool.

Fourth Sundays was our meetin' days, and everybody went to church. Us went to our white folks' church and rode in a wagon behind deir carriage. Dere was two Baptist preachers—one of 'em was Mr. John Gibson and de other was Mr. Patrick Butler. Marse Joe was a Methodist preacher hisself, but dey all went to de same church together. De niggers set in de gallery. When dey had done give de white folks de sacrament, dey called de niggers down from de gallery and given dem de sacrament, too. Church days was sure 'nough big meetin' days 'cause everybody went. Dey preached three times a day: at eleven in de mornin', three in de evenin', and den again at night. De biggest meetin' house crowds was when dey had baptizin', and dat was right often. Dey dammed up de crick on Saturday so as it would be deep enough on Sunday and dey done de baptizin' before dey preached de three o'clock sermon. At dem baptizin's dere were all sorts of shoutin', and dey would sing "Roll Jordan Roll," "De Livin' Waters," and "Lord I'se Comin' Home." . . .

When de camp-meetin' was over, den come de big baptizin': white folks first, den niggers. One time dere was a old slave woman what got so scared when dey got out in de crick dat sombody had to pull her foots out under her to get her under de water. She got out from dere and testified dat it was de devil a-holdin' her back.

8. The Dispute over Slavery

Several Baptist associations had pointed to the evils of slavery in the late eighteenth and early nineteenth centuries, but these verbal condemnations produced little tangible action. In 1822, the year of the abortive insurrection of Denmark Vesey in South Carolina, Baptists in the South stopped apologizing for slavery and defended it as a positive good, sanctioned in Scripture. Richard Furman, pastor of the First Baptist Church in Charleston and president of the Baptist State Convention of South Carolina, formulated a classic religious proslavery argument. *Source:* Richard Furman, *An Exposition of the Views of the Baptists Relative to the Coloured Population of the United States, in a Communication to the Governor of South Carolina* (Charleston: A. E. Miller, 1823), pp. 709, 17.

. . . the right of holding slaves is clearly established in the Holy Scriptures, both by precept and example. In the Old Testament, the Israelites were directed to purchase their bond-men and bond-maids of the Heathen nations; except they were of the Canaanites, for these were to be destroyed. And it is declared, that the persons purchased were to be their "bond-men forever;" and an "inheritance for them and their children." They were not to go out free in the year of jubilee, as the Hebrews, who had been purchased, were; the line being clearly drawn between them. In example, they are presented to our view as existing in the families of the Hebrews as servants, or slaves, born in the house, or bought with money; so that the children born of slaves are here considered slaves as well as their parents. And to this well known state of things, as to its reason and order, as well as to special privileges, St. Paul appears to refer, when he says, "But I was free born."

In the New Testament, the Gospel History, or representation of facts, presents us with a view correspondent with that, which is furnished by other authentic ancient histories of the state of the world at their commencement of Christianity. The powerful Romans, had succeded in empire, the polished Greeks; and, under both empires, the countries they possessed and governed were full of slaves. Many of these with their masters, were converted to the Christian Faith, and received, together with them into the Christian Church, while it was yet under the ministry of the inspired Apostles. In things purely spiritual, they appear to have enjoyed equal privileges; but their relationship, as masters and slaves, were not dissolved. Their respective duties are strictly enjoined. Their masters are not required to emancipate their slaves; but to give them the things that are just and equal, forebearing threatening; and to remember, they also have a master in Heaven. The "servants under the yoke" (bond-servants or slaves) mentioned by Paul to Timothy, as having "believing masters," are not authorized by him to demand of them emancipation, or to employ violent means to obtain it; but are directed to "account their masters worthy of all honour," and "not to despise them, because they were brethren" in religion; "but the rather to do them service, because they were faithful and beloved partakers of the Christian benefit." Similar directions are given by him in other places, and by other Apostles. And it gives great weight to the argument, that in this place, Paul follows his directions concerning servants with a charge to Timothy, as an Evangelist, to teach and exhort men to observe this doctrine.

Had the holding of slaves been a moral evil, it cannot be supposed, that the inspired Apostles, who feared not the faces of men, and were ready to lay down their lives in the cause of their God, would have tolerated it, for a moment, in the Christian Church. If they had done so on a principle of accommodation, in cases where the masters remained heathen, to avoid offences and civil commotion; yet, surely, where both master and servant were Christian, as in the case before us, they would have enforced the law of Christ, and required, that the master should liberate his slave in the first instance. But, instead of this, they let the relationship remain untouched, as being lawful and right, and insist on the relative duties.

In providing this subject justifiable by Scriptural authority, its morality is also proved; for the Divine Law never sanctions immoral actions.

While Furman spoke for a majority of Baptists in the South, many Baptists in the North became disturbed by what they increasingly perceived to be a moral evil compromising the claims of both a free republic and the Christian church. When British Baptists, who had recently contributed their influence to the movement that abolished slavery in the British West Indies in 1833, urged Baptists in America to oppose slavery in the United States more actively, they received from the Board of the General Missionary Convention an almost complacent reply. But abolitionist sentiment was rising, especially in New England, and several regional antislavery societies were formed, leading to the organization in 1839 of the American Baptist Anti-Slavery Convention. Resolutions passed by the New Hampshire Baptist Anti-Slavery Society at its first annual meeting (held in conjunction with the State Baptist Convention) typify the stance of the movement.

Source: Minutes of the New Hampshire Baptist Anti-Slavery Society, 1838. Archives, American Baptist Historical Society.

An adjourned meeting was held in the meeting house in the evening. After singing and prayer, the following resolutions were presented and passed.

1. Resolved, That we regard the institution of American Slavery, as it exists in the Southern States, opposed to the gospel of Christ, and morally wrong.

2. Resolved, That we view the plan of immediate and entire emancipation as the only safe and practicable mode of freeing our nation from the shame and sin of Slavery.

3. Resolved, That in view of the glorious triumph effected through the instrumentality of British Abolitionists over West India despotism, we will use all christian means for the immediate overthrow of oppression in our own land.

4. Resolved, That the signs of the times indicate the dawning of a bright and peaceful morn in the prison of the American slave.

5. Resolved, That we request all our brethren to unite in prayer on the 4th Monday evening in every month, for the speedy and peaceful termination of Slavery.

Addresses were made by brethren Worth, Jones, Foss and P. Richardson, who presented the above, and O. Tracy, Caswell and Ranney. Bro. Caswell related some facts with which he became acquainted while in Charleston, S.C., where he saw families sold under the hammer and separated among different purchasers: and saw two slaves, members of the Baptist church, Sambo and Prince, publicly whipped 39 lashes each on the bare back for the crime of giving religious instruction to their fellow slaves. A christian spirit was manifested by the speakers, and their remarks were solemn and appropriate, and secured the undivided attention of the assembly about three hours. The choir attended and gave several pieces of select music in fine style. May the time soon come when every christian shall remember those in bonds as bound with them, and unite in their prayers and efforts for their peaceful deliverance.

The dispute soon arose and focused in the national Baptist societies; and as acerbity turned to acrimony, Baptists North and South became profoundly alienated from each other. In 1840 the American Baptist Anti-Slavery Convention warned Baptists in the

South that if they continued perversely to adhere to the slave system, further Christian fellowship would be impossible. The Alabama State Convention responded by instructing its treasurer not to forward money to the national societies until clear evidence indicated that the leaders of such societies were not involved in abolitionism. The Board of the General Missionary Convention promptly declared its neutrality in the matter (Selection A).

The General Missionary Convention met the next year, 1841, at Baltimore and confirmed the Board's neutrality statement. Antislavery Baptists, however, found the "Baltimore Compromise" highly unsatisfactory and proposed to form a "free" missionary society as an agency through which their contributions could be transmitted without taint by any connection with slavery. The General Missionary Convention gathered at Philadelphia for its regular triennial meeting in 1844 and made a final effort to preserve its unity by urging silence on the slavery issue (Selection B). *Sources:* A. *Twenty-Ninth Annual Report of the Board of Managers of the Baptist General Convention for Foreign Missions,* 1843, pp. 49-50. B. *Minutes of the Eleventh Triennial Meeting,* 1844, pp. 157–158.

[A. A Declaration of Neutrality—1843]

The primary and exclusive object of the founders of the General Convention, as expressed in the preamble to the constitution, was to "send the glad tidings of salvation to the heathen, and to nations destitute of pure gospel light." For the prosecution of this one object the Board of Managers was created, and empowered to act on their behalf; and to this alone (with the exception of a temporary, authorized, divergence to Home Missions and Education,) have the operations of the Board down to the present moment been restricted.

Our venerated fathers who constituted the original Convention, contemplating in the new organization the prosecution of the Foreign Missionary enterprise alone, and justly appreciating the vast extent of the work and the demands which it would make upon the sympathies and resources of all benevolent hearts within the bounds of the community whom the Convention was designed to represent, were careful to lay no obstruction in the way of any individual who might be disposed to communicate to its funds, nor any restriction on the liberty of counsel or direction in its concerns, further than was judged indispensable to their efficient and safe administration. Their purpose, distinctly avowed in the preamble alluded to, was the "eliciting, combining, and directing the energies of the whole denomination in one sacred effort."

Such being the design of the organization of the Convention, and such the principles on which cooperation may be tendered and accepted, the Board are unable to discover any sufficient reason for the withdrawal of support on the part of any of their contributors, in view of facts or considerations wholly extrinsic and irrelevant. That the influences which at the present time are apparently set toward this result, are wholly irrelevant and should be steadfastly withstood, is evident not only in view of the object and principles of the Convention above stated, but from a just consideration of the relations and responsibilities of the Board. These relations and responsibilities have to some extent been misapprehended by brethren near and remote, and the consequence of the misapprehension has been to hold the Board accountable for things done and not done, in relation to all of which alike the Board has done nothing, because it had nothing to do. With respect to such things the Board has, so to speak, neither a name nor existence. Its vitality and power are wholly derived, and can by its present constitution act only to one end. As to all other intents and purposes, the Board can have power and will, only when first it shall have been endued with them by the Convention, from whom it emanates. The Board is the executive of the Convention: the Convention alone is legislative. It is the province of the Board simply to carry into effect the will of the Convention.

[B. Unity for the Sake of Mission—1844]
The following resolution was adopted with great unanimity.

Whereas there exists, in various sections of the country, an impression that our present organization involves the fellowship of the institution of domestic slavery, or of certain associations which are designed to oppose that institution,

Therefore Resolved, That, in cooperating together as members of this Convention in the work of Foreign Missions, we disclaim all sanction, either express or implied, whether of slavery or of antislavery; but, as individuals, we are perfectly free both to express and to promote, elsewhere, our own views on these subjects in a Christian manner and spirit.

The American Baptist Home Mission Society was equally a cockpit of controversy. Shortly after the 1844 meeting of the General Missionary Convention it faced a test case designed by the Georgia State Convention, which proposed to guarantee the support of the Rev. James E. Reeve, a slaveholder, if the ABHMS would appoint him as a missionary to the Cherokee Indians. After several months of agonizing, the Executive Board of the Society declared in October that "it is not expedient to introduce the subjects of slavery or antislavery into our deliberations, nor to entertain applications in which they are introduced''; and therefore the Board declined to consider Reeve's application. Spencer Cone, a member of the Board since its inception in 1832, wrote to John Leadley Dagg, president of Mercer University and an influential leader among Georgia Baptists, about his distress over the case. *Source:* Edward W. Cone, *The Life of Spencer H. Cone* (New York: Livermore and Rudd, 1856), pp. 277-278.

"After five meetings upon the subject, each meeting of at least three hours' continuance, the Board of the American Baptist Home Mission Society, adopted, by a vote of 7 to 5, the accompanying preamble and resolutions (adverse to appointing Mr. Reeves). One brother was excused from voting, on the ground that the question was pressed, before he had had time to make up his mind upon its merits. The final question was taken by yeas and nays (the first instance of the kind since the formation of the society), by which you may learn that the brethren deemed it of importance 'to define their position.'

"I regret this result, and did all in my power to prevent it; believing as I do, that the constitution knows nothing of slavery or anti-slavery, I besought the brethren to act as we always had done, until the constitution should be altered. I suppose there will be a separation between the North and South next April, in our Home Mission operations; as many brethren have declared their unwillingness to commission a slaveholder as a missionary, although I have assured them that we must appoint such ministers as the South fellowship and recommend, or the society must be dissolved. Some of the members of our Board, who have the same constitutional views with myself, would have voted for the application from Georgia, if nothing had been said about Brother Reeves being a slaveholder; but they construed this mere matter of information into an ungenerous and offensive 'test,' and upon that word 'test'—resolutions and amendments were hung—in every possible shape and form, until I was sick at heart.''

The division of national denominations along sectional lines stirred profound apprehensions over what effect these schisms would have on the federal union. One of the warnings about the political impact of severing religious ties appeared in the *Baptist Banner and Western Pioneer,* edited in Louisville by John Lightfoot Waller. *Source: Baptist Banner and Western Pioneer,* 1 May 1845.

. . . we think a Convention of all, (not a part only,) the Southern Baptists and the friends of Baptist Union in the United States, should be called; not for the inevitable purpose of effecting a separation, but, for the purpose of ascertaining whether the causes of difficulty cannot be removed and the union of the denomination be preserved. . . .

[W]e object to this State line division, because, it will not only separate those brethren, churches and Associations, that now hold sweet intercourse and fellowship, across these lines, but it will tend to gender sectional strife and divisions; it will produce alienation of heart, and lead to contentions, turmoil and warfare, along the whole line of division: and who can contemplate this state of things without pain and trepidation?

. . . Let the three great denominations of christians be divided, by State lines, upon the subject of abolitionism, and who does not see that all social intercourse between the parties will be sundered, and the parts continually recede? . . . Who does not see . . . that if the religious and consequently the social interests of the country are divided by State lines, that more than half of the bonds which hold the political compact in harmony are dissolved, and that the ground work is laid for the ultimate dissolution of the Union, and the destruction of the fairest fabric of civil and religious liberty the world ever saw?

We forbear to disturb the evil that hides the fearful scene which lies behind the dissolution of this Union—we pray God that it may never be seen or realized; and we are, hence, anxious to do all we can to prevent its occurrence.

At the time of the division between northern and southern Baptists, each missionary serving under the Board of the General Missionary Convention was given the choice of remaining with the old Board or going with the southern Board. Only one chose to accept appointment by the latter, and that was John Lewis Shuck (1814–1863) of Virginia, who had been in China since 1836. Shuck wrote to Solomon Peck, secretary of the Board of the General Missionary Convention, describing his reaction to the Baptist schism. *Source:* J. Lewis Shuck to Solomon Peck, 23 August 1845, Correspondence Files, ABFMS. Archives, American Baptist Historical Society.

Canton 23rd Aug. 1846

Rev. Mr. Peck
  My Dear Bro:
    You will perceive that the inclosed was written nearly a month ago—no opportunity for sending has occurred—the Royal Steamer with overland Mail leaves Hong Kong 1st Sept.—the first of the regular monthly line—by her I send this. Today I received your two very welcome and truly friendly letters of 31 of May—to my deep concern

I find by these letters that the dreaded division has really taken place—alas! alas! how few real friends the ascended Saviour has on earth. This intelligence weighs me to the dust. A thousand and one things I should like to say but the fact is this news has so addled me that I absolutely don't know *how* to say *what* I would. I have been foolishly hoping that *some* plan would have been hit upon to put off the crisis at least until after the meeting of the Convention at Cincinnati—but no, the Rubicon is passed, the deed done, and *another* Bap. Board for For. Missions formed! What is to be the issue is known only in the councils of Heaven. *My* position is an embarrassing one, embarrassing above my missionary brethren generally. I feel that my attachment to the Board with whom, under such varied circumstances, I have so long worked, is neither slight nor (to me) unimportant, although "Ocean floods" have rolled between us, and the bare thought of a severance causes me unhappiness, and on the other hand, how can I be expected, with my views of the Bible, to sympathize with that strange system of studied invective whose fundamental principles seem to say that men's souls are *less* precious than their bodies, that it is a matter of *less* importance that men be delivered from the slavery of lust and idolatry than from the bondage of an earthly master, and that the peace and union of the Church of the Lord Jesus is of *less* consequence than the success of certain dogmas, dogmas too which are regarded as doubtful to say the least by hosts of men eminent for their humanity, intelligence, and godliness. Now I do not believe that you or your immediate coadjutors for a moment hold any such views, but are you not *now* committed to men who do? And if so soon the red flag of abolition will be unfurled in heathen lands, tearing asunder our tremblingly interesting little churches, breaking up our Missions, making enemies of those who are now brethren, and causing the certain expulsion of all the Missionaries from such communities as China, for the various ramifications of slavery in the whole Chinese empire are thorough and systematic. It is good to believe that *Jehovah reigns!!!* For the present I feel that we are brethren in heart and labor—for the future, God, in whose boundless sympathies it is a privilege to trust, will guide. I hope to see you face to face in a few months and speak fraternally over the troublous times upon which we have fallen. . . .

In November, 1844, the Alabama State Convention determined to present to the Board of the General Missionary Convention a hypothetical case in order to force a declaration of the Board's sentiments with regard to the appointment of slaveholders (Selection A). The "Alabama Resolutions" were received by the Acting Board, a small group that met monthly and functioned as the executive committee of the full Board. The Acting Board framed a careful reply to Alabama on December 17, 1844.

While deploring Alabama's demand that they answer a hypothetical question and reaffirming the position that being neither a slaveholder nor nonslaveholder was a relevant qualification for appointment as a missionary, the members of the Board nevertheless went on to say that they had never knowingly appointed a slaveholder. The operating sentences of their lengthy letter—and the one which gave immediate offense to the majority of Baptists in the South—stated: "If, however, any one should offer himself as a missionary, having slaves, and should insist on retaining them as his property, we could not appoint him. One thing is certain (:) we can never be a party to any arrangement which would imply approbation of slavery." The letter was not released immediately because of continuing reservations about the propriety of replying at all. In Selection B, Solomon Peck, the Foreign Secretary of the Board, presented on February 24, 1845 a statement that reveals something of the anguished reasoning behind the Board's decision. *Sources:* A. *Journal of the Proceedings of the Baptist State Convention in Alabama,* 1844, p. 8. B. *Minutes of the Acting Board,* ABFMS, 24 February 1845. Archives, American Baptist Historical Society.

[A. The "Alabama Resolutions"]

Whereas the holding of property in African negro slaves has for some years excited discussion, as a question of morals, between different portions of the Baptist denomination united in benevolent enterprize; and, by a large portion of our brethren, is now imputed to the slave-holders in these Southern and South Western States as a sin, at once grievous, palpable, and disqualifying:

1. Resolved, by the Convention of the Baptist denomination in the State of Alabama, that when one party to a voluntary compact among christian brethren is not willing to acknowledge the entire social equality of the other, as to all the privileges and benefits of the Union, nor even to refrain from impeachment and annoyance, united efforts between such parties, even in the sacred cause of Christian benevolence, cease to be agreeable, useful, or proper.

2. Resolved, That our duty, at this crisis, requires us to demand from the proper authorities in all those bodies to whose funds we have contributed, or with whom we have in any way been connected, the distinct explicit avowal, that slave-holders are eligible and entitled, equally with nonslave-holders, to all the privileges and immunities of their several unions; and especially, to receive any agency mission or

other appointment, which may fall within the scope of their operations or duties.

Resolved, also, That the Treasurer of this body be, and he is, hereby instructed not to pay any money, intended to be applied without the limits of this State, except at the written order of the President of this Convention, with the concurrence of the board of officers before mentioned; and this body, profoundly sensible of the vast issues dependent on the principles herein advanced, will await, in prayerful expectation, the responses of our non-slave-holding brethren.

[B. Response of the Acting Board]

"In giving my vote on the adoption of the letter to the Baptist State Convention of Alabama, I beg leave to state to the Board, briefly, my position and grounds of action. Conceding the constitutionality of refusing for *adequate cause* to appoint a slaveholder a missionary. I have objected to giving an answer to the inquiry of the Convention whether the Acting Board *would* in any case appoint one, for the following reasons: 1. The question is a hypothetical one, and it is contrary to our usage and our avowed policy to answer hypothetical inquiries. The policy and usage are good and not to be departed from needlessly. 2. There is an additional reason for refusing to entertain the present inquiry, as merely hypothetical, since no case of the kind has ever occurred and there is no apparent reason for expecting that one ever will. 3. The question is one of peculiar delicacy, and decide it as we may, will involve great dissatisfaction on one part or other, which it would be better if possible to forestall. 4. It verges closely, *at best,* on the *limits* of our constitutional power, and it is wise to avoid in the eyes of *all* members of the Convention the least approach to a violation of constitutional rights. 5. It threatens to be virtually an act of *division* of the Convention, and it does not become the Acting Board who are merely agents of the Convention, to assume the responsibility of such division, except from *necessity* such as would justify in civil government a revolution. The responsibility should be devolved on the members of Convention, who are the principals and would act for themselves. These are a part of the reasons I have alleged against the measure about to be adopted, considered in its *own* light and on its *own* merits. But the case has associated with it, in the course of discussion, *another element* which changes its character. . . .

It has become manifest, in the course of debate, that there is a decided *contrarity of views,* as to the policy proper to be pursued, both *in* and *out* of the Acting Board; and that, if the inquiry of the Alabama State Convention be not answered explicitly, those who dissent from the views above expressed, *will retire,* the most if not all, from their present relations to the Board and the General Convention; and the Acting Board, itself reduced perhaps to a minority of its present members, will be left with a minority of northern supporters and contributors to co-operate with southern contributors in sustaining our missionary operations. And the inevitable consequence of this would be either a speedy and lamentable reduction of our missions and stations, or the early transfer of most, if not all of them, to a new missionary organization. In other words, the question before my mind, under this new aspect, is not whether a course shall be adopted which would threaten a dismemberment of the General Convention by severing the South from the North, but which of two divisions would be least disastrous to the Missions; a division between the North and South, or a division in the North, leaving, as already intimated, an ever-diminishing minority at the North to cooperate with the South. This, as it appears to me, is the alternative now presented. I regret that it is so; *I disclaim all responsibility for its being so:* I have done what I could do to prevent it. But *being presented,* it is necessarily taken into account in determining what is best to be done; and constrains me to *accede* to a measure in its *own* light and on its *own* merits I should deem unnecessary and unwise.

Colporteur Baptism

Schism and Reorganization

Baptists in the South withdrew from both national societies and formed a separatist convention in 1845. (Methodists and Presbyterians were having the same problems with the same results; so the formation of the Southern Baptist Convention was not an isolated event.) While the controversy over slavery precipitated and in large part caused the break, differences in ecclesiological perspective were also at work. Centralizing denominations had always been stronger in the South. The Baptist southerners, therefore, intentionally organized an all-embracing body, while the northerners continued to operate with single-purpose societies. When the nation broke apart and plunged into fratricidal war, each regional denomination loyally supported and sought to supply the religious needs of its army. After emancipation, blacks withdrew from the white churches *en masse* and organized their own associations and conventions—another legacy of the long period of slavery and the racism on which it was predicated.

At the end of the war and "reconstruction," Baptist unity remained un-reconstructed. Yet all Baptist groups continued to grow. In spite of many clashes yet to come between a Southern Convention whose constitution recognized no geographical boundaries and a Home Mission Society whose motto remained "North America for Christ," at the close of the war a Southern Baptist could travel to New York City and speak with confidence about "the progress of Baptist principles."

1. The Southern Baptist Convention

The Virginia Foreign Mission Society inserted in *The Religious Herald* of 13 March, 1845, a sweeping critique of the national societies' responses and a resolution declaring "that in the present exigency, it is important that those brethren who are aggrieved by the recent decision of the Board in Boston, should hold a Convention, to confer on the best means of promoting the Foreign Mission cause, and other interests of the Baptist denomination in the South." The notice added that "in the judgment of this Board, Augusta, Ga., is a suitable place for holding such a Convention; and the Thursday before the second Lord's day in May next is a suitable time." Other Baptist periodicals in the South quickly circulated the proposal, many with unreserved approval. Amid rising excitement, J. B. Taylor, the president of the Virginia Foreign Mission Society, published his views of the direction the impending convention should take. *Source: The Religious Herald,* 10 April 1845.

---

1. We wish not to have a merely *sectional* Convention. From the Boston Board we separate, not because we reside at the South, but because they have adopted an unconstitutional and unscriptural principle to govern their future course. The principle is this—That holding slaves is, under all circumstances, incompatible with the office of the Christian ministry. On this point we take issue with them; and verily believe, that, when the mists of prejudice shall have been scattered, we shall stand justified in the eyes of the world. For ourselves we cordially invite all our brethren, North and South, East and West, who "are aggrieved by the recent decision of the Board in Boston," and believe that their usefulness may be increased by co-operating with us, to attend the proposed meeting.

2. We are desirous to see a *full* Convention. Let us, brethren, have a meeting concentrating in a good measure, the wisdom, experience, and sentiments of the denomination in the South, and South West, and such portions of our brethren in other places as may deem it best to unite with us. As we shall have no principle of representation, churches, associations, mission societies, or other religious bodies, may send as many delegates as they choose. Application has been made to the Railroad and Steamboat lines to furnish the delegates free return tickets. Should the application prove successful, as we hope it will, the cost of going and returning from Richmond, will not much, if at all, exceed twenty five dollars. Should our application result favorably, the earliest possible information shall be given of it.

3. *Several important subjects,* beside the question of organizing a Foreign Mission Society, will, we presume, come under the consideration of the Convention. We will mention them, that our brethren in Virginia, may learn, as far as practicable, the wishes of the denomination. Whether it be better to organize a separate Bible and Publication

Society, or to continue union with the existing institutions, are questions which must be discussed. It is quite likely, too, that the subject of building up a common Southern Theological Institution will claim a share of attention.

John Lewis Shuck returned to the United States permanently from China in 1854 and transferred to the Southern Baptist Convention's Board of Domestic Missions, which wanted him to work among the Chinese in California. He is credited with organizing, at Sacramento, the first Chinese Baptist Church in the United States. The Board's 1855 report describes the beginning of the Chinese chapel. *Source: Proceedings of the Fifth Biennial Meeting of the Southern Baptist Convention,* 1855, pp. 32-33.

CHINESE MISSION

Eight months after the adjournment of the (1854) Convention at Baltimore, were employed by Bro. Shuck in traveling to solicit funds to defray the expenses of himself and family to California, and aid in sustaining him on that field. One month was required for the passage, so that he has yet been actively engaged on the ground only a little over one year. On his arrival at San Francisco, he explored carefully that city, and then went to Sacramento for a similar purpose. Having surveyed both cities with anxious attention, the following reasons, among others, determined his mind in favor of the latter, as the place for the Baptist Mission to the Chinese in California: "A Christian Mission was already in operation among the Chinese in San Francisco;" "In Sacramento are as many respectable Chinese as in San Francisco, although the whole number is not so great;" "A growing prejudice on the part of the Americans against the Chinese, rendered it absolutely necessary to meet it publicly. The pulpit and pastor at Sacramento offered direct and palpable facilities." In addition to these and other reasons, Bro. Shuck was advised to locate in Sacramento by friends and brethren who had an intimate knowledge of both cities. After correspondence had with the Presbyterian Board of Missions, and letters received from Rev. Mr. Rollinson and other ministers in California, the salary of Mr. Shuck was fixed at $3,000, and to enable the Board to meet this draft upon the treasury, he was allowed to supply, for a season, the pulpit of the Baptist Church in Sacramento city, that church agreeing to pay a portion of his salary. This arrangement, however, is only to continue till the church can obtain a pastor, and the Chinese Chapel, now in course of erection, shall have been completed.

The most serious internal controversy troubling Southern Baptists before the Civil War was Landmarkism. Led by James Robinson Graves (1820–1893), editor of *The Tennessee Baptist* and pastor of the Second Baptist Church in Nashville, Landmarkers affirmed a stiff exclusivism that left in the Southern Baptist Convention a long-lasting deposit of suspicion toward ecumenical relationships. *Source:* James R. Graves, *Old Landmarkism: What Is It?* (Memphis: Graves, 1880), pp. 139-141.

What Is The Mission of Landmark Baptists?

1. As Baptists, we are to stand for the supreme authority of the New Testament as our only and sufficient rule of faith and practice. The New Testament, and that alone, as opposed to all human tradition in matters, both of faith and practice, we must claim as containing *the* distinguishing doctrine of our denomination—a doctrine for which we are called earnestly to contend.

2. As Baptists, we are to stand for the ordinances of Christ as he enjoined them upon his followers, the same in *number,* in *mode,* in *order,* and in *symbolic meaning,* unchanged and unchangeable till he come.

3. As Baptists, we are to stand for a spiritual and regenerated church, and that none shall be received into Christ's church, or be welcomed to its ordinances, without confessing a personal faith in Christ, and giving credible evidence of piety.

The motto on our banner is:

CHRIST BEFORE THE CHURCH, BLOOD BEFORE WATER

4. To protest, and to use all our influence against the recognition, on the part of Baptists, of human societies as scriptural churches, by affiliation, ministerial or ecclesiastical, or any alliance or co-operation that is susceptible of being apparently or logically construed by our members, or theirs, or the world, into a recognition of their ecclesiastical or ministerial equality with Baptist Churches.

5. To preserve and perpetuate the doctrine of the divine origin and sanctity of the churches of Christ, and the unbroken continuity of Christ's kingdom, "from the days of John the Baptist until now," according to the express words of Christ.

6. To preserve and perpetuate the *divine, inalienable,* and *sole* prerogatives of a Christian church—1, To preach the gospel of the Son of God; 2, To select and ordain her own officers; 3, To control absolutely her own ordinances.

7. To preserve and perpetuate the scriptural design of baptism, and

its validity and recognition only when scripturally administered by a gospel church.

8. To preserve and perpetuate the true design and symbolism of the Lord's Supper, as a local church ordinance, and for but *one* purpose— the commemoration of the sacrificial death of Christ—and not as a denominational ordinance, nor as an act expressive of our Christian or personal fellowship, and much less of *courtesy* towards others.

9. To preserve and perpetuate the doctrine of a divinely called and scripturally qualified and ordained ministry, to proclaim the gospel, and to administer the ordinances, not upon their own responsibility, but for, and under the direction of, local churches alone.

10. To preserve and perpetuate that primitive fealty and faithfulness to the truth, that shunned not to declare the whole counsel of God, and to teach men to observe all things whatsoever Christ commanded to be believed and obeyed.

Not the belief and advocacy of one or two of these principles, are the marks of the divinely patterned church, but the cordial reception and advocacy of all of them, constitutes a full "Old Landmark Baptist."

2. Northern Baptists Reorganize

After the withdrawal of the Southerners, the General Missionary Convention reincorporated as the American Baptist Missionary Union. The new constitution, adopted in 1846, was significantly different from the constitution of the original convention (see pages 170-171) in membership requirements and governance (Selection A). Most missionaries, however, were little affected by the dramatic changes in Baptist organizational structures in the United States. As Selection B shows, for Lucy Lord in China, life and ministry went on as before. *Sources:* A. *Thirty-Second Annual Report of the Board of Managers of the Baptist General Convention . . . and the American Baptist Missionary Union,* 1846, pp. 68-70. B. Lucy Lord, *Memoir of Mrs. Lucy T. Lord of the Chinese Baptist Mission* (Philadelphia: ABPS, 1854), pp. 171-173.

[A. Constitution of the ABMU]

1. This Association shall be styled THE AMERICAN BAPTIST MISSIONARY UNION.

2. The single object of this Union shall be to diffuse the knowledge of the religion of Jesus Christ, by means of missions throughout the world.

3. This Union shall be composed of Life Members. All the members of the Baptist General Convention who may be present at the adoption

of this Constitution, shall be members for life of the Union. Other persons may be constituted Life Members by the payment, at one time, of not less than one hundred dollars.

4. The Union shall meet annually on the third Thursday of May, or at such other time, and at such place, as it may appoint. At every such annual meeting the Union shall elect by ballot a President, two Vice Presidents, a Recording Secretary, and one third of a Board of Managers.

At a meeting to be held immediately after the adoption of this Constitution, the Union shall elect an entire Board of Managers, consisting of seventy-five persons, at least one third of whom shall not be ministers of the gospel. Said Board shall be elected in three equal classes, the first to go out of office at the first annual meeting; and thus, in regular succession, one-third of the Board shall go out of office at each annual meeting, and their places shall be supplied by a new election. In every case, the members whose term of service shall thus expire, shall be re-eligible. . . .

8. All members of the Union may attend the meetings of the Board of Managers, and deliberate on all questions, but members of the Board only, shall vote.

9. Immediately after the annual meeting of the Union, the Board of Managers shall meet and elect by ballot a Chairman; a Recording Secretary; an Executive Committee of nine, not more than five of whom shall be ministers of the gospel; as many Corresponding Secretaries as they may judge to be necessary; a Treasurer; and an Auditing Committee of two, who shall not be ministers of the gospel. At this meeting the Board shall determine the salaries of the Corresponding Secretaries and Treasurer, and give such instructions to the Executive Committee as may be necessary to regulate their plans of action for the ensuing year.

[B. Lucy Lord in China]

On the 24th of January, 1848, Mrs. Lord's family, and her family cares and comforts, were increased by the birth of her first child.

Writing to her aunt Mary Lyon, a short time after the birth of her babe, she says: "Of course the care of this child will tax my time considerably, and my wisdom and patience *more;* but to make amends for it, I propose to lessen my correspondence. This perhaps can be done without any material injury, either to myself or others. And this must be my apology for sending you this little note instead of a long letter. I daily think of the instructions I have received from you, and endeavor to put them in practice in all my duties. You may be interested to know, that we are proposing to take a Chinese boy, seven years old, to bring up. He is to come on trial to-morrow. We think some also of taking another somewhat older, for several years. If we take them, we must support them at our own expense.

"One day, as my woman servant was sewing in my room, and I was reading, she asked me if I understood books, saying, 'Ningpo women do not understand books—*men* understand, but *women* do not.' Some time afterwards I repeated her remark to our native assistant, and asked him how large a portion of the women at Ningpo could read. He replied, 'Perhaps one in ten thousand.' Lately my woman, of her own accord, has commenced learning to read. For a time she concealed it from me, because it took her frequently to the teacher's room, with which she thought I would not be pleased. When I ascertained that she was learning to read, I told her I was pleased, and endeavored to encourage her. She then brought up a Christian tract, and repeated some seven pages which she had learned. Almost every day I hear her reading during her leisure moments. Our men servants are required to learn a lesson in the catechism, which they recite every Sabbath evening.

"I would like to tell you more about our plans of usefulness, had I time. I am happy in my family and missionary relations; and my dear husband seems happy and devoted to his work. So far from hindering me in my benevolent purposes, *he* is usually the one to propose them."

Following an investigation in 1848, the American Baptist Home Mission Society was found to have "no relation or action which involves directly or indirectly the countenance of Slavery." Indeed, the Society had taken special interest in freed slaves, especially their educational needs, and by 1869 one third of the missionary force was laboring in the South. The reminiscences of Joanna Patterson Moore (1832–1916), who taught at Helena, Arkansas, furnish a glimpse of the missionary teachers. The response of one of her pupils reveals the impact of her ministry. *Sources:* A. Joanna P. Moore, *In Christ's Stead: Autobiographical Sketches* (Chicago: WABHMS, 1903), p. 28. B. George Gaines to Joanna P. Moore, 26 June 1865, in "Joanna P. Moore Autograph Book." Archives, American Baptist Historical Society.

[A. Ms. Moore's Recollections]

The Home Farm, about three miles from Helena, was a contraband camp something like Island No. 10. Here were gathered a great company of women and children and helpless old men. A company of soldiers in a fort near by guarded it. There were no white people there, and no one was teaching or helping those people to a better life. I offered to go and live there. The other teachers called me presumptuous and crazy, but I went. We fixed up a room in a cabin with a colored woman. I got the soldiers to make me an arbor and some rude seats, made by driving posts in the ground and fastened on them a split sapling; nailed my blackboard to a tree, and divided the colony into four divisions. The very little children, older children, adults who could read a very little, or rather those who wanted to learn, and the old people who could only listen as I read to them. Each division had about one hour and a half in school. . . .

After this I began to teach the colored soldiers that were guarding Helena. I found none that could read well; several others could read a little, having been taught occasionally by officers of the regiment. I found only one who was a Christian. I opened a school in four or five companies which I taught at different hours of the day. I never had more than ten at once, and yet I had more than one hundred on my list. Each day I taught all one verse of the Scripture till they knew it perfectly; giving them plain, easily understood texts, such as "All have sinned and come short of the Glory of God."

One day I said to the boys in each division: "All of you who are sorry for your sins and want to be forgiven, come to the children's school room at 7 o'clock." When I entered that school room, there sat three of my boys in tears. "My sins, my sins. How can I be forgiven?" . . .

For one week we had the meeting every night, after that we met only once a week and on the Sabbath. The good work went on till sixty of those soldiers were converted.

[B. A Grateful Student]

Kind Teacher

I want to write a few words in your Album because you have asked me to do so And first I wish you all the good possible and that you may enjoy the greatest happiness. O that I could dear Teacher reward you for your great kindness to me and our poor degraded and long oppressed people I know not my future but whatever it is I intend you shall here it and I also intend that with the help of God you shall hear nothing bad of me. Your people have often said that the colord man could not be made an intelligent people of and you know how many more terrible hard things they have said about us. But I for one am determined that shoe shall not fit me. I will try as you have so often told me to choose for my companions the moral the sensible and especially the religious. I do want to be useful in this world and try to do good to all I meet whether white or black. I never will with Jesus to help me forget the promises I have made to God and to you to live so on earth that at last I may meet my teacher who has been my dearest earthly friend in immortal Glory where parting is no more

My home was in St. Francis Co., and Maine Township Mo.

my occupation farmer

Your most obedient Scholar and friend George Gaines Co. B. 56th US. C. I. Helena, Arkansas, June 26th [1865].

3. The Civil War

As the sectional conflict propelled the nation toward rupture and war, the divided churches not only supported their respective sides but engaged in denunciation and mutual recrimination which further alienated North and South. Typical of the Southern Baptist approval of southern nationalism was the action of the Charleston Association in 1860 (Selection A). Equally typical of the attitude of northern Baptists in the developing conflict was the Circular Letter of the Oneida (New York) Association (Selection B), which in September, 1861, declared its revulsion toward Baptist supporters of the Confederacy. Finally, a third selection shows that Freewill Baptists, while mostly northern antislavery and pro-Union, recognized in the war—as President Lincoln did—a judgment of God upon the collective sins of the whole nation. *Sources:* A. *Minutes of the One Hundred and Ninth Session of the Charleston Baptist Association,* 1860, p. 4. B. *Minutes of the Forty First Anniversary of the Oneida Baptist Association,* 1861, pp. 12-14. C. Minutes of the Freewill Baptist General Conference, 1862. Archives, American Baptist Historical Society.

[A. Southern Nationalism]

Whereas, our predecessors, the members of this Association, did, at their meeting in the city of Charleston, in the year of our Lord 1777, express their approbation of the American measures, and their sympathy with the Colony of South Carolina, in the struggle for Independence, we, the members of this body, deem it our privilege and duty, to give utterance to our sentiments, in reference to the present crisis. Therefore, be it *Resolved,*

1. That we believe and profess that the institution of slavery, as

existing among us, is sanctioned by the SACRED SCRIPTURES.

2. That the teachings of those professed Disciples of Christ, who have occasioned the existing division between the two great sections of our Confederacy, are utterly at variance with the wholesome words of our Lord Jesus Christ, and the doctrine which is according to Godliness; and it is the duty of all faithful Christians to withdraw themselves from such, Tim. 6:1-5.

3. That we will continue to exhort masters to "give unto their servants that which is just and equal," and servants to "be obedient to their own masters, &c., that they adorn the doctrine of God our Savior in all things." Tit. 2:10.

4. That in resisting the encroachments of the enemies of our domestic institution, and opposing the "perverse disputings of men of corrupt minds, and destitute of this truth," our duty to God coincides with our duty to our country.

5. That we earnestly commend our beloved Commonwealth to the protection and guidance of Almighty God, beseeching Him to enlighten the minds and strengthen the hearts of our people, and overrule all our affairs for the advancement of His Kingdom, and the glory of His Holy Name.

[B. Preparation for War]

Dear Brethren: We address you under circumstances most novel and exciting.

After almost a century of the highest civil and religious freedom, in the midst of a consequent prosperity which has made us the envy of Christendom, millions of our countrymen, submitting to the dictates of corrupt demagogues, are clamorously denying the doctrines that made them free, and are seeking to destroy the bond and pledge of a pure and prosperous nationality. . . .

Hence it is that the land trembles under the tread of armed men, and the skies become dark with the murky promise of desolating war. . . . For it is a significant fact that the outbreak of civil war was contemporaneous with the assertion by Christian Teachers, of the divine authority and loveliness of a system which makes the wife a concubine and her children the merchandise of the oppressor; and we remember with sorrow that a *Convention of Christian Churches* was one of the earliest and most violent advocates of Secession, and that the religious press of the South has led the secular in its attacks upon the rights of man and its insane demand of vengeance for fancied wrongs.

Such facts reveal the *causes* of our peril, and as distinctly exhibit the means of its permanent removal. Civil war is, indeed, the necessity of the case; and for its terrible scenes of carnage and desolation, we must prepare ourselves. Upon its altars, willing or unwilling, we must sacrifice treasures of gold and lives of men, or endure the more dreadful alternative of a ruined country and an established despotism more vile than the world has seen. But we do well to remember that this is not the antidote, but the poisoned draught for which we have prepared our lips; and if we would gain life from the Devourer, we must secure it by the removal of the cause of his power, while penitently enduring the rod of our chastisement. War can be the destruction of evils only as it secures the removal of the wrongs which induce them. . . .

[C. War—the Judgment of God]

Every intelligent and pious mind must be impressed with the conviction that a just and all-wise Ruler is visiting severe and merited punishment upon us, for guilt of no trifling character, and wickedness of no ordinary degree; nor can the conviction be resisted, that the criminality of the nation is as great as its punishment is severe.

This bloody war, inaugurated and maintained, on the one side, by ignorance, bitter prejudice, aristocratic lust of power, and heathenish brutality, and prosecuted, on the other, through success and defeat, at first by inconstant policies and measures, which repressed and stifled the truest convictions, then with an aimless vigor, and latterly with a policy both just and wise, and measures which are abundantly hopeful to enthralled humanity, has already developed the following facts:—

1. That a very large portion of our country had become utterly and hopelessly corrupted by the aristocracy and despotism which ruled it.

2. That in other portions, the patriotism and even piety of the people had been sadly perverted and debased, and, throughout the whole land, our moral vision had become wonderfully dim.

3. That the leading commercial and aristocratic influences of England and other powerful nations were in league with traitors for the overthrow of our government and free institutions.

4. That the common people, and especially the dissenting Protestant Christians of other countries, so far as they comprehend the issue thrust

upon us, are in full sympathy with the stupendous efforts of liberty and vital Christianity to enthrone their principles throughout our common country; and,

5. That the true friends of God and man in these United States were ready to pour out their treasures and their blood, with the spirit of the early martyrs, to secure the blessings of civil and religious liberty to their country and posterity.

Who can doubt that upon the result of this contest depends the fate of Christian civilization in America?

Baptist ministers on both sides of the conflict sought to meet the religious needs of the soldiers. Most Baptist efforts in the Union forces were coordinated through the U.S. Christian Commission, an interdenominational agency spun off from the YMCA in 1861. Southern Baptist ministers responded more individually, though no less strenuously, as the report of John J. Hyman of Georgia illustrates. *Source:* John William Jones, *Christ in the Camp: Religion in Lee's Army* (Atlanta: Martin & Hoyt, 1887), pp. 504-505.

"I left my house on the 10th day of March, 1862; joined the Forty-ninth Georgia Regiment as a private soldier on the 1st day of May. I was commissioned chaplain of the Forty-ninth Georgia Regiment. The battles around Richmond prevented us from having regular Divine service. After the battles were over, the Forty-ninth Georgia Regiment was attached to General J. R. Anderson's Brigade, afterwards General E. L. Thomas's. At this time I was the only chaplain in the brigade (four regiments). I, being young, knew but little about the duties of a chaplain, but was willing to do anything in my Master's cause. Being in the command of General Jackson, we had but little time for religious service during the whole of 1862. On the 16th of December 1862, we went into quarters at Camp Gregg, six miles south of Fredericksburg, Virginia, where I opened regular night service; sometimes in the open air, at other times (when weather was bad) in tents. . . .

About the 1st of February, 1863, the good Lord poured out hundreds were seeking the Lord for pardon of sins; almost daily there were some going down into the water, being buried with Christ in baptism. At this time our brigade was so scattered that I had to preach to each regiment separately; the interest was so great that I preached for weeks from four to six times a day. Just as I was about to break down, Brother E. B. Barrett came from Georgia as a missionary and gave me much assistance. He joined himself to the Forty-fifth Georgia Regiment as chaplain, and at once entered upon the faithful discharge of his duties; about the same time Brother A. W. Moore came on as chaplain of the Fourteenth Georgia Regiment. The battle of Chancellorsville broke into our service for a few days; when we went back into camp Brother Moore left for Georgia, leaving Brother Barrett and myself in the brigade. We preached night and day, baptizing daily in a pool we prepared for the purpose. In the month of May, 1863, I divided my labors with Thomas's and Wright's Georgia Brigades. I baptized during the month fifteen in Forty-ninth Georgia and sixty-five in Wright's Brigade. The day that the army was ordered to march on the Pennsylvania campaign, yes, while the regiments were being ordered to fall in, I was baptizing near Wright's Brigade. Baptized forty-eight, all in twenty minutes.

4. Independent Black Baptists

As the war closed, black Baptists in the South were withdrawing from the white churches in large numbers. Soon they began to form associations and state conventions, such as the Virginia Baptist State Convention, formed in 1867. This convention enjoyed the assistance of the American Baptist Home Mission Society, the American Baptist Missionary Union, and the Consolidated American Baptist Missionary Convention. The last-named group was a newly formed (1865) umbrella organization embracing many black Baptists in the North and West. At its first anniversary, the Virginia Convention passed a number of resolutions (Selection A). Yet other blacks in the West regarded themselves as Freewill Baptists and petitioned in 1871 for admission to the Freewill General Conference. Selection B offers part of their petition. *Sources:* A. *Minutes of the First Anniversary of the Virginia Baptist State Convention,* 1868, pp. 18-19. B. Minutes of the Freewill Baptist General Conference, 1871. Archives, American Baptist Historical Society.

[A. Black Baptists in Virginia]
6. WHEREAS, In the providence of God, we have been permitted to form a State Convention for the gospel interests of the State of Virginia, and are permitted to hold this our first anniversary, and feeling ourselves encouraged in the great and noble work before us, therefore,

Resolved, That we are determined, by the grace of God, to go forward under the leadership of God, the author of *liberty, justice,* righteousness and *equity,* until this State shall be thoroughly evangelized, and the hills and valleys be dotted with school and meeting houses, and the knowledge of God and of Christ shall be known, felt and reverenced by all. To this end we invoke the aid of the A.B.F.M. Society, the A.B.P. Society, the C.A.B.M. Convention, the A.B.H.M. Society, churches, associations, etc., one and all, friendly to the cause of Christ, to aid us in the great and laudable work before us.

7. *Resolved,* that the funds in our treasury be always divided as follows, and to be used for the purposes for which it is divided, and no other, unless so directed by the Convention. The division shall be thus:—*One-fourth* for incidental expenses, *one-fourth* for pastors' salaries of feeble churches, *one-half* for our missionaries. This division shall be held inviolate; and any departure from it by the Treasurer, unless so ordered by this Convention, shall incur the displeasure of the Convention. . . .

Resolved, That we recommend the American Baptist, No. 37 Park Row, New York City, and the National Baptist, No. 530 Arch Street, Philadelphia, Pa., as being good, able, beneficial Baptist papers, and should be in every family, and read by all our ministers and deacons.

12. *Resolved,* that we advise our pastors who have not, to procure the benefits of the J.P Croz[er] Memorial Fund for the colored pastors of the South. The bequest is as follows: "One-fourth of the income from the said Memorial Fund shall be annually expended in furnishing colored pastors of churches with suitable books for their libraries, to aid them in their pulpit preparations."

[B. Black Freewill Baptists]

ILLINOIS SOUTHERN. "We are black, but comely," and most earnestly desire to be received as a member of your Christian body. The Y.M. was organized in 1870, and consists of 4 Q.M.'s, 35 churches, 40 ministers, 1,527 members, and 22 houses of worship. Our ministers are sound in the faith, studious and loyal, active and zealous. Our members are in sympathy with our benevolent efforts, and liberal in the support of the Gospel. Sabbath schools are sustained where there are those who can read well enough to profit by them. We are now enjoying privileges unexpected, and can hardly believe our senses, or realize the fact that we are freemen; have been organized into a Y.M., and are now knocking at the door of a Christian body of white men for admission. We can never forget the cruelties, the horrors, of the long, dark night of slavery, that so fearfully hung over us, and shut out the light of God's truth. We can all remember the deep grief and sorrow produced by the utter hopelessness of our condition. But God, in his infinite mercy, has come to our aid; has changed our darkness into light, broken the yoke of our bondage, opened our prison doors, converted us from goods and chattels into men and women, and we now feel that we are God's freemen. And to you, dear brethren of the Freewill Baptist denomination, do we feel more deeply indebted for this deliverance than to any human power. Christian denominations had baptized it into their fellowship, and claimed for it the divine sanction, we have learned that you stood up for the oppressed, and gave your voice and influence for freedom. Your prayers went up to heaven for the opening of the prison doors, and your votes were cast for our emancipation. And when we came up from the long, dark night of bondage, in poverty and ignorance, you did not forget or forsake us, but sent teachers and missionaries, whose hearts were in the great work of our elevation. They were willing to bear the taunts and slanders of our enemies, give up home comforts and associations, and share with us the poverty of our degraded condition, for the sake of lifting us up into the enjoyment of true social and moral life. Your teachers have enlightened us, your missionaries have taught us the way of God more perfectly, and we feel that the spirit of adoption is in our hearts, and that we are, with you, the children of God, and heirs with Christ.

5. The Progress of Baptist Principles

Following the Civil War, Baptists occupied a strong position in many states and at least a beachhead in most of the others. The *American Baptist Almanac* for 1868 supplied statistics (see page 246). The figures are not very reliable as absolute numbers but serve to show the relative strength of Baptists across the United States. The last column on the right refers to the total number of members, while the next to last column records the number of converts baptized during the preceding year. *Source: The American Baptist Almanac for the Year of Our Lord 1868* (Philadelphia: ABPS, 1868), p. 48.

In 1867, when Jeremiah Bell Jeter (1802–1880) traveled from his native Virginia to New York City to lecture on the mission of Baptists, he brought his rich experience as pastor, missionary, denominational executive, and editor to bear on his vision of the future of the denomination. With characteristic optimism he predicted continued growth and enlarged influence, with "usefulness chiefly among the poor and middling classes of society." *Source:* Jeremiah B. Jeter, "The Mission of Baptists" in *The Madison Avenue Lectures* (Philadelphia: ABPS, 1867), pp. 380-381.

We take encouragement from the *past history* of our principles. They have lived and spread, from time immemorial, in spite of priests, and popes, and kings, in the face of fines, and prisons, and tortures, and

TOTAL OF REGULAR BAPTISTS IN THE UNITED STATES IN 1866.

STATES.	Churches.	Baptized.	Associations.	Or. Ministers.	Total.
Alabama, 1860	29	808	429	5,481	61,219
Arkansas, 1860	16	321	149	1,272	11,341
California	2	36	45	208	1,991
Connecticut	7	114	119	1,041	18,447
Delaware	—	5	5	37	609
District of Columbia	—	7	6	321	2,102
Florida, 1860	5	134	73	553	6,483
Georgia, 1860	38	994	592	6,717	84,567
Illinois	36	719	627	5,031	46,129
Indiana	30	450	263	3,092	29,103
Indian Territory, 1860	4	45	40	400	4,300
Iowa	17	278	183	1,457	14,377
Kansas, 1865	4	46	28	35	1,119
Kentucky, 1865	47	944	424	5,038	81,631
Louisiana, 1860	10	209	113	932	10,264
Maine	13	268	172	704	19,870
Maryland	1	39	30	405	4,843
Massachusetts	14	265	307	2,720	37,948
Michigan	13	239	186	1,293	15,378
Minnesota	6	122	84	246	3,434
Mississippi, 1860	22	598	303	3,331	41,610
Missouri	37	749	432	3,804	44,877
Nebraska, 1865	1	10	4	15	217
New Hampshire	7	84	75	142	7,718
New Jersey	5	129	145	2,338	21,094
New Mexico, 1864	—	1	—	5	49
New York	45	814	701	7,962	91,928
North Carolina, 1860	27	696	375	4,818	60,532
Ohio	30	482	307	3,796	33,869
Oregon	3	29	25	47	1,082
Pennsylvania	18	427	350	5,354	47,700
Rhode Island	3	56	71	363	8,537
South Carolina, 1860	18	473	281	4,643	62,984
Tennessee, 1860	24	663	397	3,806	46,564
Texas	22	456	263	2,296	19,089
Vermont	7	108	94	321	7,714
Virginia	22	622	324	9,752	116,526
West Virginia	8	220	117	1,750	12,774
Wisconsin	12	172	120	606	8,891
German and Dutch Churches	2	76	56	425	3,896
Swedish Churches, 1860	1	13	11	150	600
Welsh Churches, 1860	3	34	20	250	1,400
Total in the United States	609	12,955	8,346	92,957	1,094,806
Nova Scotia	3	155	93	861	16,308
New Brunswick	2	119	73	274	8,755
Canada	11	275	239	901	15,091
West India Islands	4	101	39	—	22,261
Grand Total in North America	629	13,605	8,790	94,993	1,157,221

OTHER DENOMINATIONS THAT PRACTICE IMMERSION.

	Churches.	Baptized.	Associations.	Or. Ministers.	Total.
Anti-Mission Baptists	180	1,800	850	—	105,000
Free-Will Baptists	147	1,264	1,076	2,496	56,258
Six-Principle Baptists, 1860	—	18	16	—	3,000
Seventh-Day Baptists	4	68	80	467	7,038
Church of God, (Winebrennarians)*	10	360	350	1,000	32,000
Disciples, (Campbellites)	—	5,000	2,500	—	500,000
Tunkers, 1860	—	200	150	—	20,000

*We have obtained from two prominent ministers of this denomination the statistics for 1866. The statements, however, differ essentially, the one giving the total membership as 25,000, the other as 40,000. We have taken the average of these figures as most likely to be correct.

fires, yielding a noble army of heroes, confessors and martyrs. And these achievements have been won, not by the advantages of wealth, and learning, and secular authority, but mostly by the toils, sacrifices, and sufferings of the poor and the illiterate, and by the inherent force of truths wholly uncongenial with depraved human nature. Principles which have made progress under such disadvantages, must be vital, vigorous, and aggressive, promising far more brilliant victories in the future than they have secured in the past.

The United States is the only civilized country in which these principles have had free course. In all other lands they have been interdicted, or restrained by discriminating taxes, or have prevailed by mere sufferance. In this land they have found a congenial soil, and have flourished steadily, and without a parallel. This success appears, not only in the increase of the Baptist denomination in numbers, learning, and resources, but in the influence which their principles have exerted in other Christian denominations. Infant baptism, in defiance of the most strenuous efforts to defend and propagate it, has been gradually decreasing, relatively to the number of communicants, in, perhaps, all Pedobaptist sects. The belief in the regenerating efficacy of infant baptism has been driven almost entirely beyond the pale of evangelical Christendom. Immersion, too, as Christian baptism, though ridiculed as superstitious and indecent, has won its way into all Pedobaptist churches, and their pastors have been constrained to lead candidates for the ordinance "down into the water," or permit them to pass into Baptist churches; and they have usually preferred the former alternative. By this means, persons embracing our sentiments, though not consistently maintaining them, are to be found, not only in every Pedobaptist denomination, but in almost every separate congregation of it.

We do not expect all the world to become Baptists in name; but we do anticipate the gradual, steady and successful diffusion of our principles among all Christian sects. If the progress of our denomination, in the future, should be in the same ratio as it has been in the last fifty years, many centuries will not have elapsed before the triumph of our principles throughout the world will be complete. But may we not reasonably hope that our denominational progress will be accelerated? If Baptists have accomplished so much in their poverty and weakness, amid reproach and persecutions, what may we not expect from them, with their schools, colleges, literature, and various organizations for the diffusion of the gospel and the advancement of the kingdom of Christ? It is not, however, on the resources and activities of the denomination that we chiefly rely for the spread of these principles; but on the changeless purposes, the unbounded resources, and the inexhaustible grace, of their Divine Author. He cannot lack means for their diffusion. He can raise up Judsons, and Onckens, and Spurgeons, in every land, to disseminate and vindicate them; and in the absence of human advocates, he can, by the gracious, potent, influence of his Spirit, so influence the hearts and minds of men, that they will discern these principles in the Bible, and cordially embrace and support them.

Suggestions for Further Study

Investigation of American Baptist life, 1812–1877, rightly begins with organized mission endeavors. To understand the nature of these voluntary associations in general, see Winthrop S. Hudson, *The Great Tradition of the American Churches* (New York: Harper & Row, Publishers Inc., 1963). For specific Baptist organizations, W. H. Eaton, *Historical Sketch of the Massachusetts Baptist Missionary Society 1802–1902* (Boston: Massachusetts Baptist Convention, 1902) is the prelude; Robert G. Torbet traces the national foreign society in *Venture of Faith: The Story of the American Baptist Foreign Mission Society 1814-54* (Valley Forge: Judson Press, 1955); while *The Missionary Jubilee . . . with Commemorative Papers and Discourses* (New York: Sheldon Co., 1865) contains statistical and biographical data not found elsewhere.

On domestic missions, consult *Baptist Home Missions in North America 1832–1882* (New York: Baptist Home Mission Rooms, 1883) and Charles L. White, *A Century of Faith* (Valley Forge: Judson Press, 1932). For literary and educational endeavors, see Lemuel C. Barnes, *Pioneers of Light* (Philadelphia: ABPS, 1924) or Daniel G. Stevens, *The First Hundred Years of the American Baptist Publication Society* (Philadelphia: ABPS, 1925).

The story of black Baptist missions is told in Leroy Fitts, *Lott Carey: First Black Missionary to Africa* (Valley Forge: Judson Press, 1978), and the best book thus far on Baptist work among American Indians is George A. Schultz, *An Indian Canaan: Isaac McCoy and the Vision of an Indian State* (Norman: University of Oklahoma Press, 1972).

During the Civil War, Baptists were active on both sides, as illustrated in Lemuel Moss, *Annuals of the U.S. Christian Commission* (Philadelphia: J. B. Lippincott Co., 1868) and John W. Jones, *Christ in the Camp; Or Religion in Lee's Army* (Richmond, Va.: B. F. Johnson, 1887).

Published documentary resources for the Middle Period are useful. F. A. Cox and J. Hoby, *The Baptists in America* (London: T. Ward, 1836). *The Feast of Fat Things* (Salisbury, Md.: 1981) brings together the main items of Primitive Baptists, including the Black Rock, Maryland, resolutions; and William H. Wyckoff, editor, *Documentary History of the American Bible Union,* 3 vols. (New York: American Bible Union, 1857) tells the story of Bible translations. Finally, Robert A. Baker, *A Baptist Sourcebook*

(Nashville: Broadman Press, 1966) presents documents of Southern Baptist history and Sydnor L. Stealey, editor, *A Baptist Treasury* (New York: Thos. Crowell, 1958) provides excerpts from the writings of John Broadus, Jesse Mercer, and Francis Wayland.

Since this period for Baptists is preeminently one of expansion, organizational and educational developments are significant. A general study of regional growth is Ellwood L. Goss, "A Survey of the Development of American Baptist State Conventions" (Th.D. Dissertation, Central Baptist Seminary, 1951). On single regions and states, the works are numerous, with the following worth special consideration: Leo T. Crismon, editor, *Baptists in Kentucky 1776–1976* (Middletown, Ky.: State Convention, 1976); Sandford Fleming, *God's Gold: The Story of Baptist Beginnings in California* 1849-1860 (Valley Forge: Judson Press, 1949); J. S. Rogers, *History of Arkansas Baptists* (Little Rock: State Convention, 1948); and Albert W. Wardin, *Baptists in Oregon* (Portland: Judson College, 1969).

Two fine studies of education have been completed in recent years: Sandford Fleming, *American Baptists and Higher Education,* 6 vols. (Valley Forge: American Baptist Board of Education, 1965), and Charles D. Johnson, *Higher Education of Southern Baptists: An Institutional History 1826–1954* (Waco: Baylor University, 1955). Individual college stories are told in Ernest C. Marriner, *The History of Colby College* (Waterville, Me.: Colby College Press, 1962); Robert N. Daniel, *Furman University: A History* (Greenville: Furman University, 1951); G. Wallace Chessman, *Denison: The Story of an Ohio College* (Granville: Denison University, 1957); and Robert S. Langley, *Acadia University 1838-1938* (Wolfville, N.S.: Kentville Pub. Co., 1939).

Several one-volume editions recount the development of diverse Baptist groups that originated before the Civil War: Frank H. Woyke, *Heritage and Ministry of the North American Baptist Conference* (Oakbrook Terrace: Conference Press, 1979) treats the German Baptists. Works on other groups are: J. O. Backlund, *Swedish Baptists in America* (Chicago: Conference Press, 1933); Peder Stiansen, *History of Norwegian Baptists in America* (Philadelphia: ABPS, 1939): and John I. Fredmund, *Seventy Five Years of Danish Baptist Missionary Work in America* (Philadelphia: ABPS, 1931). An important unpublished socio-historical study of an ethnic group is Eric H. Ohlmann, "The American Baptist Mission to German Americans: A Case Study of Attempted Assimilation" (Th.D. Dissertation, Graduate Theological Union, 1973).

For doctrinally diverse Baptist groups see *Minutes of the General Conference of the Freewill Baptist Connection,* 2 vols. (Dover, N.H.: Printing Establishment, 1859, 1887), James Bailey, *History of the Seventh Day Baptist General Conference 1802–1865* (Toledo: S. Bailey, 1866), and A. D. Williams, *Memorials of the Free Communion Baptists* (Dover, N.H.: Freewill Printing Establishment, 1873).

The national period was also a time of diversification and controversy for Baptists in America. The major trends, concerns, and issues are covered in a few important studies, with much more investigation needed. A well-documented recent examination of black Baptist origins is Mechal Sobel, *Trabelin' On: The Slave Journey to an Afro-Baptist Faith* (Westport, Conn.: Greenwood Press, 1979), and William C. Suttles describes slave religion in "A Trace of Soul: The Religion of Negro Slaves in the Plantations of North America" (Ph.D. Dissertation, University of Michigan, 1979). On antislavery, see the appropriate sections of Robert G. Torbet, *History of the Baptists* (Valley Forge: Judson Press, 1963) and Norman A. Baxter, *History of Freewill Bapists: A Study in New England Separatism* (Rochester: ABHS, 1957).

The antimission problem in the Ohio Valley is the subject of John F. Cady, *The Origin and Development of the Missionary Baptist Church in Indiana* (Franklin, Ind.: Franklin College, 1942), and John B. Taylor's *Thoughts on Mission* (Franklin, Ky., 1820). The Kehukee, North Carolina, Association story is found in Sylvester Hassell, *History of the Church of God from the Creation to A.D. 1855* (Middletown, N.Y.: Beebe's Sons, 1886). William H. Brackney, "Religious Antimasonry: Genesis of a Political Party 1826-30" (Ph.D. Dissertation, Temple University, 1976) examines Baptist reactions to the Lodge. Although the Baptist period of Miller's career was short, Sylvester Bliss, *The Memoirs of William Miller* (Boston: Himes, 1853, 1971) is an important beginning for Adventism. Likewise, for the Campbellite schism compare Errett Gates, *The Early Relation and Separation of Baptists and Disciples* (Chicago: R. R. Donnelly, 1904) with J. B. Jeter's contemporary southern perspective in *Campbellism Examined* (New York: Sheldon, 1855).

Much effort has been spent on the separation of the Southern Baptists in the 1840s; two accounts by southern historians are W. W. Barnes, *The Southern Baptist Convention 1845-1945* (Nashville: Broadman Press, 1954) and Robert A. Baker, *The Southern Baptist Convention and Its People, 1607-1972* (Nashville: Broadman Press, 1974). Baker's older work, *Relations Between Northern and Southern Baptists* (Ft. Worth, 1948) treats the separation and subsequent tensions, while Mary B. Putnam's *The Baptists and Slavery 1840-1845* (Ann Arbor: G. Wahr, 1913) is carefully researched from original sources and still valuable.

There are many biographies and memoirs for the era. Those that bring the issues to life are: S. W. Adams, *Memoirs of Rev. Nathaniel Kendrick, D.D.* (Philadelphia: ABPS, 1860); Rufus Babcock, editor, *Memoirs of John Mason Peck, D.D.* (Carbondale: Southern Illinois, 1965); Edward W. Cone, *Life of Spencer H. Cone* (New York: Sheldon, Blackman, 1857); Harvey Cook, *A Biography of Richard Furman* (Greenville, S.C.: Baptist Courier, 1913); Shields Hardin, *The Colgate Story* (New York: Vantage Press, 1959); William E. Hatcher, *Life of J. B. Jeter, D.D.* (Baltimore: H. M. Wharton, 1887); R. Jeffrey, editor, *Autobiography of Elder Jacob Knapp* (New York: Sheldon, 1868); J. Wheaton Smith, *Life of John P. Crozer,* (Philadelphia: ABPS, 1868); John C. Stockbridge, *The Model Pastor: A Memoir of the Life and Correspondence of Rev. Baron Stow, D.D.* (Boston: Lee and Shepard, 1881); and Francis Wayland, Jr., *A Memoir of the Life and Labors of Francis Wayland* (New York: Sheldon, 1868). Joan J. Brumberg's *Mission for Life: The Dramatic Story of the Family of Adoniram Judson* (New York: The Free Press, 1980) is the best treatment of the first American Baptist missionary and his three wives, and it is the most sensitive study of the role and identity of Baptist women in the antebellum period. Judson's colleague and promoter *par excellence,* Luther Rice, is the subject of Helen W. Thompson, *Luther Rice: Believer in Tomorrow* (Nashville: Broadman Press, 1967), recently reissued; a more scholarly treatment is L. T. Gibson, "Luther Rice's Contribution to Baptist History" (Ph.D. Dissertation, Temple University, 1944).

Concerns of theology and polity were fiercely debated throughout the era and several books illustrate the major trends and statements. In 1835 the Tract Society issued a *Baptist Manual,* which contained doctrinal and devotional materials for family use, and early in the century, attempts were made to define and standardize Baptist doctrine, including J. Newton Brown's *The Baptist Church Manual* (Philadelphia: B. R. Loxley, 1853) and later, Francis Wayland's *Principles and Practices of Baptist Churches* (New York: Sheldon, 1857). Brown had been one of the authors of the New Hampshire Confession of Faith, published as *A Short Summary and Declaration of Faith of the Baptist Churches in To Which is Added The Church Covenant* (Concord, N.H.: Eastman, Webster Co., 1833). Edward T. Hiscox, *The Baptist Church Directory* (New York: Sheldon, 1859) was also a popular revision of local church polity that influenced Baptist life in many regions for several generations. Attempts at a Baptist "system" of theology may be seen in Francis Wayland's ethical lectures, *Elements of Moral Science* (Boston: Gould, Kendall and Lincoln, 1835), and J. L. Dagg, *A Manual of Theology* (Charleston, S.C.: Southern Baptist Publication Society, 1857). Arminian Baptist principles are presented in Hosea Quinby, *Letter to the Rev. J. Butler . . . Together with a General Outline of the Doctrines of Freewill Baptists* (Limerick, Me.: 1832), and John J. Butler, *Natural and Revealed Theology* (Dover, N.H.: Morning Star, 1861). J. R. Graves began to state what he would later describe as "Landmark" Principles in a now rare tract, *The Lord's Supper, A Symbol of the Church, Not Christian Fellowship* (Nashville: Southwestern Pub., 1857).

The Baptist press came into full fruition by 1860 and there were many fine regional papers that addressed every topic of concern to Baptists. Of significant value are: *The Watchman* 1819–1911 (Boston, Massachusetts), *New York Baptist Register* 1824-1844 (Utica, New York), *The Morning Star* 1826-1911 (Dover, New Hampshire [Freewill Baptist]), *The American Baptist* 1846-1872 (New York), *Baptist Banner and Western Pioneer* 1835-1849 (Shelbyville, Kentucky), *The Religious Herald* 1828-1875 (Richmond, Virginia), and *The Confederate Baptist* 1862-1865 (Columbia, South Carolina). Three magazines rich in biography and denominational organization are: *Massachusetts Baptist Missionary Magazine* 1803-1816 (later American Baptist Magazine 1817-1836) (Boston, Massachusetts), *Latter Day Luminary* 1818-1825 (Washington, D.C.), and *The Baptist Memorial and Monthly Chronicle* 1842-1856 (New York). Each of the mission organizations also had its own publications.

Primary source materials are abundant and easily accessible. A typical, though not exhaustive, list of personal papers would suggest the following: Adoniram Judson, Luther Rice, William Colgate, John P. Crozer, John M. Peck, Jonathan Goble, Anders Wiberg, and Lucius Bolles, at the American Baptist Historical Society; Irah Chase, Jonathan Going, Baron Stow, and Miles Bronson, at Andover Newton Theological School; Francis Wayland, Frederick Denision, and Asa Messer, at Brown University; Richard Furman, Furman University; Jesse Mercer, Mercer University; William Brisbane, Wisconsin State Historical Society. For other Southern Baptist papers in general contact Southern Baptist Theological Seminary. Many microform copies are available through the Historical Commission, Southern Baptist Convention in Nashville, Tennessee. Andover Newton administers the records of the Massachusetts Baptist Missionary Society and its successors, while virtually all other extant American Baptist national archives are kept at the American Baptist Historical Society. Local church records are preserved in regional depositories, and region, state, and city organizational records are held in original or micro-format at ABHS. For a complete directory, consult ABHS.

Section IV
The Era of Progress and Protest
1877–1920

> With so large a part of the population of the country under the influence of the Baptists; with prejudices against their principles in great measure overcome . . . with a fair measure of wealth and social position and a firm hold on the middle classes of the population, the achievements of Baptists during the coming century should surpass those of the past.
>
> Albert H. Newman, 1894

The context for Baptist life and thought as the nineteenth century came to an end and the twentieth opened was one of notable growth in population, industry, wealth, urbanization, science, technology, and education. But the period was also one of mounting protests and demands for reform, both by those who felt excluded from the benefits of progress and those who sympathized with those excluded.

Improvements in transportation and communication brought distant nations nearer; many of the devout hoped for the evangelization of the world in their generation. Home missionaries still found formidable tasks in the West, but as the tides of immigration swelled in unprecedented fashion after 1880, coming increasingly from non-Protestant countries of southern and eastern Europe, the challenge of mission often focused on the burgeoning industrial cities into which so many of the new arrivals crowded.

As the level of wealth rose through technological advance and industrial development, it was very unevenly distributed: a few were able

255

to amass great riches while others were forced to live in poverty, in both rural and urban areas. Protest movements of many types emerged among laborers, reformers, populists, progressives, and socialists. In the churches, awareness of the problems of the time was especially evident in the social gospel movement.

Changes in patterns of thought inevitably helped to shape such movements. The social gospel movement, for example, was largely premised on liberal theological currents that were related to the revolutions in thought stimulated by scientific, evolutionary, and historical thought. Many of those strongly influenced by liberal theology did not add the social dimension, however, but remained rooted in the individualism that had been so pervasive in American life. That pattern also was often strong among those who resisted the revolutions in thought in order to hold on to the certainties of the past and to cling to familiar values. Among them were many Protestants who adhered to a belief in fiat creation and an inerrant Bible against a belief in evolution and biblical criticism.

The restlessness and tensions of the era, produced by the startling changes in life and thought and by resistance to them, were heightened by the military ventures of the time—the Indian wars, the Spanish-American War, and especially the "great crusade" of World War I, the war that was to end war and make the world safe for democracy.

Baptists shared in the great growth and progress of the time and also in its turmoil and tension. They grew in numbers from an estimated one and one-third million to about seven million in the major northern, southern, and black conventions. In view of the growing size, diversity, and inner complexity of the Baptists, the focus in this section and the next in this book will be largely on the Northern/American Baptists for the years after 1877, though some attention will be given to other members of the Baptist family.

Baptists and the Major Currents of American Religious Thought and Life

With their congregational polity and emphasis on believer's baptism, Baptists have been quite distinctive among evangelical Protestants; yet they have shared much with them. They participated in various voluntary society and reform movements, becoming involved in the tensions and controversies of the time.

The following documents illustrate aspects of such involvement. For example, Baptists played a prominent role in one of the most conspicuous moral reform movements of the period, the temperance crusade. Baptists generally opposed any consumption of alcoholic beverages and gave leadership and support to the campaigns for national prohibition, which was achieved by the ratification of the Eighteenth Amendment in 1919.

As a denominational family with a long history of revivalism, Baptists were deeply involved in the perpetuation and elaboration of the evangelical tradition, especially as it wrestled with the challenge of mass revivalism in the burgeoning cities. In theology, the trend toward the development of conservative and liberal evangelical parties, which often tended to obscure moderate and middle groups, affected Baptists heavily, as it affected Presbyterians and Disciples. Not only theological thought but also church practice was affected; the more liberally inclined often favored using the "institutional church" as a way to meet the challenges of city slums, while others felt this to be too radical a departure from proper evangelical emphases.

The institutional church was one of the primary channels for the social gospel as it sought to relate Christian faith and church to progressive social thought and practice. Baptists had conspicuous leaders

257

on both sides of the controversies concerning social Christianity. Other currents in the thought and life of the time, such as the woman's suffrage movement, had their supporters and critics in the evangelical denominations.

1. The Temperance Crusade

So pervasive was the temperance movement among Baptists of the period that literally hundreds of documents could be chosen to illustrate its character and flavor. Quite typical was the report on temperance adopted by the Twenty-Fifth General Conference of the Freewill Baptists, the largest of the "Arminian" Baptist groups of the nineteenth century. The gathering was held at Minneapolis, October 4 to 8, 1883. *Source:* Minutes of the Freewill Baptist General Conference, (1883), 3, p. 49. Archives, American Baptist Historical Society.

The Committee on Temperance recommends that the usual devotional service at the opening of Conference on Monday morning next be devoted specially to prayer for the success of the cause of total abstinence and prohibition in the different states of the Union and throughout the world.

Resolved, that the prohibition of the importation, manufacture and sale of intoxicating liquors for a beverage is greatly to be desired and should be an object of constant and earnest endeavor by every Christian citizen; and that every step in that direction, such as prohibition on the Sabbath or other stated times, or other restrictive measures, should be vigorously supported, provided always that no encouragement be therein given to any legal protection of the disgraceful and soul-destroying traffic.

That we respectfully petition the Congress of the United States in favor of the appointment of the proposed Congressional commission for the investigation of the liquor traffic and its effect upon the moral, educational, and business interests of the country; and that the officers of this Conference prepare and officially sign a memorial in behalf of the Conference and the denomination which it represents, and present the same to Congress through such medium as they may deem best calculated to accomplish the end sought in the memorial.

That we express our high appreciation of the policy of Ex-President Hayes and his estimable wife, in respect to temperance, and the influence of their noble example upon society in Washington and throughout the land; and we greatly deprecate the fact that the present Chief Executive of our nation—President Arthur—has not for conscience sake, or in deference to the temperance sentiment of the country, followed an example so commendable in itself and so valuable to the cause of temperance, domestic happiness and the general welfare of the country.

That the policy of prohibition of the liquor traffic is essentially and necessarily *Political,* and therefore *must* and *ought* to be recognized among the political questions in the state and nation; and, believing it to be the paramount question now before the American people, any party which ignores or opposes the cause of prohibition is unworthy of our affiliation or support.

2. The Great Revivalists

Generally committed to their revivalist traditions, Baptists followed and often supported the work of the leading urban evangelists, especially the Congregational layman, Dwight L. Moody (1837–1899) and the ordained Presbyterian, William A. (Billy) Sunday (1863–1935). These editorial reactions are from widely read periodicals of the time. *Sources:* A. *The Watchman,* 77 (10 December 1896), p. 10. B. *The Standard,* 61 (28 February 1914), p. 776.

[A.] Magnifying the Church

Mr. D. L. Moody is sensitive to the signs of the times, and he has a nice sense of the relation of means to ends in accomplishing spiritual results. He has commended himself to the sober judgment of Christian men in part by the facility with which he adjusts his methods to meet new conditions. He frankly admits that he has abandoned some of the plans that were so successful in his hands a few years ago, and that his present campaigns are conducted along new lines. The key-note of his present method is to arouse the churches to their work by presenting to church-members those truths which will deepen spiritual life, the sense of fellowship with Christ, and the impulse of devotion to His work. He appears to believe that it is the Christian Church to which we must primarily look for the evangelization of men. The great mass-meetings have given place to the audiences of two or three thousand Christians whom he seeks to inspire to larger conceptions of Christian obligation and privilege.

In this we think he is wise. The tendency of some of the popular methods of religious work has been to minimize the church. Much of the religious activity of Christians has been carried on outside the churches. When we deduct from the effective working force of the churches, as such, the young people who over-emphasize their energies into the temperance organizations, the children who are only found in the Sunday school, the women who are chiefly devoted to mission circles, the young men who labor in the Young Men's Christian Associations, and those devoted to evangelism who unite with some evangelistic association, there is very little left for the church as such, but the old men and women, or those who are indifferent to these great causes. Even revival services have often been so conducted as to obscure the place of the church. The great evangelistic mass-meetings, held in some rink or wigwam, have sometimes fostered the impression that they were accomplishing what the churches could not or would not do.

Mr. Moody's new departure is a step in the right direction. It tends to inspire the churches with the conviction that the great work of evangelism is not to be relegated to evangelists who conduct union services for a few weeks, but that this work should be undertaken by the church as a church, and that so far as possible every church-member should be enlisted in it. It tends to magnify the function of the Church in advancing the kingdom of God.

[B.] Billy Sunday

Once more is Billy Sunday a live issue. The tremendous upheaval through which Pittsburgh has been passing and the whole character of the Sunday campaign which has already achieved such unparalleled results cannot be disregarded by thinking people. No one can read of what has taken place in recent weeks in Pittsburgh without realizing that here is a movement which calls for careful consideration. Never having heard Sunday preach—we had almost said seen—and never having lived or visited in a community where a Sunday revival has been held, we are perhaps qualified to make an observation without prejudice on either side of the case.

We have read many editorial comments from as many different points of view on Mr. Sunday's characteristic limitations—his vulgarity, his harshness of judgment, his obscurantism. We are inclined to believe that both his critics and his friends have paid too much attention to this side of the case and too little to the really great secrets of this success and in so doing have failed to bring out into clear relief what is the underlying cause of his remarkable career.

We could wish indeed that Mr. Sunday had the breadth of mind of

Dwight L. Moody, who made his Northfield platform large enough to include such men as Henry Drummond and George Adam Smith; that he had the freedom from vulgarity of a Charles Haddon Spurgeon. We believe that with both these qualities, he would still be Billy Sunday, and he would be a bigger and a better, though not a busier, Billy Sunday.

It is the busier Billy Sunday that should not be forgotten in the controversy that has been aroused over his obvious limitations. As the editor of the Continent has put it, "Sunday is about the best antidote to laziness extant anywhere in the Christian world; just looking at him is enough to make a lazy Christian ashamed of himself. In a world where it is so easy to go easy, Sunday is helping a host of people to go hard in opposition to sin in themselves and in other people." His unusual platform ability does not wholly explain his success although the leading dramatic critic in Pittsburgh says that Sunday is the greatest comedian and humorist he has ever seen.

The danger many will have in judging of Sunday's work is twofold. Some will be so utterly disgusted with his violation of good taste that they will be blind to the good he actually accomplishes. Such persons should read the judgment of one of his converts who has said, "It was like going through a sewer to be converted at his meetings, but it was worth going through in order to be changed." On the other hand, not a few, we fear, will assume that his tirades against "that old gin Spencer," and others are an essential part of his message.

On the whole we believe in Billy Sunday. He cannot be judged by ordinary canons. His defects are serious, but they are not so serious as the prim conventionality, or the propriety that never blunders, which characterize far too many Christians in these days.

3. Signs of Theological Cleavage

Tension among Baptists as to the degree to which scientific and historical thinking (especially the two areas of evolutionary theory and biblical criticism) should be employed or entirely rejected became increasingly acute in the latter part of the nineteenth century. A prominent Baptist educational leader who strongly favored the liberal side was William Rainey Harper (1856–1926), a biblical scholar who became president of the new University of Chicago in 1892. This great popularizer of the study of Hebrew early became aware of the widening gulf among evangelicals on matters of biblical interpretation, as these observations in a journal he edited demonstrate. *Source: The Hebrew Student,* 2 (1882), pp. 89-90.

The Eve of an Agitation.—"All the signs of the times indicate that the American church, and, in fact, the whole of English-speaking Christendom, is upon the eve of an agitation upon the vital and fundamental question of the inspiration and infallibility of the Bible, such as it has never known before." This is the opening sentence of Professor William Henry Green's "Moses and the Prophets," which has just appeared. Our readers will find among the "General Notes" of this number another extract from the same Introduction. This statement is not an exaggerated one. It is made by one who is in a position to judge well the "signs of the times." No man in this country is better qualified to appreciate the situation than Professor Green. He is no alarmist, yet he sounds the note of alarm. He might, indeed, have gone further, for it may be soberly said that we are no longer upon the *eve* of agitation; we are in the midst of it. The time has passed when the attention of the church shall be wholly taken up with theological controversy. A fundamental question has come up, upon the decision of which rests all our faith. Is the Bible what it claims to be? *Is* it what the church, since its institution, has supposed it to be? Is it the Word of God? Nothing less than this is involved in the question at hand. Who is to decide it? Who does not feel it his duty, at least, to look into the question, and, so far as it is in his power, to fit himself to understand the points at issue? Is this not, in very truth, obligatory upon every man who professes to herald God's truth to perishing souls?

Scientific Biblical Knowledge.—"I call all teaching *scientific*," said Wolf, the critic of Homer, "which is systematically laid out and followed up to its original sources." Such teaching is scientific, and only such. The critical study of the remains of classical authority in the original languages is the only means of obtaining a scientific knowledge of that authority. This is none the less true of Biblical knowledge. Need one hope to gain a scientific knowledge of Biblical antiquity except through the medium of the languages in which it has been transmitted to us? And surely no one can be satisfied with any other than a scientific knowledge. It is for the lack of just such knowledge that the Church to-day suffers. Those who represent the Church before the world have Biblical knowledge, that is to say, some of them have; but of what sort? Many, in high position, have as little truly scientific knowledge of the Bible, as the average school-boy, of Homer. They can quote texts in proof of this or that doctrine, they can argue without limit, questions of an entirely irrelevant character: but a genuine scientific knowledge of the Bible, of its facts, and their interpretation they do not have. The reason of this is twofold: Those who are now in the active ministry did not, while in the Seminary, receive the training in this department of theological work, which they ought to have had, nor do the men who are to-day in the theological seminary, receive either the needed amount, or, in many cases, the right kind of instruction. Sufficient time is not given for the *study of the Bible,* and too often even the time allowed is frittered away in fruitless discussion. Yet the fact that a man does not obtain this knowledge in the Seminary, is no reason why he should not have it. Taken all in all, very little is even supposed to have been gotten during a theological course. Must a *pastor* give up all hope of being a *scholar?* Is it not a radical defect in our ministry that they allow their pastoral duties to draw them from their study? The common cry is "lack of time." It ought to be remembered, however, that often where time cannot be *found* for a given work, it can be *made.* In view of the present demand "for the highest Biblical scholarship" is it not well for us to consider whether more time cannot profitably be devoted to study which is strictly Biblical, whether a scientific Biblical knowledge is not within the reach of every one of us, if we will but reach out our hand and take it?

4. Toward a New Theology

Baptist theological writings demonstrated the diverse responses to the general intellectual changes of the late nineteenth century brought about in science and philosophy. During this "golden age of Baptist theologies," each major theological school produced a textbook adopted from classroom lectures. Some of them achieved great popularity in a wider public. Of those who wrote or edited systematic theologies, Alvah Hovey (1820–1903), Elias H. Johnson (1841–1906), Edgar Y. Mullins (1860–1928), George D. B. Pepper (1833–1913), and Ezekiel G. Robinson (1815–1894) are noteworthy. But the two major spokesmen were Augustus H. Strong (1836–1921) of Rochester Theological Seminary and William N. Clarke (1841–1912) of Colgate University Theological School. Both men struggled to relate doctrinal understanding to the contemporary milieu and, in many cases, broke with established traditions among American theologians.

In Selection A, Strong (whose works were popular among conservative evangelicals well into the twentieth century) recalled the tempestuous response to his theory of ethical monism, which he explained as his realization that "man is of one substance with God in Christ" and that "the union of Christ with all men by creation, involves Him in responsibility for their sin, though He is absolutely Holy." At about the same time, Clarke was helping to reshape the form of Christian theology by relating the Bible to theology by means other than proof texts. For Clarke, "theology has always changed

with the changing life of successive generations and can never cease to do so." The
result of his labors was a Christocentric evangelical liberalism that profoundly influenced
the next generation of American theologians. In Selection B, Clarke describes the task
of the theologian as personalized through his own experience. *Sources:* A. "Autobiography of Augustus Hopkins Strong," A. H. Strong Papers, 3, pp. 227-230. Archives,
American Baptist Historical Society. B. William N. Clarke, *Sixty Years with the Bible:
A Record of Experience* (New York: Charles Scribners, 1909), pp. 200-203, 210-211.

[A. A. H. Strong on Ethical Monism]

I first delivered an Essay on "Christ in Creation" at our Annual
Theological Conference. Then I waited for two years, trembling on the
brink. At last I concluded that intellectual honesty required me to
disclose my views, even if they cost me my position as theological
teacher. I felt that I could make no further progress without printing
the conclusions I had already reached. The Essay on Ethical Monism
appeared in the Examiner. I tried to show that the drift of modern
science, philosophy, literature, and theology, was all in the direction
of Monism, and that theology must make use of the new light or lose
her hold upon thinking minds. It was only Ethical Monism, however,
that in my judgment had promise of the future, and by Ethical Monism
I meant a Monism that held to freedom in man and transcendence in
God. I maintained that such Monism as this was but an interpretation
of Paul and John, when they say that Christ is all and in all, and that
in him we live and move and are. I claimed to be simply digging out
the debris from the old wells of salvation, and letting the waters flow
forth that had been long choked back. But my protestations were not
sufficient to prevent hostile criticism. While there was much favorable
notice of my work, and I received scores of letters assuring me that it
was almost a new revelation, there were many ignorant denunciations
of it, and I was called a Pantheist and a Buddhist. It was the severest
ordeal through which I ever passed. Dr. Johnson of Crozer Theological
Seminary wrote a reply, and I replied to him in a second series of
articles, printed a year after the first, namely, in October 1895. In these
articles I gathered up all the criticisms that had been made upon me
and answered them impersonally. I succeeded in doing it gently, though
I must confess that I sometimes felt as Nero did, when he wished that
the inhabitants of Rome had but one head that he might cut it off at a
single blow. I made clear the fact that I believed in freedom and
transcendence, that my Ethical Monism held to Trinity and excluded

Pantheism, and that it had originated, not in philosophical speculation, but, as I have tried in this history to show, in Scripture and in the logical necessities of a Scriptural theology.

[B. The Essence and Purpose of Theology]

In constructing a system of theology I did not find myself proceeding upon the ancient and familiar proof-text method. The proof-text idea has appeared in various forms. Texts, or quotations from Scripture, have been largely relied upon for support of doctrinal statements, and have been regarded as sufficient support for such statements. If the Bible can be quoted for a doctrine, that doctrine has been accepted as true. It has usually been held that a theologian must work into his statement of a doctrine the testimony of all the texts in the Bible that bear upon the subject in question, and must construct a statement that will include the teaching of them all. If this cannot be quite accomplished, still it is the ideal, to be reached as nearly as possible. Sometimes, again, a doctrine has been made to take its form from some classical biblical passage, felt to be so important that it must be made determinative. But I did not find myself following the proof-text method in any of these forms. A critic once remarked concerning my published result that although the pages were freely marked with Scripture references—"spattered," I think he said—the work was not really an expression of the results of exegesis. He was wrong in the deeper sense, but superficially he was right. I was not simply gathering in the meaning of passages, and fortifying my positions by the citation of texts. I was not simply reporting what the Bible said upon the Christian doctrine. I was working under a different conception of the relation of the Bible to theology.

My life had brought me entirely over to the position of my early teacher in theology, now my predecessor, from whose method I had so conscientiously dissented in my youth. I had almost demanded, as I acknowledged to him long afterward, that his theology be dictated to him by the Bible. But by this time I had learned that instead of being dictated by the Bible, a man's theology should be inspired in him by the Bible—or, more truly, inspired in him through the Bible by the Spirit that inspired the Bible. Theology should be a result of exegesis, but a second fruit, not a first. Between exegesis and theology there are intermediate processes, not only legitimate but necessary. . . . How does this principle work out in practice? What result does it yield? According to the principle that I accepted and acted upon, a system of Christian theology has God for its centre, the spirit of Jesus for its organizing principle, and congenial truth from within the Bible and from without for its material. As for the Bible, I am not bound to work all its statements into my system: nay, I am bound not to work them all in, for some of them are not congenial to the spirit of Jesus which dominates Christian theology, and some express truth in forms that cannot be of permanent validity. The glory of the Bible for my purpose as theologian is that it gives me Christ whose revealing shows me God the centre of the system, that it instructs me in that spirit of Christ which is the organizing principle, and that it provides me with abundant congenial material for the building up of doctrine. One who uses the Bible thus is using it in accordance with its character. He may fail in forming his system through insufficiency of his own, but he will not fail because his principle is wrong.

5. Institutional Churches, Pro and Con

Those churches that maintained extensive educational and service programs for their surrounding urban neighborhoods, as well as carrying on the regular activities of a worshiping congregation, had their strong proponents and sharp critics. Edward Judson (1844–1914), son of the famous missionary to Burma, was a conspicuous theoretician and practitioner of the institutional church. (One observer counted over 170 institutional churches by 1900.) Judson's objective was to keep the doors of the church building open all day every day so as to be able to reach out and serve persons of various backgrounds in "a system of organized kindness." He developed his ideas as pastor of the Berean Church in New York City, later renamed the Judson Memorial Church. A selection from his book on the institutional church provides an insight into his position.

Judson was aware that a minister's time and energy might become so absorbed in social problems that the "priestly character" of the office might be lost, but Judson felt that the problem was manageable. Others were convinced that the innovations so detracted from a church's central purpose that they should be rejected. So Amzi C. Dixon (1854–1925), a conservative Baptist pastor and evangelist, who later edited the famous series, *The Fundamentals* (twelve volumes, 1910-1915), sharply criticized institutional churches in a sermon published in a book on evangelism. *Source:* A. Edward Judson, *The Institutional Church: A Primer in Pastoral Theology* (New York: Lentilhon & Co., 1899), pp. 29-31. B. Amzi C. Dixon, *Evangelism Old and New: God's Search for Man in All Ages* (New York: American Tract Society, 1905), pp. 16-19.

[A. The Institutional Church]

Such is the problem of social alienation that confronts us in New

York. On the one side is a vast tenement-house population, insufficiently provided with the ameliorating influences of school and church; on the other, in more favored districts, the well-to-do classes, in possession of the more ample and effective educational and ecclesiastical appliances. We are like a workman who uses his strongest tools where there is the easiest work to do, or a general who turns his heaviest guns upon the weakest point in the enemy's line, or a physician who injects his medicine into the least diseased portions of his patient's body. We make the mistake of huddling our best preachers and our most amply equipped churches in that part of the city where they are least needed, and where refining influences are most abundant; and, on the other hand, just where the population is densest and materialism most strongly entrenched, we bring to bear our weakest and poorest Gospel appliances. It is as though during a cold night one should unconsciously gather the bed-clothes up around one's neck, leaving one's lower extremities stark and chill.

This is where the Institutional Church comes in as a reconciling force. The name is not one of my own choosing. It does very well, however, if you put the emphasis in the right place. Perspective is everything in morals and religion. Emphasize *Church,* not *Institution.* Everything good is haunted by evil. Dangers lurk along all right paths, but this is no reason for turning back. Goethe says: "Upon the most glorious conception which the human mind forms, there is always pressing in strange and stranger stuff." You do not want a great palatial institution with a feeble church attachment, atrophied through disuse. Our social, educational and philanthropic equipment should be saturated with the Gospel spirit. The purpose of all Institutional Churches should be gently to turn humanity around, and direct its sad, averted gaze toward the cross.

An Institutional Church, then, is an organized body of Christian believers, who, finding themselves in a hard and uncongenial social environment, supplement the ordinary methods of the Gospel—such as preaching, prayer-meetings, Sunday-school, and pastoral visitation— by a system of organized kindness, a congeries of institutions, which, by touching people on physical, social, and intellectual sides, will conciliate them and draw them within reach of the Gospel. The local church under the pressure of adverse environment tends to institutionalism.

The church contains within itself the potency for the cure of every social ill. All that good people seek to accomplish through University Settlements, Young Men's Christian Associations, Rescue Missions, and other redemptive agencies, can better be done through churches, embedded in society, each forming a center of light, which irradiates the circumjacent gloom. The human mind could not conceive of a more perfect machine for cleaning up the misery of a great city than the network of local churches distributed through it, provided each church would interest itself in the fallen and wretched immediately about it. I would be glad to see the local church girdled with philanthropic institutions, each on a small scale, meeting the needs of the neighborhood—as orphanage, dispensary, hospital, home for the aged, and so on. We like to say that Christianity is the root of our philanthropies, but plain people cannot trace the connection. If the church should directly interest itself in curing social sores, a workingman could not pass one of our ecclesiastical structures without the same softening of the heart and moistening of the eye which he feels when he passes some great hospital and sees the white faces of little children pressed against its window-panes, and thinks that his turn may come to seek shelter within its embrace.

[B. Amzi Dixon on Evangelism]

We must confess that as a means to an end it is often a dismal failure. Institutional churches lose about as many as they gain by their philanthropic work. A pastor of an institutional church in New York declared that after twelve years of philanthropic work, which involved the expenditure of thousands of dollars, he could not recall a single person who had been made a Christian and became a permanent, useful member of the church through receiving material assistance. Others who have engaged in such work can make a little better report, but those who do philanthropic work with a view to winning people to Christ are not so enthusiastic over the results as are the literati who sit in their studies writing books and lectures. The worker notices that the people he helps often disappear just as soon as they secure lucrative employment. They seem anxious to get away from the scenes and associations of their poverty. The sight of their benefactors is painfully suggestive of obligation. A practical worker in the philanthropic field finds it difficult to decide as to what kind of environment is best suited to making people good Christians. As he climbs the rickety stair of an old tenement he sometimes hears a strange mingling of praise and profanity. In one room is a family with the mother singing at her work, "Jesus, lover of my soul" or "Rock of ages cleft for me," and in another room next door is a family with father and mother both drunk and boisterous. The same kind of environment, and yet the characters developed there are as far apart as heaven and hell. When he goes into the homes of wage earners he finds piety and worship side by side with debauchery and profanity. He also learns that on the avenues of the wealthy, where the environment is all that money can make it, piety and worship still live side by side with debauchery and profanity. You need not be surprised that a practical Christian worker looks puzzled when you talk to him about a revival to be brought about by change of environment. He knows, perhaps, of the wealthy philanthropist in New York, who had heard reformers talk so much about better environment for the poor that he determined to buy an old rookery, tear it down, and build on the site a model tenement with water and baths, which he would rent to the poor for less than they were paying for their present squalid quarters. He took great pleasure in the enterprise until he learned from his agent that before the first month of the experiment had expired some of his tenants were using the bath tubs for coal bins and others had disappeared with all the gas fixtures and piping that they could rip from their places and sell in the junk shop. It cost him something to learn that swine cannot be made into sheep by change of environment.

There is a socialistic evangelism very popular in certain quarters. Society must be saved. Some have become so noble that they refuse to be saved from a sinking ship unless all the crew can be saved simultaneously. And yet we are not told how society can be saved without the salvation of the individual. Shall we refuse to build houses because we cannot lay all the bricks at one time, or shall we continue to make good bricks and carefully lay each brick one in its proper place? Shall we adopt the principles of this socialistic school and apply them to the education of our children by declaring that each one need not study for himself, for we propose to educate the bulk in some mysterious way? Is there not danger that this socialistic teaching shall push the wheels of progress back to the time before Christ asked the question, "What shall it profit a man if he gain the whole world and lose his own soul?"—the time when society was everything and the individual nothing, when men did not feel personal responsibility or realize personal worth, but were content to remain slaves in the bulk? If one would be truly altruistic he must place high value upon himself, for if he does not value himself he will not value others. If a man does not consider his own salvation of great importance, he will not regard the salvation of others as of great importance. Indeed he can do nothing toward saving others until he is himself saved. The captain of a life-saving corps would hardly commission a drowning man to rescue another drowning man. A man in the fire is in poor condition for pulling others out of the fire.

6. The Social Gospel

While Walter Rauschenbusch (1861–1918) is especially remembered as the outstanding proponent of the social gospel, many other Baptists were prominent in the movement, notably Samuel Zane Batten (1859–1925), author of *The Christian State* (1909) and *The Social Task of Christianity* (1911). A leading spokesman of the social gospel among Northern Baptists through his work in the Social Service Commission, his reports to annual meetings were generally well received, despite opposition. His 1909 statement focused on one of the most central themes of the social gospel, the relationship of the church to labor and industry. His 1910 report recommended that the Social Service Commission be made an official department with full-time leadership. This was finally done in 1913, and Batten became the secretary of the Department of Social Service and Brotherhood. *Sources:* A. *Year Book of the Northern Baptist Convention, 1909,* pp. 132-133. B. *Ibid., 1910,* pp. 143-144.

[A.] Report of the Social Service Commission, 1909

With reference to the questions of labor and industry, we beg to submit the following report, with findings and recommendations. In these latter times humanity is coming to what is called self-conscious-ness, and men are discovering that they are social beings. To-day men are learning to think of humanity, not as a race of disconnected indi-viduals, but as the interrelated members of a living society. In the most real sense we have discovered that no man lives to himself, and no man dies to himself.

As the result of their new social consciousness, men are seeing many things as they never saw them before. On the one side they are dis-covering that humanity, through the toils and sacrifices of the generations past, has come into a vast heritage of knowledge and wealth and achievement. And, on the other hand, they are discovering also that many members of the race grow up in conditions which practically make impossible a full and worthy human life. They are finding that many persons are really disinherited by society, and have no real heritage in life. And as a result, many higher possibilities of their nature are unrealized and they never make the most of themselves.

This is not all, but, adopting the statement here of the report of the Committee on the Church and Modern Industry to the Federal Council of the Churches in Philadelphia, ''there are many phases of the present industrial conditions in the United States which cry aloud for immediate remedy. . . . Multitudes are deprived, by what are called economic laws, of that opportunity to which every man has a right. When automatic movements cause injustice and disaster the autonomy should be destroyed. That to these impersonal causes are added the cruelties of greed, the heartlessness of ambition, and the cold indifference of corporate selfishness, every friend of his fellow must with grief and shame admit. The helplessness of the individual worker, the swift changes in location of industrial centers, the constant introduction of labor-saving appliances, the exactions of landlords, add uncertainty to privation. The hazard of the mine, the monotony of the shop, the poverty of the home, the sickness of the family, the closing of the doors of higher opportunity react with dreadful precision upon temperament and mar character.''

These questions of social welfare most deeply concern all Christian men. They are not, as many seem to suppose, primarily economic and political questions; they have their cause and their basis in the moral life of man; they have to do directly with the questions of human relations and human welfare. Behind and beneath all these surface questions of labor and wages are human lives and human relations, and these are the essential and sacred things in life. For this reason, if for no other, the churches are profoundly interested in the right solution of these problems, and for this reason Christian men should lead in the study and settlement of these questions.

The mission of Christ includes the salvation of the whole life of man. The Son of man is Redeemer of the world. The kingdom of God, in the Christian conception, may mean much more than a human society on earth, but it is certain it can never mean less. The program of the kingdom includes daily bread for all; it demands the removal of the things that may become temptations; and it implies the deliverance of the life from all evil. The Christian who cherishes the hope of a Christian and offers the Lord's Prayer, expects the coming of a social order where "the Beatitudes are always operative, and justice never falters, and truth excludes all lies; where people hunger no more neither thirst any more nor say they are sick—a city that lieth foursquare,'' a city where no one is wronged or trodden under foot, but where all have right to the Tree of Life. Society needs saving as much as the individual, and in the long run the power of Christianity to save individuals will be measured by its power to save society. And the individual and society are so related as cause and effect, each to the other, that the work of saving persons is conditioned upon the saving of society.

[B.] Report of the Social Service Commission, 1910

Our study and experience have led us to the conclusion that our church people should co-operate most heartily in all forms of effort for social betterment. Many people have lost interest in the churches, and no longer attend its meetings and assist in its work. Many people have taken up an attitude of indifference where it is not opposition to all forms of organized religion. There is much unrest to-day in the political world, in social life, and in religious thought. The present, every discerning man confesses, is a time of pressure and crisis. Great movements are going on around us; great changes are impending in the social and religious world. A new order is struggling to the birth; the old vine of the kingdom is producing some new wine that is bursting the wine skins. And the one question of supreme moment at this time is this: What will be the attitude of Christian men in this time of crisis and change? Will they misread the signs of the times and take up an attitude of opposition and suspicion? What will be the outcome of the mighty formative forces that are now at work in society? Will Christian men seek to infuse the religious spirit into the efforts for social amelioration? Will Christian men accept the leadership of the social faith and see that the coming age is Christian in spirit and motive?

This is not all, but discerning men confess that among Christian people there is a moral lassitude which is alarming and disconcerting. The rank and file of our churches are not living as men and women might be expected to live and work who believe that they are workers together with God and are enlisted in a divine enterprise. We need some new ideal which shall put meaning and power into life; we need some great moral and religious impulse which shall set the pulse beating with hope and enthusiasm; we need some great enterprise which shall cause the feet of young men and maidens to leap with joy, and shall send them into the morrow with bounding confidence.

We offer the following suggestions for the consideration of the Northern Baptist Convention:

1. We recommend the adoption by the churches and Brotherhoods of the social service year. And we suggest that the topic named be presented to the people in each church in such a way as the pastor may elect, either as the theme of a sermon, the topic of a lesson, or the subject of a prayer meeting.

2. We recommend that a systematic effort be made to instruct the people in the social duties of life. To this end, classes for the study of the Christian's social responsibility should be formed, and the social teachings of Jesus should be considered. We are fortunate in having at hand a text-book admirably adapted to this purpose in Dr. Shailer Mathew's new book, "The Social Gospel," and heartily recommend its general use. The Christian conception of the kingdom of God should become the inspiring ideal of our people; in addition, we suggest that classes be formed where the great question of social reform and industrial betterment be studied in the light of the teaching of Scripture; above all, we suggest that in these classes there be systematic instruction in the meaning and obligation of the home, the church, the school, and the State.

3. We recommend that an effort be made to unite the men of good will in every community in behalf of better conditions in society. In all of our communities there are many earnest and conscientious men and women who are anxious to serve their day and generation. In all of our churches there are societies and classes studying the social questions of the time. But, thus far, there has been little fearless and devoted leadership. The churches, we believe, should be the rallying centers for all the men of good will in the community.

4. We recommend that an effort be made in all churches to keep our people informed concerning the various forms of social service in their communities. To this end, we suggest that social service committees be created in each church to study the various uplifting and charitable agencies that are at work, and to co-operate with them as far as possible, so as to infuse into existing organizations the force of the religious impulse, and to afford to our people some agency through which their faith and devotion may become more effective and fruitful.

5. We recommend that the Social Service Commission for next year be encouraged to a larger work than has been possible this year. The Convention should consider again the wisdom of appointing a Social Service Secretary to press the work. An official organ is also a necessity. In view of the generous co-operation of the Publication Society, it might be possible to have one of its publications officially designated as the organ of this work.

6. In view of the fact that the Convention has taken no definite steps toward prosecuting effective educational work in the cause of temperance, and in view of the fact that the recent return of many prohibition communities to the saloon system shows the great need of effective work in the creation and maintenance of temperance sentiment, we recommend that the Convention authorize the Social Service Commission to prosecute temperance education in all ways that shall be open to it.

7. Changing Roles of Women

Walter Rauschenbusch (1861–1918) has been generally understood to have been the leading American Christian social prophet of his time. A graduate of Rochester Theological Seminary, after more than a decade in a New York pastorate on the edge of Hell's Kitchen, he returned to his alma mater, soon becoming professor of church history. From that position he lectured widely and produced the books that made him famous, especially *Christianity and the Social Crisis* (1907) and *A Theology for the Social Gospel* (1917). He was deeply concerned with social currents of all kinds, among them what he called the "woman movement." In a brief article, the first part of which is given, he explained that the increasing roles of women in industry, education, reform, and politics added up to a social revolution; in his conclusion he indicated his own belief and support for the woman's movement. *Source:* "Some Moral Aspects of the 'Woman Movement'," *The Biblical World*, 42 (1913), pp. 195-196.

I was walking through a factory district when the whistle blew in the evening. In a moment the sidewalk was flooded with a tide of human beings, wave on wave, and they were nearly all girls.

I passed along the corridors of a great university when the bell rang. The students were hurrying through the hall and filling the lecture rooms. Their ranks were alive with the bright colors of women's dress, the saucy flash of hats and ribbons, the loose tendrils of hair, the passing glances and smiles of sex challenge.

I sat in the convention of a great political party. There were women all around me and women on the platform, not ladies who had come to see their men-folks perform, but women who were there to do the performing, earnest, watchful, ready to assert themselves and to fight for a cause on the same level as men.

Women have arrived—in industry, in education, in politics. They pervade all domains of life, not passively as adjuncts, but with a sense of equal rights and a feeling of new-found destiny.

This is a tremendous fact. In our age of social transformations what other social process is of equal import? It would be a great thing if we could abolish child-labor. It would be an immense achievement if all public utilities could be brought under public ownership. But what is that compared with a forward movement in which half of the entire nation is surging up out of the semi-seclusion of the past, out of a world with a fair but narrow horizon, out of self-imposed limitations of purpose, and marching out into a future which none knows or understands? This thing through which we are passing is a social revolution.

If this social change stopped after readjusting the equilibrium of the sexes, it would constitute an epoch in the history of humanity. Every little brother and sister playing together, every man and maiden mating, every father and mother governing a household in common; every man and woman meeting in society would henceforth act differently on account of this great change. But this change is only the beginning of more changes. The emancipation of half the race must release a vast reservoir of stored energy. What will it do and not do?

They are realizing these unknown potencies concretely in Illinois just now. What changes will votes for women make in the political alignment of the state? Who will get hurt? How will the game of politics have to be played from now on? What new tremolo stops will have to be pulled out on the organ of political eloquence to get those votes? Who knows?

This political adjustment is sudden and conscious. But similar adjustments of even greater importance have long ago begun to take place quietly and for the most part unconsciously.

For instance, it would be hard to formulate the influence of the feminine invasion on the methods, the spirit, and the subject matter of higher education. But every professor who has had to pass from the old to the new must have felt that the presence of women affected him. Some liked it; some did not. A public speaker would be strangely unresponsive to the electric currents of humanity if he talked in precisely the same strain and temper to an audience composed of men only and to another in which women predominate. But in most educational audiences women do predominate.

The ascendancy of woman has long begun its work in religion. In our American Protestant churches women, who have been mute and passive in the church for ages, have found a voice and have freely uttered their religious ideas and sentiments, molding the vital and working religion of the country. They have accented morality according to their ethical tastes and interests. The anti-saloon movement is one of the results; there are others. What changes in our theology have been due to the transition of women from a passive to an active participation in church life? Anyone who would answer that question adequately would make a real contribution of church history. Women have not occupied our pulpits, but the men in the pulpits were conscious of talking to women who could speak their mind and who did their own thinking. The profoundest changes in theology come by silences. Things are left unsaid because they sound awkward or arouse contradiction; after awhile these things have quietly dropped out of the religious consciousness of an entire generation.

We are far too deeply immersed in these currents of change to see clearly whither they will carry us. God knows. Plainly women are here as our equals in religion, in the intellectual life, in industry, and in the life of our commonwealths. When a thing is both right and inevitable we might as well accept it and go ahead.

The results will not be all to the good. No great historic movement worked out 99.6 percent—not even Christianity. The rise of women will cut some knots and tie others. But no admixture of evil must make us waver in the faith that it is right to do right, and that a larger freedom will in the end work out the larger good.

Polity and Piety

Baptists have put great stress on congregational polity and the autonomy of the local church. The congregation is also the major locus of popular piety; hence debates about local church polity provide clues for understanding changing currents of piety. For example, as the cause of temperance was taken up with religious zeal by most Baptists, it became part of their style of piety in this period and, consequently, affected the way congregations governed themselves.

Baptists have also followed the associational principle by which congregations cooperate for common aims, but questions as to what degree and how to cooperate emerge in somewhat differing ways in each generation. After the organization of the Southern Baptist Convention in 1845, Baptists in the North carried on the older societies for mission and publication but lacked a center of unity. Because of the multiple and often conflicting appeals for support to the local congregations, much attention and energy had to be devoted to problems of polity at state and national levels. Finally it was decided in Washington in 1907 to form the Northern Baptist Convention; constitution and bylaws were adopted the next year at Oklahoma City, and incorporation followed in 1910.

1. Communion Controversy: Wine or Grape Juice?

As the cause of temperance (by which they usually meant total abstinence) became part of their piety, many Baptists came to believe that their Lord did not use wine that had alcoholic content. A medical doctor, Abraham Coles (1813–1891), argued for that conclusion in an address delivered in 1878; his own concise summary of his position is reprinted (Selection A).

Others thought that such interpretations simply could not be sustained. For example,

277

Alvah Hovey (1820–1903), for fifty years on the faculty of Newton Theological Institution and president for more than half of that time, responded to such views in a long article. Explaining that though his sympathies were "heartily with the active friends of temperance," he reported that his careful examination of biblical passages had led him to a different conclusion from the one held by many of them. His own brief recapitulation of his argument is provided (Selection B).

Concurrently, many congregations were changing from the use of the common cup to individual Communion cups, influenced by considerations of personal and public health. As an illustration, part of a typed report (which incorporated some unidentified clippings) to a local committee to its congregation, which adopted it, is given. *Sources:* A. Abraham Coles, *Wine in the Word: An Inquiry Concerning the Wine Christ Made, The Wine of the Supper, Etc.* (New York: Nelson & Phillips, 1878), pp. 46-47. B. Alvah Hovey, "What Was the 'Fruit of the Vine' Which Jesus gave His Disciples at the Institution of the Supper?" *Baptist Quarterly Review,* 9 (1887), pp. 302-303. C. "Report of Committee on Individual Communion Cups" (to Philadelphia [Pennsylvania] Fifth Baptist Church), 10 December 1897. Archives, American Baptist Historical Society.

[A.] Wine in the Word

. . . I claim to have established the following propositions:—

1. That the Greek word, *oinos,* translated wine, is generic, and includes unfermented grape juice, known as must, new wine, and sweet wine—and that, too, without any defining adjective; but more specifically and explicitly, of course, when associated with an explanatory epithet like *neos,* new; and that the Bible does demonstrably speak of two kinds of wine.

2. That the wine Christ made corresponded to the wine of nature, and was unfermented and unintoxicating.

3. That the wine of the Supper was unfermented.

4. That the only wine which Christ is known to have drunk was new wine; and that total abstinence from intoxicating wine is enjoined in the Epistles, inferentially by his authority.

5. That whatever intoxicates is, as the word implies, a poison; that opium is no more a poison than alcohol; that to use either, except to meet a rare need as a medicine, is inexpedient; and that the only remedy for the dreadful evils of intemperance is total abstinence.

[B.] What was the Fruit of the Vine?

But it is not the clearness, or odor, or color, or taste, or slightly exhilarating quality, or comparative freedom from yeast germs, or stability of composition, by reason of which it is easily preserved and carried without change to any part of the world, which leads me to call in question our right to substitute any other drink for wine in the cup of the Lord, but rather my conviction that what Christ gave to his disciples, saying, *this cup* (not something else) *is the new covenant in my blood,* was the proper wine, the fermented juice of grapes. For I seem to myself to have shown: (1) that there is no biblical foundation for the two-wine theory; (2) that there is no biblical proof of Christ's giving simple grape juice to his disciples in the cup; and (3) that there is strong extra-biblical evidence of "this fruit of the vine" being the *wine mingled with water.* It is then easy for me to honor the intention of those who have put grape-juice, or raisin-juice, or some other liquid into the cup to represent the blood of the Lamb, but it is not easy for me to perceive the soundness of their reasons for so doing. I heartily wish they would re-examine the case, and if they find the evidence to be against their practice, yield to it promptly and without fear. There is no body of Christians that is under more sacred obligations to ascertain and follow the law of Christ in this matter than the one to which we belong. But the writer's principal object will be accomplished if his brethren are led to act with full intelligence in observing the holy supper, whether they do or do not agree with him.

[C.] Individual Communion Cups

The promiscuous and common use of a cup or other drinking vessel, has much about it that is traditional, conventional and customary; it is seen in public and in private; in institutions both sacred and secular; at ceremonies of a solemn or sentimental, jovial, lively, or boisterous nature. The use of a single cup we believe is not consistent with the preservation and improvement of personal and public health. Among the maladies which may be carried from mouth to mouth by a common cup are . . . cancer, tuberculosis, diphtheria, scarlatina, influenza, tonsillitis, whooping cough, and others; the greatest of these is tuberculosis, the "Great White Plague," which, like the poor, we have always with us, principally because, not occuring in acute and alarming epidemic form, as do smallpox, diphtheria, cholera, etc., the fact of its contagiousness in insidious ways is not recognized generally by the public. Dentists urge strongly the importance of avoiding the common cup, because so many mouths are in an uncleanly, if not an unhealthy condition; neglected teeth, vitiated oral secretions, diseased gums, . . .

may be mentioned. "Sanitas," of London, writes: "In 1894-5, when influenza was very prevalent in England, the spread of it was noticed and put down to the same cause (common communion cup), in several of the church and other papers." Although the committee are not able to prove a single instance of any one person contracting a disease from the Communion Cup, we fully believe the time has come when the Individual Cup should be adopted by our churches for Communion Service.

So far as our knowledge extends, the first church to use individual communion cups for sanitary reasons was the First Congregational Church of Saco, Maine, in November, 1893. It may be of interest to quote from a deacon's letter to us: "Having officiated at the communion service for many years and observing the mustaches, sore and tobacco-stained lips, the idea suggested itself to me that there must be some better way. Then, too, the hurried manner in which the cup was passed from one to another took from the solemnity of the occasion and I thought if each one could have a cup of his own more time would be given for meditation and prayer and it would be of greater benefit to each communicant; and, as at our tea-table we have individual cups, why not at our communion table! The change has been very satisfactory." The first extensive use of individual communion cups was made in Rochester, N.Y., where on the first Sunday in May, 1894, the Central Presbyterian Church used the outfit designed by Dr. Forbes, a member, for its 1,800 communicants; although on the Sunday previous the outfit was first put to practical test in the North Baptist Church, with its 240 communicants. It seems that the Baptists and Presbyterians had the courage, liberty, adaptability and foresight to unite on this question, if not on questions of doctrine and polity. Other churches of the same and various other denominations in Rochester soon followed in adopting individual communion cups, so that within one month fourteen had them in use and six signified their intention of adopting them. In July 1894, a Congregational Church in Lima, Ohio, adopted the individual cups invented by Rev. J. H. Thomas of that city. In September 1894, the Fourth Baptist Church of Philadelphia, voted in favor of the change. A half dozen other churches, Methodist, Presbyterian, Reformed and Congregational fell into line before long, and several other Philadelphia churches are now contemplating using individual cups.

Perhaps the number of churches now using individual cups is greater by half a score or more than we have learned of, as replies from some sources have not been received.

We may summarize as follows: According to denominations: Congregational churches 65; Baptist 42; Presbyterian 33; Methodist Episcopal 20; Lutheran 5; Reformed 4; Protestant Episcopal 2; Universalist 1; Disciples of Christ 1; Welsh Calvinistic 1; unknown denominations 50. Total 224. According to States: New York 33 churches; Massachusetts 39; Ohio 25; Pennsylvania 23; California 23; New Jersey 18; Connecticut 11; Wisconsin 9; New Hampshire 8; Maine 7; Illinois 5; Vermont 4; Michigan 4; Indiana 3; Iowa 3; Rhode Island, North Carolina, Maryland, Colorado, Texas, New Mexico, Oregon, Nova Scotia and Japan, each 1.

The number of communicants in the various churches range from 36 to 2,000. The approximate average number of communicants is about 450 to a church: about 100,000 altogether.

Wherever individual communion cups have been adopted, the testimony of pastor and people has been expressive of the utmost satisfaction. They would not be persuaded to return to the old method. There is a sense of relief in using a clean, sanitary cup, devotion is promoted, the ceremony reverenced. Ministers say that individual cups are more convenient, and that there is less time occupied in serving them, and without any confusion, than by using common cups. Again, from nearly all churches now using the individual cups come replies stating that the number of church-members who attend communion service has increased, and in some instances greatly so; in one Reformed church in New York the number of communicants was doubled; in a Presbyterian church ''about 200 more communicants,''. . .

2. Problems of Baptist Unity

The Baptist Congress was an annual gathering of Baptist leaders, largely from the North. It provided a forum for presentation, debate, and discussion and flourished from 1882 to 1914. Many persons who were then (or later) conspicuous in the denomination participated in the Congress. When he addressed the assembly in 1903, Russell H. Conwell (1843–1925) was already famous. A successful Boston publisher, his activities as a layman led to his decision to enter the ordained ministry. In 1882 he was called to a small church in Philadelphia that under his leadership grew into the Baptist Temple, largest institutional church in America, from which Temple University and several hospitals were spawned. Today Conwell is often remembered for his espousal of the ''gospel of wealth'' in his immensely popular, oft-repeated address, ''Acres of Diamonds.'' Before the Congress, Conwell argued for a closer cooperation among Baptists in accordance with the association principle. This selection is from the early part of his long address. *Source:* Russell H. Conwell, "How Can Baptists Secure for Themselves a More Practical Working Union?" *1903 Proceedings of the Baptist Congress, Philadelphia, Pa.* (New York: Baptist Congress Publishing Co., 1904), pp. 14-18.

The chief need in the progress of our work as a denomination now, is a closer fraternal union without encroaching on the legal independency of the churches. The strength of union, the deepening of interest, in all forms of work for Christ, require that as a people we should be brought more into acquaintance with each other. We need the stimulus of large gatherings, and the instruction to be obtained from the teaching of our great men. We need that the powerful force recognized as "public opinion" in our denomination should be focused on our missionary enterprises; and that comprehensive views of the magnitude of our denomination as it is, should encourage all the membership to labor more hopefully for the further advance so reasonably to be made by such a body of Christian people. Churches must be strengthened in every city by what others have done; new churches should be started in a thousand cities or villages; larger sums of money could be raised for missionary work abroad; and the great gain which the Presbyterian, Methodist, or Catholic churches have secured by legal organization of the churches in a legislative union, the Baptists can as fully accomplish without a sacrifice of our jealously-guarded soul liberty, or of our independence among the churches.

The speaker, therefore, places unhesitatingly before this Congress the necessity and feasibility of opening at once a National or International Congress of the Baptist Churches of like faith and order with those the Congress now, in a measure, represents; and that a call be issued at once by this body, for the first meeting next Spring. That this exceptional change which will for once make this Congress a doer as well as a debater, will be a grand result worthy* of the founders and supporters of this honorable organization. That the proposition may be more clearly set before you, the speaker advances these additional suggestions:

NAME

The name of the proposed organization may well be the National or International Baptist Association, following directly in the path of the district and state associations, which have been held from time immemorial.

The delegates which would form this Association or Congress would be sent directly from each Baptist Church in the land, and no church could be compelled to join the association or prevented from withdrawing therefrom at any time.

PURPOSE

The purpose of the organization would be similar to that of the State associations now existing, and would in its larger constituency naturally consider the larger questions in which the whole denomination has a general interest. There need be no legislation. The influence of a broader fraternity would lead naturally to a more practical fellowship, and the consciousness of power which such a representative gathering would give would awaken enterprises and encourage effort in those larger measures where other denominations now lead us because of their compact organization.

The speaker feels that the time is ripe for this larger movement and a closer union of all the churches in the denomination, and that a great duty has been placed on this Congress by the hand of Divine Providence. The fact that the general public regards this Congress now as a representative body of the Baptists of the nation, and takes our utterances as the fiat of the whole denomination—contradictory and confusing as they have often been—suggests the great influence upon public opinion which the opinion of a really national association would have. Such an influence would greatly assist the local churches in their work among the people and would be of special helpfulness to the missionaries beginning Sunday-schools and churches in new or deserted fields.

But a greater gain would be secured to our Missionary Societies, which, while children of the denomination, are left to wander, clothe and feed themselves, unmothered and unfathered by the power which gave them birth. A meeting of the societies is not a meeting of the denomination as a denomination, and cannot act for the denomination in matters affecting the whole body. The difficulties which must continually arise between the societies, in their independence of each other and working in the same field, with their boundaries and duties undefined by a higher power, can only be avoided by a meeting of the whole denomination in solemn council. The appeals to the churches for aid to carry on their work partakes in the minds now more or less of a supine begging of the laymen; and the responsibility for the work, which ought to be assumed by the churches, now is transferred to the officers of the societies. Those societies would be greatly strengthened and their work made much easier by the moral backing of a body whose word is the word of the denomination at large.

3. Steps Toward the Organization of the Northern Baptist Convention

Like Conwell, many persons favored a more efficient national organization of Baptists in the North and outlined ways of putting one together; the actual process was a very complex one, as the selection indicates. To commemorate its tenth anniversary, the denomination's executive committee had a manual prepared; its "Historical Preface," most of which follows, is a concise summary of the steps that led to the formation of the Northern Baptist Convention. The manual was largely the work of William C. Bitting (1857–1931), for many years pastor of the Second Baptist Church of St. Louis and the first corresponding secretary of the Convention. *Source: A Manual of the Northern Baptist Convention* (Philadelphia: ABPS, n.d.), pp. 3-10.

1. In May, 1896, at Asbury Park, N.J., "A Commission on Systematic Beneficence" was created, by the adoption of a series of resolutions presented by the Finance Committee of the American Baptist Missionary Union. These resolutions were also adopted by the American Baptist Home Mission Society, and the American Baptist Publication Society. Rev. F. M. Ellis, D.D., of Baltimore, Md., then declared, "We have unified the denomination at the contribution-box, and that is next to the throne of grace."

2. In May, 1897, the Woman's Baptist Home Mission Society adopted resolutions, urging Northern Baptists to combine all their missionary periodicals into one, and pointed out the waste occasioned by the current method of publishing numerous journals. At the Anniversaries the same year, the report of the Commission on Systematic Beneficence called attention to the significant and the suggestive example of the joint efforts which had been made during the previous year by the three general Societies to cancel their debts.

3. In November, 1898, at the meeting of the Baptist Congress in Buffalo, N.Y., Rev. George E. Horr, D.D., then editor of "The Watchman," declared: "There is a great opportunity for the denomination to harmonize its missionary work. . . . There is just as much necessity that the work of the Missionary Union, the Home Mission Society, and the Publication Society should be harmonized—note that I do not use the word *unified*—should be *harmonized*, as there ever was that our

controversies in regard to the Bible question should be adjusted, as they were at Saratoga a number of years ago." This significant deliverance was the subject of much comment. The denominational press, particularly "The Standard," started discussion which increased the sentiment in favor of a closer relation between the organizations that were conducting our denominational work.

4. So far the discussion had related principally to the harmonious cooperation of distinct organizations. It was inevitable that such discussions should produce a feeling in the hearts, and a conviction in the minds, of many intelligent Baptists that our brotherhood should be more pronounced and an exhibition of it in Christian work more manifest.

5. In May, 1900, at the Anniversaries in Detroit, Mich., "A Commission on Coordination," composed of representatives of the general Societies, including the women's organizations, with Mr. Stephen Greene, of Massachusetts, as chairman, was appointed to consider the better coordination of our denominational work. The duties of this commission were, "To consider the relative amounts which the denomination should be asked to furnish for our different benevolent enterprises, and also to consider the practicability of more closely coordinating the different departments of our denominational work, and to make such other recommendations as in their judgment they may deem wise."

6. In May, 1901, in Springfield, Mass., there was held the first of several general meetings of the denomination. This was a mass-meeting on "Coordination." The report of Mr. Stephen Greene, of Newton Center, Mass., chairman of the committee, made six notable suggestions. Among them was one that "The best interests of our work as a denomination require that the annual gatherings of the American Baptist Home Mission Society, the American Baptist Missionary Union, and the American Baptist Publication Society should be representative and delegated bodies, having the same basis of representation, so that the delegates to the three Societies shall be, so far as possible, identical.

"As a step necessary toward this end we recommend that the several Societies, at the earliest possible date, and after mutual consultation through their executive boards, change their constitutions so as to require the same qualifications of voters at their Anniversaries.

"It is believed that such action is fundamental, and if taken would create an atmosphere in which a "better coordination" would be pos-

sible. If the executive officers and boards of our several Societies could
be brought to realize, as such action would help them to see, that their
constituencies were actually one, a distinct advantage would be gained,
and if the representatives of our churches could go up to the Anniversaries with the clear conviction that an actual responsibility concerning
the entire work of the denomination rested upon them, it is certain that
a better coordination of the different departments of our work would
be the result.''

It was at this *general denominational meeting* that many remarks
were made upon the need for reforming the method of conducting our
Anniversaries, and for improving the existing scheme of representation.
Objections to the proposed uniform basis of representation were raised
to the effect that it was a step toward consolidation. There were also
vague references to an impression that there was competition and rivalry
between the Societies.

The Woman's Home Mission Society, during these Anniversaries,
adopted resolutions favoring coordination, and advising that a period
of five years be devoted to adjusting existing interests without the injury
of any.

At these Anniversaries also another recommendation of the committee
of which Mr. Greene was chairman was adopted, providing for an
annual joint meeting of executive boards or committees of the Societies,
but a recommendation to publish a joint missionary periodical was
rejected.

Another recommendation was adopted to appoint a committee of
nine, to consider the matter of district secretaryships of the Societies,
and the relations of collection agencies.

This was a most notable meeting. It had a marked influence upon
the growing desire for coordination and orderly procedure. It is claimed
that from this meeting, and from the report presented by Mr. Greene,
dates the denominational movement resulting in the formation of the
Northern Baptist Convention.

7. In December, 1901, in New York City, there was held an important
conference of the executive boards and committees of the Societies, in
accordance with a recommendation adopted at Springfield. At this
conference, among the questions discussed was, ''What Changes, if
Any, Are Desirable and Feasible in our Denominational Work?'' A
committee was also appointed to take into consideration the matter of

the relations of the collection agencies of the Societies. It was voted to submit the methods involved in the operation of the several Societies to a general meeting of the Societies to be held in St. Paul.

8. In May, 1902, at the Anniversaries in St. Paul, Minn., resolutions offered by Dr. Lemuel Moss, at a meeting of the American Baptist Missionary Union, were almost unanimously adopted, providing for a committee of fifteen persons who were to ascertain whether there was any lack of proper adjustment and cooperation between the three Societies, including organizations associated with them, as to fields of labor, collecting and other agencies, and methods of work, and whether there could be an improvement in the mutual relations of these agencies. These resolutions were also adopted by the American Baptist Home Mission Society and the American Baptist Publication Society. . . .

10. In May, 1904, at the Anniversaries in Cleveland, Ohio, there was another general denominational meeting at which, however, no opportunity was given to discuss general denominational matters. At this meeting, a committee was appointed to represent the Baptists of the North, in cooperation with other committees, in a proposed Baptist World Congress to be held in London. This Congress met in 1905 and was not only suggestive, but decidedly helpful to the movement for denominational solidarity. The same effect was produced by the formation of the General Convention of the Baptists of North America, in St. Louis in May, 1905.

11. In September, 1906, the Chicago Baptist Association, after listening to a notable paper, entitled "An Awakening Consciousness of Denominational Unity, What Does it Demand?" adopted the following resolution:

For years there has been a growing belief among our churches that there should be more coherence in our missionary work, and especially that our Baptist Anniversaries should be made more helpful to denominational unity. The splendid work now carried on by our several missionary Societies ought to be more widely extended; and there should be some platform from which may be voiced the sentiments of the denomination upon movements and policies which concern the denomination as a whole, and are not germane to the work of any one of our present Societies exclusively.

In view of the wide-spread dissatisfaction with present arrangements for conducting our Baptist Anniversaries, dissatisfaction which in no degree concerns the honored leaders of our denominational Societies, but which concerns arrangements and policies and precedents growing out of the nature of the organizations and their history, therefore,

Resolved, That the Chicago Baptist Association, consisting of over twenty thousand Baptists, put upon record its earnest desire for greater effectiveness in the conduct of our great annual meetings, known popularly as the Baptist Anniversaries.

In order that reasonable steps may be taken looking to improvements, this association urges the executives of our national Societies to call a joint meeting of all Societies in connection with the Anniversaries of May, 1907; that for this meeting a suitable program be provided by the executive boards of the Societies; that provision be made for the permanent organization of a general association or convention representing all the Northern Baptist churches; that one of the special functions of this association or convention shall be the appointments of a representative committee on arrangements to act in connection with the boards of the Societies in unifying and improving the exercises of all the meetings of all the Societies whose anniversaries are held each May; that this general association or convention be so organized and its objects be so stated that it shall voice to a large degree the trend of denominational sentiment and policy in such matters as touch the welfare of all the churches, leaving to the Societies the management of the great missionary and publication work which they are now conducting.

Resolved, That if no steps are taken by the boards of the Societies before April 1, 1907, to call such a general or joint meeting as proposed, the moderator of this association be empowered to appoint a committee to act in conjunction with other committees and representatives of churches in this and other States to consider the advisability of calling a general convention or association for the purposes specified.

12. In November, 1906, at a meeting of the Baptist Congress in St. Louis, Mo., a conference was held in which brethren from different parts of the country participated. It was decided to call the attention of the general Societies to the wide-spread demand for an organized expression of denominational unity. The following petition, numerously signed by prominent ministers and laymen from all parts of the country, was addressed to the secretaries of the Societies:

To the Corresponding Secretaries of   .
    The American Baptist Missionary Union; and

The American Baptist Home Mission Society; and
The American Baptist Publication Society,

DEAR BRETHREN: In view of the growing desire, most recently shown by State Conventions, district associations, and persons, for an organization through which Northern Baptists may consider the manifold interests of the Kingdom of God, and express a denominational opinion thereon, we respectfully request you to set apart, during the Anniversaries of the Societies in 1907, at least one morning and afternoon, as near the middle of the week as possible, for a meeting to consider the expediency of such an organization.

We suggest that in your call for this meeting, if you consent to issue it, each church be requested to appoint its pastor and two delegates, who shall represent it at this meeting, with power to effect the organization if found desirable.

This request is addressed to you in order to avoid even an apparent expression of any unfriendly attitude toward our heartily appreciated denominational Societies or their executive officers.

13. December 11, 1906, in compliance with the request of those brethren, the following call was issued for the meeting at which the Convention was provisionally organized:

Whereas, in various quarters a desire has been expressed for a meeting in connection with the Anniversaries at Washington, D.C., in 1907, to consider the question of a general organization of Baptists as represented in the constituencies of the American Baptist Missionary Union, The American Baptist Home Mission Society, and the American Baptist Publication Society; the undersigned acting upon the request of those interested in the subject, and with the approval of their respective boards, and representing their joint committee on the Anniversaries, do hereby formally call a meeting of those who shall be entitled to membership in these Societies, and of others who shall be formally appointed by their churches to participate in the deliberations, on Thursday evening, May 16, and Friday forenoon, May 17, at the Calvary Baptist Church, Washington, D.C., for the purpose of effecting a general organization, if it shall be deemed desirable to do so; and suggest that Thursday evening, Rev. W. C. Bitting, D.D., of St. Louis, Mo., address the body for fifteen minutes upon a motion to form such an organization, to be followed by Rev. A. J. Rowland, D.D., of Philadelphia, Pa., in an address of ten minutes in seconding the motion; these to be followed by general discussion in which speakers shall be limited to five minutes each; and that Friday forenoon be devoted to the consideration of the report of the committee on organization with an address of twenty minutes by Prof. Shailer Mathews on the functions of such an organization, followed by general discussion, speakers being limited to five minutes each.

H. L. Morehouse,

T. S. Barbour,

A. J. Rowland,

Committee.

In accordance with the arrangements indicated above, the meeting was held in the Calvary Baptist Church, Washington, D.C., on the evening of May 16, 1907. The following was unanimously adopted:

Resolved, That we, representatives of Baptist churches, in convention assembled, do hereby declare our belief in the independence of the local church, in the advisory and representative nature of the local and State associations, and our loyalty to the work of our missionary and educational Societies; and,

Resolved, That we do also affirm our conviction that, in view of the growth of our country and denomination, there is further need of a general body that shall serve the common interests of our entire brotherhood, as the individual church, the district and State associations minister to the interests of their several constituencies; and,

Resolved, That we do now proceed to organize ourselves into such a body.

It was also

Resolved, That a committee of fifteen brethren be appointed to draft a plan of organization; to which committee the matters now under discussion shall be referred for further consideration; said committee to report at the session to-morrow morning.

4. The Making and Mission of a Denomination

The spirit of a denomination cannot be very fully discerned from its patterns of organization, though they are not unimportant. In 1912 Henry L. Morehouse (1834–1917) preached the annual sermon to the Northern Baptist Convention in session at Des Moines; from that stirring address, reprinted here in substance, something of the self-understanding, goals, and spirit of the Northern Baptists in their early years can be discerned. After serving for some fifteen years in two pastorates, in 1879 Morehouse was called as corresponding secretary of the American Baptist Home Mission Society, serving in that capacity (with one interruption as field secretary) for the rest of his life. He was deeply involved in many aspects of Baptist life, for he was deeply devoted to foreign missions, was the decisive figure in the founding of the American Baptist Education Society, and was the principal originator of the denomination's pension plan, the Ministers and Missionaries Benefit Board. He deserved the tribute paid to him by one of his colleagues, "a master builder of the denomination." *Source: The Making and Mission of a Denomination* (Philadelphia: ABPS, 1912), pp. 8-11, 16-19.

In the making of our own denomination there was no man or group of men "higher up," to lay out the architectural or, if you please, the anatomical features of a comprehensive organization in accordance with which all details and specifications should be exactly followed. There was large margin for the divine factor in fashioning the structure. First came local Associations, then larger bodies, then our general missionary agencies. Each came in the fulness of the times, as it was required. There was a divine timing of events in the development step by step, stage by stage, of denominational life and power. In our own time we seem to have entered upon another stage in such development. What our fathers did in their time is not necessarily the inflexible order for us in a very different time. This is not saying that their methods were inefficient; rather, that for to-day, they are insufficient.

To-day we are engaged in the effort more closely to articulate and unify the numerous organizations of the denomination. The conception of a general organization for the United States, and even of a Baptist World Alliance is no new thing. As far back as 1824, an organization was advocated which should have direction of the missionary and educational concerns of the denomination and which eventually might become so related to European Baptists that "Baptists on both sides of the Atlantic would be united in a solid phalanx." ("Life of Wayland," also Vail on "Mobilization," etc.) "There were reformers before the Reformation." In our present endeavor, running over five years we have made progress, but apparently have not reached finality. Perhaps we have leaned too much on our own judgment, and not enough upon the wisdom that cometh from above; and so have been left to tinker at the task until the conceit be taken out of us, and we come to a keener recognition of the truth that, "unless the Lord build the house, they labor in vain that build it."

In this making of the denomination have we a clear conception of the architectural character and of the structural principles of the edifice?

What do we want? What is evidently in accord with the mind of the Spirit? We take it for granted that for substance of doctrine we are in essential accord, even though there be occasionally individual variations and aberrations. Our concern is about working methods for greater efficiency and larger achievement. We venture to formulate a statement of what our aim is, hoping that it may elicit from others something more satisfactory: Such a vital union of all our forces as shall constitute a harmonious and symmetrical whole, wherein there shall be the largest possible liberty for individual expression and initiative, and the exercise by each member thereof of its own proper functions, with wise provision for comprehensive administration of affairs in which all are or should be concerned, so that all members shall sustain conscious relationship to the entire body and the welfare of each shall be the concern of the whole; all together being a most effective instrumentality of the Spirit of God.

Were every existing organization, except the local churches, at once blotted out and the making of the denomination in this respect begun *de novo,* the task might be somewhat simplified, although probably ninety percent of these organizations would naturally be reproduced. Some of these have become deeply rooted in the life and love of the denomination for fifty, seventy-five, and even a hundred years, and for much of the time have been organically unrelated to other organizations. In the process of making, or remaking, there must be readjustments, concessions; and it jars some of these fearfully in trying to get them out of their grooves. In the bounds of the Northern Baptist Convention there are, in round numbers, one million two hundred and fifty thousand Baptists, eleven thousand churches, five hundred and sixty local Associations, thirty-nine State Conventions, ten education societies, fifty-seven institutions of learning; twenty-five charitable institutions; three general missionary and publication societies; three Women's Missionary Societies, a Baptist Young People's Union, a Brotherhood, a Laymen's Missionary Movement, and other minor organizations too numerous to mention. Many are incorporated and autonomous bodies. Now, to get all, or most of these, into one harmonious, homogeneous body is no simple task, especially when the sensitive spirit of Baptist independence resents suggestion of interference with its prerogatives, and "each individual hair doth stand on end like quills upon a fretful porcupine." Probably we have about reached the limit of such organizations. The problem is what to do with them in the making of a more coherent denomination. Principal Fairbairn says: "The Christian idea created two novel notions as to man; the value of the unit and the unity of the race." ("Philosophy of Christianity," p. 544.) We have properly emphasized individualism; it is now for us to harmonize this with the larger unity of all.

The primary unit in our denominational organization is the local church. There is no other above it. These eleven thousand churches constitute the denomination, so far as we are concerned. No local Association, no State Convention, no general missionary organization, not even the Northern Baptist Convention, is the denomination. Two thousand people at our anniversaries, half of whom came from the adjacent region, are not the denomination; are only about one six-hundredth part of it. But they may be said fairly to represent the denomination if every reasonable facility has been afforded churches to send messengers to these annual convocations. . . .

Now, *as to our mission.* We have a distinctive mission. We have also a conjoint mission. In some vital matters we differ from others. In many things we are in accord with them. We stand alone where we must; we work together where we can. No denomination has a monopoly of the favor of heaven.

What was our original distinctive mission? Was it not in and for Christendom itself? Was it not preeminently a protest against the errors in faith and practice into which Christendom in general had fallen, and an attempt to reestablish Christianity on a simple, spiritual basis? Our fathers contended for the right of private judgment in religious matters against the bitter intolerance of their time; for the authority and sufficiency of the Scripture, as against imposed creeds of human councils; for the direct communication of divine grace to receptive souls, as against all sacerdotalism and sacramentalism; for the administration of baptism according to the teachings of the New Testament, both as to mode and subjects; for the simple democracy of the early church, as against distinctions between clergy and laity and an ecclesiastical ruling body; for a spiritual church composed of regenerate souls; and for the separation of Church and State as against entrenched State-established churches. In matters of such vital moment to Christianity itself, they believed they had a divinely appointed mission, to which they addressed themselves heroically, suffering severe persecutions both in Europe and

America, being the sect everywhere spoken against for trying to turn
the religious world upside down. They were neither fools nor fanatics.
Among the leaders were men of wide learning and great ability whose
course was incomprehensible to their self-satisfied and easy-going associates in the established bodies of their day.

To what extent has this mission in and for Christendom been accomplished, and is there need still for our testimony and our activity? In
some things, other bodies formerly arrayed against us, have come to
our way of thinking. But by no means all, or even the majority. Many
are just where they were two hundred and fifty years ago.

In the matter of separation of Church and State, the leading evangelical denominations in this land are generally at one with us. But
even here, some that were importations from Europe, while accepting
the fact, only half believe in it, for in European countries where they
are dominant they hold tenaciously to this unholy union. Furthermore,
while the first amendment to the Constitution says: "Congress shall
make no law respecting an establishment of religion or prohibiting the
free exercise thereof," municipal authorities, State legislatures, and
Congress are manipulated to appropriate millions of public monies for
sectarian institutions and the avowed policy in some quarters is to press
for more. What care they for a constitutional amendment so long as at
the side door they secure generous appropriations?

In this respect our mission is not local, but world-wide, as in Russia
and other countries where our brethren suffer great disabilities and
persecution from the established order. We must make the statement of
Ambassador Bryce more conspicuously true than ever:

The lamp kindled by Roger Williams on the banks of the Seekonk
has spread its light and illuminated the minds of Christian men all over
the world. (Address at Brown Univ., 1904.)

As to baptism. We maintain that there is but one scriptural mode
with its significant symbolism, and that any other is an unwarranted
perversion and destructive of the intended symbolism; that it is only
for professed believers and not for unconscious babes; that it is binding
upon all believers in connection with their union with Christian churches,
everywhere and for all time. It is not a question of much or little water,
but of doing the right thing for which we have the weight of the world's
scholarship in our favor. While millions have adopted these views,
Christendom in general has not. We have a mission still in this respect.

And when here and there, even in our own ranks, the question is mooted whether, after all, baptism is not an outgrown rite which we may discard altogether; it behooves us for ourselves and for all Christendom to hark back to the divine authority which instituted it. Not only has it the authority and the force of the example of Jesus and his disciples, but pre-eminently also of the administrative Spirit of God on the day of Pentecost, when the apostles "spake as the Spirit gave them utterance," saying to the converted multitude: "Be baptized, *every one of you*"— "*every one of you*"; and not only so, but directed Philip "full of the Spirit," after his wonderful mission in Samaria, to baptize, "both men and women" as also the Ethiopian eunuch; and through Peter "commanded" Cornelius and his household to be baptized; and at Ephesus, inspired Paul to require the rebaptism of John's disciples upon whom, when baptized, the Spirit fell with power. Has the Holy Spirit become a forgotten factor in the authority for the institution of Christian baptism? Let us beware lest in our pedantic spirit we expose ourselves to the charge of lack of love and loyalty to Jesus Christ, and to the belittling of the Holy Spirit's supplemental and reaffirmatory teachings concerning this impressive ordinance.

John A. Broadus

Henry Morehouse

Russell H. Conwell

Ellen Cushing

Missions, Evangelism, and Education

Much of the work in missions, evangelism, and education done on behalf of the local congregations and associations was staffed and supervised by the national societies. The activities of the foreign and home mission, the publication and education societies were manifold; their annual reports, not to mention the individual reports and other writings of missionaries and agents, provide a vast mine of information. Out of a wealth of materials a few samples have been chosen to illustrate the extent and nature of outreach under the Northern Baptist banner and to point to some of the difficulties and controversies that inevitably accompanied such extensive enterprises.

1. Foreign Missions

In the 1870s the cause of foreign missions was seen as one of the major reasons for cooperation among Baptist congregations and associations. The administrative work was carried out chiefly by the various boards and societies, each of which had its own ways of working and distinctive history. A new factor in Protestant missions in those years was the formation of separate women's societies for missions, which cooperated with the existing agencies and were active in stimulating interest in missions among church women, in raising funds, and in appointing women missionaries for service abroad. In 1871 two such Woman's Baptist Missionary Societies were formed, one with headquarters in Boston and the other in Chicago; they eventually merged as the Woman's American Baptist Foreign Mission Society in 1913. In the later nineteenth century, the women's societies worked in close cooperation with the American Baptist Missionary Union, which changed its name to the American Baptist Foreign Mission Society in 1910.

Soon after its founding, the Boston women's society was engaged in encouraging the formation of missionary circles in local congregations, in promoting organizations of women at associational and state levels, in carrying on the work of publication and fund raising, and especially in appointing missionaries for mission stations, primarily in Burma but also in China and Japan. The report of the society for 1877–1878 (Selection A) lends insight into its expanding work.

One of the prominent leaders in the expansion of Baptist work in the Belgian Congo (now Zaire) was a medical missionary, William H. Leslie (1868–1935). As an appointee of the American Baptist Missionary Union, he began his work in Africa in 1893. Active in the field for thirty-eight years, he became well known as a founder of schools and a builder of hospitals. Among those he served, he was known as "Nganga Buca"—the doctor who really cares. His report for 1905 (Selection B) gives a vivid picture of missionary work in the Belgian Congo; his attitude toward Roman Catholicism was not untypical of many Protestant missionaries at that time. *Source:* A. *Seven Years of the Woman's Missionary Society, 1871–1878* (Boston: 1878), pp. 17-19. B. Correspondence Files, American Baptist Missionary Union. Archives, American Baptist Historical Society.

[A. Woman's Baptist Missionary Society]

In our seventh year, just closed, we sent out Miss Clara Bromley to Prome; Miss Ella F. McAllister to Bassein; Miss L. E. Rathbun to the Kemendine school; and Miss Mary M. Day to the Teloogoo Mission, of which her father was the founder. Miss Gage and Miss Manning returned to this country for rest and the recovery of health. Miss R. E. Batson and Miss M. Russell have been appointed missionaries at our request, and hope to go in a few months to the foreign field.

In November, 1877, Mrs. Colby, the President, went to Europe with her husband, for the restoration of his health. Her place in the meetings of the Board, and at the public meetings of the Society, has been ably filled by the Vice-President, Mrs. J. N. Murdock.

At the request of Mrs. E. E. Stevens, $1000 has been paid to build a house at Prome for the accommodation of the sick, on land given for the purpose by Government. More than half the amount has been contributed by friends in New York, Brooklyn, and New Jersey.

An appropriation has been made for a school for the Christian training of Chinese boys at Zaohying, in care of Mr. Jenkins, and one to aid in the erection of a new school-house in the Sgau Karen Mission of Mr. Vinton at Kemendine. We have now 25 missionaries, 37 schools, about 1000 auxiliaries and bands, 1,170 life members. As many new circles have been formed as in any previous year; but some have become discouraged, and failed to contribute. Receipts of the seventh year, $39,260.43.

It will be seen from this brief survey that much of the educational work of our missions has gradually come to be supported by our Society. This is in accordance with the appeals and the motives which led to the formation of the Society. It is our hope that we may be able to enlarge and strengthen this department to just the extent needed for the best interest of the cause of Christ. We long, also, to have more native Bible women going from house to house, wherever such workers are adapted to the character and customs of the people, to tell the women and children of the Saviour. But there must be missionaries fitted by character and education for the work of training these Bible women.

As we look over our foreign field, we have reason to be grateful for those whom we have been allowed to send there. They prove that unmarried women can be as brave and steady and devoted as any class of workers. God bless them every one, and supply all their need, according to his riches in glory by Christ Jesus!

What shall we say of our success at home? Year by year we have rejoiced in the increasing number of active workers, and of contributors to the treasury; and most of those who have joined us are actually learning something of the work of God in foreign lands, and of the circumstances under which it goes on. The constant demand for missionary literature is in itself an encouragement. The instruction given to thousands of children will make them more wise and willing supporters of missions than we are in the present generation. We rejoice in the assurance that the Woman's Mission Circle is in many churches what it is intended to be—a quickener of piety, a stimulating agent to love for souls, to prayer, to all forms of Christian growth and work. Its members call attention, by word and example, to the need of foreign mission work in accomplishing the object of all Christian effort—the bringing of every human soul into Christ's kingdom. And we hope our Society is helping effectively, though unobtrusively, to speed the day when every Christian shall, of necessity, as one who owes all to Christ, give and labor according to his or her ability, in making the gospel known to every creature. When that day comes,—when even the Baptist women of America may be counted on as sure, because of their abiding principle, to do their share in this great work,—we will gladly consider our mission as a separate organization at an end. But as yet we may not relax our efforts, but must rather persevere, with greater zeal and riper wisdom as the years go by.

[B. Report of Dr. Leslie]

The opening year found us still in the homeland but just beyond the time limit of the doctor's edict to abstain from all work. Three months were spent in revising and printing a larger edition of the New Testament History translated and printed on our station press during our last term of service. This beside speaking among the churches and packing fully occupied our time until we sailed from Philadelphia, April thirtieth. Our welcome when we arrived on the field was some little compensation for the pain of parting from our little ones at home. A few days and we were back in the hospital and dispensary, were repairing, building and translating as though there had been no broken health and long furlough.

The Banza Manteke district is now pretty well evangelized; but the work is scattered in a hundred little hamlets, cared for by the natives, requires attentive supervision if there shall be an all round vigorous development. As there is as great a need for medical as for evangelistic and educational work among the out-stations, I was glad to take up this department. To the isolated worker plodding along in the face of discouragement and opposition these visits are doubly welcome. One of my personal boys stationed at a far distant frontier post after bidding me a most hearty welcome looked into my face with shining eyes and said "Do you know its more than six months since I have seen a white face." They will often sit far into the night seeking the explanation of some difficult passages of Scripture found in their study and reading. Much opposition to the Gospel and many perplexing problems arise with which the young evangelist with his inexperience and lack of authority can not cope. At one new post where work had looked most promising we found the school empty and the teacher quite discouraged. The old chief who was suffering from double cataract had sent a long distance for a famous witch-doctor to discover the cause of his failing sight. After a mysterious investigation it was announced that the two most promising boys in the school were guilty of this felony. All children were forbidden to attend the school. Upon our arrival a few days later we explained the real cause of the loss of vision to a meeting of the chiefs and warned them that they would be held responsible if anything happened to the boys.

The opposition and false teaching of the Roman Catholics is an obstacle hard to endure and difficult to overcome. In one district where the people were just learning that to lay hold of salvation they must renounce their evil practices, a Catholic teacher came and told them that the demands of the Protestants were entirely unnecessary. He then put a pinch of salt on their tongues and pronounced their absolution complete. At another place not able to intimidate the teacher or completely deceive the people the chief who favored the Protestants was accused of the death of a Catholic adherent. If the chief had not been able to produce the man alive at the trial it would probably have gone hard with him. When the Catholic catechist confessed before a meeting of chiefs that he had knowingly made this charge, the people withdrew their allegiance from that faith, which precipitated another false charge against the innocent kind-hearted old chief for which he suffered a month's imprisonment since the false witnesses outnumbered the true. But the ultimate triumph of truth is certain. This affair is opening other villages to our men and closing them to Catholic teachers. At a large Belgian coffee plantation the superintendent is very friendly to our work. He says to me, "Workmen from Banza Manteke district are in general faithful from Catholic districts unfaithful. You send a many intelligent fellow to teach the people the Pere sent two boys and a harlot."

The real heathen are frequently afraid of our medicines and refuse to take them even in their extreme need. I had walked one day several miles to see a young woman who was very ill. We found her in great pain, much emaciated and very weak, but assured her that she would recover if she would take the medicine we could send. She pointed to her husband and said "Diampu diandi" (it is his affair whether I take or not.) But tho he was told she would die without our help, he neither came nor sent for medicines. But usually in this part of the country where the people have either seen or heard of the wonderful power of the white man's medicine there is no hesitation in taking any thing we give them, often with wonderful results considering the condition under which the remedies are administered. A few days previous to this in one town, a girl was brought to the tent in a dying condition. She was carefully attended that night and next morning before leaving I gave the mother medicine and careful instructions for its administration but with small hopes of her recovery. Two months later the woman came two days journey, beaming with gratitude and happiness to show me her daughter well and strong; and to be examined for baptism.

For several years our eyes have been turned toward the great valley of the Kwango river, lying about 250 miles east from here which has hitherto been untouched by the gospel. In January our conference appointed a committee to investigate the advisability of opening a new station in that region. I was the only one who seemed free to make the long journey, so attempted the work alone. With a small caravan of ten men I started about the middle of August. A few days marching took us beyond where any knowledge of the gospel had penetrated and for weeks we traveled in the most oppressive moral darkness. The great Mayaka tribe inhabiting a large part of the Kwango district was reached only after seventeen days march. They were reported to be a fierce warlike, cannibalistic people with whom no outsiders had any intercourse. Our first meeting with them seemed to verify this report, but when they were really convinced of the peacefulness of our mission, all their hostility disappeared and they became quite friendly, and offered us presents of food. To our delight we found their dialect so like that spoken on the Lower Congo that we were able to converse freely with them, even more so than with the tribes thro which we had passed. From my carriers they learned that I was an "Nganga" (medicine-man) and straightway began to bring their sick to me to be treated. Even the great chief Nlele took medicine internally without fear. Such a degree of confidence in the white man has never been shown by any other tribes in Congo, until white men have lived with them for years.

Having obtained the desired information regarding language, etc. of Mayakas, we took a trail running to the southwest to see the country and people in the Portuguese Territory. This route soon brought us again to the Zompos, the tribe to the west of the Mayakas and just across the Portuguese boundary. Many natives in this section have fled across the border to escape the oppression of the Gov't. of the Free (?) State. I was mistaken for a State official by the Zombos, and the entire expedition was in imminent danger of annihilation. For two days we were met by mob after mob of demon-like savages, each one more fierce and threatening than the last. There seemed no hope of escape but we kept pushing forward until by the Lord's help and a bold face, we not only escaped without the loss of any of our goods, but had forced our way thro where the inhabitants had sworn no white man should ever pass alive. Six days later we arrived at the English Baptist Mission station, Kibokolo, in a rather dilapidated condition, but able to continue the journey after a day or two's rest. One week after leaving Kibokolo we were safe at home, having covered 600 mountainous sandy miles in less than seven weeks. A definite site was not selected but the necessary knowledge of the country was obtained and we hope to choose a site and open work next season.

The medical work of the station which has been carried on by Dr. Mabie during my absence has little that is new to report. Sleeping sickness has claimed fewer victims than any previous year since I came to this country, but this decrease is probably only temporary and its harvest may be averaged up another year. The source of the infection is now known to be a variety of the tsetse fly and experts are seeking a remedy. The death rate has been again lowered.

The work at Mpalabala has been left in my care during the last months of the year as Mr. Harvey had to take his wife to England on account of her continued ill health. That has necessitated my making a trip down to that station once a month. The work has proceeded without interruption under the faithful native evangelists.

The year.has been an unusually trying one but Jehovah has verified to us His promise that "As thy days so shall thy strength be."

2. Home Missions

Baptist home mission work also expanded significantly in this period. During the years in which Henry Morehouse guided the American Baptist Home Mission Society, its roll of missionaries and teachers went from 236 in 1879 to 1,274 in 1917. The outreach became increasingly specialized as particular approaches to racial, ethnic, language, and religious groups were developed. The society worked especially with Indians, Germans, Scandinavians, French Canadians, Mormons, Blacks, and Mexicans as well as carrying out its missionary, evangelistic, educational, and church extension work among English-speaking Americans on the frontiers and in the cities. One of its major concerns under Morehouse was the education of the newly freed blacks; students in schools maintained for them in the South increased from one to seven thousand. It was an appropriate gesture when Atlanta Baptist College was renamed Morehouse College in 1913. A glimpse of a few items from the minutes of the ABHMS (Selection A) gives some impression of the range of the work.

As in foreign missions, women also formed their own home missionary societies, first at local and state levels and then, on the national level in 1877, an eastern and a western society. These societies became the Woman's American Baptist Home Mission Society in 1909.

One of the early prominent missionaries appointed by the western society was Isabel Alice Hartley Crawford (1865–1961), who served among the Kiowa Indians. Like many field missionaries, she kept a journal; the entry for May 10, 1898 is reproduced (Selection B). In 1906, however, Isabel Crawford resigned her post. In one of the "little churches" (Saddle Mountain, Oklahoma), which did not have a pastor, she allowed a layman,

Lucius Altsan, to administer Communion. When the Chicago-based society did not approve, she sent a letter of resignation, hitherto unpublished. After a period of rest, she continued with the WABHMS until her retirement in 1930, traveling widely among the Indian missions and in deputation work among Baptist congregations across the country. *Sources:* A. *Annual Report of the American Baptist Home Mission Society, 1879,* pp. 18-19; *1880,* pp. 16; *1881,* pp. 48-49. B. Isabel Crawford, *Kiowa: The History of a Blanket Indian Mission* (New York: Fleming H. Revell Co., 1915), p. 86. C. Isabel Crawford to the Board of the WABHMS, Chicago, 1905. Isabel Crawford Papers, American Baptist Historical Society.

[A. ABHMS Minutes, 1879]

The Committee on Indian Missions, through Rev. R. L. Luther, presented the following report, which was adopted:

The Committee on Missions to the American Indians would respectfully report:

That, while we recognize with gratitude the efficient nature of the work done during the past year by the preaching missionaries and teachers of this Society who have labored among this much neglected people, and recognizing also the success attendant upon the labors of the Southern Baptist Convention, of the Woman's American Baptist Missionary Society, and also of the Woman's Baptist Home Mission Society, we yet believe that the last command of our risen Lord, and the memory of years of unredressed wrong, demand of us a more vigorous effort than has yet been made to convey to the American Indians the blessings of the Gospel of Jesus Christ.

We therefore respectfully yet earnestly recommend to the Executive Board a more vigorous prosecution of the Indian Missions, together with such extension of the field and more thorough organization of the whole service, as may, in their judgment, be found practicable.

The Committee would also respectfully present the following resolutions:

Resolved, That we heartily commend the Proclamation of the President of the United States warning off unauthorized settlers who have encroached on the Territory, the occupancy of which is guaranteed to the Indians by treaty; and that we appeal to the Executive and to the Houses of Congress to use all needful means to protect the Indians in the enjoyment of their rightful possessions.

Resolved, That we commend to the special attention of the Executive Board the colored people formerly held in bondage among the Choctaws and Chickasaws, who have no share in the lands or school funds of the tribes; and that we earnestly request the United States Government to continue and extend the support of schools among these needy people.

The Committee on Missions to Non-English Speaking Peoples reported, through Rev. R. S. MacArthur, as follows:

The Committee on the above-named topic beg leave to report:

That they have not included in their deliberations on the subject the Indians or the Chinese, as it is understood that special committees have been appointed in the case of both these nationalities. The committee confined their attention to our work among the Germans, the French Canadians, and the Scandinavians. . . .

GERMANS

As far as the Committee have learned, the thirty-two Missionaries of this Society at work upon the German field, have reported results which are prophetic of a brightening future. Despite the most disheartening difficulties, arising from the mighty sway of Rationalism on the one hand, and Romanism on the other, among the five millions of Germans in this country, the annals of the Society indicate a series of advancements which assure us of a regular progress toward glorious and permanent results.

[1880]

The Committee on Chinese Missions reported, through Rev. Dr. Bixby, R.I., as follows:

Your Committee submit the following resolutions as their report on the Chinese Missions:

WHEREAS, God seems to be testing the genuineness of our Missionary spirit by sending the heathen of China to this country, and bringing them even into our congregations, our bible schools, and our homes; therefore

Resolved, That our Home Mission Society be requested to press this department of its work with constantly increasing energy and effort.

Resolved, That as the Chinese themselves have already given $400 towards the erection of a Chinese Baptist Chapel on the Pacific Coast, we accept this as a hopeful augury of the greater things which these people will do under proper training in this same line of direction in the future.

Resolved, That as God has so signally smiled upon the efforts of the Home Mission Society in raising up Freedmen preachers and teachers to labor among their own people in the South and in Africa, we have reason to believe that He will graciously grant His blessing upon similar efforts to raise up Chinese Evangelists and pastors to labor among their own race on the Pacific slope, in other parts of the country, and also in the Chinese Empire itself.

After an address by the Rev. Dr. J. B. Simmons, N.Y., on the "Evangelization of the Chinese," the report was adopted.

[1881]

In November the Board commissioned a man, carefully chosen, to preach the Gospel "where Satan's seat is"—in Utah. This is the first serious settled attempt in this direction. An exploring missionary was on the field a short time in 1872, but with no tangible results. Already we have a church organized in Ogden, a Sabbath-school gathered, lots secured for a church edifice which is to be erected as soon as the funds can be obtained for the purpose. It should be done at once. There are prospects also for the organization of a church in Salt Lake City. A Christian school is an indispensable auxiliary in missionary work in Utah. Ogden, the great railroad centre of the region, is the natural location for such a school. For $10,000 suitable buildings could be erected and considerable local assistance secured. The Society is prepared to proceed with the enterprise the moment the means are furnished. Other denominations, longer on the field, are doing much in this direction. One denomination expends $20,000 this year for a Christian school at Salt Lake City. The hour has come for the Baptists of the United States to have a hand in the overthrow of the immoral Mormon monstrosity which has too long disgraced our civilization. . . .

The year has witnessed decided advance in our work among the Freedmen. Ten established schools now receive our assistance. This is an increase of two over last year. These are the schools at Selma, Ala., and at Live Oak, Fla. Sixty-three teachers have been under appointment in these schools—last year there were 38. Last year 1,191 pupils were enrolled; this year 1,592. Males, 1,046; females, 546. Unconverted students who promise well are admitted to the schools. From this number 123 conversions are reported. Profound religious interest has prevailed in several institutions. Reports show that 367 students have the ministry in view. The students have paid a larger sum for tuition than ever before.

In several of the States the freed people have taken deep interest in the maintenance of these schools. In Alabama they have contributed over $2,000 for the support of teachers and for other school purposes.

In South Carolina they raised nearly $1,000 for furnishing "Colby Hall." In Florida they gave about $400 for improvement of the building at Live Oak. In Texas and the Southwest, through the agency of Dr. Marston, they have paid about $2,000 on the school property at Marshall, and have nearly as much more pledged. In Georgia they are raising funds for the erection of a building at Atlanta for the education of young women. In other States, also, something has been done, and larger things are contemplated. It is estimated that the freed people have contributed not less than $7,000 during the year for educational purposes in connection with our schools.

[B. A Blanket Indian Mission]

May 10, 1898

While the air is full of "wars and rumors of war" and letters are pouring in asking: "Are the missionaries safe?" . . . an organization was formed today that breathes of peace. It isn't a church and it isn't a women's mission circle exactly.

Our nearest Baptist church is seventeen miles away. It is into this church that all converts are baptized.

After prayerful and careful consideration we decided that it would be better to retain our membership at Rainy Mountain instead of forming a new organization.

Therefore we wrote to Chicago and asked if the Woman's Baptist Home Mission Society would recognize a mission circle composed of men as well as women.

The matter was brought before the Board and we were informed that there was no reason in the world why men as well as women might not belong to the circles *especially if they paid their dues.*

All morning we sewed on quilt-tops and after dinner the new road was explained.

"Before Jesus went away He asked all who loved him to spread the good news everywhere.

Little churches were formed and many meetings were held on the sly. The devil was mad and killed many of the first Christians. Men went out two by two to carry the news and walked till they were tired. The women did what they could and all prayed and prayed and prayed.

Men work at big things and when they stop they sit down. Women work at many little things. Their work is never done.

Their work for Jesus is different also. Men organize churches and become pastors. Women organize little mission circles in these churches and meet to pray, study, pack barrels, give and push. They do all this to obey Jesus' last command. . . .

The Woman's Baptist Home Missions Society is the name of the organization composed of all the little mission circles in our churches that sent her (Miss Reeside) to the Kiowas.

Today we are going to stand with those praying women, organize a circle and give money to send the Gospel to another tribe.

We will give money also for a church but giving the Gospel to others is way ahead. . . ."

. . . (A) man facing the sea of earnest upturned faces said: "We never heard anything like this before. We thought we just gave our hearts to Jesus, cut off our bad roads and walked as straight as we could up, up, up to the Beautiful Home.

We never knew before that we could give money to Jesus. We have heard great news today. Now I am ready to be baptized and I will give money to Jesus for my children and grandchildren as long as I live. I have spoken. . . . Isn't it kind of Jesus to *let the poor Indian give to send His Gospel to somebody else!"*

[C. Isabel Crawford to WABHMS Board, 1905]

My Dear Sisters:

I have considered very carefully your proposition that I change my resignation to an indefinite leave of absence.

Gladly would I do this if it were in my power. I love the work, am perfectly content to live and die in it, but the conditions are such that I am powerless to act other than I have.

I am a Baptist through and through from very strong convictions and to remain teacher and guide of a church not "of the same faith and order" is derogatory to the promptings of the Holy Spirit in my heart.

From the very first I have tried to impress upon the minds of the Indians the Divine origin of the church.

No organization on earth can compare with it. W.C.T.U.'s— Y.W.C.A.'s—Associations—Conventions—Anniversaries are all inventions of men, for the promotion of good, but none of them are to be compared with the church, nor in any way whatsoever pass any law binding upon the same.

To the *Church* has been committed two ordinances and the individual churches and they alone are responsible for their observance.

The pastors as the recognized heads of the churches are naturally the administrators, but when a church is pastorless it has no *right* to omit the Lord's Supper.

It may invite a neighboring pastor to come and officiate or it may appoint one of its own members to do so.

Thinking it to be in the best interests of the church I recommended that they appoint Mr. Lucius Aitsan your much beloved and consecrated interpreter to act in this capacity.

The vote was perfectly unanimous and the service was conducted with so much feeling that every heart overflowed and tears sparkled in many eyes.

Never once did we dream of trouble.

In obeying the command of the Master we supposed that everyone interested would rejoice.

Dark days came upon us unawares. We were denounced from the pulpit and reported to headquarters, threatened with exclusion from the Asso.—voted against—and finally Bro. Clouse, the only minister near enough to be with us regularly refused to come unless *I* promise *that the church* would postpone the ordinance, if for any reason he failed to appear at the appointed time.

Having no right to make any such arrangement I simply said: "If you fail us *the church* can vote to postpone the ordinance."

At Xmas time Rev. A. J. Scott expected to be with us and the ordinance was announced.

He failed us and when asked to postpone the ordinance the church said: "Let it go. We won't vote."

At that moment the Baptist Church at Saddle Mt. ceased to exist. A church without the power to observe the Lord's Supper is not a Baptist Church!

A church that bows down to any authority higher than the Holy Scriptures (sic) is not a Baptist Church! The Saddle Mt. Church is adrift: heading toward popery.

I resign. I cannot stay.

My heart rebells, my whole being rebells against the unjust, unnecessary, unscriptural pressure that is being forced upon this church to have a pastor.

May God in his infinite mercy and wisdom bring right out of wrong, peace out of turmoil, and a disposition to let the Holy Spirit rule into every heart related in any way to the work.

Sincerely,

Isabel Crawford

3. Interpreting the Publication Society's Work

Both home and foreign missions had a strong appeal among Baptists; it was harder to enlist enthusiasm for the work of publication. The American Baptist Publication Society issued a pamphlet in 1879 to make clear its functions; its brief preface presented a capsule view of its many activities.

The clipped phrases of such an overview, however, give little picture of the way the work went in the field. The account of Walter H. Brooks (1851–1945), an ABPS missionary in Louisiana who later was pastor of the Nineteenth Street Baptist Church in Washington, D.C. for more than sixty years, provides a look in greater depth at one of the many strands of the publication society's outreach. *Sources:* A. *The Work of the American Baptist Publication Society Defined* (Philadelphia: ABPS, [1879]), preface. B. W. H. Brooks, "Experiences in Louisiana," *The National Baptist,* 17 (9 June 1881), p. 364.

[A. The Work of the Publication Society]
Facts All Should Know
WHAT THE SOCIETY IS.

It is at once, a Bible Society, Book Concern, Tract Society, Colporteur Agency, and Sunday School Union of the Baptists of the United States— as provided in its Constitution, Article II.: "THE OBJECT OF THIS SOCIETY SHALL BE TO PROMOTE EVANGELICAL RELIGION BY MEANS OF THE BIBLE, THE PRINTING PRESS, COLPORTAGE, AND THE SUNDAY-SCHOOL."

HOW IT IS THIS.

As a BIBLE SOCIETY, it provides and circulates the Holy Scriptures. As a BOOK CONCERN and a TRACT SOCIETY, it publishes to the world a purely Evangelical literature, in single volumes and libraries; also tracts and periodicals, adapted to all classes of people. As a COLPORTEUR AGENCY, it employs earnest Christian laborers, who go among the neglected and destitute, carrying forth the Bible and other good books, selected from the 1,200 different publications of the Society, preaching the gospel, also, as they go, at the homes of the people, and laboring in all Christian ways for the salvation of souls. As a SUNDAY-SCHOOL UNION, it organizes Sunday-Schools, extends help to poor Schools, provides an ample literature for all, and seeks to raise all to a higher standard of excellence. As a SOCIETY OF THE BAPTISTS, its publications and work are all conformed to their convictions of the teachings of the word of God.

WHERE IT WORKS.

The field for the Society's work is the wide world, although its efforts have hitherto been mainly expended upon our own country—in the more destitute portions of the older States in the East; the newer States and Territories of the West, including those on the Pacific; among the Red men of the Indian Territory, and the Freedmen, as well as the White population of the South; and in Sweden, Italy, and Germany, in Europe. But it is equally adapted to do good to all lands, home and Foreign; and all people might alike be blessed through it, were the contributions to its treasury according to the ability of its friends.

WHAT IT HAS DONE.

During the fifty-five years of its history, it has given the world *over ninety millions of copies* of *religious publications,* large and small, making over four billions of pages that have been published; and twice that number have been circulated. Grants of libraries, in whole or in part, have been made to *fifteen hundred Ministers* and to over *seven thousand Sunday-Schools.* The Colporteurs and Sunday-School Missionaries of the Society have together performed labor equal to that of one man for about *six hundred years,* and have baptized well nigh *fourteen thousand converts,* organized nearly *five hundred Baptist churches* and *four thousand Sunday-Schools*—besides distributing an untold amount of religious literature by sales and grants.

[B. W. H. Brooks in Louisiana]

It is almost unnecessary to be ever telling the same story of ignorance and woe which we have so often told, but the more we see of Louisiana, the more we are convinced that a hundredfold more missionary work ought to be done here by the Baptists of the country. I was at a church, some days ago, and listened to the story of some little children, nine and ten years of age, who sat before the pastor, in the assembled church, and most positively declared that they had been to hell, had been to heaven, and recounted scenes which they had witnessed in hell and conversations they had held in heaven. They were received for baptism with a hearty shout by the church, and the approbation of pastor and officers. This was on a Saturday night. On Sunday, twenty-six candidates were baptized. They were all required to dress in white cotton suits, and wear a white handkerchief on their heads. The pastor, deacons, "steward sisters," "mothers of the church," and other dignataries (sic) had their heads tied up in white handkerchiefs also. In this style of dress, they marched to the Bayou La Fourche.

The sisters of the church had been appointed, the previous night, "to toat" the female candidates from the place of baptizing to the house, about a half block away, where they were to change their clothes. The "brothers" were appointed to perform the same duty for the male candidates.

The baptizing was rather a disorderly and disgraceful one. The candidates carried on at such a rate that, notwithstanding the pastor was assisted by his "head deacon," at least six of those who went down into the water were only partially immersed, the hands and arms not going under the water. As I stood near the bank of the river, I informed the preacher, when the first case occurred, that he was not burying the candidates. He thanked me, and got the next one under; but in a moment, things were worse than before.

As the candidates came up out of the water they threw themselves on the ground, miring their wet white garments, sometimes exposing themselves in an unbecoming manner. As they fell and rolled in the dust, mud and dirt, the men and women of the church would seize them and hurry them away to their dressing apartments. Of course, but a few of the sisters could attend church that night, after toiling with heavy women, carrying them by main force, from one place to another. In the afternoon, after the baptizing, the parties all dressed in white, again tied up their heads as before, (the "Steward sisters," "mothers of the church," and such high officials, wore, in addition to the regular regalia, blue sashes and silk neckties of the same color), and marched back to the church. The Lord's Supper was administered after extending the hand of fellowship to the recently baptized. Then began a scene I had never witnessed before in all my life. The preacher took the emblems each time, and turning his back to the congregation, lifted them nearly as high as his chair and muttered an inaudible prayer. Then two young preachers passed the bread and the wine, preaching in a wild and disconnected manner as they went, both crying at the top of their voices. The people groaned and mourned. Then, in the midst of it all, some

one began to sing "a shouting hymn." This caused the excitement to
reach so high a pitch that the whole congregation, saints and sinners,
came to their feet, and finally stood up on the benches and shouted and
sang in the wildest manner imaginable. It was a strange sight to see
several hundred people, singing, partaking of the Lord's Supper, standing on the benches, clapping their hands, rolling, jumping, shouting,
falling, all at the same time. This is what that people call "a glorious
time." At night, I went to this church again, and preached the best
sermon I was capable of delivering. The people were all quiet and
perfectly orderly until I was through. When I had finished, however, a
young woman began to sing, and in a moment was walking up and
down the aisles of the church, in quick, measured steps, and singing
in a rapid, wild, exciting style. As she sang and moved to and fro to
her own music, the church rose to their feet and united in the song,
and sang, and intensified the excitement until the young woman fell,
exhausted and almost breathless, into the arms of one of the "mothers
of the church." She groaned fearfully, but in ten or fifteen minutes was
herself again. The collection being taken, the church closed, and I went
home exclaiming, "My people perish for lack of knowledge.". . .

4. The Religious Education of Negroes—a Southern View

Much of the religious educational material for southern blacks in the nineteenth century
was furnished by the American Baptist Publication Society. For many Southern Baptists,
such literature was not sufficiently rigorous on doctrinal issues. Many felt the need for
a strong, centralized Southern Baptist organization to produce educational materials for
church schools and general use among both whites and blacks. This led to the formation
of the Sunday School Board in Nashville in 1891; it was soon producing an increasing
volume of literature expressive of Southern Baptist views. A typical expression of the
sentiments that lay behind the action was written the year before by George S. Anderson
(1847–1923). The substance of his article is reproduced. The Dr. Stifler mentioned was
William H. Stifler (1841–1895), pastor of churches in Illinois and Iowa and active in
Sunday school work. *Source:* G. S. Anderson, "The Southern Publication Board,"
Western Recorder (17 April 1890), p. 1.

The necessity for the Sunday-school literature published under the
auspices of the Southern Baptist Convention is apparent from the following considerations:

I. *We need the literature with which to train our children.* The
responsibility of training our children has been fixed upon us by the

Almighty and cannot be shifted to another. Religious literature is a prime means by which we meet this obligation.

The religious interests of our children transcend all others and no mistake should be made as to the character of the means by which this interest is to be subserved. Our literature, in the first place, must be sound in doctrine. Brilliant thought, profound learning, biblical lore, elegant diction, pure style, costly execution do not supply its place, but often become its greatest enemies. This is the world's age of manifold and diversified heresies. Rottenness is a fundamental characteristic of the theology of this age. The pure Baptist belief of the South is constantly menaced by the vitiated spirituality and rationalism of Germany, the depraved morality of France, the commercialism and latitudinarianism of England, and the politic-religious mixture and doctrinal looseness of the North.

But a few months ago, Southern men exposed heresy fostered upon us by the American Baptist Publication Society which resulted in Dr. Stifler's vacating his position as writer for the *Teacher*. And though it was a heresy, and though he did retire in consequence of it, the phenomenal fact exists that Southern men bear the odium of the exposure. Whilst we saved the doctrine, our good name suffered in the necessary duty of exposing the heresy.

Sound religious literature can only come from the bosom of religious society in which unyielding integrity to sound doctrine is maintained. As the fountain so will the stream be. Southern Baptists voice no uncertain sound in doctrine, and are alone qualified to supply their own literature.

In the second place, our Sunday school literature should inculcate the spirit of missions in unison with the plans and enterprises of our Southern Convention. . . .

II. They are necessary, for we must have them with which to train the negroes. The leadership and training of the Southern negroes are a responsibility that rests upon the Southern whites. In the providence of God the relation of owner and slave first existed, the two races being thus united in the same territory.

This bond has given place to that of citizenship. Thus the stronger and the weaker, the wiser and the less favored are indissolubly linked together in interest and destiny. Former relations and present conditions fix upon us the responsibility for his religious advancement. We understand his aptitudes, necessities and possibilities best, and are in deeper sympathy with him than any of his boasted friends. The self-instituted leadership of the negro from abroad is a violation of the normal relations of the two races in the South. . . .

III. The third argument for the Board and its publications is that of patriotism. It is of great moment that the South have their own institutions. Her civilization is peculiar, and the advancement of its interests should be the aim of her sons. This will best promote not only our own section, but the interests of all other sections, and of the general government. Institutions make men, men and institutions stereotype Christianity and mould civilization. A country without institutions makes no men. Men and institutions are both essential to civil life. Institutions are the foundation of society, and if we would elevate and purify the latter we must have and sustain the former. To buy our literature is to do so at the expense of our character.

. . . The South has but little literature. The publishing houses and literati are most all in the North, though many of them are contributers (sic) from the South. Religious literature gives cast to all other literature. Sunday-school literature gives genius to religious literature. Sunday-school literature is therefore the foundation of our learning. It is the soil out of which the next question will grow. It will, therefore, contribute influences which will sustain or destroy the Southern Baptist Convention, and its Boards. It is the bedrock of civilization and upon it we stand, without it we fall. The prestige and the hope of the South, honored by the integrity and ennobled by the blood, of our fathers and our brothers, demand that we perfect the plans and press the work committed to us. We have the money, the brains, the opportunity and the prospects, and will be culpable if we fall. Southern Baptists present the world's highest type of Bible Christianity. The responsibility therefore of leading the world is upon us, but if we buy our Sunday-school literature from abroad, we make others, in doing so, our leaders and thus forfeit this high trust. Previous efforts at such a Board failed for want of ability, but the difficulty is removed. The new South comes to the front in her herculean strength. . . .

5. Northern Baptists and Education

The expanding educational work of Baptists in this period was carried out through many channels and at many levels, from Sunday schools to theological seminaries. The mission and publication societies regularly planted educational institutions of various kinds as part of their work at home and abroad. One of the projects encouraged by the American Baptist Publication Society was the Baptist Young People's Union of America in 1891 in Chicago. The introduction (Selection A) to the report of the organizational meeting stated the hopes of the founders. Conspicuous among them was Frank L. Wilkins (1851–1926), who became the union's first general secretary.

New theological seminaries founded in this period often reflected the growing theological tension among Northern Baptists. For example, the statement (Selection B) issued by the Northern Baptist Theological Seminary at its founding in Chicago in 1913 made clear its conservative stance, for many Baptists in that area were disturbed by liberal trends at the Divinity School of the University of Chicago. An expression of some of the characteristic positions espoused by liberal theological educators was given at a Conference of Baptist Theological Seminaries in Massachusetts in 1918 by Gerald Birney Smith (1868–1929) of the University of Chicago's Divinity School; the paper he presented is reproduced in part. *Sources:* A. The Baptist Young People's Union of America, *Proceedings of the First National Meeting, Chicago, July 7th and 8th,* 1891 (Chicago: J. C. Drake, 1891), pp. 3-4. B. First Annual of the Northern Baptist Theological Seminary, 1914-1915, pp. 12-14. C. Gerald B. Smith, "The Indispensable Minimum of the Theological Curriculum," *Conference of Baptist Theological Seminaries . . . ,* 1918 (Chicago: University of Chicago Press, n.d.), pp. 15-16.

[A.   Baptist Young People's Union]

Christ's predicted baptism was one of fire as well as water. He was to winnow as well as save. The finest work of the forge requires the intensest heat. Truth polarizes and separates. Ephraim Peabody said of Lyman Beecher: "He has good aims and feelings, but his intellect is totally depraved." This is a sweeping statement, but it applies often to men who think that truth is a child of feeling emotion. "No matter what a man thinks if he lives right," has never been Baptist doctrine. As a man "thinketh in his heart so is he"—or, *that* he is. Baptists, per force of their thinking, have been obliged to act often singularly different from other people. Standing squarely for the word of God, taking it as the only, supreme and unalterable rule of faith and practice, they have been obliged to be as narrow as a railroad train that runs upon the identical track laid for it; narrow as the boat that must, in order to secure safety, keep the channel; narrow as the nurse who uses the doctor's prescription rather than her own.

"The Baptist Young People's Union of America," has been formed not in *protest* or in *opposition*. It is not a new organization really, but a reorganization. If, as we have sometimes been told, we represent the "department of navy," we have only sought to organize the navy so as to accomplish the most good. "For Christ and the church." We fall in with that, pledge to work might and main for Christ, and nominate the Baptist church as our most immediate and practical field of operation.

No love is genuine or sincere that asks sacrifice of principle or conscience. Equality of inspiration, unity of enthusiasm, or oneness of purpose expressed in mass convention, will not hide nor diminish honest points of difference. The exoteric clock, foreign, and with all the value of an import, must keep time so as to rightly guide the humblest few, or, for truth's sake, they must go by their *own* little watch, even if they be deemed esoteric and narrow. We say to all men, far and near, "Brothers, we believe that as things are we can help the cause of Christ, help you—of whatever Christian name—help our own church, and the world, the most by this organization." Our work is organized. It was a memorable day for us when it was done. We came to the supreme moment carefully, prayerfully, well-advised, and the convention herein faithfully pictured, was the result of honest, manly, sincere love, sacred conviction, open and free discussion.

Perhaps it will be the most timely and just thing to say, and not invidious when said, that to Rev. F. L. Wilkins belongs, in this place, a few words of merited approbation. Nobly did he labor, faithful was he in every detail of plan, fair in every argument, and sweet but firm in his purposes as a Luther or a Knox. Asking only the most reasonable things, he and his co-workers were at last rewarded, by seeing organized, officered, located—headquarters at Chicago—the Baptist Young People's Union of America. With no organic relation with other bodies; free to co-operate with any strictly Christian and philanthropic movements that may have in them Christ's glory and the weal of men; fraternal and sweet towards its older sister, the Young People's Society of Christian Endeavor, yet thoroughly Baptistic—this newest society of Baptists was born. The utmost harmony prevailed. It was done. This convention will certainly mark the beginning of a new era and development in the life of our denomination, and fulfill, we believe, some of the highest purposes and plans to which, as a people, we have aspired.

The Union, if only true to the brilliant prophecies uttered above its infant head, will mean better education in Bible lore, more thorough training for religious work, more intelligent consecration to Christ (and his and our church), more aggressive measures in missions, and a finer social and denominational *esprit de corps* than our Baptist boys and girls have ever known. Of course, it is another wheel in the machine, and it looks, now, as if it might be a drive-wheel, which means a loftier, nobler speed toward the millennium glory heaven promised and Christ foretold.

All the things set forth in this faithful stenographic copy of proceedings were done in love, and out of fair, sweet fidelity to principle. Such fidelity evermore has had its reward. When all was dark, as the midnight of despair, and no future shone upon the Gethsemane that should grow green through his tears and blood moistening it, the Lord Christ flinched not, but was true. The last generation of downy cheeks and bearded faces mingled in awful sacrifice for freedom and native land in the red tide of war, and so ennobled the flag we love as that its crimson stripes will forever speak to us of their blood. Baptist history is a monument, as we see it, of the fidelity of our fathers. They have left us principles distinctive, scriptural, and eternal. By these principles, and for His sake who loved the church and gave himself for it, let us stand.

[B.] A Statement Concerning The Northern Baptist Theological Seminary of Chicago

"The things which thou hast heard from me, among many witnesses, the same commit thou to faithful men who shall be able to teach others also."

Brethren of the Baptist Churches, Greetings:

After a full year of prayerful consideration a representative group of Baptists has opened a new School of Theology in the city of Chicago. The majority of these brethren having membership in the Second Baptist Church petitioned that body to endorse and co-operate in the solemn enterprise. On condition that the new seminary should be founded upon a sound doctrinal basis in general agreement with the New Hampshire Confession of Faith and should select a majority of its trustees or directors from members in good standing of the Second Baptist Church, the church unanimously voted its approval, and extended to the seminary, if started, the services of its pastors so far as they might be needed, and the use of class rooms and library rooms within the church meetinghouse until the seminary should have fit quarters of its own.

The general opinion of the denomination was accorded due respect in the ascertaining from many denominational leaders their probable attitude toward the new seminary. The replies from numerous pastors, professors, presidents and other representative Baptists of marked ability and devotion were so cordial and commendatory as to confirm the founders in their conviction as to the will of God.

The Divine Hand was observed in a quick succession of providences and The Northern Baptist Theological Seminary held its first assembly on the 23rd of September, 1913.

Its first session was one of marked spiritual power. Among those present were two pastors who had studied theology under Nathaniel Colver, the first pastor of the Second Church and the founder of the Chicago Baptist Theological Seminary.

The provisioned faculty had been carefully selected by the board of trustees and leaves little to be desired in either scholarship or reverence toward the Word of God.

The courses are marked by eight characteristics:

I. They aim at sound scholarship. The instructors are men of learning; the text books are the most comprehensive and thorough known in the Christian vocation, and the library facilities are excellent.

II. The courses aim to embody the principles, methods and matter of the great constructive Baptist educators, such as John A. Broadus, Augustus H. Strong, A. J. Gordon, Henry G. Weston, B. H. Carroll, A. H. Newman, H. C. Mabie, and Francis Wayland.

III. They stress the positive, changeless and glorious doctrines of grace as opposed to the negations of the New Rationalism.

IV. They do not neglect the study of the original languages of the Word of God, and in fact urge all students without exception to undertake at least New Testament Greek and elementary Hebrew, but they give the premier place to thorough courses in the English Bible.

V. They are so constructed as to give due prominence to the practical problems of Christian leadership in all departments of the Christian worker's activities. Schools of Method in Evangelism, Sunday School, Social Service, Young People's Work and Missions are emphasized more than usual. The "How" of the evangelist, the pastor and the missionary is considered most important.

VI. The courses are taught in an atmosphere of prayer and reverence. The co-operation of the Holy Spirit as the "Spirit of power and love and of a sound mind" is constantly reckoned with and depended upon. The spiritual life of the student is considered of the first importance.

VII. The courses are blended with the practical activities of the

BAPTIST LIFE AND THOUGHT: 1600-1980

students in the great laboratory of the heart of Chicago's most needy wards. The location of the school is of profound value for the practical efficiency of its students. All students must do practical Christian service. A small but definite parish is assigned to each pair of students.

VIII. The courses aim to add to the regular Baptist Seminary instruction the best features of the Bible Institutes of the country. The doctrinal basis of the school, however, is uncompromisingly Baptist.

For these reasons the founders of the Seminary venture to ask the prayers and kindly co-operation of their brethren throughout the country and especially in the field of the Northern Baptist Convention where the doctrinal statements of the vast majority of the churches are in full accord with that of the Seminary, which is substantially the New Hampshire Confession of Faith.

Brethren! the Baptist hour in history is upon us!
This is no time to abandon our position and enter into vain compromises either with Rationalists or Pedo Baptists, Romanists or Materialists. The need of today is for well-equipped, devoted, unselfish, accredited Baptist pastors, evangelists, teachers and missionaries, men who are not ashamed of the unchangeable Gospel of Redemption as revealed in the inspired Word of God.

[C.] The Indispensable Minimum of the Theological Curriculum
In discussing this subject I cannot do any better than to lead you through some of the considerations which have emerged in our own conferences at Chicago concerning the demands of the present crisis on a theological curriculum.

However much we may talk about living in a totally new world and having totally new tasks before us, it is inevitable that anything which we may attempt will have its historical connection with what men have been doing previously. We cannot start *de novo*. Nevertheless, the curriculum which we have inherited and which we have recently been modifying to a greater or lesser extent rests upon a certain conception of Christian thought which is being sharply challenged in our day. That conception, briefly stated, is this: that Christianity is to be regarded as a religion which came into existence, not through historical development but as an authorized system given through revelation, and which has been in the world complete from the first. The task of the Christian minister, on this conception, is to derive from this divinely revealed system such aid and strength as the world may need.

Theological education from this point of view would consist in making a religious leader a complete master of the system. Since, by hypothesis, that system was given to us fundamentally, if not exclusively, in the Bible, the mastery of the Bible would be the primary aim of a theological curriculum.

Systematic theology and practical theology simply reinforced and made effective this view, which was dominant in all the other departments. This ideal gave an education and technique admirably adapted to the age in which it was developed, and built itself into great and noble systems of theology.

Within the past generation or two we have become aware of a shifting interest. Everyone is more or less conscious that the kind of ideals we have in our modern religious life are not exactly coincident with those that have come down to us.

The following characteristics of the new interest and emphasis may be mentioned: (1) The conception of divine rights has given way to a conception of popular and democratic rights. We appeal no longer to the "divine right of kings" but to the human rights of the people. This is a movement which so far as we can judge is likely to go on gathering momentum. It is what we really mean by the growth of democracy. (2) Akin to the first change is the shift of emphasis from the idea of conformity to the idea of investigation, exploration, and discovery. The world is full of this kind of experimental activity; and it is coming to be true, even in religious work, that the man who has made experiments is likely to speak with more authority than the man who simply expounds precedents. (3) A third characteristic which seems to be dominating the world today is the shift from what I may call classical study to technical and vocational study. The students who are engaged in scientific study are more serious as a rule than the classical students, the reason being that at every step the student in engineering is distinctly preparing himself for a vocation, while in the classical course a man seldom sees how he can use his Greek and Latin in a vocation. The adverse criticism of our theological seminaries is largely due to the suspicion that they are providing a somewhat impractical kind of classical education. The attitude of criticism, however, soon disappears if men discover that the seminary is doing something besides digging at Hebrew roots. (4) A fourth change, which is perhaps the most important, is that which is being greatly accelerated by this world-war. That is the disappearance of provincialism and the acquiring of a world-conscience. We are not thinking in the terms of our little locality or our country. We are not even stopping with Europe, but are going to Asia, China, and Africa. We cannot read the newspapers without learning that the whole world is tied up together.

What, now, shall be the attitude of the seminary toward these changing ideals? Shall it set itself deliberately to combat these movements and to re-establish in greater vigor a conception of a rigid ecclesiastical control, wherein a man's religious duty is not to reason why or to question but to obey orders? We have in our own denomination, as in other denominations, a strong demand for the revival of a kind of literalistic education which will make conformity to authority the sufficient basis for religious education and church work. But the seminaries represented here have all been working toward a different conception. They have been honestly attempting to shift the emphasis, so as to serve this new world in which we are living. To use President Mullins' fine phrase, "The most important thing for a minister is that he shall live as a citizen in the world in which he has got to live."

In the endeavor to free themselves from petty ecclesiastical prejudice, theological teachers have been increasingly adopting the method of free critical scholarship in the realms of biblical and historical study. A somewhat elaborate technical apparatus has been developed, and much freedom of judgment has been encouraged. But does this critical biblical and historical scholarship really serve the demands of the modern age?

Back in the nineties many ministers believed higher criticism to be a new kind of gospel, and it was looked upon as a preliminary to a genuine religious revival. Young men went out and attempted to introduce into their churches critical methods of studying the Bible, and that method has gained considerable headway among the leaders of education.

But the process of elaborate literary criticism furnishes a minister with a high brow technique which he cannot use in the pastorate as he could in the seminary. Indeed, much critical teaching leads to a scholasticism which is as dry as the older scholasticism. Mere critical scholarship has not solved the problem. With all our endeavors to bring the scholastic curriculum into touch with the modern world, we have been in danger of developing just a different kind of scholastic curriculum.

The first essential of a virile theological education is that the student shall learn to think of his Christianity, not as a scholastic system, but in terms of a new world-vision. People are today rising out of their provincialism.

How are we to get the men to think in terms of a new world-vision? Either the modern minister must have the best type of a college course—for that is where you get acquainted with the world-movement—or there must be provided for the student who is not a college graduate something entirely different from the traditional curriculum. Such a student should have a theological-college course. This course should be orientated, not from the traditional point of view of the seminaries, which made one acquainted merely with standardized Christianity, but from the point of view of the broadest possible practical knowledge of modern life. So among the minimum prescriptions should be such courses as "The Rise of the Modern World," "The History of Democracy in the Modern World," "Religion in the Modern World," "Modern Social Problems," and the like.

The second indispensable element is a sense of historical growth. The minister should know how the Old Testament religion came to be what it was. He should know that New Testament religion is a historical movement. He should understand the Nicene Creed as the result of a historical process. And he should realize that Christianity is still growing and developing. . . .

Mexican Mission Orphanage, 1899

Spelman College Campus, 1883

Relationships with Other Baptists and Christian Groups

After the Civil War, there was some hope that Baptists North and South might reunite; however, continuing sectional, racial, and theological differences were too great. As both conventions grew in size and as they pursued their evangelistic and missionary purposes, they did come into conflict with one another over practical issues. Various meetings were called to provide ways to adjudicate differences, assign boundaries, and promote cooperation in advancing the Baptist cause. As new territories were opened in the West and were gained as a consequence of the Spanish-American War, giving both conventions room to expand, comity arrangements were made. How the two major predominantly white conventions should relate to black Baptists involved considerable tension, negotiation, and adjustment.

The spirit of cooperation was further encouraged in the early twentieth century by the emergence of the Baptist World Alliance in 1905. The leading Baptist conventions of the United States joined this international body. To go beyond cooperation into union between Baptist conventions with their congregational polity is no easy matter. Yet the Northern and Free Baptists did accomplish a union in 1911.

As the movement for wider cooperation among evangelical Protestant churches expanded in the early twentieth century, its leading institutional expression became the Federal Council of the Churches of Christ in America, organized in 1908. Charter members included Northern, National, Free, and Seventh Day Baptist conventions.

1. Efforts Toward Cooperation in Home Missions

A move by the American Baptist Home Mission Society in 1868 to bring about more effective cooperation with the Southern Baptist Convention bore little fruit. In 1879 a southern college president, Isaac T. Tichenor (1825–1902), offered a resolution at the annual meeting of the Southern Baptist Convention. As he later explained, the resolution was intended to encourage cooperation, but not at the expense of diminishing separate Southern Baptist organizations. However, this was not entirely clear at the time. A substitute motion, introduced by John A. Broadus (1827–1895) of the Southern Baptist Theological Seminary at Louisville, was adopted. Both resolutions are given.

In 1882 Tichenor was named the executive head of the SBC's Home Mission Board and provided strong leadership for its expansion. The two home mission agencies, North and South, largely went their individual ways. Their conflicts from time to time necessitated a series of conferences beginning at Fortress Monroe in 1894 to adjudicate differences. *Source: Annual of the Southern Baptist Convention, 1879*, pp. 14, 26.

[Tichenor]

WHEREAS, the time has come when all who believe in Jesus should work mightily for the deliverance of the nation from the bondage of sin; when the voice of Divine Providence calls us to greater sacrifices and nobler efforts to secure the triumphant coming of His kingdom; and,

Whereas, the cordial co-operation of the Baptists of the United States would tend greatly to promote their efficiency in this grand work; and,

Whereas, the love of Jesus and the wants of dying men demand that, allowing "the dead past to bury its dead," we, leaving the things which are behind, should press forward to deliver the kindreds of the earth, from ignorance and vice, and bring them into the liberty wherewith Christ is able to set them free: therefore,

Resolved, That five brethren be appointed by this Convention to bear to our Baptist brethren of the Northern States, at their approaching anniversaries, expressions of our fraternal regard and assurances of our readiness to co-operate cordially with them in promoting the cause of Christ in our own and all foreign lands.

Resolved, That we respectfully suggest to them the propriety of holding, at some convenient time and place, a meeting of representative men from all sections of our common country, to devise and propose such plans of co-operation between this Convention and other Baptist bodies of the United States as may best contribute to the more efficient working of the Baptist brotherhood, to the good of all men, and to the glory of our Redeemer.

[Broadus]

The committee, to whom were referred the resolutions on co-operation with our Northern Brethren, have had the same under consideration, and instruct me to report the following resolution:

Resolved, That five brethren be appointed by this Convention to bear to our Baptist brethren of the Northern States, at their approaching anniversaries, expressions of our fraternal regard, and assurances that, while firmly holding to the wisdom and policy of preserving our separate organizations, we are ready, as in the past, to co-operate cordially with them in promoting the cause of Christ in our own and foreign lands.

2. Comity in Puerto Rico and Cuba

Though there was conflict between Northern and Southern Baptist interests in the southern and southwestern states, when Puerto Rico and Cuba came under American control in 1898, an amicable division of territory was accepted. A conference between representatives of the SBC's Home Mission Board and the ABHMS was held, where the following resolution was adopted, and later approved by both the principal organizations. *Source:* Minutes of the Board of Managers, 1898, ABHMS. Archives, American Baptist Historical Society.

The principal matter for consideration by the conference was to determine the relations of the two bodies in prosecuting work in the islands of Cuba and Porto Rico. After a full and frank discussion of the whole subject, the following preamble and resolution was unanimously agreed to:

Whereas, in the providence of God, Porto Rico has become a part of the United States territory, and Cuba has been brought under our temporary military control, thus liberating these islands from the dominion of Spain; and, whereas, there is an urgent call for the vigorous prosecution of evangelical missionary work among the people on these islands; therefore,

Resolved, That in the opinion of the conference, held this 23d day of November, 1898, in the City of Washington, D.C., and representing the two great Home Mission Societies of American Baptists, North and South, with a constituency of two and one half million communicants, it is expedient that the following division of territory should be adopted by the Societies represented, viz: that the American Baptist Home Mission Society should prosecute its work in the Island of Porto Rico, and in the two eastern provinces of Cuba, while the Home Mission Board of the Southern Baptist Convention should prosecute its work in the remaining provinces of the Island of Cuba.

3. Cooperation in Mission: Black and Northern Baptists

Black Baptist Congregations, associations, missionary societies, and state conventions grew rapidly after emancipation as the newly freed people found that the churches were the main public institutions under their own control. Yet, until the twentieth century, blacks were predominantly rural people and of limited economic ability; hence the assistance of other Baptists was important to them. However, they had good reason to want to keep control of their own agencies. For example, the following letter to the American Baptist Missionary Union from the first president of the Lot Carey Foreign Missionary Convention, a group that separated from the National Baptist Convention in 1897, illustrates the point. The letter was written by Calvin Scott Brown (1859–1936), founder and president of the Waters Normal Institute. *Source:* C. S. Brown to H. C. Mabie, Correspondence Files, American Baptist Missionary Union. Archives, American Baptist Historical Society.

Rev. H. C. Mabie, D.D.,
Boston, Mass.

My Dear Brother:—Your letter of the 7th instant came to me today; and, being anxious to arrange terms of cooperation between the (American Baptist) Missionary Union and the Lot Carey Foreign Mission Convention, I hasten to write again. I am aware of the fact that the terms offered us are in harmony with suggestions made when I was in Boston in May; but, submitting them to our board, I find they do not fully satisfy my brethren. I therefore renew my efforts and labors in this direction, hoping that we may be able to agree on terms that will be acceptable to both parties. Our brethren seem to be exceedingly jealous about their rights and want recognition in the management of affairs; and, while it is needful that there be ''some central authority whose voice shall be decisive on all questions of policy, etc.,'' still, for the good of the work among us, the matter might be so adjusted as to have my brethren feel that they share in a measure this honor and responsibility. I appreciate what you say regarding the position assigned our organization as not being subordinate, but rather ''auxiliary and coordinate,'' and yet if the terms are made public, it will be hard to explain to the people that we maintain a separate and coordinate exist-ence. I would not have you think, however, that we mistrust you, or think that you would deprive us willingly of any right or privilege essential to our existence as an executive body. Your aim is to do the best thing in the best way. Now allow me to make a few suggestions concerning terms which would very likely meet the approval of our board.

In relation to cooperation between the Lot Carey Foreign Mission Convention and the Missionary Union in Mission Work, the following terms are hereby endorsed:

1. All cooperation missionaries shall be elected by the Lot Carey Convention subject to the approval of the Union.

2. The Lot Carey Convention shall regulate and pay the salaries of all missionaries so chosen, sending all remittances through the Secretary (Treasurer) of the Union.

3. The Lot Carey Convention shall also provide funds for the outfits, transportation, and working expenses of the missionaries.

4. The Lot Carey Convention shall maintain its own organization, raise its own funds, and be consulted on all matters affecting the work of their missionaries in the foreign field.

5. The Union shall afford a base of operation on the field, so far as its resources will permit, and as, in its judgement, may be thought wise and best, make all remittances abroad, and exercise immediate supervision over the work.

6. Each missionary shall be required to send a report quarterly to the Secretary of the Lot Carey Convention, and a duplicate report to the Missionary Union.

7. This plan of cooperation may be terminated by the Convention or the Union at six months notice.

Now, my dear brother, these terms would very likely suit our brethren, and would produce no serious disadvantage to you. If we can get started (at) once, we can from time to time work the terms to suit the situation better. Cooperation is right, is desirable; please indulge our presumption, until we can get our brethren to see. Brother (C.C.) Boone desires to go to the Congo, and he wishes to labor as a Cooperation Missionary. An early reply is respectfully solicited.

Yours very truly,
C. S. Brown.

4. Cooperation for Negro Education: Northern and Southern Conventions

Racial tensions in the early twentieth century, when patterns of segregation were widespread and "Jim Crow" legislation made a travesty of "separate but equal" shibboleths, had their continuing impact on Baptist life. Efforts to deal with problems involving relations between white and black Baptists led to the naming of a Joint Commission, which presented the following report, adopted by both Northern and Southern conventions. The seminary mentioned was founded at Nashville in 1924 as the American Baptist Theological Seminary. *Source: Year Book of the Northern Baptist Convention,* 1919, pp. 222-224, and *Annual of the Southern Baptist Convention,* 1919, pp. 64-68.

Report of the Joint Commission
OF THE NORTHERN BAPTIST CONVENTION AND THE SOUTH-
ERN BAPTIST CONVENTION APPOINTED TO STUDY OUR RE-
LATIONS AS BAPTISTS TO THE NEGRO QUESTION IN THE
UNITED STATES, AND TO REPORT TO THE TWO CONVEN-
TIONS THEIR FINDINGS, TOGETHER WITH SUCH RECOM-
MENDATIONS AS TO THEM MIGHT SEEM WISE AND PROPER.
To the Northern Baptist Convention:

Your Commission have held two meetings; one at Mount Eagle, Tennessee, in the summer of 1918, and one at Washington, D.C., early in the year 1919. A majority of the members appointed by both Conventions were present at the first meeting: all were present at the second.

The Commission organized by electing Rev. J. B. Gambrell, D.D., of Fort Worth, Texas, as chairman; Rev. Carter Helm Jones, D.D., of Philadelphia, as vice-chairman; and Rev. Clifton D. Gray, Ph.D., of Chicago, as secretary.

The data necessary to enable the Commission to arrive at conclusions and to formulate recommendations were available only in the field of Christian Education. The specific recommendations in this report are limited, therefore, to this one field.

Your Commission desire, however, to express their conviction that possibilities for helpful cooperation will be found in every field where need for Christian helpfulness and service exists. It is their conviction, therefore, that the Commission should be continued and made a permanent Commission of the two Conventions, and they so recommend.

The following facts with respect to the education of our Negro Baptists give much food for thought:

The Baptists, with two-thirds of all church-members of the race—that is, with twice as many as all other denominations put together—have but one-fourth the total number of schools, but one-third of the secondary and college students, and but one-fourth of the annual income for the schools. In other words the other denominations have about six times as many schools in proportion to their church-membership, about four and one-half times as many secondary students and about five times as many college students in proportion to their church-membership, about six times as much income and about five times as much school property in proportion to their church-membership as have the Baptists.

The figures with respect to theological training are equally disquieting. The available figures are only approximately correct but it is fair to assume that as regards the different denominations they are relatively correct. These figures indicate that *the other denominations are educating in their schools sixteen times as many men for the ministry in proportion to their church-members* as we are educating. There is no doubt that the Baptists are falling far behind their brethren of other names, and that there is a most urgent call upon our denomination to multiply its efforts for the ministerial training of Negro Baptist preachers. The opportunity to provide Christian leadership for the Negro is open to us above all others.

After a full discussion of the educational needs of the Negro, and of what is involved in creating for the race an adequate trained leadership, the Commission are unanimously of the opinion that the time has come when it is the part of wisdom for the two Conventions to cooperate fully and on equal terms in the maintenance of higher training-schools for the Negro, to the end that Christian leaders of his own race may be raised up who shall be equal to the tremendous responsibilities that must rest upon them in the days to come. Your Commission therefore recommend:

First, That the principle of cooperation in our educational work for the Negro be approved by both Conventions. Secondly, That this cooperation be put into effect as soon as practicable;

(a) In connection with all of the "Major Schools" for the Negro which are now maintained by the American Baptist Home Mission Society;

(b) In connection with the new Theological Seminary for the Negro in which the Southern Baptist Convention is interested; and

(c) In connection with such other institutions as may be agreed upon in the future.

Thirdly, That, after deducting the income from present endowments, the amount remaining in the budgets for these schools to be raised among the churches and individuals shall be assumed in equal proportions by the proper Society or Board of the Northern Baptist Convention, and by the proper Board or Society of the Southern Baptist Convention each year.

Your Commission believe it to be to the best interests of the cause of Christ that there should be cooperation between the Northern and Southern Baptist Conventions and the National Baptist Convention, and possibly with other Negro Baptist organizations also, in their efforts to promote Christian education for the Negroes in our land. But we hold "denominational control" through genuinely representative Baptist bodies to be essential to all effective cooperation between organized Baptist forces. We hope, therefore, that such changes will be made in the constitution of the National Baptist Convention as may be necessary to make it a genuinely representative body, and as will place its Convention officers on the same basis as the unsalaried officers of the Northern and Southern Baptist Conventions.

Fourthly, That, whenever the constitution of the National Baptist Convention has been so changed, it be invited to enter into full cooperation with the Northern and Southern Conventions in the field of Christian education for the Negro.

Fifthly, That general responsibility for any school maintained by the Joint support of the cooperating bodies be vested in a local Board of Trustees made up of members nominated or appointed by these bodies; that each cooperating body as quickly as possible assume its full pro rata share of the expense of maintaining the school; that it then have equal representation on the Board of Trustees with the other cooperating bodies; and that such changes in the charters of the schools as may be necessary to provide for such representation be secured if, and when, the above recommendations have been adopted by the two Conventions.

Respectfully submitted,
The Joint Commission.

(Signed) Members from the Southern Baptist Convention

J. B. Gambrell,
W. J. McGlothlin,
O. L. Hailey,
R. H. Pitt,
E. W. Stevens,
Z. T. Cody,
B. J. W. Graham.

Members from the Northern Baptist Convention	Carter Helm Jones,
	F. M. Goodchild,
	F. T. Galpin,
	A. S. Hobart,
	Geo. R. Hovey,
	Smith Young,
	Clifton D. Gray.

5. The Baptist World Alliance

A major Baptist achievement in the early twentieth century was the formation of what has come to be called in ecumenical circles a "Christian World Communion." Supported by the great majority of Baptists in America, the Baptist World Alliance, which has met every five or six years (with some irregularities), has come to play an important part in Baptist life. John H. Shakespeare (1857–1928), a British Baptist leader, wrote an introduction to the published proceedings of the first Baptist World Congress in London in 1905 out of which the Alliance grew; the piece provides an illuminating reflection on an event of Baptist history. *Source: The Baptist World Congress, London, July 11-19, 1905; Authorized Record of Proceedings* (London: Baptist Union Publication Department, 1905), pp. v-vi.

In issuing the official report of the proceedings of the first Baptist World Congress, it seems fitting to put on record an introductory statement as to the origin of the Congress, the method of organisation adopted, and some general impressions of its value, influence and lessons.

The desire for a world gathering of Baptists has been expressed by several influential men within the last five years, but it was left to Dr. J. N. Prestridge, of Louisville, Kentucky, to give the necessary driving force to the suggestion. In an editorial in his paper, *The Baptist Argus,* two years ago, he pleaded for a meeting of the leading officers of the various Baptist Unions with a view to a Congress. Later, he appealed to Dr. Clifford and myself. We favoured the holding of the Congress itself at an early date. Dr. Prestridge obtained opinions from Baptists in different parts of the world, published them in his paper, and when it was found that the project would meet with universal acceptance, a resolution of invitation was adopted by the Baptist Union, assembled at Bristol, October, 1904, for the Congress to be held in London in July, 1905. A strong Baptist Union Committee was elected, representatives were added from the Committee of the Baptist Missionary Society, and the work of preparation began. Special Committees were formed to deal with the different sections of this great undertaking.

At this point a serious initial difficulty arose. It was clearly impossible, in the short time available, for me to carry through the details of the organisation without assistance of a very high order, unless I could be entirely liberated from the regular secretarial work of the Baptist Union. The unanimous choice of the Committee fell upon the Rev. W. T. Whitley, M.A., LL.D., the pastor of Fishergate Church, Preston, as my assistant secretary, and on Mr. Harold Knott, M.A., as assistant organising secretary. Dr. Whitley had the great advantage of being known in Australasia and America by most of the leaders of the Baptist Societies in the two continents. His church freely liberated him for an average of three days a week, and during the last month for continuous service. His patience, courtesy, untiring industry and business-like method have been beyond praise. A pleasant episode during the preparation for the Congress was that he won the Jay Gould prize of £200 for the best work on the Douay Version of the Bible. Mr. Harold Knott was able generously to give his whole time to the work of the Congress. Trained by Dr. Maclaren, he has been recognised among Baptists for some years as one of their finest characters and ablest workers. For three years he laboured as the secretary for Lancashire on behalf of the Twentieth Century Fund. Deeply imbued with the spirit of the Quakers, and disliking any recognition other than that of the Great Master, he might easily escape the tribute which is his due. As general secretary I have the happiness to record that, through a time of strain and tension, the harmony and good understanding between my assistant secretaries and myself have been absolute and complete.

The most important fact of the Congress is that it has been a World Congress in the sense that representatives came from almost every country upon earth. We scarcely expected that the representation would be so large or so varied. Of course, the largest contingent was from America. Canada, Germany and Sweden also contributed a great number of delegates. Considering the distance, Australia nobly supported the gathering. Never before had we realised the strength, determination and consecration of our brethren in the various countries of Europe. The Russian delegates, headed by Baron Uixkiull, who had suffered so much and who had most of them been imprisoned or fined, were undoubtedly the heroes of the Congress. One Baptist preacher came even from far Tiflis. The picturesque element was supplied by the negro brethren, of whom about fifty were present, and who were cheered and seen everywhere. Indeed, the cordiality of their reception was so marked that one American was heard to say, ''Would you rather be the governor of your State or a negro delegate in London?''

The tone of the Congress has been marked pre-eminently in two directions. First, it has been distinctly evangelical. It was not only that from the simpler negro delegates there was the unqualified declaration of loyalty to the Gospel and the Bible, but the Congress sermon preached by Dr. Strong, one of the profoundest theologians of the United States of America, asserted with the utmost vehemence the essential doctrines of Christianity. From first to last there was no wavering note on any of the great realities of faith. The other note was that of optimism. The American host was naturally jubilant, but even from those countries where the Baptists are few in number, poor and, in some cases, persecuted, there was the same certainty that at the end of the day the Baptist propaganda would triumph, and that the Evangelical Church, under the pressure of sacramentarianism, would be led back to primitive doctrine and practice with regard to baptism.

6. A Black Leader Addresses the Alliance

Many addresses were delivered at Baptist World Alliance congresses; some were routine reports, while others stirred the great audiences. A memorable address, reprinted in part, was presented at the second Alliance congress in Philadelphia in 1911 by Elias C. Morris (1855–1922), who served for twenty-seven years as the president of the National Baptist Convention, Inc. *Source:* Elias C. Morris, ''The Negro Work for the Negro,'' *The Baptist World Alliance, Second Congress, Philadelphia, June 19-25, 1911, Record of Proceedings* (Philadelphia: Harper & Brothers, 1911), pp. 286-290.

BROTHER PRESIDENT, LADIES AND GENTLEMEN:

Having had the honor of attending the first meeting of the Baptist World Alliance, and having enjoyed the privilege of making a few remarks in that meeting, I deem it extraordinary to be given a place on the program at this time, and beg to assure you that I fully appreciate the distinction that this appointment gives.

I recognize that I am speaking to the representatives of an irresistible army of Christians—those who are in line with the direct successors of the apostles of Jesus Christ and who, upon the doctrines of Jesus Christ, are as firm as Gibraltar. To be in the presence of such representatives is sufficient to give renewed inspiration and courage to any speaker.

You will pardon reference to the fact, that while I appear to you as a Baptist, yet I come as the representative of a denomination of Christian people commonly known in the United States as Negro Baptists, whose principal missionary organization is the National Baptist Convention. While these are not different in doctrine or practice, they are separate and distinct from the white Baptists in many things. But we are proud of the fact that we represent one-third of all the Baptists in the world, having a certified membership of two million two hundred and sixty-one thousand communicants.

I am asked to speak upon "The Negro Work for the Negro." This theme as indicated is in plain accord with the polity of American Baptists as well as with my own ideas as to the most effective way to direct religious efforts among any people. It is not to be understood, however, that there are or should be any color or racial lines drawn in the kingdom of grace, but rather it is my purpose to give emphasis to the fact that in undertaking any great work the matter of adaptability must be taken into account in the employment of factors, if success is to abundantly follow the effort. . . .

Let me localize my subject for a brief moment. For a number of years following the close of the Civil War in this country, the great heart of the Christian people North and South went out to the emancipated, and many devout white Christians came to the Negro people to do missionary and educational work among them. Their effort met with signal success. But as the Negro people became educated, it developed that they preferred teachers and preachers from among their own race; hence, the strength of the race was turned towards educating teachers and preachers, so as to supply their schools and churches. The Negroes felt, and rightly so, I think, that their ministers and teachers should associate with them, should eat and drink in their humble homes, and do by contact, by social example much that could not be done by anyone in the schoolroom or pulpit alone. Owing to the wide race distinctions, this could not become a rule with the white ministers and teachers, and the most that they could do without sacrificing their social standing among their own people, was to preach, teach, and baptize the Negroes. The Negroes, as a rule, were opposed to the social intermingling of the races, preferring to maintain their peculiar racial identity. Hence, the demand for Negro churches and Negro preachers became imperative.

In the matter of separation in the church life of the people on this continent, the blacks have been the beneficiaries to a very large extent. This has enabled them in the forty-five years of their freedom to establish more than one hundred high schools and colleges, twenty-seven thousand church houses with a valuation of forty million dollars. They have also twenty-five thousand ordained ministers, and more than ten thousand well-educated men and women who are teaching in schools and preaching in churches, while others are successfully following the professions of law and medicine and all other vocations. Then, again, the Negroes have enrolled fully fifty per cent of the entire race in this country in Christian churches. This, in my opinion, is a showing which cannot be made by any other race in so short a time, and is due largely to the fact that the Negro people regard their ministers as their God-appointed leaders, and, as a rule, accept their teaching without question.

But in speaking of the Negro work for the Negro, we are including a larger range of thought and territory than that which applies to the Negroes of the United States, and we hope to make it plain that the Negroes of the United States are the logical Christian leaders of the black people of the world.

In the beginning of the Negroes' life as freemen in the United States, a wise Providence directed that the race should make as the base of its future the principles of Christianity, taking as guide, that Scripture which says. "Seek ye first the kingdom of God and His righteousness, and all these things shall be added unto you." They believed then and believe now that whatever else is necessary to complete a well-rounded Christian civilization must follow in its time. That their choice was wise will be seen by making comparison with other emancipated people who were emancipated during the past century. . . .

But, my friends, I would have you know that it is a condition which warrants what I have here said. For I firmly believe that the time will come when there will be "neither Jew nor Greek, bond nor free," white nor black, European nor American, Asiatic or African in the kingdom of God, but all will be one in Christ Jesus.

But until that time shall come, we should work along, recognizing the metes and bounds set by an All-Wise Creator, who will, in His own time and way level the hills and mountains: and raise up the valleys, until this division of labor and distribution of tasks shall unite to promote the oneness of Christ and His cause the world over. . . .

7. Tensions of Church Union

Though the General Conference of Free Baptists was a much smaller body, the differences between it and the Northern Baptist Convention were minimal. Their polities were essentially the same, and as the historic Calvinist emphases of Baptists in the North had modified somewhat (largely in consequence of nineteenth-century evangelical trends), the theological differences between them and the more "Arminian" Free Baptists had largely evaporated. The move to unite the two was strong; yet when a small denomination enters into a union with a larger one, the small one's fear of being swallowed up usually emerges. The following letter by Alfred Williams Anthony (1860–1939) to Alvah S. Hobart (1847–1930) discloses such anxieties and reveals a familiar phenomenon of merger negotiations—members of each side will break away rather than enter into such an arrangement.

Anthony, a direct descendant of Rogers Williams, was a prominent figure among Free Baptists. A New Testament scholar, he taught at Cobb Divinity School, a department of Bates College in Maine. He chaired the committee to work out the details of the union.

The doubts to which he referred were largely resolved. The second, "general" letter outlines the way the Free Baptist interests were to be safeguarded in the union. When the merger took place in 1911, Anthony resigned his teaching post to become secretary and treasurer of the General Conference so that funds and property would not be misused and the Free Baptist witness would not be lost. *Sources:* A. A. W. Anthony to A. S. Hobart, 18 January 1909. Alfred Williams Anthony Papers, American Baptist Historical Society. B. A. S. Hobart and others, general letter, 1 October 1910. *Ibid.*

[A. A. W. Anthony to A. S. Hobart, 18 January 1909]

Your favor of the 16th instant is received. I confess to entertaining a good many anxieties. I am exceedingly sorry for the situation which has arisen. I do not quite know how serious it is, for I do not yet understand the attitude of your people. I hope the attitude of the Free Baptists is plain. I have tried to be frank, and explicit, and I am confident that the majority of our people are disposed to be generous in their attitude and action. I am confident that most of us feel sure that if Union, as proposed in the Basis, can be inaugurated, these various matters will in time work out to a satisfactory conclusion. We cannot, however, preserve our self-respect, and hopefulness, if we look forward to a straight-jacket, or the lash of discipline. We wish to anticipate nothing more and nothing less than toleration. We do not ask for approval, for any position which seems to our brethren "irregular"; and we ask for nothing which we are not ourselves perfectly willing to grant. We do not ask that Baptists should become as we are. We know full well that there are a great many things in the Baptist bodies which do not represent the Free Baptist position; and it is to these things that some of us in the associations and yearly meetings which have not voted unanimously for Union, have objected; and yet the majority of us have, and eventually, I am confident, all of us will raise no objection, provided we are allowed the same degree of liberty and toleration. I do not know how real union can otherwise be anticipated excepting upon this basis of toleration; and it seems to me that the platform which has been framed admirably meets the necessity of the situation, and promises, if carried out in spirit, a real union, however one might term it, whether co-operation, or Union.

The most serious situation now, so far as Free Baptists are concerned, arises from the disturbance in their work which this whole discussion has caused. You Baptists have hardly given the matter consideration, I mean referring to the rank and file of the church. It has not stirred your people profoundly. Only a few now are interested in any way; but Free Baptists in New England, and the middle states (I am excluding only those along the Southern borders of our constituency) have been deeply stirred; it is a matter which has been discussed in all their local bodies, and in most of their local churches; and now if the whole subject is held in suspense, or is finally defeated, then we are sure to have internal conditions which will seriously threaten our peace and prosperity. We have gone too far to easily turn back. Did I not profoundly believe in an overruling providence, which shapes all things for good, when intended righteously, I should be alarmed for the welfare of our Zion. We have preserved in the midst of this discussion, and the unrest which is inevitable, a remarkable unanimity. Now if this Union fails, or even appears to fail, there will be those who will say "I told you so"; some will break away, as some have already done; others will be discouraged; some may flare up and go elsewhere.

It has been a serious matter with us Free Baptists, this whole question of Union. We have not taken it lightly; but have considered it a question which related to our very existence. I do not think you Baptists are justified, for any slight cause, in rejecting the plan. There is a kind of honor which should hold you, if it is possible for you to continue, steadily to the execution of the plan. I know it is difficult to see far ahead in situations of this kind; but it is exceedingly unfortunate that a condition like this should now arise which had not been several years ago anticipated.

It is true that the final action of the Free Baptists has not yet been taken; and may not be taken for one or two years yet; but in their constituent bodies action has in reality already been taken, and a commitment to the plan of Union made. What remains to be done by Free Baptists would be in reality but formal and technical.

I await your further advice and wishes in this matter, with a great deal of anxiety. I am writing to no one but you for the present. Should I write to anyone else? Is there anyone who ought to hear from me directly? I am not quite sure how your committees are organized, whether I shall appear to have left out some Secretary, or other Chairman, with whom I ought to correspond. Kindly advise me, as I do not wish to leave anything undone which may reasonably be expected of me.

[B. Alvah Hobart to the Free Baptists]

Allston-Boston
October 1, 1910

DEAR BROTHER:

A committee representing the Baptist missionary societies, and the General Conference of the Free Baptists met in New York Sept. 19 to complete the arrangements for consummating the union of Baptists and Free Baptists as already provided for by votes of the denominational meetings.

Having formulated the plan for the immediate steps it was thought desirable that the various local organizations such as Yearly Meetings, Associations and State Conventions should be informed of the steps taken.

The undersigned were appointed a committee to draft and send to them a statement of the case and to suggest some things which seem to be desirable for all the constituency of the denominations to do.

The action taken by the conference committee was as follows:—

Voted; That a Committee representing each Baptist organization be appointed which shall send to the conventions and yearly meetings, a communication counselling that steps be taken by each to send fraternal delegates to each other, and to caution both parties that the Free Baptist Yearly Meetings or churches should not be disbanded until they are notified by the General Conference Board that it is legally safe to do so.

The general plan for co-operation as recommended by this Committee shall also be made plain to the Conventions and Yearly Meetings.

It seems desirable also that the various state organizations should as the autumn meetings come on seek to have fraternal delegates, in attendance on the meetings of the other denomination, mutual acquaintance being necessary for the promotion of that union which we seek to bring about. We suggest therefore that fraternal delegates be appointed by the State Convention of Baptists and the Yearly Meeting of Free Baptists.

It is also very important that the original caution which has been kept in mind by both parties in all the conferences—namely to keep the Free Baptist organizations intact until they are notified that the disbanding of organizations can be done with safety to the denominational funds and property—should be now observed, and that in whatever unions may be made with Baptist organizations by Free Baptists the old Free Baptist organizations be kept up in form. This will not necessitate a separate place or time of meeting, but a meeting for business may be held by the old Free Baptist organizations at some convenient hour in connection with the union meetings. As soon as all the legal necessities are complied with the General Conference will notify the Free Baptist organizations.

The spirit of the conference at New York was very gratifying to all the committee, and is a token of coming fellowship which will not disappoint the best expectation of those who have labored so long for its accomplishment.

Fraternally yours,

> REV. ALVAH S. HOBART, D.D.
> 4 Seminary Avenue, Chester, Penna. representing the American Baptist Home Mission Society.
>
> REV. THOMAS H. STACY, D.D.
> Concord, N.H.
>
> and REV. R. D. LORD, D.D.
> 593 Bedford Avenue, Brooklyn, N.Y. representing the General Conference of Free Baptists.
>
> REV. A. J. ROWLAND, D.D.
> 1701 Chestnut St., Philadelphia, Penna. rep-

resenting the American Baptist Publication
Society,

REV. E. P. TULLER, D.D.
Allston-Boston, Mass. representing the
American Baptist Foreign Mission Society,

8. The Federal Council of Churches

The emergence of official cooperation among Protestant churches has been a divisive
issue among Baptists. When the Federal Council of the Churches of Christ in America
was organized in 1908, thirty-three denominations joined; among them were four Baptist
conventions: Northern, Free, Seventh Day, and National. But many Baptists, both in the
conventions that joined and even more in those that did not, were reserved about the
council, while others were opposed to it. Selections from articles in Baptist weeklies
show some of the nuances. In *The Standard* the report was descriptive but affirmative;
in *The Watchman*, the response was much more guarded. *Sources:* A. Jane A. Stewart
"Protest and Churches in Federation," *Standard*, 56 (19 December 1908), p. 456. B.
James W. Willmarth, "The Federal Council, Part 1," *Watchman*, 90 (17 December
1908), p. 20.

[A. Report on the Federal Council]
The first assembly of the great Federal Council of the Churches of
Christ in America, at Philadelphia, the first week in December, has
attracted wide attention and focused public interest on the development
of the spirit of cooperation among the different divisions of Protestantism.

"While churches are separate as the billows, they are yet one as the
sea," was the basic principle of Christian unity, illustrated by the
gathering, which was composed of over 300 delegated representatives
from twenty-eight different denominations, backed by a constituency
of more than 15,000,000 confessed Christians.

The entire group of Protestant churches was thus brought into close
contact. Episcopal bishops fraternized with those of the Methodist
church. Baptists, Presbyterians, Congregationalists and Lutherans clasped
hands in brotherhood. Friends, Moravians, Mennonites, Disciples of
Christ, and representatives of nearly a score of less numerous denominations, extended brotherly greetings to each other and to the preachers
of the Negro churches, who were conspicuous in the assembly.

Moderators and bishops, editors of religious journals, presidents and
professors of theological seminaries, colleges and universities, heads

of mission boards, leading clergymen and laymen, senators and congressmen were among the members of the council. The Governor of Kansas, the New Jersey state commissioner of charities, and a judge of a federal court were listed among the delegates. Each denomination in sending its delegates seems to have selected its leading men. But there were no women delegates—an omission it is almost impossible to understand, for there are in most denominations, consecrated and able women in positions of high responsibility in the work of the church.

The Delegates.

Of bishops there were more than a score—thirteen of them being Methodists, three Southern Methodist, seven Negro Methodist, three Episcopal, one Mennonnite, five United Brethren and four Negro Zion Methodist.

Among the thirty-four Baptist delegates were President Judson and Dean Mathews, of the University of Chicago; Congressman Henry K. Porter, of Pittsburgh; Secretary Sears, of the Pennsylvania Baptist State Convention; Samuel A. Crozer, of Upland, Pa.; Dr. J. B. Calvert, of The Examiner, New York; Rev. R. G. Boville, secretary of the National Vacation Bible-school Committee; Dr. H. B. Grose, of the American Baptist Home Mission Society; and W. N. Hartshorn, of the International Sunday-school Association. . . .

The Federal Council does not pose as a legislative body. Its purpose is simply to effect a combination for harmonious work in all problems outside of church doctrine and administration. It has long been recognized that there are many questions of morals and public interest, settlement and missionary work in which all denominations can do better work by uniting and conferring than by acting alone. The council consequently becomes a great clearing house for the suggestions and interchange of methods and plans as well as a consolidation for concerted action. It acts through its standing committees, each one of which was given a place upon the program for a presentation of its previously prepared and carefully digested statement on the topics assigned. These included "Week Day Instruction in Religion"; "Interdenominational Organizations"; "Cooperation in Foreign Missions"; "State Federations"; "Local Federations"; "Organization and Development"; "The Maintenance of the Council"; "The Church and the Immigrant"; "The Church and Modern Industry"; "Home Missions"; "Temperance"; "Sunday Observance"; "Family Life"; "Religious Instruction in Higher Institutions"; "International Relations"; and "Religious Instruction Through the Sunday-school"; all printed and distributed in a 100-page paper covered book, to the delegates who thus had opportunity beforehand to read and digest the text of the questions to be presented for discussion.

Discussion

Nearly every chairman in presenting the report of the committee, followed it by the introduction of concise, clear resolutions or recommendations of a practical nature, to be acted upon by the council; and if endorsed, thus made part of the future propaganda. Some of these subjects, as that of Sabbath observance, peace, Sunday-school work, etc., embodied the common consensus of opinion already established in the churches and carried without discussion. Others were of a more radical nature and called forth amendments and active discussion before adoption. Still others were quite strenuously opposed. . . .

[B. A Reluctant Response]

It seems to me that the true path to unity or towards unity is in another direction. If all "evangelical Christians" would heartily adopt the principle that the New Testament ONLY is our authoritative and absolute rule of faith and practice, it would be a long step in advance. It would not bring outward unity at once—for "the meaning of the Bible, that is the Bible" and men differ in their interpretations. But this principle would lead to the discarding of all causes of division growing out of the creeds, forms and traditions of men. Then coming to the study of the New Testament, relying on the guidance of the Holy Spirit, would not spiritual men gradually come to such an understanding of the truth, that outward union would inevitably follow?

For example, the scholarship of the world now justifies our contention that the baptism of the New Testament was the immersion of believers. Suppose that all the bodies represented in the Federal Council were to adopt this view practically, an enormous hindrance to the oneness of Christ's people would instantly vanish. Some other examples could be mentioned.

I should hope much more from an attitude, even approximate to what I have set forth, than from a good natured acceptance of all manner of sectarian differences, at the same time minimizing their importance.

What if in such an attitude the absolute authority of Christ should be lost sight of and the traditions of men be put on a level with the teachings of divine revelation? Where would this process stop? Might it not divert attention from the supreme importance of obedience to Christ, and with baleful results?

Suggestions for Further Study

A good general approach to this period is Albred H. Newman, editor, *A Century of Baptist Achievement* (Philadelphia: ABPS, 1901) which focuses on the nineteenth century in the characteristic optimism so evident among Baptists, North and South. The appropriate sections of Robert G. Torbet, *History of the Baptists* (Valley Forge: Judson Press, 1963) and Robert A. Baker, *Relations Between Northern and Southern Baptists* (Ft. Worth: 1948) are also informative. Black Baptist history is the subject of Edward A. Freeman, *The Epoch of Negro Baptists and the Foreign Mission Board* (Kansas City: Central Seminary Press, 1953) and James M. Washington, "The Origin and Emergence of Black Baptist Separatism, 1863–1897" (Ph.D. Dissertation, Yale University, 1979). There are two books about Baptist women in this era: Eleanor Hull, *Women Who Carried the Good News* (Valley Forge: Judson Press, 1975) and Bertha G. Judd, *Fifty Golden Years: The First Half Century of the Woman's American Baptist Home Mission Society 1877–1927* (Rochester: Dubois Press, 1927).

For northern Baptists, denominational unification and reunion were important issues. The creation of the Northern Baptist Convention is documented and explained in W. C. Bitting, editor, *A Manual of the Northern Baptist Convention* (Philadelphia: ABPS, 1918) and the union with the Free Baptists is described in Alfred W. Anthony, *Further Steps in Union* (Lewiston, Me.: n.p., 1915). Free Baptist organizational life and missions are detailed in a series of essays entitled *The Centennial Record of Freewill Baptists 1780–1880* (Dover, N.H.: Printing Est., 1881) and Mary A. Davis, *History of the Free Baptist Women's Missionary Society* (Boston: Morning Star Pub., 1900).

In addition to strictly denominational identity, Baptists also participated in various forms of cooperative Christianity. A scholarly prelude was the Baptist Congress, the *Proceedings* of which were published annually, 1880 to 1913. Northern and Southern Baptists joined the Baptist World Alliance, whose early story is told in J. H. Rushbrooke, *The Baptist World Alliance in Retrospect and Prospect* (London: B.W.A., n.d.). Northern Baptists joined the Federal Council; this story is the thrust of Samuel M. Cavert, *The Churches Allied for Common Tasks . . . 1916–1920* (New York: Federal Council of Churches, 1921). The application of ecumenical principles to mission is recounted in Robert T. Handy, *We Witness Together: A History of Cooperative Home Missions* (New

York: Friendship Press, 1956), which also contains data about prominent Baptists in the movement.

To varying degrees, Baptists were also respondent to the new thrusts in evangelism, the institutional church, and the social gospel. On revivals and evangelism, compare William G. McLoughlin, *Modern Revivalism: Charles Grandison Finney to Billy Graham* (New York: Ronald Press, 1959) with W. L. Muncy, *Evangelism in the United States* (Kansas City: Central Seminary Press, 1945). Marion L. Bell has examined a specific series of revivals in which Baptists were involved in *Crusade in the City* (Lewisburg, Pa.: Bucknell University Press, 1977). The institutional church is styled in Edward Judson, *The Institutional Church: A Primer in Pastoral Theology* (New York: Lentilhon & Co., 1899) and promoted in Russell H. Conwell, "The Institutional Church," *Temple Magazine* (June 1893). Robert T. Handy, editor, *The Social Gospel in America 1870–1920* (New York: Oxford University Press, 1966) is the standard introduction to accompany Walter Rauschenbusch, *A Theology for the Social Gospel* (New York: Macmillan, 1917), Samuel Z. Batten, *The Christian State* (Philadelphia: Griffith and Rowland Press, 1909) and Shailer Mathews, *The Social Gospel* (Boston: Pilgrim Press, 1910).

Henry C. Vedder, *A Short History of Baptist Missions* (Valley Forge: Judson Press, 1927) provides a summary of northern and southern Baptist mission endeavors. For foreign fields, consult A. H. Strong, *A Tour of the Missions* (Philadelphia: Griffith and Rowland Press, 1918) for specific status reports from an astute observer. SBC work is detailed in Mary E. Wright, *The Missionary Works of the Southern Baptist Convention* (Philadelphia: ABPS, 1902), and Lewis G. Jordan, *Up the Ladder in Foreign Missions* (Nashville: National Baptist Pub. Bd., 1903) traces developments among black Baptists. Two good examples of overseas mission work in the era are: Dana M. Albaugh, *Between Two Centuries* (Valley Forge: Judson Press, 1935) and Charles K. Harrington, *Captain Bickel of the Inland Sea* (New York: Fleming H. Revell, 1919).

The starting point for information on home mission efforts is undoubtedly Henry L. Morehouse, editor, *Baptist Home Missions in North America 1832–1882* (New York: ABHMS, 1883); of particular relevance are the reports and histories of educational efforts among the Freedmen and the development of the ethnically diverse mission conferences. Other important individual treatments are Wilmoth A. Carter, *Shaw's Universe: A Monument to Educational Innovation* (Rockville, Md.: Natl. Pub. Co., 1973); A. J. Holt, *Pioneering in the Southwest* (Nashville: Sunday School Board, 1923); Joanna P. Moore, *In Christ's Stead* (Chicago: WBHMS, 1902). Charles H. Sears, *Baptist City Planning and City Man* (Valley Forge: Judson Press, 1926, 1928) are classics on urban mission strategy.

As in other periods, biographies provide useful information for the era plus personal insights. See especially the following: Charles H. Banes, *Benjamin Griffith: Biographical Sketches* (Philadelphia: ABPS, n.d.); Joseph R. Carter, *The 'Acres of Diamonds' Man: A Memorial Archive of Russell H. Conwell*, 3 vols. (Philadelphia: Temple University, 1981); Helen C. A. Dixon, *A. C. Dixon: A Romance of Preaching* (New York: G. C. Putnam's Sons, 1931); George R. Hovey, *Alvah Hovey: His Life and Letters* (Valley Forge: Judson Press, 1928); Herbert W. Hines, *Clough: Kingdom-Builder in South India* (Valley Forge: Judson Press, 1929); Asahel C. Kendrick, *Martin B. Anderson: A Biog-*

raphy (Philadelphia: ABPS, 1895); Jeff D. Ray, *B. H. Carroll* (Nashville: Sunday School Board, 1927); A. T. Robertson, *The Life and Letters of John Albert Broadus* (Philadelphia: ABPS, 1910); W. O. Stearns, *et. al., William Newton Clarke: A Biography* (New York: Charles Scribners Sons, 1916); Augustus H. Strong, *Autobiography,* edited by Crerar Douglas (Valley Forge: Judson Press, 1981); Charles H. Sears, *Edward Judson, Interpreter of God* (Philadelphia: Griffith & Rowland, 1917); Dores R. Sharpe, *Walter Rauschenbusch: A Biography* (New York: Macmillan, 1942).

The era of 1880 to 1920 may well be the "golden age of Baptist theologies." In addition to the well-known William Newton Clarke, *An Outline of Christian Theology* (New York: Charles Scribners, 1898), Edgar Y. Mullins, *The Christian Religion in Its Doctrinal Expression* (Valley Forge: Judson Press, 1917), and A. H. Strong, *Systematic Theology: A Compendium and Commonplace Book Designed for Students* (Rochester: E. R. Andrews, 1886), major texts were authored by G. D.B. Pepper (1873), E. H. Johnson (1891), and Ezekiel G. Robinson (1894); also much in demand was Charles A. Jenkins, *Baptist Doctrines* (St. Louis: Burns, 1880). On matters relating to worship, T. H. Pattison's *Public Worship* (Philadelphia: ABPS, 1900) usually accompanied John A. Broadus, *On the Preparation and Delivery of Sermons* (New York: Sheldon, 1870). Edward T. Hiscox's, *Standard Manual for Baptist Churches* (Valley Forge: Judson Press, 1890) and *The Star Book for Ministers* (Valley Forge: Judson Press, 1877) were the popular guides to church practice, while Free Baptists relied upon *The Book of Worship* (Dover, N.H.: Freewill Baptist Printers, 1866). Northern and Southern Baptists cooperatively produced *The Baptist Praisebook for Congregational Singing* (New York: A. S. Barnes, 1871), which served churches for several generations.

Original sources for this era include organizational records, personal papers and periodicals. ABHS administers the archives of the Northern Baptist Convention and societies plus the Baptist Missionary Training School, the Baptist Institute, Leland College, and the Spanish American Baptist Seminary; also, the personal papers of Samuel Z. Batten, John E. Clough, Ellen Cushing, William H. Doane, J. C. Massee, Grace Nuveen, Walter Rauschenbusch, John R. Straton, Augustus H. Strong, Henry C. Vedder, and Cornelius Woelfkin. Andover Newton has collections for Alvah Hovey and W. H. P. Faunce and the University of Chicago manages the papers of William R. Harper and Shailer Mathews. Major periodicals for Northern Baptists include *The Watchman* (Boston) and *Examiner* (New York; merged in 1911), The *National Baptist* (Philadelphia), *The Standard* (Chicago) and the *Baptist Home Mission Monthly;* for Southern Baptists, *The Baptist Argus, Foreign Mission Journal* and *Home Field;* for Baptists in Canada, *The Canadian Baptists* and *The Maritime Baptist;* for Freewill Baptists, *The Morning Star* and for the German Conference, *Der Sendbote.* All of these titles are available in microform through ABHS.

Section V
The Modern Era
1920–1980

Still unresolved for American Baptists was the problem of disunity among Baptist bodies within the United States, the degree to which they should become more involved in the deepening ecumenical developments within Protestantism, and the quest for self-identity and a discovery of the true meaning of the church and ministry in a rapidly changing culture. In some respects American Baptists had come of age; in other respects they stood with uncertainty upon the threshold of a new age.

Robert G. Torbet, 1963

Baptist life in America since 1920 has been set in a time of rapid change, startling contradictions, serious troubles and also great challenges and opportunities. The period began with a depression following World War I. But that was nothing like the Great Depression that came in the 1930s, an especially difficult time for all aspects of American life including organized religion. In this modern era also were periods of marked prosperity, notably the 1920s and the 1950s, but even in such times all too many lived in poverty, which often bore with particular weight on racial and ethnic minorities. The period opened with dreams of lasting peace, but the realities turned out quite differently as World War II occurred, followed by the Korean and Vietnam wars, a continuing arms race, and the fear of nuclear destruction.

The modern era was also a time of striking technological advance: the development of automobiles and the highway system, the improvement in radio and then television communication, the shift from railroads to jet planes in passenger transportation, and the spectacular achievements in space travel. Advances in medicine and sanitation increased life expectancies. That factor plus continuing immigration meant that the population of the United States more than doubled in this period from just over 105 million to about 225 million sixty years later. To maintain an increasingly highly organized industrial civilization required higher levels of education. The percentages of the population with high school, college, and graduate education went up; and vast universities, public and private, became a sign of the times.

Sociologists have pointed out that modernization has been accompanied by secularization as secular modes of thought have become more evident in the common life. Yet the era was also marked by a period of general religious revival and renewal in the 1950s and early 1960s, when estimated church membership involved some 64 percent of the population. Certain religious groupings, especially conservative Evangelicals and Pentecostals, continued to grow rapidly.

The Protestant world was torn early in the period by the bitter Fundamentalist/Modernist confrontations. In more moderate form the tension between variant perspectives has continued. The search for forms of cooperation and unity among Christians gave vigorous life to the ecumenical movement, especially in the middle decades of the era. The National Association of Evangelicals was formed (1943), the Federal Council of Churches joined with other cooperative agencies to become the National Council of Churches (1950), and many American denominations joined the World Council of Churches (1948).

The neoorthodox movement in theology then hoped to find a middle way between liberals and conservatives. Though the movement had wide influence, it was not long lasting and was followed by such differing trends as resurgent neoevangelicalism and various forms of liberation theology.

Roman Catholicism entered a new phase of ecumenical openness to other churches as a consequence of the pontificate of John XXIII (1958–1963), the Second Vatican Council (1962–1965), and the election of a Catholic, John F. Kennedy (1917–1963), to the American presidency. With the passage at the Second Vatican Council of the Declaration of Religious Freedom and the Decree on Ecumenism, the way was cleared for increasing dialogue and cooperation with other churches. At the same time criticism came, from both inside and outside the churches, of former "triumphalist" and "imperialist" motifs in Christian life. Even so, churches placed a greater emphasis on the value of dialogues with those of other religions, especially Judaism. In the shadow of the horror of the holocaust, anti-Semitism was deplored by many Christians.

Baptist life and thought could not but be affected by the achievements, strains, troubles, and tensions of such a paradoxical and disturbing era. As in the previous period, the primary focus here is on Northern/ American Baptists.

Reuben E. Nelson

Helen Barrett Montgomery

Walter Rauschenbusch

John Roach Straton

Baptists and the Major Currents of American Religious Life and Thought

According to rough estimates, probably somewhat inflated, the number of Baptists in the United States increased from some seven million persons to nearly four times that number from 1920 to the present. Significant growth occurred among Southern and National Baptists; the Northern Baptists (since 1950, the American Baptists) have netted more moderate increases, from about 1,300,000 to about 1,600,000. In part this limited growth resulted from inner theological tensions and the departure of dissenting groups, for the Fundamentalist/Modernist controversies of the period had a divisive impact on Northern/American Baptists.

American Baptists were deeply involved in the ecumenical movement, though they preferred cooperative and conciliar approaches to church union movements. National Baptists were somewhat less involved, and Southern Baptists were involved very little as they did not join the National or World Council of Churches.

Neoorthodox theology, a strong current in ecumenical life in the 1950s, influenced almost all theological thinking when it was at its peak, having its most direct influence on American Baptists. The more recent resurgence of conservative evangelical theology has been congenial to many Baptists in all of the conventions; a number of the conspicuous leaders of the neoevangelical movements have been Baptists.

Baptists have also played leading roles in the movements for racial equality, civil rights, and peace with justice during the troubled decades of the modern era. Though such movements have aroused controversy, various official statements from the Baptist conventions support them.

355

Also controversial has been the movement for women's rights and for larger roles for women in church and society. Women have won the support of many Baptist conventions both at the outset of the period, when woman's suffrage had just been won nationally, and then more recently as the new feminist movement emerged.

1. The Fundamentalist/Modernist Controversy

The growing tension between liberal and conservative religious and theological perspectives came to a head in the decade of the 1920s. Some of the leaders of liberalism had moved away from the evangelical or Christocentric liberal position to a more anthropocentric view; they were strongly influenced by evolutionary thought and critical approaches to the Bible. In their view of "last things" their stance was postmillennial as they sought to "build the kingdom of God on earth." The leadership of conservative forces was often seized by fundamentalist leaders, who generally favored supernaturalist and premillennial interpretations of Christian faith and a literal interpretation of the Bible. Moderate middle ground was largely obscured as the cleavage widened.

Baptists played a prominent role in the World's Christian Fundamentals Association, founded in 1919. A Baptist Bible Union was formed, and at a meeting in Kansas City, Missouri, in 1923 it adopted bylaws, aims, and resolutions (Selection A has excerpts). It frankly committed itself to driving its opponents out of the Northern Baptist Convention. It had no hesitation in naming those opponents, especially Cornelius Woelfkin (1859–1928), pastor of Park Avenue Baptist Church in New York, and Harry Emerson Fosdick (1878–1969), a prominent liberal preacher who favored open membership (the reception of members from other Christian bodies without requiring them to be baptized by immersion).

The latter had their strong supporters, both in their own settings and nationally. For example, when Dr. Woelfkin resigned from the Park Avenue Church, the church chose Dr. Fosdick as pastor, thereby committing itself to inclusive church membership, a larger building in the vicinity of Columbia University, and a new name (it became The Riverside Church). A long statement on the matter was issued by congregational leaders, from which several paragraphs are excerpted. *Sources:* A. *A Call to Arms!* Pamphlet issued by the Executive Committee of the Baptist Bible Union of North America (n.p., n.d.[1924]), pp. 14-15, 17-18. B. "Statement Made by Mr. James C. Colgate on behalf of the Joint Board of Deacons and Trustees at the Church Business Meeting, held Friday Evening May 22nd, 1925, . . ." Archives, American Baptist Historical Society.

[A. Resolutions of the Baptist Bible Union]

Whereas, the unproven hypothesis of evolution is being increasingly advocated in the name of science, thereby deceiving the unsophisticated undergraduate of the day into a supposition that it is an established verity, and

Whereas, many professors in our state and increasingly in our denominational schools, having themselves been prejudiced in their student days in this direction, are now telling our sons and daughters that this theory is demonstrable and ought to be accepted, and

Whereas, the theory itself, in addition to being unscientific, is unscriptural, anti-Christian and even atheistic in its entire nature and tendencies:

Therefore Be It Resolved, that we, The Baptist Bible Union of America, in session in Kansas City, Mo., this 15th day of May, 1923, declare our unqualified opposition to this God-dishonouring, Bible-denying, man-degrading doctrine, and we call upon the tax-payers of this and other States to exercise their inalienable rights as citizens in protesting such teaching, and if need be, in serving injunctions against such teachers, on the manifest legal grounds that this teaching is by nature and character a false religion, and to instruct in it is contrary to the Constitution of the United States.

We further plead with those professors in our Baptist schools who have been inoculated with this virus, not to spread the unholy contagion among students committed by godly parents to their care. We appeal to the Boards of Governors of our denominational schools to investigate the entire teaching force with a view to discovering who in the force adopts this anti-Christian philosophy and removing every such professor from his chair. . . .

We further remind our Baptist brethren of the fact that the Mission Boards are, to a large extent, shut up to the sources of supply provided by our colleges and theological seminaries, and that unless both these institutions of higher education, including even schools of second grade, are freed from the utterly destructive influence of evolutionary rationalism and kindred forms of unbelief, it will be impossible for true Baptists to retain interest in and fellowship with the great cause of missions so named. As members of churches that are known to be liberal in their contributions to all Christian calls, we plead earnestly for relief from the intolerable situation now confronting us, which compels us either to withhold funds we would gladly give, or contribute them to a cause we believe to be not only dishonouring to, but a fresh crucifixion of Christ. It is therefore hereby ordered that a copy of this resolution be sent to every Baptist Educational Institution and to every Baptist Mission Board of the North American Continent. . . .

WHEREAS at the meeting of the Northern Baptist Convention held in Indianapolis, at its Eighth Session, Friday, June 16th, 1922, a motion was proposed that the Convention recommend to the local Baptist churches within the bounds of the Convention the adoption of the New Hampshire Confession of Faith; and

WHEREAS the Rev. Cornelius Woelfkin, D.D., of New York, moved as a substitute for the said Confession of Faith, a motion in the following terms:

"The Northern Baptist Convention affirms that the New Testament is the all-sufficient ground of our faith and practice, and we need no other statement;" which motion was carried by a vote of 1264 to 637; and

Whereas the mover of the said motion affirming acceptance of the New Testament, the said Dr. Woelfkin, preaching in the Park Ave. Baptist Church, April 29th, 1923, declared (according to a report in the New York Tribune, which was followed by the publication in the same paper the next day of a personal interview in which the said report was not repudiated) his belief that

(1) Baptists should abandon the practice of requiring baptism by immersion on profession of faith as a term of church membership, which step he believed logically followed his own church's practice of open communion; and that

(2) Baptists need greater tolerance of the various sects springing up about the fringes of the older churches, which sects he says he does not regard as heretical, mentioning as among them Spiritism and Christian Science; and that

(3) He declares himself to be "a Modernist out and out, as opposed to Fundamentalists and Traditionalists"; and that

(4) He is in step with Dr. Harry Emerson Fosdick; and

WHEREAS Dr. Woelfkin, as the mover of the said substitute motion must be regarded as the chief interpreter of the Convention's action in rejecting the New Hampshire Confession of Faith for the motion proposed by himself, to which action the Northern Baptist Convention still stands committed; and

WHEREAS the said mover of the said motion affirming acceptance of the New Testament as the all-sufficient ground of faith and practice now proposes that Baptists

1. Consent to the New Testament ordinance of believer's baptism, and

2. To the practice of open membership; while he

3. Expresses sympathy with the anti-Christian cults of Spiritism and Christian Science; and

4. Declares himself a Modernist out and out, as opposed to Fundamentalists and Traditionalists; and that

5. He is in step with Dr. Fosdick, the said Dr. Fosdick being on record as denying practically every fundamental doctrine of the New Testament and of Evangelical Christianity;

THEREFORE BE IT RESOLVED:

That the Baptist Bible Union of North America, in Conference assembled, hereby declares its uncompromising opposition to the theological position taken and announced by Dr. Cornelius Woelfkin, and to which the Northern Baptist Convention stands implicitly committed until it shall officially declare itself to the contrary. . . .

[B. Park Ave. Church Statement]

In regard to the character of the church, it is the belief of your Boards and of Dr. Fosdick that in moving to the new location the church would bring its present membership with its traditions, its substantial character, its strong spirit of fellowship, furnishing a sound foundation for future development; and that this body united and earnest would absorb into its membership, and imbue with its spirit, those desiring to join in its work and purpose. He has no desire to preach to a transient congregation. It is his purpose and hope to build up a strong working church which would be a powerful influence for good.

The principle of inclusive membership your Boards have tried to make clear in their statement to the church. This does not involve any question of infant membership. The church takes a position similar to that taken by the Baptist Churches in England and on the Continent. Dr. Fosdick's own position is clear. He himself has been immersed and believes in that form of baptism. On Easter Sunday he baptised in the Baptist Church of Montclair his two daughters. He is not willing, however, that failure to accept this form should bar any true believer from admission to our church.

As to the relationship of our church to the denomination, Dr. Fosdick is equally clear. He expects us to remain a Baptist Church in fellowship with the Southern New York Baptist Association, ready and willing to take our share of denominational burdens and our part in all denominational enterprises. On the other hand, he wishes to emphasize the Christian rather than the denominational aspect of the church, and would leave out the word "Baptist" from the church name when change of locality necessitates a change of name; retaining it, however, in the subtitle.

2. The Impact of Neoorthodoxy

The neoorthodox theological movement in American Protestantism was somewhat less rigorous than the "crisis" or "dialectical" theology of Europe in which Karl Barth (1886–1968) was such a seminal figure. The American movement was seeking to find a way beyond the Fundamentalist/Modernist stalemate and was conducive to ecumenical effort. Its leading figures were Reinhold Neibuhr (1892–1971) and H. Richard Niebuhr (1894–1962). It was influenced strongly by and contributed to the resurgence of biblical theology in the 1930s and 1940s with its stress on revelation. It had an impact on many of the younger American Baptist pastors and teachers from both liberal and conservative backgrounds. The high-water mark of neoorthodox thinking in the denomination came in a series of theological conferences in the 1950s that began with a major conference in 1954 at Green Lake, Wisconsin. The 1954 findings were summarized in ten brief statements, of which the first follows. It was written by Old Testament scholar, Walter J. Harrelson (1919–   ), who has taught at Chicago and Vanderbilt Universities. *Source: Ten Theological Papers: Conference on Theology, Green Lake, Wisconsin, June 15-July 3, 1954* (n.p., n.d.), pp. 4-6.

1. The authority of the Bible
   When one begins with the Bible as the authoritative story of God's saving deeds, he is immediately faced with certain issues. Since the deeds are prior to the record of them, the authority which the Bible has is seen to rest in its making these deeds our own possession. The authority of the Bible thus rests on more than the words alone. The words must be given life. Moreover, these words live most fully within the fellowship of believers, where the Holy Spirit gives power and direction to the Church and to its individual members. In addition, the Bible has a personal center—God's own Son given for our redemption. He is both the focus of the story and the central fact which makes the Bible authoritative. Thus we are required to judge the Bible on the basis of its presentation of the Christ to us, and yet we do not know the Christ apart from the Bible. The Bible is therefore much more than the factual account of certain experiences of the ancient Hebrews and the early followers of Jesus. It had to be written because significant things had come to pass in the life of a people which demanded recording and preserving. . . .

3. The Witness of the Spirit

The Holy Spirit, breathed into the Body of Christ which is the Church, makes this authoritative and single Book a living one. The Bible fulfills its mission as the Word of God when the Spirit acts on the words in the life of the believing community or in the heart of the believer. An individual may indeed receive God's Word apart from any earthly meditation, but most commonly this genuine Word will speak from the Bible's words in the context of the worshiping and believing fellowship of the Church.

4. Faith and reason

Faith and reason also have their very great importance for the question of the biblical basis of the Gospel. The Gospel is presented through the Bible under the guidance of the Spirit, but this by no means suggests that human reason has no role to play. On the contrary, the revelation of God's Word to man is itself a revelation compounded of faith and reason. God does not reveal His truth through reason alone, nor does He speak independently of man's rational faculties. The words of the Bible become vital when they are fully appropriated by the whole man, by man as rational and man as believer. The way back to some greater harmony between faith and reason must first lead to a restoration to the term 'reason' of its rich and positive content, not contained in its technical usage. Then there must be a return to that depth of life characteristic of the Bible in which faith and reason clearly appear as partners, not in conflict with each other. The Church must come again to a more vital understanding of the biblical pictures and images used to convey realities not capable of adequate description in abstract terms. Faith must be freed, moreover, from its obscure and sentimental features which make difficult, if not impossible, sound theological conversation.

. . .

3. The Resurgence of Conservative Evangelicalism

With the defeat of its efforts to take over major denominations in the 1920s, the Fundamentalist movement became less conspicuous and militant. Some of its supporters withdrew from the Northern Baptist Convention to form such bodies as the General Association of Regular Baptists (1933) and later the Conservative Baptist Association of America (1947). But many remained in the Convention. (The same thing occurred in other major denominations.)

A leader, who regrouped such people into what swelled into an important theological current, was an American Baptist minister and professor, Carl F. H. Henry (1912–   ), a prolific author, speaker, and the founding editor in 1956 of the periodical *Christianity*

Today. The following year he wrote a series of articles under the general title, "Dare We Renew the Modernistic-Fundamentalist Controversy?" The opening pages of the fourth and final article are reprinted. Throughout the series, Henry was critical of the older fundamentalism and of its neoorthodox alternative and urged evangelicals to emphasize a biblical super-naturalism. *Source:* Carl F. H. Henry, "Dare We Renew the Controversy? The Evangelical Responsibility," *Christianity Today,* 1 (22 July 1957), pp. 23-25.

A higher spirit to quicken and to fulfill the theological fortunes of this century will require more than the displacement of modernism, more than the revision of neo-orthodoxy, more than the revival of fundamentalism. Recovery of apostolic perspective and dedication of the evangelical movement to biblical realities are foundational to this hope.

EXALT BIBLICAL THEOLOGY

Evangelical theology has nothing to fear, and much to gain, from aligning itself earnestly with the current plea for a return to biblical theology. To measure this moving front of creative theology sympathetically, to understand its concern and courage and to name its weaknesses without depreciating its strength will best preserve relevant theological interaction with the contemporary debate. The evangelical movement must make its very own the passionate concern for the reality of special divine revelation, for a theology of the Word of God, for attentive hearing of the witness of the Bible, for a return to biblical theology.

POSITIVE PREACHING

Rededication to positive and triumphant preaching is the evangelical pulpit's great need. The note of Christ's Lordship over this dark century, of the victory of Christianity, has been obscured. If it be evangelical, preaching must enforce the living communication of the changeless realities of divine redemption. The minister whose pulpit does not become the life-giving center of his community fails in his major mission. Perspective in Christianity's current gains and final triumph will avoid a myopic and melancholy discipleship. The Christian pulpit must present the invisible and exalted Head of the body of Christ; linked to him this earthly colony of heaven moves to inevitable vindication and glory. The perplexing problems of our perverse social orders find their hopeful solution only in this regenerative union. Out of its spiritual power must spring the incentives to creative cultural contributions.

ENLARGE CHRISTIAN LIVING

The evangelical fellowship needs a fresh and pervading conception of the Christian life. Too long fundamentalists have swiftly referred the question, "What distinguishes Christian living?" to personal abstinence from dubious social externals. The Christian conscience, of course, will always need to justify outward behavior, in home, in vocation and in leisure. But Christian ethics probes deeper. It bares the invisible zone of personality wherein lurk pride, covetousness and hatred.

Unfortunately, fundamentalism minimized the exemplary Jesus in the sphere of personal ethics. The theme of Christ's oneness with God was developed so exclusively in terms of his deity that the import of his dependence upon God for all human nature was lost. The manhood of Jesus is essentially one with ours, its uniqueness is in the zone of sinlessness, not of humanness. His uncompromised devotion and dependence upon God, his sustained relationship of mutual love, embodied the ideal pattern of human life in perfect fellowship with God. In view of his unbroken union with God, his humanity holds a central significance for all humanity.

In this light, a new importance attaches to the Nazarene's learning of the Father's will in the course of obedient dependence. His struggle with temptation to magnificent victory over all the assaults of evil, his exemplary trust, his unwavering reliance on God even in the darkest hours, his interior calm of soul, the wellspring of love that flowed from his being—in all these experiences Christ models for us an ideal spiritual relationship with God. In Jesus of Nazareth, God is fully resident; in God, Jesus is fully at home. He lives out the "rest in God" that actualizes the "abiding" to which we are called.

Another way in which evangelicals need to move beyond the fundamentalist ethic is in comprehending the whole of the moral law in fuller exposition of love for God and neighbor, and in the larger experience of the Holy Spirit in New Testament terms of ethical virtue. Often quite legalistically, and with an absoluteness beyond New Testament authority, fundamentalism's doctrine of surrender, of rededication, has merely proscripted worldly practices, from which the believer was discouraged. Unemphasized, however, are the fruit of the Spirit and those many virtues, which differentiate dedicated living in terms of biblical Christianity.

SOCIAL CONCERN

We need a new concern for the individual in the entirety of his Christian experience. He is a member of all life's communities, of faith, of the family, of labor, of the state, of culture. Christianity is by no means the social gospel of modernism, but is nonetheless vibrant with social implications as a religion of redemptive transformation. To express and continue the vitality of the gospel message, marriage and the home, labor and economics, politics and the state, culture and the arts, in fact, every sphere of life, must evidence the lordship of Christ.

Obviously, the social application of Christian theology is no easy task. For one thing, fundamentalism fails to elaborate principles and programs of Christian social action because it fails to recognize the relevance of the gospel to the sociocultural sphere. Modernism defines Christian social imperatives in secular terms and uses the Church to reorganize unregenerate humanity. Its social sensitivity gave modernism no license to neglect the imperative of personal regeneration. Evangelistic and missionary priorities, on the other hand, gave fundamentalism no license to conceal the imperative of Christian socal ethics. Despite the perils, no evasion of responsibility for meaningfully relating the gospel to the pressing problems of modern life is tolerable.

The divine life is a "being in love," a social or a family fellowship in which personality expresses the outgoing, creative relationship of redemption. A worker by God's creation, man sees vocation as a divinely entrusted stewardship by which to demonstrate love to God and service to man. As divinely ordained, the state declares God's intention and the dignity of man's responsibility for preserving justice and repressing iniquity in a sinful order. This world challenges man to interpret literature, art, music, and other media in reference to eternal order and values. . . .

PRECISION IN BELIEFS

Evangelical emphasis on an indispensable doctrinal basis for Church unity needs, however, to be defined with greater precision. Such concern accounts for evangelical uneasiness over the creedal vagrancy of the World Council of Churches whose nebulous emphasis is only on "Jesus Christ as Lord and Savior." Since the evangelical movement includes churches that are both creedal and noncreedal in heritage, a specific creedal unity has not been elaborated, although common theological tenets are listed. This evangelical listing of a doctrinal minimum raises difficulties for creedal churches, inasmuch as they consider no article of faith dispensable. To Reformed churchmen, evangelical formulas often appear open to objectionable development. They prefer a strict creedal fellowship, a restriction that excludes progress toward the unity of diverse evangelical elements. The evangelical failure to fully elaborate essential doctrines has resulted in fragmentation by granting priority to secondary emphases (in such matters as eschatology). Evangelical Christianity has been slow to establish study conferences in biblical doctrine, to encourage mutual growth and understanding. Ironically, study sessions on theological issues are now often associated with movements whose doctrinal depth and concern are widely questioned. The significance of Christian doctrine, its dispensability or indispensability, its definition as witness or revelation, the elements identified respectively as core and periphery—these are issues on which evangelical Christianity must be vocal.

4. The Ecumenical Involvement

American and National Baptist conventions have participated in many aspects of the ecumenical movement, whereas the Southern Baptist Convention generally has not. In 1961 John E. Skoglund (1912–   ), former foreign secretary of the ABFMS and then professor of homiletics at Colgate Rochester Divinity School and for many years a member of the Commission on Faith and Order of the World Council of Churches, wrote a summary, given here in part, of the long-standing commitment of American Baptists to ecumenical relations. Selection A contains the action referred to in the opening paragraph of Skoglund's statement. *Sources:* A. *Year Book of the American Baptist Convention,* 1960, p. 46. B. John E. Skoglund, "American Baptists and the Ecumenical Movement After 50 Years," *Foundations: A Baptist Journal of Theology and History,* 4 (1961), pp. 112-114.

[A.] Resolution on National Council of Churches, 1960

WHEREAS, from the beginning American Baptists have stood in the forefront of co-operative Christianity, repeatedly reaffirming our American Baptist position as a part of the National Council of Churches, and

WHEREAS, Distinguished American Baptists in our times are providing trustworthy leadership in national, state and local councils of churches in complete consistency with our historic position,

Be it hereby resolved, that we reaffirm our participation in the National Council of Churches and our faith in its purposes, politics and leadership.

In keeping with our basic Baptist principle of the autonomy of the individual church, we also reaffirm the right of any local church to express dissent and to withhold its financial support from the National Council of Churches. Provision shall be made whereby individual churches, if they so desire, may indicate that they are not affiliated with the National Council of Churches through the American Baptist Convention and that such churches shall be so listed in the annual year book of the American Baptist Convention.

[B.] American Baptists and the Ecumenical Movement After 50 Years.

The most recent action of the American Baptist Convention concerning its relationship to the ecumenical movement was taken at its convention in Rochester in 1960. Asked by a strong middle-western church to adopt a resolution urging that all reference to the National Council and related ecumenical organizations be taken out of literature printed by the American Baptist Convention, and after a presentation of both sides of the issue, the delegates voted overwhelmingly against the church's resolution and went on to reaffirm continued membership in the National Council of Churches and cooperation in the whole ecumenical movement.

However, the Rochester action was no new innovation. It stood firmly in line with the long-established policy of American Baptists. In 1911, only four years after the American (then Northern) Baptist Convention was organized, the delegates in response to an invitation from the Protestant Episcopal Church and the Congregational Churches of the United States to participate in a world wide Faith and Order movement adopted the following resolution:

WHEREAS, there exists, we believe, a wide-spread feeling among members of all Christian bodies that the divisions of the Church of Christ, while necessary in time past to secure liberty of thought and worship, have largely fulfilled this mission and should now gradually advance to closer forms of cooperation in order to accomplish with economy and efficiency work too great for any single body; and

WHEREAS, this growing sense of brotherhood in Christ surely being realized by all who bear His name, is, we trust, the manifest working of God in our own day and generation, whereby He seeks to heal for His Church the estrangements of former times and to restore unto her the unity of the Spirit to the bond of peace; and

WHEREAS, that great principle of free personal faith with liberty of conscience in matters of belief and worship, unto which our fathers were made apostles and we their heirs in stewardship, is not in any sense the exclusive possession of Baptists, but is the heritage of the whole Christian world. Therefore,
BE IT RESOLVED that with readiness to share our apprehension of the truth as it is in Jesus with all His followers, and with both willingness and humility to learn from others any aspect of the way of life which we may not have in due proportion, we will gladly enter into a conference of all the Churches of Christ looking toward a more perfect mutual understanding and a clearer insight into the mind of our Saviour; and we hereby appoint a committee of five as our representatives to act with similar appointees from other Christian bodies in making arrangements for such a proposed conference (Minutes, Northern Baptist Convention, 1911).

Behind this resolution stood a long history of American Baptist participation in cooperative Christianity. In 1796 Baptists joined hands with Presbyterians, Dutch Reformed and Associate Reformed laymen and ministers to establish the New York Missionary Society. The Society began work on an interdenominational basis among the Seneca and Tuscarora Indians in the vicinity of Niagara Falls. American Baptists joined with other Christians to help establish the American Bible Society (1816), the Sunday and Adult School Union (1817), the American Sunday School Union (1824), the Foreign Missions Conference of North America (1893), the Missionary Education Movement (1902), the Federal Council of Churches (1908), the Home Missions Council of North America (1908), and the National Protestant Council of Higher Education (1911); and, even later, the United Stewardship Council (1920) and the United Council of Church Women (1940). Cooperative world missions drew American Baptists in 1878 to Liverpool, England, to the first Central Conference on Foreign Missions. The American Baptist Foreign Mission Society, then known as the American Baptist Missionary Union, brought a Burmese pastor to this gathering. He was the only non-occidental present. Today in similar gatherings the members of the so-called younger churches have a dominant voice. Ten years later John Murdock, home secretary of the Foreign Society, represented American Baptists at the London Missionary Conference. In 1910 American Baptists participated in the famed Edinburgh International Missionary Conference which led to the formation of the International Missionary Council.

In more recent times American Baptists have been active in each World Conference on Faith and Order, and Life and Work. They joined with others in 1948 to form the World Council of Churches. The National Council of Churches of Christ in the United States of America was formed in 1950 with the American Baptist Convention among the charter members. Since that time American Baptists have participated actively in the National Council and all its divisions. They have been honored in the most recent period by having Edwin T. Dahlberg as president of National Council and Mrs. William S. Terrill as president of the United Church Women. At the recent assembly of the National Council of Churches in San Francisco it was discovered that American Baptists have proportionately more secretaries of state and local councils of churches than any other single denomination. A number of American Baptists are in executive positions in national and world ecumenical organizations. Men and women like Edwin Espy, Kenneth Maxwell, Paul Albrecht, Irene Jones, George Carpenter, Eugene Nida and Oliver Hasselblad give ample evidence that some of the ablest American Baptists are at work in the heart of the ecumenical movement.

5. New Roles for Church Women

As has been noted, the role of women in American life increased in the years before World War I especially through their work in foreign and home missions. The passage of the Nineteenth (woman suffrage) Amendment in 1919 opened new avenues of civic involvement for them at a time when the social gospel encouraged wider participation in solving social problems. A brief article (Selection A) that appeared in the month the amendment was ratified pointed out new opportunities for service for Christian women. The author was Helen Barrett Montgomery (1861–1934), who had long been prominent in Baptist life as an author and leader and who became the first woman president of the Northern Baptist Convention in 1921.

The emergence of a new feminist movement after midcentury created a changed situation for women in church and society. A heightened consciousness of the restrictions they had long faced arose among church women as among others. New sensitivities concerning the use of sexist language and the realities of unequal pay and opportunities for promotion in church life and secular life were aroused. In 1976 Gail Hinand (1937–

) compiled from various denominational sources a statement on "The Process of Consciousness Raising and the Formation of Support Groups." *Sources:* A. Helen B. Montgomery, "Civic Opportunities of Christian Women," *The Baptist,* 1 (August 28, 1920); p. 1073. B. Gail Hinand, comp., "The Process of Consciousness Raising and the Formation of Support Groups,'' American Baptist Churches Women's Packet, issued by American Baptist Women, 1976, Valley Forge, Pennsylvania.

[A. New Opportunities for Women]

With the complete enfranchisement of women assured in the near future, Christian women are looking about them to see what opportunities of service the new conditions will bring them. In many states there are legislative councils and voters' leagues being formed for the purpose of keeping women in touch with legislation, both state and national. One of the best examples of such organizations is the Women's Legislative Council of Washington of which one of our Baptist women, Mrs. Sophy L. W. Clark of Seattle, is president. Miss Carrie M. Barr of Yakima is vice president.

This organization came into being several years ago, and has been actively and practically engaged in furthering legislation drawn in the public interest ever since. The object of the Women's Legislative Council is to coordinate the legislative committees in existing societies so that their cumulative influence may be exercised in the furtherance of good legislative and in opposition to evil measures.

The legislative bureau of the council functions actively at the state capitol during the sessions of the state legislature. The women's society in the University Place Baptist Church of Seattle has been a member of the county and state councils since their organization, but many local organizations of church women have not yet seen that organizations such as this offer an opportunity to make the conscience of the nation effective in legislative halls.

Since the organization of the Council in 1913, the women have succeeded in securing the passage of a great part of their proposed legislation, while before that time the separate groups of women interested in various reforms were unable to secure the passage of their measures. It is a strange thing that in our modern American life the voice of the Grange, the Federation of Women's Clubs, the labor unions or the chamber of commerce is much more effective in state and national legislation than that of the Christian church. But this is only because these other bodies are organized, know exactly what they want and work unitedly. There are, to be sure, political questions on which Christians differ widely. These have no proper place in the program of the National Women's Voters' League or bodies like that in Washington. But questions affecting education, the protection of young girls, child welfare, the milk supply, and temperance are those on which the public opinion of the Christian church is overwhelmingly one. Women, moreover, because of their closer connection with the home and the child, have a more uniform body of opinion than has any other group in the nation. There is no doubt where the women stand on these questions of public health, morals and education.

The moral of it all is that the great organizations of Christian woman, the home and foreign mission societies, should as soon as may be add a committee on legislation to their other activities. Some one woman should be selected in each circle, whose duty it will be to keep watch on the course of state and national legislation, to circulate petitions when those are needed, to induce the women to write letters or send telegrams when these may be powerfully utilized to inform legislators in regard to the wishes of their constituencies, and in every legitimate way to exert the pressure of intelligent public opinion upon state and national Government. The woman elected to this position ought to be the sanest and strongest and most practical woman in the church.

Influence can be dissipated if the women attempt to do too many things, or to take action before they are thoroughly informed in regard to the facts. By connecting themselves with these state and national organizations, it will be possible for them to learn the facts and to associate themselves with other organizations seeking the same ends.

[B.] The Process of Consciousness Raising

We all know what it means to be newly conscious of something. Very often that consciousness will alter the way we respond to a situation. Upon learning of a particular concern or issue in the community, for example, a pastor might "shift gears" to incorporate this concern into the life of the church. We could say that the consciousness of the pastor had been raised to another level.

In a more personal way, this process of consciousness raising has been going on among groups of women throughout the country. Consciousness raising happens when women from their different perspectives share with each other how things look to them; what it means to be a woman in this culture. We are realizing that our roles, our goals, our values, and our dreams are more often the result of the expectations of others—rarely our expectations of ourselves. As a result of honest encounter each is led to see with increased vision what was not visible or clearly defined before. It is an "aha!" moment.

By sharing our experiences of being a woman in our unique situation; by daring to ask who we are and what we are becoming; by affirming personhood, choices, rights and responsibilities for women; we are discovering emerging possibilities for ourselves as persons. In discovering our common experiences as women, we can identify and oppose patterns of oppression in our lives, feel new sympathies for each other and for strangers who touch our lives, and discover sources of strength in togetherness. As women we have begun to experience a freedom, a renewed sense of self, a sense of really being alive once we discover that questions and feelings previously assumed unique were literally shared by all other women. . . . Many of us have been taught from a very early age to distrust other females, to be protective of our families and bosses, to see marriage as the ultimate form of happiness and fulfillment, and to be both emotionally and economically dependent on the various men in our lives. These are but a few of the things we have learned that have tended to keep us powerless and isolated from one another. Furthermore, our problems often seem childish and insignificant when compared to the real problems men face as they go out to make their way in the world. Consequently, many of us feel that everything limiting and painful in our lives is due to our own failings, and that if something weren't wrong with us in the first place, we would be happy and fulfilled in our female role. The consciousness raising (or support, as we prefer to call it) group is a place where we can be free, where we can be honest, where we can explore, and we will find supportive and non-judging friends with whom we can share our frustration, fears, successes and failures. It's a place where we learn that many of our feelings and problems are not ours alone but are shared by many women. It's a place for self-examination and exploration of the alternatives that are available to all of us. . . .

The goals of consciousness raising are coming to a new awareness of ourselves as women and acting on that awareness. The goal of a support group is to provide a supportive setting where each woman can share and express her feelings about being a woman. The ultimate goal is wholeness in the Christian community and in society; when women and men will share responsibilities for breadwinning, childrearing, housekeeping, government, and care of the earth as partners and citizens in the world as well as in the kingdom.

Because we are all individuals—we have different pasts, presents and futures—there are no "right answers" as to what that awareness should be. We will find, though, that many of us have been channeled in the same directions because we are women. And we have experienced the same frustrations about finding employment that is in line with our talents, spending the day at home without the enriching companionship of another adult, feeling our contributions to society are not valued, or being relegated to the usual "feminine" responsibilities in the church. It is the awareness of these common frustrations women share that brings us together and enables us to support each other as we are searching for emerging ways of being women.

The actions we take as a result of our awareness will reflect our individual needs, but will find expression within the groups of people who share our awareness. It is important we become involved lest our experience in consciousness raising turn into "navel gazing" with no outward expression. Consciousness without action is not really consciousness. The evidence of the change of consciousness of the pastor mentioned previously was in the action, not in the fact that the pastor learned of the concern. . . . The leadership of women can be utilized by the church only as women are affirmed as persons and encouraged to use their talents and abilities in the church and the world. These support groups can thus be one means of leadership discovery and development, especially when followed by concerted action at all levels of the church. . . . A group of women can begin a support group in many different ways. There may be six to ten of your friends with whom you would like to talk and from whom you would like support. Or ask friends to bring friends—it isn't necessary to know everyone. Or you may even wish to form or join a group of women whom you do not presently know.

6. Concerns for Justice and Peace

Many Baptists were involved in various causes that were devoted to a more just and peaceful society and world. Deeply influenced by Walter Rauschenbusch, Harry Emerson Fosdick (1878–1969) spoke on behalf of various movements for equality and a higher level of justice in American life. Though he had supported American participation in World War I, ministering to troops in France, he soon had second thoughts about the war and became a convinced pacifist, even through the trying days of World War II. Several passages have been chosen from his Armistice Day sermon (Selection A), preached first at The Riverside Church, November 12, 1933.

A generation later, Martin Luther King, Jr. (1929–1968), a minister in both American and National Baptist conventions and one who had also expressed his indebtedness to Rauschenbusch, became the outstanding leader of the civil rights movements of the 1950s and 1960s. About a year before his tragic assassination, he came out openly against the war in Vietnam; for him the two causes of civil rights and peace could not be separated. At the fiftieth anniversary of the American Baptist Convention meetings, King was invited by the Division of Christian Social Concerns to address the plenary session on the subject of civil rights and Christian responsibility. The address was a brilliant use of allegory and reflects the classic style and thought of a premier advocate of social justice. *Sources:* A. Harry Emerson Fosdick, "The Unknown Soldier." Harry Emerson Fosdick Papers, Union Theological Seminary, New York. B. Martin Luther King, Jr., "Paul's Letter to the American Churches," Speech at the American Baptist Convention (Philadelphia), 1957. Records of the American Baptist Convention; Tapes 49, 50; Archives; American Baptist Historical Society.

[A.] "The Unknown Soldier"

It was an interesting idea to deposit the body of an unrecognized soldier in the national memorial of the Great War, and yet, when one stops to think of it, how strange it is! Yesterday, in Rome, Paris, London, Washington, and how many capitals beside, the most stirring military pageantry, decked with flags and exultant with music, centered about the bodies of unknown soldiers. That is strange. So this is the outcome of Western civilization, which for nearly two thousand years has worshiped Christ, and in which democracy and science have had their widest opportunity, that the whole nation pauses, its acclamations rise, its colorful pageantry centers, its patriotic oratory flourishes, around the unrecognizable body of a soldier blown to bits on the battlefield. That is strange.

It was the war-lords themselves who picked him out as the symbol of war. So be it! As a symbol of war we accept him from their hands.

You may not say that I, being a Christian minister, did not know him. I knew him well. From the north of Scotland, where they planted the sea with mines, to the trenches of France, I lived with him and his fellows, British, Australian, New Zealander, French, American. The places where he fought, from Ypres through the Somme battlefield to the southern trenches, I saw while he was still there. I lived with him in his dugouts in the trenches, and on destroyers searching for submarines off the shores of France. Short of actual battle, from training camp to hospital, from the fleet to No-Man's Land, I, a Christian minister, saw the war. Moreover, I, a Christian minister, participated in it. I too was persuaded that it was a war to end war. I too was a gullible fool and thought that modern war could somehow make the world safe for democracy. They sent men like me to explain to the army the high meanings of war and, by every argument we could command, to strengthen their morale. I wonder if I ever spoke to the unknown soldier.

One night, in a ruined barn behind the lines I spoke at sunset to a company of hand-grenaders who were going out that night to raid the German trenches. They told me that on the average no more than half a company came back from such a raid, and I, a minister of Christ, tried to nerve them for their suicidal and murderous endeavor. I wonder if the unknown soldier was in that barn that night.

Once in a dugout which in other days had been a French wine cellar I bade Godspeed at two in the morning to a detail of men going out on patrol in No-Man's Land. They were a fine company of American boys fresh from home. I recall that, huddled in the dark, underground chamber, they sang

"Lead, kindly Light, amid th' encircling gloom,
    Lead thou me on.
The night is dark, and I am far from home,—
    Lead thou me on."

Then, with my admonitions in their ears, they went down from the second to the first-line trenches and so out to No-Man's Land. I wonder if the Unknown Soldier was in that dugout.

You here this morning may listen to the rest of this sermon or not, as you please. It makes much less difference to me than usual what you do think. I have an account to settle in this pulpit today between my soul and the Unknown Soldier.

He is not so utterly unknown as we sometimes think. Of one thing we can be certain: he was sound of mind and body. We made sure of that. All primitive gods who demanded bloody sacrifices on their altars insisted that the animals should be of the best, without mar or hurt. Turn to the Old Testament and you find it written there: "Whether male or female, he shall offer it without blemish before Jehovah." The god of war still maintains the old demand. These men to be sacrificed upon his altars were sound and strong. Once there might have been guessing about that. Not now. Now we have medical science which tests the prospective soldier's body. Now we have psychiatry which tests his mind. We used them both to make sure that these sacrifices for the god of war were without blemish. Of all insane and suicidal procedures can you imagine anything madder than this, that all the nations should pick out their best, use their scientific skill to make certain that they are the best, and then in one mighty holocaust offer ten million of them on the battlefields of one war?

I have an account to settle between my soul and the Unknown Soldier. I deceived him. I deceived myself first, unwittingly, and then I deceived him, assuring him that good consequence could come out of that. As a matter of hard-headed, biological fact, what good can come out of that? Mad civilization, you cannot sacrifice on bloody altars the best of your breed and expect anything to compensate for the loss.

Of another thing we may be fairly sure concerning the Unknown Soldier—that he was a conscript. He may have been a volunteer but on an actuarial average he probably was a conscript. The long arm of the nation reached into his home, touched him on the shoulder, saying, You must go to France and fight. . . .

He was a son, the hope of the family, and the nation coerced him . . . He was, maybe, a husband and a father, and already by that slow and beautiful gradation which all fathers know, he had felt the deep ambitions of his heart being transferred from himself to his children. And the nation coerced him . . . Do I not have an account to settle between my soul and him? They sent men like me into the camps to awaken his idealism, to touch those secret, holy springs within him so that with devotion, fidelity, loyalty, and self-sacrifice he might go out to war. O war, I hate you most of all for this, that you do lay your hands on the noblest elements in human character, with which we might make a heaven on earth, and you use them to make a hell on earth instead. You take your science, the fruit of our dedicated intelligence, by means of which we might build here the City of God and, using it, you fill the earth instead with new ways of slaughtering men. You take our loyalty, our unselfishness, with which we might make the earth beautiful, and, using these our finest qualities, you make death fall from the sky and burst up from the sea and hurtle from unseen am-buscades sixty miles away; you blast fathers in the trenches with gas while you are starving their children at home with blockades; and you so bedevil the world that fifteen years after the Armistice we cannot be sure who won the war, so sunk in the same disaster are victors and vanquished alike. If war were fought simply with evil things, like hate, it would be bad enough but, when one sees the deeds of war done with the loveliest faculties of the human spirit, he looks into the very pit of hell.

Suppose one thing more—that the Unknown Soldier was a Christian. Maybe he was not, but suppose he was, a Christian like Sergeant York, who at the beginning intended to take Jesus so seriously as to refuse to fight but afterward, otherwise persuaded, made a real soldier. For these Christians do make soldiers. Religion is a force. When religious faith supports war, when, there is one by one, but the wholesale destruction of children, starving them by millions, impoverishing them, spoiling the chances of unborn generations of them, as in the Great War. [sic]

My friends, I am not trying to make you sentimental about this. I want you to be hard headed. We can have this monstrous thing or we can have Christ, but we cannot have both. O my country, stay out of war! Cooperate with the nations in every movement that has any hope for peace; enter the World Court, support the League of Nations, contend undiscourageably for disarmament, but set your face steadfastly and forever against being drawn into another war. O church of Christ, stay out of war. Withdraw from every alliance that maintains or encourages it. It was not a pacifist, it was Field-Marshal Earl Haig who said, "It is the business of the churches to make my business impossible." And O my soul, stay out of war!

At any rate, I will myself do the best I can to settle my account with the Unknown Soldier. I renounce war. I renounce war because of what it does to our own men. I have watched them coming gassed from the front line trenches. I have seen the long, long hospital trains filled with their mutilated bodies. I have heard the cries of the crazed and the prayers of those who wanted to die and could not, and I remember the maimed and ruined men for whom the war is not yet over. I renounce war because of what it compels us to do to our enemies, bombing their mothers in villages, starving their children by blockades, laughing over our coffee cups about every damnable thing we have been able to do to them. I renounce war for its consequences, for the lies it lives on and propagates, for the undying hatreds it arouses, for the dictatorships it puts in the place of democracy, for the starvation that stalks after it. I renounce war and never again, directly or indirectly, will I sanction or support another! O Unknown Soldier, in penitent reparation I make you that pledge.

[B.] ''Paul's Letter to the American Churches''
My Christian Friends:
I would like to share with you this evening an imaginary letter which comes from the pen of the apostle Paul. The postmark reveals that it comes from the Island of Crete. After opening the letter, I discovered that it was written in ill-formed, sprawling Greek. At the top of the letter was this request: ''Please read when the people assemble themselves together, and pass on to the other churches.''

For several weeks now I have labored assiduously with the translation; at times it has been difficult. But now I believe I have deciphered its true meaning. May I hasten to say that if, in presenting the letter, the contents sound strangely Kingian instead of Paulinian, attribute it to my lack of objectivity rather than Paul's lack of clarity. It is miraculous indeed how the apostle Paul could be writing a letter to you and to me almost nineteen hundred years after his last letter appeared in the New Testament. How this is possible, I do not know, and I do not really care. The important thing is that I can imagine the apostle Paul writing a letter to American Christians in 1957 A.D. . . .

''The hour is late. The clock of destiny is ticking out. You can't afford to slow up because your nation has a date with destiny. You must keep moving. Someone in this nation . . . must rise up and cry out in the prophetic tones of an Amos, 'Let judgment run down like waters, and righteousness like a mighty stream.' This is your challenge, America.

''I must say just a word to those who are struggling against this evil system. I must say just a word to those who are victimized with the system. You must struggle passionately and unrelentingly to remove this evil. But be sure that your hands are clean in the struggle. Never struggle with bitterness. Never allow yourself to hate in the struggle. Never let anybody pull you so low as to hate them. Never fall to the point of using violence. For if you succumb to the temptation of using violence in your struggle, unborn generations will be the recipients of a long and desolate night of bitterness, and your chief legacy to the future will be an endless reign of meaningless chaos. You must somehow once again hear the words of Jesus saying, 'Love your enemies, bless them that curse you, pray for them that despitefully use you.'

''This is the thing you must follow. Your aim must never be to defeat or humiliate the white man or to pay the reactionary forces in the white community back for things they've done to you over so many years. Your aim must be to win their friendship and understanding. Sometimes as you struggle, you might have to boycott. But remember, American Christians, those of you who will have to struggle through boycotts and other means, remember that a boycott is not an end within itself. A boycott is merely a means to awake a sense of shame within the oppressor and say to him you don't like the way he's treating you. But the end is reconciliation. The end is redemption. The end is the creation of the beloved community. Your aim must be to work to that point. You, by the grace of God, will create a society where men will live together as brothers and respect the dignity and worth of all human personality. This is what stands before you as you struggle ahead.

"There will be many persons who will see the need for struggling against this evil. Many Negroes will devote their lives to the cause of justice. Many white persons of good will and deep moral sensitivity will be allies in the struggle and will dare to take a stand for freedom and justice. Realism impels me to admit that if you take this stand, you must be prepared for suffering and sacrifice. If you will take a stand for freedom and justice, you must be prepared for condemnation.

"So don't despair when you are condemned and persecuted for righteousness' sake. You will be called an impractical idealist at times, and sometimes you will be referred to as a dangerous radical. If you take this stand, it might even be necessary for you to go to jail. But if such is the case you must humbly grace the jail with your presence. It might even mean physical death. But if physical death is the price that some must pay to free their children from a permanent life of psychological death, then nothing could be more Christian. Oh, don't worry about persecution. If you stand up for truth and righteousness, you will be persecuted from time to time.

"But I say to you, stand up and don't worry about it; and I can say this to you, America, with a bit of authority because my life was something of a continual round of persecution. After my conversion, I was denied by the disciples at Jerusalem. Later I was tried for heresy at Jerusalem. I was jailed at Philippi, beaten at Thessalonica, mocked at Ephesus, and oppressed at Athens. You see, I'm still going. And I left all of these experiences and all of these persecutions more persuaded than ever before that 'neither death, nor life, nor angels, nor principalities, nor things present, nor things to come, . . . [can] separate us from the love of God in Christ Jesus our Lord.'

"Oh, American Christians, I must say to you that standing up for the righteousness and the truth of Jesus Christ and for the truth of God is the greatest thing in all the world. This is the end of life. The end of life is not to be happy. The end of life is not to achieve pleasure and avoid pain. The end of life is to do the will of God, come what may. This is what you must see, America, if you are to face the days ahead. . . ."

Polity and Piety

In Northern Baptist life, differing styles of piety sometimes came into conflict at national conventions, as happened at Grand Rapids, Michigan, in 1946. Soon after that convention, the communion adopted a new name and made changes in its national polity that were designed to help the various patterns of piety to live together in relative harmony. The development of a national assembly ground at Green Lake, Wisconsin, was also a step toward that end.

In the intense debate over the relocation of the national headquarters at Valley Forge, Pennsylvania, the diversities of interpretation of denominational theology, piety, and polity were further complicated by regional interests. Differences in style were also increased by the flexibility of congregational polity, which permitted the "dual alignment" of a local church with more than one denomination so that some congregations enjoyed relationships with both Northern and Southern conventions, others with the Northern and one of the National Baptist bodies.

The growing complexities of a modern denomination were important factors in the negotiations and debates that led to another name change and a decision to shift from a "societal" to a more "churchly" form of organization in the 1970s.

1. Controversy at Grand Rapids

The clipped words of the official report that appears below hardly catch the turmoil and excitement of a stormy seventh session of the Northern Baptist Convention meeting at Grand Rapids on May 23, 1946. An effort of conservative forces to win the convention to their way of interpreting the New Testament led to a confusing debate; at length a substitute resolution was moved and adopted. Thus the denomination reasserted its historic position and its inclusive policy. Many of those dissatisfied with the action and with the defeat of their slate of candidates for elected offices organized what soon became a new denomination, the Conservative Baptist Association of America. *Source: Year Book of the Northern Baptist Convention,* 1946, pp. 96-97.

94. The following resolution was presented by F. W. Fickett of Arizona, who moved its adoption:

WHEREAS, The Northern Baptist Convention declared in the Indianapolis Convention that

"The Northern Baptist Convention affirms that the New Testament is the all-sufficient ground of our faith and practice, and we need no other statement"; and

WHEREAS, The Agencies of the Convention have interpreted this action inclusively under what is termed the "Inclusive Policy," in confusion as to our testimony on the Gospel of Christ and great division and controversy among the churches; be it,

Resolved, That the Northern Baptist Convention in session at Grand Rapids, Michigan, May 23, 1946, advises its Agencies, Councils, and Committees representative of the Convention in its work that they should not employ as secretaries or appoint as missionaries any persons who refuse to affirm the following:

(a) That the record of the Incarnation of our Lord Jesus Christ as stated in Matthew 1 and Luke 1 and 2 is true and trustworthy.

(b) That the record of the Resurrection of Christ as stated in Matthew 28, Mark 16, Luke 24, and John 20, 21, is true and trustworthy.

(c) That the record of the miracles of Jesus as given in the Gospels is true and trustworthy.

(d) That the New Testament is inspired of God in all its contents and that the acceptance of its historical facts, revelation, teachings, and doctrines is obligatory in Christian faith and practice.

This motion was seconded by Rev. C. P. White, of California, and discussed by F. W. Fickett and by Rev. E. H. Pruden, of the District of Columbia: Rev. C. P. White of California: Rev. H. C. Phillips of Ohio: E. L. Delbey, of Illinois: Rev. Winfield Edson, of California: Rev. Sam Bradford, of Colorado: W. C. Coleman, of Kansas: Mrs. C. V. Englund, of Colorado: Rev. W. R. Cole, of Michigan: Rev. C. S. Thomas, of Pennsylvania: Rev. R. E. Nelson, of New York: Rev. H. H. Straton, of Massachusetts.

95. A substitute motion was presented by Rev. Winfield Edson, of

California, and seconded by W. C. Coleman of Kansas; and after discussion by Rev. J. R. Turnbull, of Oregon; Rev. H. V. Jensen, of Washington; Rev. V. L. Shontz, of Illinois; Rev. J. B. Colton, of California; it was adopted in the following form.

Be it resolved: That we reaffirm our faith in the New Testament as a divinely inspired record and therefore a trustworthy, authorative and all-sufficient rule of our faith and practice. We rededicate ourselves to Jesus Christ as Lord and Savior and call our entire denomination to the common task of sharing the whole Gospel with the whole world.

On motion of Rev. C. S. Thomas, of Pennsylvania, the substitute was adopted in place of the original resolution.

2. Facing Denominational Problems

The Northern Baptist Convention was basically a "family of missionary societies," an arrangement that had certain strengths but led to various administrative tangles and caused multiple approaches to the local congregations. A Commission of Review, chaired by a former NBC president, Edwin T. Dahlberg (1892–   ), presented its report in 1949; accepted by the convention, it resulted in the change of the name "Northern Baptist Convention" to the "American Baptist Convention" and provided for the election of a general secretary for the denomination. Reuben E. Nelson (1905–1960) was the first one chosen.

The first two sections of the report are reprinted; the third asked that "a thorough restudy of our collecting and promotional procedure" be undertaken, and the remaining sections attempted to improve details of denominational governance and administration. *Source: Year Book of the Northern Baptist Convention,* 1949, pp. 115-116.

To The Northern Baptist Convention:

The Commission of Review, consisting of nine members, of whom five are laymen and laywomen, with the President of the Convention as an ex-officio member was appointed by the Convention in 1947 to make a thoroughgoing study of our whole denominational structure, with a view to making it more efficient, democratic, and responsive to the will of the churches.

We have had six meetings up to the present time, in Cleveland, Chicago, St. Louis, and San Francisco. Two of the most helpful of these have been open meetings, where any pastor, missionary, secretary, or member of a local church could present his thoughts concerning a more effective witness on the part of Northern Baptists to a world in need of the gospel.

The complete report of the Commission will be given in Boston in

1950, at which time we trust the Program Committee will set apart a major session of the Convention for discussion and action.

In the meantime, we submit to this session of the San Francisco Convention the following recommendations, with such necessary amendments to the By-laws and Standing Resolutions as in the judgment of the Law Committee and the General Council shall bring the procedure into accordance with corporation law and the rules of the Convention.

(1) A change of name from the Northern Baptist Convention to the American Baptist Convention.

Our Convention is a family of missionary societies nearly all of which have borne the name of American for more than a hundred years: American Baptist Foreign Mission Society, American Baptist Home Mission Society, Woman's American Baptist Foreign Mission and Home Mission Societies, American Baptist Publication Society and Board of Education, American Baptist Historical Society, and others. We believe the Convention should revive and cherish this historic tradition of its constitute societies by adopting the name American Baptist Convention, thus renewing our true genius, and widening our fellowship to those churches that today shrink from the territorial implications involved in the names Northern and Southern.

(2) The election of a General Secretary of the Convention.

We believe that steps should immediately be taken towards the combining of the present offices of Corresponding Secretary and Recording Secretary, and that at the end of the present year, such a combined office should be lifted above the mere clerical duties involved into a significant office that would make its occupant a recognized spokesman for the denomination and a correlator of the many scattered functions of our present system. We believe there is a precedent for such an office in our state convention practice and in the practice of the Southern Baptist Convention. The General Secretary should be one of the wisest, ablest, and most consecrated Christian leaders of the Denomination, with special gifts as an administrator and platform leader alike. He should be nominated by the General Council and elected by the Convention, with such tenure of office as the Convention might direct.

3. The American Baptist Assembly

Located in Green Lake, Wisconsin, the American Baptist Assembly quickly became an important center of American Baptist life, a place where persons of many backgrounds and viewpoints meet to find inspiration and discuss matters of mutual concern. The site was purchased in 1944 at a cost of $300,000; originally named the Northern Baptist Assembly, it soon became the scene of many conferences and a meeting place for committees and boards. Many improvements were made and new buildings added through the years. What follows is a brief history of Green Lake, prepared at midcentury. *Source: Year Book of the Northern Baptist Convention,* 1950, pp. 182-184.

It was fifty years ago that Victor E. Lawson, a great public-spirited Christian gentleman, purchased ten acres of land on the northern slope of beautiful Green Lake. To this lovely spot he brought his wife and together they began to build what was to be their country home.

Little by little the Lawsons began to add to their original investment acre upon acre and farm upon farm until finally they had acquired nearly 1,100 acres of the nation's finest countryside. Those high, rolling and heavily wooded acres, fronting for two and a half miles on the emerald-hued waters of Green Lake, provided the foundation for what was to become one of the world's most beautiful country estates. For you see, whatever the Lawsons set out to do they did well!

Quaint stone walls, sweeping lawns, colorful sunken gardens, myriads of birds and flowers, trees and shrubbery, buildings and road— these are the contributions of two fine Christian people of wealth and culture, who, without thought of ultimate profit and solely to satisfy their inherent love of beauty, gave of their abundant means and the best years of their lives to the development of what we now enjoy at Green Lake.

After the death of Mr. Lawson in 1925, the property was taken over by a Chicago real estate firm. What had been known throughout the lifetime of the Lawsons as the Lone Tree Point Farm now became the Lawsonia Country Club. The eleven hundred acres of rolling countryside was divided into literally hundreds of smaller estates and home sites. These were sold to people of wealth at what even today would be considered fabulous prices.

As part of this new development the real estate company erected a large number of buildings for housing purposes. The principal structure is a beautiful modern fireproof hotel with 81 bedrooms each equipped with a tiled bath. This building alone is valued at more than $500,000 without taking in account the furnishings which cost nearly $200,000 more.

No less than 35 summer homes were built ranging in cost from $7,500 to $10,000 each. Recreational features were added on the same lavish scale including a modern outdoor swimming pool; a yacht harbor and boathouse; tennis courts; a series of bridle paths twelve and a half miles long; and an 18 hole golf course, one of the finest in the entire Middle West.

Life at Green Lake took on a distinctly worldly character and the name "Lawsonia" became synonymous with expensive leisure for the moneyed few. Small wonder, then, that with the coming of the great depression the swanky country club idea failed and the property into which had gone at least ten million dollars went into the hands of receivers.

While the hotel and some of the summer houses continued to operate throughout most of the depression, even these were closed in the early days of the second world war as a result of gas rationing.

For many years a number of our denominational leaders have been praying and planning in the hope that some day we might acquire an adequate and beautiful place of retreat to which our laymen, women, youth, church school leaders, and ministers can go for periods of meditation, refreshment, inspiration, training and fellowship.

And so when Northern Baptists met in Atlantic City the proposal to purchase the Green Lake property for the establishment of a Northern Baptist Assembly was approved.

At the Milwaukee Convention in May, 1948, Mr. J. L. Kraft, our president, stated in presenting The Northern Baptist Assembly Report:

"Deep in the hearts of Northern Baptists is a prayer, 'Use me, O God, to do thy will . . . help me, O God, to walk in the steps of our Lord and Saviour Jesus Christ that I may know thy will. Show me how to work toward it and then give me the strength and courage to do it.'

"In answer to a part of that prayer, God has allowed us to possess a beautiful training ground. He has given us Green Lake for the use of the Northern Baptist Convention. Our Heavenly Father anticipated that prayer nearly fifty years ago when he inspired Victor Lawson to acquire about one thousand acres of that fairyland of waters, Green Lake.

"I believe, too, that the landscaping, the planting, the roadbuilding and every plan of beautification developed by Victor and Mrs. Lawson was inspired and in anticipation of answering the prayer by providing a place of inspiration from which might flow the spirit of Christ through the hearts of men to all the world.

"We feel that our Heavenly Father must have given us Green Lake so that by the inspiration of all its tranquility and beauty, we might render unto him a more devoted service, and discover in that environment a closer walk with God.''

4. The Headquarters Debate

The headquarters of the Northern/American Baptist Convention as a "family of societies" were long divided, principally between New York and Philadelphia. It was felt, as part of the process of denominational consolidation, that the major offices of the convention should be in the same city, preferably in the same building. But what city? By the middle 1950s the debate was raging in denominational publications and in the General Council. Three cities emerged as the leading contenders: (1) New York, at the new Interchurch Center; (2) Chicago, which was nearer the center of the communion's growing edge, its proponents argued, but they could not agree on a site—on the Midway near the University of Chicago or in the suburbs; and (3) Valley Forge, near to Philadelphia and adjacent to a historic American shrine. After careful analysis and extensive reflection, a Headquarters Commission recommended by an eight-to-four vote that the administrative headquarters be at the Interchurch Center in New York and the publishing offices and plant be at Valley Forge. The way the issue was finally decided at the ABC 1958 convention in Cincinnati was informatively summarized in a denominational magazine. *Source:* "Cincinnati, 1958 . . . Togetherness," *Crusader,* 13 (Summer, 1958), p. 3.

The Baptist Road is a rough one, strewn with every man's opinions. Last month in Cincinnati, in a "people's convention," American Baptists quickly and decisively declared themselves against a New York headquarters. But then they divided as two in the choice between Chicago and Valley Forge. And they made little progress along the Democratic Way until the spirit of sacrifice entered their midst. When they were joined—like the two on the way to Emmaus—by reconciling Wisdom, their hearts burned with conviction and the road ahead became bright with promise.

Friday the 13th was a day to remember. On that day—despite the 2-to-1 recommendation of the Headquarters Commission and the General Council, and after long and tense but respectful debate—the delegates voted against the New York Interchurch Center proposal by a 65% majority.

What they voted against was variously interpreted, on the negative side. On the positive, the vote was recognized as democracy's right to reject—without which it is weak and futile. More than likely it was an expression of the people's long-felt desire to be all together, in one place apart. The New York proposal (with part of the Board of Publication at Valley Forge) would have meant a divided house.

The Commission had done a thorough and conscientious job of fact-finding. Although two-thirds of its members favored the New York recommendation, it had concluded "that the Convention could operate with a good measure of success from any one of the three sites—New York, Chicago, or Valley Forge." The main differences, aside from costs and matters of efficiency, lay in "certain intangibles and spiritual witness." These proved to be factors of prime importance to the delegates.

Friday evening, with the hopes of Midwest proponents running high, the ballots were cast for a headquarters "in or near Chicago, with regional offices east and west." The votes in favor tallied just above 51%—short of the 55% majority previously agreed on.

Saturday afternoon the "Valley Forge boys" tried their case. The night before, in the debate on Chicago, Chairman E. J. Holt had swung his support to Valley Forge as the "second best choice of the Commission." Now the Rev. Emil Kontz, who wrote the case for New York in the June Crusader, also switched his allegiance to Valley Forge. Nevertheless, when the ballots were counted, the votes for Valley Forge were only seven more than those against.

Chicago advocates—divided in their preferences between the Midway (University of Chicago) and a suburban site—now decided to test the Midway proposal alone. Such a motion was presented at the close of the Saturday evening program. A rash of substitute motions availed nothing. Parliamentary confusion quickened the excitement. Adjournment was called for at 10:50 p.m., with action on the Midway motion deferred until Monday.

Over the Lord's Day it became clear that conciliation must supplant competition. The General Council met and decided—32 to 4—that on Monday, should the Chicago Midway vote not reach the required 55%, the Council would propose a final reconsideration of Valley Forge as a rallying choice, and this failing, that we remain just as we are.

Monday morning. First Vice-president Norman Paullin explains the Council's recommendation. The Chicago Midway motion is debated pro and con—with applause omitted. The ballots are marked and counted. Deadlocked again, at 51%.

Monday, 4:15 p.m. Rev. Randle Mixon presents the Council's motion to reconsider Valley Forge and regional offices. Prof. Lloyd Short, a Commission member, seconds the motion. Debate begins, with strong voices pleading for agreement on this "acceptable, if not agreeable" compromise. Among them is that of the Rev. Everett P. Quinton of Sioux Falls, S. Dak. A former supporter of a Midwest location, he now calls for unity at Valley Forge and decisive action so that the Convention might move on to evangelism and advance. (They were his last public words. He suffered a cerebral hemorrhage thereafter and died within two hours.)

Chairman Holt makes another stirring appeal for Valley Forge. And John Lavender, leader of the Chicago forces, makes the great sacrifice. He refers to the General Secretary's message in the June Crusader. He offers to go the "second mile" for the sake of unity in the family. He asks all to reconsider Valley Forge with the determination to be in one place and in one spirit.

A decisive standing vote approves reconsideration. Further discussion is suspended after repeated calls for the question. The ballots are marked and counted. Valley Forge is approved as the "happy mean" by a 69% majority!

No one could feel elated over the defeat of another's hopes. But there was a victory—one that belonged to the democratic process and the Christian spirit.

5. Dual Alignment

In a communion that is congregationally ordered and emphasizes the autonomy of the local church, a problem arises when congregations wish to align themselves with more than one convention. A standing resolution on the matter of the dual alignment of a congregation with more than one national body was worked out and adopted by the ABC General Council and follows. In areas where there are a number of both Southern and American congregations, as in the District of Columbia, the dual alignment pattern has been in effect for many years. Also, congregations primarily of black constituents, usually affiliated with the National Baptist Convention, Inc., or the Progressive National Baptist Convention, can participate in the life and work of the predominantly white American Baptist denomination. Congregational polity is sufficiently flexible to allow and encourage such developments, which of course further increases the variety of styles of piety within a communion. Dual alignment can be a two-way street, as is illustrated in an action of a state convention: "Inasmuch as the Negro Baptist Churches of the Pacific Northwest have been dually aligned with the American Baptist Churches of the Pacific Northwest for many years, Be it Resolved by this Convention that the predominantly white churches be encouraged to dually align themselves with one or more of the National (Negro)

Baptist Conventions." *Source: Year Book of the American Baptist Convention*, 1965/ 1966, pp. 525-526.

Resolved, That the following statement be adopted as a Statement of Policy on Matters Relating to Dual Alignment:

a. The Meaning of Membership in the American Baptist Convention

In the course of providing procedures for receiving churches, which are already members of other Baptist bodies, into the American Baptist Convention, it becomes necessary to define the philosophy of membership in the American Baptist Convention.

Historically the American Baptist Convention was formed to evangelize the world with the purpose of sending missionaries. Expanded, modified, and refined, this remains as the primary basis of American Baptist life and fellowship.

Therefore, the consideration of terms under which any church shall join the denomination must give due weight to this basic purpose. This implies that a church applying for membership shall do so with a sense of commitment to this underlying purpose and will give evidence of this through financial support as well as through participation in the educational, fellowship and program concerns of the American Baptist Convention. Recognizing the varied resources of leadership and income of the churches, it is obvious that the kind and amount of participation will reflect this varying capacity. Nevertheless, definite program goals and financial objectives should be placed before each church applying for membership.

These should include a beginning minimal amount to be increased annually looking to an ultimate goal of as much for missions as for current operation and at least equal shares to American Baptist Missions as to the other denominational body of which it is a member.

It should rest with the denominational unit, city, state or national, receiving such church into membership to negotiate the beginning amount as well as graduated scale by which the church expresses its commitment to this missionary purpose. This negotiation should take place prior to acceptance by any denominational unit, and should include a review of the chief features of the American Baptist ministry under the assumption that any church applying for membership will want to give its wholehearted endorsement to these features and standards, and further that favorable action by the denominational unit on the application of any church shall include evidence in support of such wholehearted endorsement.

It is further understood that there is an open door and wholehearted welcome for all such churches which seek membership in the American Baptist Convention, with full opportunity to share in the privileges and responsibilities that go with such membership.

6. Restructure in the 1970s: The American Baptist Churches in the U.S.A.

The various steps toward the organization (1907) and reorganization of the Northern/American Baptist Convention did not basically change the societal organizational structure of the denomination. In an effort to resolve some of the tensions between the national societies and between congregational independence and denominational order, a Study Commission on Denominational Structure (SCODS) was appointed in 1968. Its final report was accepted by the convention at Denver in 1972. The report provided for the new name and a radically revised governmental structure, vested quite sweeping authority in a General Board of some two hundred members, and called for a biennial rather than annual meeting of the denomination.

The matter of the proper relation of the state conventions and city societies to the denomination remained to be redefined; a Study Committee on Relationships (SCOR) made its final report in 1976.

At the ABC biennial meeting in San Diego in 1977, a new set of bylaws was adopted, incorporating all of the changes that had been approved. The bylaws went into effect on January 1, 1979. The main considerations behind these changes were stated quite compactly in the early pages of the 110-page final report SCODS presented in 1972. *Source:* Study Commission on Denominational Structure of the American Baptist Convention, "Final Report" (1972), pp. 9-14.

SCODS discussed the name of the American Baptist Convention at great length and sounded the constituency on the matter.* The Commission, after consideration of many concerns, recommends the new name "American Baptist Churches in the U.S.A."

The term "convention" came into the national organization in 1907 when the title "Northern Baptist Convention" was adopted. It was retained in 1950 with the adoption of the name "American Baptist Convention." Difficulty has existed with this name because for most people "convention" means "meeting" rather than "churchly body." SCODS wants to end that confusion.

*Commission hearings found strong support for a name change. Tallies ran: American Baptist Convention, 261; American Baptist Church, 579; American Baptist Churches, 561.

SCODS definitely wanted to emphasize the churchly aspect of the national organization and struggled over "Church" versus "Churches" in the proposed new name. It found in the hearings that the word "Church" seemed to imply to many of the constituency a national ownership of property, a connectional system, a creed other than the New Testament, the making of policy other than by the constituency, and a possible violation of local autonomy. None of these was the desire of SCODS and, consequently, it moved to the word "Churches" in the name.

Since SCODS proposals on A.B.C. polity underscore the significant change from a collection of societies to a national organization, the Commission saw the importance of recognizing the change by changing the name. "American Baptist Churches in the U.S.A." symbolizes the "churchly and national" dimensions of the national structure and underscores the principle that the constituency of the A.B.C. is "churches." "In the U.S.A." is needed for incorporation purposes, but will not be used except in legal documents. Further, the name reflects that a connectional system is neither the intention of SCODS nor the desire of a majority of the constituency. The new name clearly displays the interdependence as well as the independence of the A.B.C. and its units.

Specific Recommendations:

SCODS recommends to the A.B.C.:

A (1) The convention's name "American Baptist Convention" shall be changed to "American Baptist Churches in the U.S.A."

Statement of Principles and Process

SCODS decisions on representative structures were made after much debate, proposal, reaction, and change. Among the many principles guiding the Commission were the following:

—accepting and building upon the local church as the constituency of the denomination

—providing ways that local church concerns can be heard at the national level

—recognizing present groupings (congregations, associations, areas, clusters) for purposes of Election District Assemblies or Caucuses to select Representatives

—involving more local church Delegates in selecting those who will nominate persons for office on their behalf or who will frame Resolutions expressing their will on issues

—simplifying the mechanisms for the selection of Representatives to the Boards of the A.B.C.

—insuring the widest possible involvement of the diversity in the A.B.C. in the decision-making process by assuring participation of all groups in the denomination, Boards, Commissions, Committees, etc., at the points of decision

—creating a structure with flexibility to insure that the diversity and plurality in the A.B.C. can appeal to and be recognized by the national organization

—building a structure in which both lay and clergy (men and women in professional church leadership) have voices complementing without dominating the other

—providing for a regular flow of the abundant resources of the A.B.C. to all elements of its constituency

—emphasizing the oneness of the family through the establishment of a representative process linking the General Board and its Related Boards

—clarifying the roles and functions of the various structures for the mission of the A.B.C.

—devising a truly representative structure whereby the legislative function is meaningful, significant, and inclusive

—clarifying the roles of national meetings where local churches which cannot afford to send Delegates are represented

—clarifying the roles of legislative bodies where Representatives of local churches do the business of the A.B.C.

—electing Representatives by whom the entire constituency is enfranchised rather than creating the illusion of maximum democratic process through the "town-hall meeting" format of annual meetings.

NATIONAL MEETINGS OF A.B.C

SCODS has examined carefully the concerns about the annual meeting of the A.B.C. Attendance at convention has averaged 3,249 Delegates. Policy provides for over 21,000 to participate in these sessions. In the 1971 meeting in Minneapolis slightly more than one out of every five (22%) congregations in the A.B.C. were represented. Of the Delegates present, seventy percent were pastors or pastors' wives. The unrepresentative nature of the annual meetings raises the question of ability and the right of such meetings to take legislative action and to handle the business of the A.B.C.

SCODS recognizes the growing needs, however, for celebration for the enrichment of the fellowship and the inspiration for the mission of the A.B.C. Likewise, it is cognizant of providing the professional leadership regular and supported opportunity for continuing education and feels that the years between Biennial Meetings offer that possibility.

To achieve better stewardship of funds and more inclusive representation of the local congregation's interests at the National Meetings of the A.B.C., SCODS is recommending that the local church Delegates meet biennially in the odd years, at a time and place to be set by the General Board. At that meeting the local church Delegates become the membership of the A.B.C. They are responsible for the election of the President, Vice President of the A.B.C. and Representatives at-large of the General Board. The Biennial Meeting will consider and adopt Statements of Concern and conduct such other business as shall be presented, including any amendments to the bylaws of the A.B.C.

Education, Mission, and Evangelism

When an eminent Baptist historian of Christian missions, Kenneth Scott Latourette (1884–1968) came to the last of his seven-volume series, *A History of the Expansion of Christianity,* he focused it on the years 1914–1945 and entitled it *Advance Through Storm* (New York: Harper & Bros., 1945). So for Northern/American Baptists, advances in mission, evangelism, and education were made, but they were made in the face of difficulties. Problems were posed by the changing world scene: for example, the closing of mainland China as a mission field because of the victory of the Chinese Communists; and at home, the formidable obstacles to the carrying out of witness in the overcrowded, heterogeneous, secularizing metropolises. Problems were also arising out of the continuing storms of the Fundamentalist/Modernist controversy. Yet the tasks of mission, evangelism, and education were advanced by devoted workers at home and abroad with the active support of the congregations across the land. Though some of the historic Baptist educational institutions were not able to survive and a few became nondenominational, others continued to affirm their ties to the denomination, and some new ones were founded.

1. Investigating Educational Institutions

At the meeting of the Northern Baptist Convention in Buffalo in 1920, when strong resolutions were proposed that a commission investigate the various schools, colleges, and seminaries to see if they measured up to conservative theological standards, a stormy debate followed. Finally more moderate substitute resolutions were moved and were adopted; they are reprinted as Selection A.

Not surprisingly the action evoked considerable discussion across the denomination. John Roach Straton (1875–1929), prominent New York pastor and Fundamentalist leader, penned an article, "Is It Right and Wise to Investigate Our Theological Seminaries?" and concluded that it was, as an excerpt (Selection B) shows. But others resisted. For example, William Herbert Perry Faunce (1859–1930), liberal president of Brown University, the first of the Baptist institutions of higher education to sever its formal ties with the denomination (some years later), wrote to the chairman of the investigating committee, resisting any effort to impose theological tests on schools and colleges. *Sources:* A. *Year Book of the Northern Baptist Convention, 1920,* pp. 60-61. B. *The Baptist,* 1 (28 August 1920), pp. 1071-1072. C. W. H. P. Faunce to Frank M. Goodchild, 16 February 1921. Archives, American Baptist Historical Society.

[A. The Substitute Resolutions]

32. After discussion by Rev. J. C. Massee, of New York, Rev. H. J. White, of Connecticut, presented the following resolutions and moved that they be accepted as a substitute for the resolutions before the Convention.

WHEREAS, With unshaken faith in God our Father, revealed in Jesus Christ his Son, in dependence upon the constant guidance of the Holy Spirit, we hold in grateful remembrance our Baptist heritage, and

WHEREAS, Baptists have steadfastly contended for the competency of every soul in the sight of God, refusing to concur in the imposition of any doctrinal test by either political or ecclesiastical authority, now therefore be it

Resolved, That in solemn recognition of our responsibility for maintaining and transmitting unimpaired to others this heritage of faith and this liberty which we have in our Lord and Master, we reaffirm our loyalty to him; and we call upon all ministers and members of our churches, all teachers in our schools, colleges, and seminaries, and all officers of the Northern Baptist Convention, to maintain and proclaim the gospel of Jesus Christ in all its simplicity, purity and power; and be it further

Resolved, That, reaffirming the competency of every soul in the sight of God and its direct responsibility to God, and affirming also our confidence in one another as brethren in Christ, we declare that we will not seek to have dominion over one another's faith, but that we will by our fidelity to our common Master and by our Christian service to those for whom he died, seek to provoke one another to good works, earnestly praying for the coming of the day when every knee shall bow and every tongue confess that Jesus Christ is Lord to the glory of God the Father; be it further

Resolved, That, to the end that our schools may efficiently and adequately contribute to the cause of pure religion, and may send forth into our churches men and women fitted to be leaders in the defence of the faith and the building up of the churches of Christ, we request the trustees and faculties of all our schools carefully to examine their work, to correct evils which they may discover, and to put forth a statement of their purpose and work, which may give assurance to the denomination of their fidelity to the Saviour, and to the gospel as held and proclaimed by Baptists immemorially; and be it further

Resolved, That the Northern Baptist Convention appoint a representative committee of nine, who shall inquire into the loyalty of our Baptist schools to Jesus Christ and his gospel and to the historic faith and practice of the Baptists and their efficiency in producing men and women of Christian character and capacity for Christian service, and that this committee report to the Northern Baptist Convention at its meeting in 1921. Be it further

Resolved, That the Committee be instructed to investigate the method of election or appointment of trustees in all our secondary schools, colleges, and theological seminaries, and that they report upon the entire question of the control of these institutions.

[B. John Roach Straton's Response]

The action taken at the recent session of the Northern Baptist Convention, providing for a committee to investigate our schools and seminaries, was highly significant. There is a widespread feeling today that many of our theological seminaries are not teaching their students the great fundamental truths for which our Christian brotherhood historically stands. In a recent series of articles in one of the religious papers of the country statements were made by the presidents of a number of the seminaries as to what their institutions believed and were teaching. A brother speaking for one of the great seminaries said in that symposium:

"We conceive our task in the seminaries to be, not to impose upon our students a set of dogmas or opinions even, but rather to inspire them with a passion for truth, to show them the way which leads to it, to acquaint them with the tools, methods, and results of scholarship, and to assist them, as far as we can, to arrive at definite convictions for themselves. That is Baptistically and educationally orthodox."

But is this really orthodox from either the denominational or the educational viewpoint? What would we say, for example, of a law school that laid down such a program as that as the basis for its work, and did not impart to its students any clearly defined and authoritative principles and facts? What would we say of a medical college that did not impart definite principles and processes of healing to its students, or did not venture to give them "opinions even," but simply turned them out with certain "tools" and "inspired with a passion for truth?" Would anyone who was sick want one of these impassioned young doctors, who was nosing around seeking for "truth," to use his "tools" upon him? Let every doctor begin practicing medicine according to his own whim and impulse, in fulfillment of his "passion for truth," and would not the undertakers and manufacturers of tombstones become speedily the most prosperous citizens in the community?

And suppose that, as a result of what they were given in the medical schools, numbers of young physicians either came out without any great enthusiasm for their life work, or with a decision to give up entirely the practice of medicine, because the aimless teaching of the medical school had led them to believe that the profession was not much worthwhile after all. If such a thing as this came to pass, would not a tremendous chorus of indignation go up from the constituencies of the medical schools?

But have we not an exactly parallel case in connection with many theological seminaries today?

Is there anything at last more tragic than this? Here is a young man who feels called of God to preach the gospel. He is full of spiritual warmth and enthusiasm. Because of his work as a layman in his local church, and under the inspiration of earnest preaching by a faithful pastor, he has a zeal for souls and a desire to give his whole life to the work of saving souls. To these high and sacred ends he is set apart by his church; and then he goes away to a theological seminary. But instead of finding there an atmosphere surcharged with the same passion for souls that is in his own breast, he finds a rationalistic atmosphere with strong over-emphasis on intellectualism. Step by step his enthusiasm is cooled down by these things. There is so much uncertainty concerning religious truths, and there are so many question marks and negations in his class room, that he finds himself not being equipped for doing his appointed work in the world, but growing cold spiritually and losing his great, overwhelming, life-dominating convictions on the authority of the Scriptures, the deity of Christ, and the fact that without Christ souls are entirely lost. And so he reaches the point where he either leaves the ministry or drags along in a perfunctory way. Is there anything more tragic than this? . . .

[C. W. H. P. Faunce to Frank M. Goodchild]

My dear Dr. Goodchild:

In reply to your letter of February 11th, I would say that I fully recognize the delicate duties imposed upon your committee by the vote of the Northern Baptist Convention and I desire, personally, to render all possible help. The cause of Christian education is dear to us all, and only through cooperation can progress be made.

When, however, it is proposed to impose any theological tests upon schools and colleges, Brown University is obliged by its charter to decline such imposition. The charter, whose date is 1764, represents the historic attitude of the Baptist denomination when it declares: "Into this liberal and catholic institution shall never be admitted any religious tests, but on the contrary, all the members hereof shall forever enjoy full, free, absolute, uninterrupted liberty of conscience." If, therefore, we should respond to your questionnaire, we would violate our charter and subject ourselves to legal action.

The question, however, is very much broader than the legal one. Baptists have from time immemorial enjoyed the freedom which is affirmed by the Brown Charter. It was to escape from the imposition of tests that this University was founded. The Baptists of Philadelphia came to Rhode Island in order that they might escape from the tests imposed in other colonies and find here in the land of Roger Williams freedom from all man-made creeds. If they now submit to any theological formulas imposed by ecclesiastical authority, they thereby part with their birth-right. May we not ask that your committee respect the historic position of the denomination? I earnestly hope that all the schools founded by Baptists in this country will affirm once again the conviction of our fathers and stand fast in the "soul liberty" of Roger Williams and in the original faith of the founders of Brown University.

Sincerely yours,

W. H. P. Faunce

2. Church-Related Educational Institutions

In the nineteenth and twentieth centuries, Baptists have been active in the founding of many academies, colleges, and seminaries. Though some have not survived into the later twentieth century and others have become private or nondenominational institutions, a number of recognized, usually fully accredited, institutions have continued to serve in variously defined ways both church and academic constituencies. A list of schools related to American Baptists provides an overview of the situation at this high-water mark in 1940 (see page 401). *Source: Annual Report of the Northern Baptist Board of Education,* 1940, pp. 24-25.

3. The Inclusive Policy Defended

The conservative criticism of certain trends in education was also applied to the American Baptist Foreign Mission Society. Its Board of Managers issued a statement defending its policy. The first two (of three) parts of the open letter follow. The letter was signed by Frederick L. Anderson (1862–1938) and William B. Lipphard (1886–1971), respectively chairman and recording secretary of the Board. *Source:* "A Statement by the Board of Managers of the American Baptist Foreign Mission Society, New York, November 15, 1923." Archives, American Baptist Historical Society.

TO THE NORTHERN BAPTISTS,
Dear Brothers and Sisters:

The Fundamentalist, a paper edited by Dr. John Roach Straton and issued by the Baptist Fundamentalist League of Greater New York, has attacked the policy and good faith of the Board of Managers of the American Baptist Foreign Mission Society in its last three numbers, which it has sent broadcast through the Denomination. The charges may be reduced to three, (1) that the Board neglects the work of personal evangelism for education and social service, (2) that the Board permits the teaching of liberal doctrines by its missionaries, (3) that the Board has not been straightforward in its dealings with the Denomination. We now proceed to reply to the charges in order.

I.

The Board of Managers of the American Baptist Foreign Mission Society recalls that the corporate object of the Society, as stated in its charter, is "the diffusion of the knowledge of the religion of Jesus Christ by means of missions throughout the world," and now reaffirms that in pursuance of that object the proclamation of the gospel of Christ is its primary aim. It rejoices that in general the evangelistic results in the foreign mission work of the Denomination have steadily increased through the years, until in 1922 the number of reported conversions and baptisms was larger than ever before. It is the full purpose of the Board of Managers to maintain this emphasis on direct evangelism.

NAME	LOCATION	NAME	LOCATION

THEOLOGICAL SEMINARIES

NAME	LOCATION
1. Andover Newton	Newton Center, Mass.
2. Berkeley	Berkeley, Calif.
3. Bethel	St. Paul, Minn.
4. Chicago	Chicago, Ill.
5. Colgate Rochester	Rochester, N. Y.
6. Crozer	Chester, Pa.
7. Eastern	Philadelphia, Pa.
8. German	Rochester, N. Y.
9. Kansas City	Kansas City, Kans.
10. Northern	Chicago, Ill.

10 Seminaries

JUNIOR COLLEGES

NAME	LOCATION
1. Alderson-Broaddus	Philippi, W. Va
2. Bacone	Bacone, Okla.
3. Bethel	St. Paul, Minn.
4. Bucknell	Wilkes-Barre, Pa.
5. Colby	New London, N. H.
6. Colorado	Denver, Colo.
7. Frances Shimer	Mt. Carroll, Ill.
8. Rio Grande	Rio Grande, Ohio
9. Stephens	Columbia, Mo.
10. Scranton-Keystone	La Plume, Pa.

10 Junior Colleges.

TRAINING SCHOOLS

NAME	LOCATION
1. Chicago	Chicago, Ill.
2. International	East Orange, N. J.
3. Kansas City	Kansas City, Kans.
4. Norwegian	Chicago, Ill.
5. Philadelphia	Philadelphia, Pa.
6. Spanish-American	Los Angeles, Calif.

6 Training Schools

ACADEMIES

NAME	LOCATION
1. Coburn	Waterville, Me.
2. Cook	Montour Falls, N. Y.
3. Hebron	Hebron, Me.
4. Higgins	Charleston, Me.
5. Maine Central	Pittsfield, Me.
6. Peddie	Hightstown, N. J.
7. Pillsbury	Owatonna, Minn.
8. Ricker	Houlton, Me.
9. Suffield	Suffield, Conn.
10. Vermont	Saxtons River, Vt.
11. Wayland	Beaver Dam, Wis.

11 Academies

UNIVERSITIES AND COLLEGES

NAME	LOCATION
1. Bates	Lewiston, Me.
2. Brown	Providence, R. I.
3. Bucknell	Lewisburg, Pa.
4. Carleton	Northfield, Minn.
5. Chicago	Chicago, Ill.
6. Colby	Waterville, Me.
7. Colgate	Hamilton, N. Y.
8. Denison	Granville, Ohio
9. Franklin	Franklin, Ind.
10. Hillsdale	Hillsdale, Mich.
11. Kalamazoo	Kalamazoo, Mich.
12. Keuka	Keuka Park, N. Y.
13. Linfield	McMinnville, Ore.
14. Ottawa	Ottawa, Kans.
15. Redlands	Redlands, Calif.
16. Rochester	Rochester, N. Y.
17. Shurtleff	Alton, Ill.
18. Sioux Falls	Sioux Falls, S. Dak.
19. William Jewell	Liberty, Mo.

19 Colleges

NEGRO SCHOOLS

NAME	LOCATION
1. Benedict	Columbia, S. C.
2. Bishop	Marshall, Texas
3. Jackson	Jackson, Miss.
4. Leland	Baker, La.
5. Morehouse	Atlanta, Ga.
6. Storer	Harpers Ferry, W. Va.
7. Virginia Union	Richmond, Va.
8. Florida Normal	St. Augustine, Fla.
9. Shaw	Raleigh, N.C.
10. Spelman	Atlanta, Ga.

10 Negro Schools   66 Schools
Grand Total

Sometimes indeed in the history of the Society it has not been possible to balance the direct evangelistic, the educational, the medical and general humanitarian features of the work according to our best judgment. In the work abroad, as in the churches in this country, there are periods of sowing and reaping, and it is very easy to mention certain places or times in which results have not been satisfactory either to the missionary or to the Board.

The evangelization of vast Oriental and African populations can never be accomplished by white foreigners alone. It must be the task of capable native Christian leaders, who can be developed only by a thorough Christian education. In more than one instance it has been discovered that where there have been mass movements toward Christianity without trained native leaders to guide the new converts, a reaction toward paganism has followed. The increased emphasis on Christian education has been with a view to a wider proclamation of the gospel and also to the training of native leaders capable of developing self-supporting, self-governing and self-propagating churches and other Christian institutions, and of taking a large part in the direction of affairs in general in their own lands. We have learned from experience that in certain countries the denominations which have neglected Christian education have fallen far behind others in evangelistic results.

Nor should it be forgotten that upon certain fields a large proportion of all the baptisms reported (sometimes more than half) are in the schools, not to mention the large numbers who are reached in the hospitals. It is a mistake to assume that all the evangelistic results are in the work of the so-called evangelistic missionaries. Some of the most successful soul-winners are teachers and physicians. Many of the very best are native Christians. The Board of Managers endeavors to promote a spirit of evangelism in the hearts of all missionaries and in every form of work.

We definitely and positively repudiate the idea that social service is the supreme thing, and so far as we are aware, no one connected with our Society would think of substituting it for salvation. At the same time, we believe that we are following in the steps of our Master when we establish hospitals for the sick, and support other efforts to relieve human poverty and suffering. Moreover, through such service many are brought into acquaintance with the Christ, who Himself healed the sick, and had compassion on the hungry multitudes. The oral proclamation of the gospel must be accompanied by visible forms of service which illustrate the spirit of Christ. So far from substituting social service for salvation, we teach that salvation of the individual and the world must be found in Christ, and we point men to Him and His Cross as the moving power for every form of service.

II.

It is charged that the Board permits the teaching of liberal doctrines by its missionaries. Our Board has frankly stated to its constituency that it gives to its officers and missionaries a considerable degree of liberty of theological opinion in accordance with the long standing policy of the Denomination, and that it firmly and kindly declines to reverse that policy. Our Denomination, like our individual churches, is made up of men and women of diverse views, and our Board, most appropriately made up in the same way, thinks it only right, fair and wise that our missionary force should reflect the situation in our churches at home. We have no intention of restricting our appointees and missionaries to any one group. We represent the whole Denomination and we treat all our constituency as brothers and sisters in the faith.

This does not mean that individually we are neutral, ''indifferent,'' or hesitant about important doctrinal differences. Each one of us holds his views strongly, and earnestly seeks to inculcate them, but, as a Board, entrusted by the whole Denomination with its vast and varied foreign work, we seek the firm ground common to us all and stand together on that. It is on this common ground that we administer our great trust with mutual respect and brotherly love.

Our great foreign work has been done by all kinds of Baptists. It belongs to the whole Denomination, and cannot bear its richest and largest fruits without the hearty cooperation of all. If we are united in heart and in loyalty to the Savior, whom we all love, diversity of view is an advantage and a blessing, giving our work a balance, a sanity and a manysidedness, which helps us constantly to rise to higher things. We earnestly believe that Northern Baptists are in the deepest sense one body, and Paul long ago said that it takes many diverse members to make up a living and growing body (I Cor. 12).

This does not mean that we will appoint or retain any Baptist in good standing, regardless of what he may or may not believe. There are limits beyond which we will not go at either end of the line. We will not knowingly appoint any brother, conservative or liberal, who holds such personal views and gives such expression to them as would impair his fellowship with his colleagues on the field or obscure the vital message of the gospel of Christ. In every case, too, we are just as anxious to discover the fruits of a regenerate life, a passion for the souls of men, and a personal devotion to our Lord Jesus Christ, as correctness of intellectual belief. We want men and women so full of the Spirit and with hearts so warm that they can fuse the souls of men to Christ.

The exact limits of theological liberty have slowly changed in our Denomination with the years, and will doubtless further change in the future. Our Board represents the *present* feeling of our constituency. Freely elected, it is the Denomination's living voice in its sphere and its decisions are, we humbly believe, made in the spirit of Christ. Future Boards, with new light and facing new conditions, may decide somewhat differently, and doubtless will. We, today, must act as kindly, truly and wisely as we can. We ask not only the generous consideration of all our brethren, but their prayers that we may be led aright. . . .

4. Baptist City Planning

Home mission leaders learned many things about modern cities as they carried on their evangelistic and educational tasks among heterogeneous populations. A leader in such efforts was Charles Hatch Sears (1870–1943), who served as the executive secretary of the New York Baptist City Mission Society and then of the Baptist Church Extension Society. Early in 1925 a planning conference on urban church work was held in Washington, D.C.; Sears edited a book made up largely of the committee reports given at the conference and revised in the light of discussion. The final, summary chapter, reprinted in substance, presented the formal "Findings of the Washington City Planning Conference," which illustrated trends in urban home mission planning at that time. *Source:* Charles H. Sears, ed., *Baptist City Planning* (Valley Forge: Judson Press, 1926), pp. 266-270.

City Planning

As Christian citizens our people should be urged to interest themselves in cooperation with the municipalities, with a view to safeguarding the interests of the churches in the City Planning Movement. Special attention is called to unfortunate zoning regulations in certain cities where churches are debarred from certain residence areas. It is neither fair nor safe for churchmen to disregard city planning.

Protestant City Planning

In view of the vast areas of spiritual destitution in the cities, we advise our churches to determine their united policy in the light of the needs of the neighborhoods and population groups as well as the growth or prestige of the denomination. To this end there should be hearty cooperation with other evangelical bodies in the local Council or Federation of Churches of the city or the section in which such an organization is needed.

Baptist City Planning

We call upon our constituency in the cities to face their task, not as separate church units, but as a united denomination and to seek to develop the sense of denominational responsibility for the Baptist share in a ministry to the whole city, with loyalty to the local church as a means to the larger end. This involves the substitution of denominational solidarity for congregational selfishness.

The Down-town District

That it should be the general policy of the denomination, and where necessary, involving cooperation of the city organization, to maintain strongly at least one down-town church which (1) may minister to the adjacent populations, including transients; (2) may sustain an intimate relation to the moral and civic problems of the city's life, and (3) may furnish a rallying-center for the denomination easily accessible from all parts of the city. We observe that some down-town churches are providing equipment with income-bearing features in order to assure a larger ministry to make their future secure.

The Newer Residence District

That according to the consensus of successful experience in establishing churches in newer residential districts of our cities, (1) the building sites provided should be located with a view to the fullest advantage of publicity and convenience and should be ample for future expansion and, (2) the educational unit usually should be erected thereon first. We find that in most cases where these newer churches cherish a purpose or recognize an obligation to serve the entire unchurched community some form of associate or affiliate membership is provided for and has proved generally successful.

The Polyglot and Foreign District

The Conference concurs in the judgment of the subcommittee that in training workers for leadership among foreign-speaking people some provision should be made for augmenting the regular course of study in a foreign language by a course of advance study in the English language if possible at a standard seminary.

An adequate salary standard for our foreign-speaking pastors should be recognized and the workers encouraged to qualify for it. The needs of the younger generation for services in the English language must be recognized and met.

A constant and careful check-up on the program of activities in Christian Centers must be kept in order to assure the desired results in view of the fact that we are still in the initial and experimental stage of developing this work. English-speaking churches that find themselves situated in contact with foreign-speaking or polyglot population groups should adopt this program with the design of meeting the needs of this element of the community life.

In view of the fact that many city churches find themselves in close proximity to Jewish people who are religiously adrift it is urged that all possible avenues of approach and ministry to them be thoroughly explored.

The Negro District

We recommend that the leaders in white churches take steps to promote contacts with the colored leaders, and arrange frequent conferences with them so that, together, they may make a careful study of local Negro situations. That in order to develop a strong leadership the entire matter of training such a leadership should be given fresh consideration by the two Home Mission Societies.

Social Service

We recommend that the Northern Baptist Convention immediately enlarge and strengthen its Department of Social Service, and give itself whole-heartedly to the instruction and inspiration of every pastor in the convention, to make him a leader of his people in the application of the teachings of Jesus to modern conditions, and sympathetic with the importance of the service of young people as well as older men and women in various wider avenues of social welfare and social service, both community and interdenominational.

The Church and the Industrial Problems

The growth of cities is directly associated with the growth of modern industry, with its concentration of machinery, mass production, and consequent concentration of manual workers. The church in the city therefore is confronted with and is involved in the social problems created by industry. Church leaders must be intelligent concerning the issues and problems involved and make diligent inquiry as to the mind of Christ regarding them. The Conference calls attention to the available material and suggested methods of group study of these problems put forth by the Committee of Inquiry as to the Christian Way of Life and Industry.

The Church and Social Welfare

In considering this and the closely related matter involving the Church and Social Service, the Conference was reminded that the relation of social service and social welfare was analogous to that of relief and aid demanded by a railroad wreck and the primary problem of safeguarding life with a view to preventing wrecks.

The State City Plan

The Conference is strongly of the opinion that the State Conventions should prosecute with greater vigor their cooperative denominational work in smaller cities through a Baptist City Union, and that care should be exercised to promote the closer coordination of city and State work in the larger cities.

The City Plan of Evangelism

In giving most earnest consideration to the vital importance of a city-wide program of evangelism as well as evangelism in the local church, the Conference urges that no single method be exclusively relied upon. The most wholesome and satisfactory results are to be obtained by enlisting and training for constant, intelligent service the largest possible number of wise and consecrated personal workers.

5. Last Days in China

Something of the meaning of the revolution for missionaries and local populations can be seen in these excerpts (Selection A) from personal letters of Willie P. Harris, R.N. (1897–1977) to friends back home. They were written from Hwa Mei Hospital, Ningpo, not long before missionaries in China had to be recalled.

The second selection is from an educational missionary's "home letter" from Chengtu, Szechuan. Many of the missionaries who were recalled were assigned to other foreign missionary fields. Others retired or accepted posts at home. *Sources:* A. Willie Harris, to the Board, October 15, and November 18, 1949. Correspondence Files, ABFMS. Archives, American Baptist Historical Society. B. Clarence G. Vichert, to the Board, February 10, 1950. Correspondence Files, ABFMS. Archives, American Baptist Historical Society.

[A. Willie P. Harris]

October 15, 1949

After the severe bombing of Sept. 17 and the burning of Sept. 22 the populace leaves the city at 5:00 a.m. and returns at 6:00 p.m. We took turns here at the hospital after the 29th doing just this but only for three days. I'm getting ahead of my story.

We were all on duty except the less brave students when about 10:30 a.m. on Sept. 29 a heavy bomb was dropped on the oil tank in the river right by the Thomas house. This tank belonged to the Electric Light and Power Co. which is just over our back wall. Three other bombs were dropped within a city block of us.

After all four had dropped and the noise of the plane had stopped we dared step out. I was sitting, holding Anne-Ruth, Jr. when the first bomb fell—the door opposite me blew in, the transom of the door behind me fell! When I went over to my apartment it was a mess but not quite as bad as Thomas's home which got the worst of it. Thirty-five window panes in my apartment were broken! Several window frames blown out or off. The ceiling in every room fell. How lucky I was not to be in bed when I should have been, as I had a very heavy cold and a temperature of 102. The truth of the matter is I was afraid to be caught in such a wreck with my shoes and glasses off—so I wouldn't stay in bed. Now I have cystitis as a complication!

For several days we left only a skeleton staff to care for the few patients who couldn't be discharged and the rest of us went to the country at 5:00 a.m. and returned at 6:00 p.m. As nothing happened in our section after that we began to run again as usual but had classes only at night. Today a plane came over and dropped leaflets saying they would bomb the city even worse and the targets were clearly stated. Three of the targets are within a city block of our hospital—north, west and south. The river is to our east so we decided to get all the patients out tonight. We have a small branch hospital opened last week in a temple in the country. We will go there every a.m. and return here to have O.P.D. from 7-9 p.m. and then to sleep but leave each a.m. by 5:00 o'clock. How many days we can do that I do not know.

The school is disbanded—we said for all students to go home. We hope to open again next term. We will let them know when to return. We have 20 graduate nurses who can run the several O.P.D. places we now have.

November 18, 1949

The cablegrams told you of the destruction and the temporary closing of the school and the opening of country clinics. I also wrote a general letter telling of some things in more detail and that letter has probably reached you.

In the cablegram it said I was in the country. I spent nearly three weeks at the clinic there and it was running smoothly but things in the main hospital needed attention so I moved back into the city and am now working in the main hospital every day trying to salvage as much as possible and make a new inventory of what is here. . . . The loss of all I own (except some of my winter clothing and bedding) did not sadden me one-hundredth as much as the talk of closing the school. For this school has been my life work. All of the students who have graduated (200 in all) have been graduated since I came.

It so happens that just now in this time of turmoil we have a few graduates here who are less loyal to us than to the new government and one of them happens to be the principal of the school, so their attitude has saddened us all and at times made one wonder if it had all been in vain, but the loyalty of a few others has more than made up for it.

I have lived in a room 9 x 12 with stone floor and no ceiling (three weeks in the country and ten weeks in the city) and eaten common Chinese food and proved that I can take it so I am willing to stay here and carry on this way if that is best or I am willing to go to the U.S.A. if I can do more for the hospital and school there.

[B. Clarence G. Vichert]

February 10, 1950

The past year has been one of waiting for the arrival of the Liberation Army. After the fall of Nanking and Shanghai the Szechuanese knew the occupation of their province was inevitable. It was hoped there would be a peaceful turnover but this proved impossible. Since Chengtu was the last KMT capital on the mainland KMT officials and armies concentrated in this area. A delaying action was fought to allow as many officials as possible to escape by air to Formosa. There was heavy fighting near the Chengtu air fields and for days we could hear the boom of big guns. On Christmas Eve the sound of firing ceased and Christmas Day we knew the battle was over. Several days after Christmas the Liberation Army made its formal entry into the city.

The entrance of a victorious army into a captured city is a highly emotional experience. In this case the Red Star Army had obtained an objective for which they had been working and sacrificing since their Long March fifteen years ago. The soldiers, who had been marching and fighting for weeks, came into the city happy but too tired to respond to the enthusiastic welcome of the students. After the victory parade the armies were allowed several days of rest before going on to their next objective.

The immediate period after Liberation was one of festivity and general relaxation. The students paraded, sang Liberation songs and danced the Yang Ko. The business people opened their shops and the farmers began to bring their products to market. The Red Star soldiers were uniformly polite and anxious to make a good impression on the common people. Foreigners were not mistreated in any way.

Later, after the celebrations had died down, it became evident that victory has a price tag on it. Taxes had to be levied to support both the Liberation troops and the armies which turned over. In addition there are all the agencies and institutions connected with the New Government to be supported. The taxes have, of necessity, been heavy and there are those who look with longing upon the past. Chairman Mao has said that 1950 will be a difficult year and we have no reason to doubt his word. . . .

So far our work has been affected only indirectly. There has been no interference with our regular services and under the constitution of the New Democracy we are assured religious liberty. However the basic philosophy of Communism is materialistic and Chairman Mao has said the leaders of the government cannot approve of religion. Mission activities which serve the physical needs of the people will be allowed to continue but other activities may have to be curtailed.

There are certain changes in the new society which we particularly welcome. Class distinctions are being removed and the standard of living is being equalized. Administrative procedure in government, business, industry and education is democratic in the sense that all concerned have the right to discuss and vote. Emphasis is put upon propaganda work that all classes may know the fundamental principles of the New Democracy. There is an honest recognition of personal mistakes and failures. The party members seem to be sincere in their desire to establish a Socialist State. Their enthusiasm is contagious. . . .

Next term the number of students in our schools will be greatly reduced because of taxation and because of the government need for educated personnel. With smaller student bodies the professors will be able to give more time to class discussions and this is a method which has the endorsement of the University Advisors from the Military Bureau. All classes in religion will have to be optional and no credit will be given for them.

6. Continuing Witness in India

From the beginning of overseas missions, India has been a primary field for both Northern and Free Baptists. With the closing of China, American Baptists redoubled their Asian efforts in Assam, Bengal-Orissa-Bihar, and South India, where in 1960 a total of 102 personnel were employed in India alone. Frederick S. Downs (1932–   ), associated with Eastern Theological College, Jorhat, Assam, for over twenty years as faculty member and president, reported in a 1964 letter the multifaceted involvement of an American Baptist witness in the face of food shortages, political strife, and difficult terrain. *Source:* Frederick S. Downs to ABFMS Board, 9 November 1964. Correspondence Files, ABFMS. Archives, American Baptist Historical Society.

. . .This has also been a year of important political developments. The most important was the death of Jawaharlal Nehru. He had led the country through its first 17 years of independence and had a personal mystique that no successor can inherit. The food crisis of the past summer and the resultant spiraling inflation have not made it easier for the new government. Agricultural production is simply not keeping up with human production. The future of India in large measure depends upon its success in controlling the size of its population. This is often said, but it strikes home when one sees the panic of a near famine.

On a more local level we are greatly encouraged by political developments in the neighboring state of Nagaland. We are especially concerned with this area because almost half of the churches that make up the Council of Baptist Churches in North East India, of which we are a part, are located there. For ten years there has been rebellion against the Government in Nagaland. Violence and suffering have been the rule rather than the exception throughout this period. Now, primarily through the efforts of Church leaders, a cease fire has been declared and representatives of the rebel movement are sitting down to negotiate with representatives of the Government. A positive witness is being given to the reconciling Gospel. The leadership of the Naga Christians in this peace effort has been a source of inspiration to Christians throughout India—as I have learned on my several trips outside the area this year.

In October, Mary and I had an opportunity to attend a young people's convention in Nagaland. Previously, we had been unable to get permits to enter the area. The trip was a very difficult one—over roads of such quality that it took us 10 hours to travel just under 100 miles. Often we had to use the compound-low 4-wheel drive of our Jeep station wagon. But it was well worth the trip. We had four days together with 3,000 young people and visitors in a village perched on top of a mountain. The Nagas always build their villages on high places, even if it means having to go down more than 1,000 feet to get water. This goes back to the days when they had to defend themselves against neighboring villages and tribes. Now they just like the sensation of being on top of the world! It is less easy to enjoy when one's legs haven't been conditioned to it. This was one of those occasions from which one gains a great deal more than one gives. . . .

7. Billy Graham

One of the best-known religious leaders in the world in the last half of the twentieth century is William F. (Billy) Graham (1918–   ). A member of a Southern Baptist congregation, Graham is supported by his own evangelistic institute and has conducted revivals in many cities of the world during his long career as evangelist. Many American Baptists have actively supported his campaigns. One of his most successful early crusades that attracted worldwide attention was held in London in 1954. The selection that follows is from an address he gave at a ministers' meeting in the Assembly Hall of the Church House, Westminster, on March 20, 1954. *Source:* Billy Graham, *The Work of an Evangelist* (London: The Evangelical Alliance, 1953), pp. 14-21.

Now there are several dangers to this business of mass evangelism. The first is *the danger of false emotion*. I tell you quite frankly that it is possible for an orator to stand up and sweep a mass of people off their feet by his eloquence. It is possible for him to use bed-time stories and death-bed tales and moving illustrations, and for people to come forward with great emotion and in tears—and it may look genuine; but the people are weeping over the story told and not over the conviction of sin by the Holy Spirit. I learned this very lesson about two or three years ago, and we've cut out all stories and illustrations at the end of our messages—and all emotional stories whatsoever. If you were to come to our meetings you would say that there is no emotion whatsoever. You would wonder how anybody made a decision. A man must be convinced intellectually. His emotions must be touched—yes, because emotions have drive and will; but it is the will of man that exerts all feeling in making a decision for Christ. His will must change to the will of God. And unless that will is touched and unless that will is transformed and changed, the man is not converted to Christ. Just a little emotional upset is nothing. The person who makes a purely emotional decision is far worse than before. . . . Then secondly, there comes the old criticism: *Converts don't last.* Jesus must have heard it, because in the Parable of the Sower He had something to say about this. "Those by the wayside are they that hear; then cometh the devil, and taketh away the word out of their hearts, lest they should believe and be saved." Jesus said that in the case of some hearers the devil is going to come along and take the Word out of their hearts, lest they be saved.

Did the Lord Jesus tell us that because so much seed-sowing is apparently fruitless that we are not to sow? Never! But let me tell you, you clergymen and ministers and pastors, you face exactly the same problem in your church work as we face in our evangelistic missions. You receive ten people into your church on a Sunday. You are going to do well if three or four of those ten people are faithful in church attendance every Sunday for the next year. . . . Now, concerning converts not lasting, I want to say a word about the follow-up programme that we have inaugurated. I do not think—and I say it humbly before God, for we give Him the praise for giving it to us—I do not think it has any parallel possibly in the history of modern evangelism. In explaining our follow-up work I'd like to start way back before our campaign. Suppose we are going to a city like Washington, D.C. . . . We always have, six months in advance of our campaign, classes for personal workers or counsellors. These classes are taught by members of our Team who go ahead, or they are taught by some local man who has been chosen by the local committee. . . . For example, John Smith makes a decision for Christ in the evening service. Immediately a process, a machine, starts into motion. We have learned that it takes about 5 per cent effort to win a man to Christ and 95 per cent to keep him resting in Christ and growing into maturity in Christ and in the church. And so our major effort is to get the man to grow in Christ.

We now have on our Team thirteen men in follow-up—full time in follow-up—headed by Dawson Trotman. Thus it is that when John Smith comes forward to make a decision for Christ he is dealt with in the inquiry room by a counsellor who has been trained over a long period of time. We choose these counsellors not only because they are church leaders and because they are spiritual people, and because they have a knowledge of the Work, but because they look decent. We tell them how to dress and deport themselves; we give them every type of instruction. John Smith is carefully dealt with by a man of his own age group, of his own social standing. We have them divided into all of these classifications. He is dealt with from anywhere between fifteen minutes and an hour—or it may be sometimes two hours—in personal counselling. That's in addition to the little message that I or one of my colleagues give in the inquiry room.

The counsellor forwards to the office all relevant information concerning the convert. Statistics are kept as to age groups, church preference, and so on. A card is sent immediately to the church of his preference. If he has no preference the card is sent to a committee of ministers appointed by the churches of the city. That committee of ministers chooses a church that is geographically close to him or one that they consider he could fit into. And so he is passed on immediately to that particular pastor and that church. Next the convert receives letters, and then we start him on a Bible study programme. . . . In Seattle, Washington, we had approximately 9,000 who made decisions for Christ in the campaign there.

There is another criticism that comes to evangelism. There is *too much excitement*. People find the evangelistic service so different from the worship service. They go to the evangelistic service and hear the evangelist speak with a certain amount of vigour and he hits the pulpit. And they go to their church on Sunday and the minister doesn't hit the pulpit. What's the matter with him? Why is he so dead?

First of all, I'd like to say that perhaps it might do the minister good and the church good if he did hit the pulpit once in a while—if he doesn't frighten himself too much. Because I do think that we are living in such an era to-day when we need to become slightly excited over these affairs. We are in such a spiritual condition that we need to become somewhat vigorous in our presentation of the Gospel to the people. The Communists are. . . . I don't know about Britain, but I know that in America any evangelism that is to be successful and is to do any permanent good must be integrated into the church. I've been severely criticized by both the fundamentalist groups in our country for the all-inclusive policy that we have adopted in our campaigns. But I tell you this, I would never pull a punch from the Word of God in order to compromise with one man—I don't care who it may be—who might be in the audience. I welcome all the men of every theological structure to come and join with us if they will lift up Christ. On the Executive Committee of our campaigns we have only men who accept the deity of the Lord Jesus Christ, which includes the Virgin birth, the vicarious atonement and the bodily resurrection. . . . And then there is a final criticism of evangelism. It is said that *there is too much emphasis on finance*. How do we manage in regard to that? I am going to tell you. When we go to a city we never handle the finances ourselves. We have nothing to do with it. We advise those concerned on the different methods of spending money on advertising and all the rest of it, but we never handle the funds ourselves. The only requirement we have is that the accounts be audited and published in the newspapers when the campaign is over so that everybody knows where every penny went. The local ministers handle all the money. They receive all funds—and they distribute all funds.

8. The Baptist Jubilee Advance, 1959–1964

The Advance, a cooperative endeavor in evangelism and mission of seven Baptist conventions, was a six-year commemoration of the 150th anniversary of the national organization of Baptist work in America, 1814. It was supported (in whole or in part) by the American Baptist Convention, the Baptist Federation of Canada, the Southern Baptist Convention, the National Baptist Convention of America, the National Baptist Convention, Inc., the Northern American Baptist General Conference, and the Seventh Day Baptist General Conference. As the Advance drew near to its conclusion, the committee that guided the·work of the ABC presented a rather full report to the General Council; selections from the "Findings and Recommendations" of that report are reproduced. *Source:* "Report to the General Council by the National Committee and Executive Director of the Baptist Jubilee Advance, 1959-64," pp. 12-14. Records of the American Baptist Convention, Archives, American Baptist Historical Society.

The five years of the Baptist Jubilee Advance, coming as they did at a strategic moment in our history, have injected into the life of our Convention something which warrants recognition as a turning point in our approach to program. With foresight born of willingness to see and confess the growing impotence of the church as presently constituted while the secular power structures determine the shape of modern life, the BJA committee made a crucial decision. . . . The decision was to structure the BJA in terms of the church's need for rigorous self-examination and recovery of the full Biblical implications of its commission to preach the gospel and disciple the nations, in witness to Christ as Lord over the world. This required the creation of programs emphasizing year by year all the elements of change and reconstruction needed in its ministry if the church is to fulfill the purpose for which it exists. . . .

Today the task has become bewilderingly complex. To have strong preachers and missionaries does not suffice. We as American Baptists face the staggering complexity of an urban metropolis, and the church has come almost to a halt. The suburban churches face the question, "How can these congregations become the people of God?" We are at a loss to know how to penetrate the social structures which shape and determine modern life. Ministries assumed by the church in the past are assumed by the state, and the church feels edged out from the mainstream of human events. The social revolution sweeping through the world has severed its religious roots and has become secular. Ancient non-Christian faiths are again on the march with evangelizing zeal.

Strong men are bewildered. Requests for help and pleas for understanding are coming from the thoughtful and concerned men of the church. It is thoughtless and unjust to assume that tireless effort and dedication alone can accomplish the mission. For the denomination to assume that it has grasped the answers would not be facing the magnitude of the situation.

What then can we do? We can confess with integrity that we are desperate. We need to reassure heroic pastors and laymen that their troubled spirit is no reflection on their competence, their consecration, or their faith in the adequacy of Christ. God summons us to understand this baffling world more deeply, to listen with keener discernment to the Spirit of Christ, and to live in such obedience as to discover his way of redemption for the 20th century. This is why theological engagement is so necessary.

By theological engagement is meant discerning the nature and purpose of God's mission in the world and participating with faithfulness and obedience in that mission. Theological engagement involves study and action, worship and work, reflection and witness. Theological engagement is the total response of the church in missionary obedience. Then what does this mean for American Baptists?

Nature and Purpose of Mission

God is calling us to a theological engagement *to discern what is the nature and purpose of mission,* which raises the fundamental question of God's mission and purpose for the world. Paul speaks of it as, "His purpose which He set forth in Christ." (Eph. 1:9) Our fathers spoke of "God's Plan for the Ages," while modern man might call it "the Christian Philosophy of History" . . . .

We can scarcely understand the church's mission except as we see the larger cosmic purpose of God, what it is that He is bringing about in the world. The Bible uses such terms as Shalom, the Kingdom of God, the New Heaven and the New Earth. We have focused on one narrow aspect of the Biblical witness, the Church, and we are imperiled with distortion when we do not see the Church in the context of God's larger purpose.

Baptist World Alliance, London, 1955

The Riverside Church, New York City

Valley Forge Offices, American Baptist Churches in the U.S.A.

Relationships with Other Baptists and Christian Groups

The various Baptist conventions, large and small, have generally been reluctant to merge with each other or with other denominations (though there have been some exceptions; see the discussion of the Northern/Free Baptist Union of 1911, pages 338-341). Some of the smaller ethnic conventions have merged with larger conventions, while others have rejected that option. Efforts to merge American Baptists with the Disciples of Christ, another congregationally ordered, believers' baptism denomination, came to naught after a number of attempts.

Yet Baptists have found ways of working together for stated purposes, such as the defense and extension of the principle of religious freedom. The Baptist World Alliance, which has met six times on the North American Continent, has been a positive force toward further cooperation. One of the outcomes of the Baptist Jubilee Advance was the organization by seven conventions of the North American Baptist Fellowship. A more formal type of Baptist cooperation was the working out of an "associated relationship" between the American and Progressive National Baptist conventions. Though some Baptist bodies wanted no relationship with the National and/or World Councils of Churches, others, such as the American and National Conventions, have participated faithfully (see the article by John E. Skoglund, pages 366-368). Despite the great differences in the Baptist family, there is a core of principles and attitudes that gives it a certain coherence and identifiability.

1. American Baptists and Ethnic Conventions

As various small Baptist bodies representing particular nationality groups became fully Americanized and largely English-speaking, there seemed to be less reason, to themselves and others, for continuing their independent existence as small denominations. So the Danish-Norwegian Baptist Conference of America at first affiliated with Northern Baptists and then became so closely related to its structures that the Conference dissolved in 1956 and became fully a part of the American Baptist Convention. But when the somewhat larger General Conference of German Baptist Churches in America (now the North American Baptist Conference) was invited to enter an "associated" status with the Northern Baptist Convention in 1938, it responded two years later in a gracious but firm resolution that declined the invitation. *Source: Verhandlungen der 26. Bundes-Konferenz der Deutschen Baptisten Gemeinden von Nord-Amerika, . . . 1940,* p.12.

WHEREAS the Northern Baptist Convention has extended to the General Conference as to all other foreign language Baptist groups, which have been in a measure the outgrowth of her missionary activities, a most cordial invitation to enter into an associate relation with her entitling the General Conference to a representative in the General Council, but involving no financial obligation nor any abridgement of the independence of the General Conference, and

WHEREAS the relation between the German Baptists and the American Baptists in the territory of the Northern Baptist Convention as well as in that of the Southern Baptist Convention and the Canadian Baptist Convention has always been most cordial, and the English brethren have always and everywhere been most gracious in their attitude toward the brethren of the General Conference, but

WHEREAS our territory extends over that of the Southern Convention and the Canadian Convention also, and

WHEREAS no such affiliate relation with reference to the latter Baptist Conventions is in contemplation, and

WHEREAS such an affiliation would place a portion of the General Conference into a different status than that which other areas of said Conference enjoy with reference to their numerically stronger brethren, and such difference might become divisive in effect, and

WHEREAS the affiliation might be a step which would lead to further involvements for which the General Conference seems not ready at this time, therefore

BE IT RESOLVED, that we express to the Northern Baptist Convention our most hearty greetings and our gratitude for the kind solicitude which they have always manifested on our behalf, and

BE IT FURTHER RESOLVED, that we advise them as to our present status with regard to our territory and as to how it overlaps and goes beyond the border of their convention, making the suggested arrangement appear impracticable and that we, therefore, find it inadvisable for the present to accept their gracious invitation. But we do assure the brethren of the Northern Baptist Convention that we are one with them in spirit, in fellowship, and in the furtherance of Christ's Kingdom on earth.

BE IT FURTHER RESOLVED THEREFORE that we encourage our churches to cooperate with the Associations and Conventions of the Northern Baptist Convention to the best of their ability, as they have done in the past and that a copy of these resolutions be sent to the General Secretary of the Northern Baptist Convention.

Unanimously adopted as is.

2. Should Baptists and Disciples Unite?

As denominations that were somewhat parallel in size and belief, both Northern/ American Baptists and Disciples of Christ have periodically been interested in discussing a possible merger. The question came up again in 1947; a Joint Commission was appointed. As its work progressed, the newsmagazine *Crusader* gathered a group of promient Baptists to discuss the matter. Much background information was provided by the chair of the Baptist delegation in the joint commission, Hillyer H. Straton (1905–1969), a pastor in Massachusetts.

The substance of the issue never came to a vote before the Baptists; sensing that the opposition, especially in the Midwest and Southwest, was very strong and that the question would be very divisive, at its own suggestion the commission was dismissed in 1952. The Disciples went on to reorganize as the Christian Church (Disciples of Christ) and to enter the Consultation on Church Union (1962–   ). Baptists did not enter the Consultation except as observers. *Source:* "Should Baptist and Disciples Unite?" *Crusader,* 4, (November 1949), pp. 2-5.

Let me begin with a word or two of history. Over 100 years ago the people who are now known as Disciples of Christ were a part of the American Baptist group. (That was before the division into Northern and Southern Baptists.) For 17 years we were one people together. Following the division, about 1830, one of the main problems that the Disciple group had was the problem of a name. A section of them continued to be known as Reformed Baptists. One of their first publications for years had been the title: REFORMED BAPTIST. But they kept coming back to the idea that they didn't want non-Biblical names to be connected with the united church they were trying to establish. And so they said, "Well, we are simply Christians, we are Disciples of Christ." And so today many churches may be known by some such title as "Union Avenue Christian Church," and then you will find under the sign on the wall of that church: "Affiliated with the Disciples of Christ."

There have been a number of different times during the past 100 years when Baptists and Disciples have considered this matter of union or reunion of their two groups. If I remember the dates correctly, one of the first was in 1866 when Dr. W. T. Broaddus of revered memory in Southern Baptist history had something to do with a discussion between Disciples and Baptists. The subject was broached two or three other times between that date and 1928. In that year Dr. Edgar DeWitt Jones, then pastor of the Central Woodward Avenue Christian Church in Detroit, delivered an address at the Northern Baptist Convention in Detroit in which he made a plea for Christian unity.

Following his address there was a committee appointed by the Northern Baptists to go into the whole matter. A report was brought to the Northern Baptist Convention at Cleveland in 1930. One of the members of that committee, Dr. Frederick L. Anderson, professor of New Testament at the Newton Theological Institution, brought in a minority report, and after long debate that minority report was accepted by the Convention. The minority report in effect killed further talk between Northern Baptists and Disciples at that time.

The burden of Dr. Anderson's plea was that if Northern Baptists continued to talk or possibly united with the Disciples, it would jeopardize very seriously Northern and Southern Baptist relations. It was hoped that Southern Baptists and Northern Baptists would reunite in the foreseeable future, and that if Northern Baptists and Disciples effected a union, then this would impede the possibility of Northern and Southern Baptists uniting.

The matter was dropped for a period of 10-odd years, and then in the early 1940's a committee was again appointed to explore relations with the Disciples of Christ. The committee was headed by Dr. Edwin T. Dahlberg who was later elected president of the Northern Baptist Convention. At the time he was elected he asked me to serve as chairman of that committee. In 1947 we were asked point blank by the Disciples, what did we intend? Were we really interested in a possible union or were we just interested in some pleasant words with each other?

Now when we were faced as frankly as that with this question on the part of the Disciples' leaders—and it was uttered in all kindness and in every good faith—we had to face it ourselves. We felt that we were interested in the possibilities of reunion with the Disciples if that were in the will of God. So we went to the Northern Baptist Convention meeting in Atlantic City and asked what they would do. And at the Convention it was unanimously voted that we explore *again* the possibility of union with the Disciples of Christ. That word *again* was put in purposely and it was put in with emphasis because of the previous contacts we had had. At that time it was requested that our committee be elevated to the status of a commission with special standing and prerogatives to do this task.

Well, from that moment on we have gone forward with a sense of directive to actually explore the possibility and the wisdom of union with the Disciples of Christ. Now that has been misinterpreted by some in our Convention. They have felt that our only task was to survey the history of the two groups, and make a report of that history. In my judgment that was not the directive of the Convention. It was clearly stated that we were to explore again the possibility of union. So we do have to explore history and theology. But one of the most vital factors we have to explore is where Disciples and Baptists stand at the present time, not necessarily where our great-grandfathers stood, but where we stand.

Now that has involved contact with the Disciples. It has involved a meeting with them, because if you are ever going to find out what a man thinks or believes, you've got to have some contact with him. Just studying antecedents or parentage is not enough. So we have felt that we were within our prerogatives to have joint meetings of Baptists and Disciples, to have youth conventions, to propose the possibility of a joint or simultaneous Northern Baptist and Disciples convention. Well now, I think that brings us up to date. . . .

3. Joint Witness for Religious Liberty

The historic and continuing Baptist concern for religious freedom was clearly stated in 1939 in a statement unanimously passed at the annual session of the Southern Baptist Convention (May 20, 1939), the Northern Baptist Convention (June 21, 1939), and the National Baptist Convention (September 7, 1939). The pronouncement, given in full, was published in 1940 by the Associated Committees on Public Relations, claiming to speak for more than ten million persons, and widely circulated. *Source:* The American Baptist Bill of Rights: A Pronouncement upon Religious Liberty (Leaflet, Associated Committees on Public Relations, 1940), pp. 2-4.

A Pronouncement upon Religious Liberty

No issue in modern life is more urgent or more complicated than the relation of organized religion to organized society. The sudden rise of the European dictators to power has changed fundamentally the organic law of the governments through which they exercise sovereignty, and as a result, the institutions of religion are either suppressed or made subservient to the ambitious national programs of these new totalitarian states. . . .

Baptists Stress Spirituality

The principles that animate the activities of the Baptists, principles which they hold clearly to be taught in the New Testament are the worth of the individual; the necessity of the new birth; the preservation of Christian truth in Christian symbols; spirituality, or the free pursuit of Christian piety; the persuading of others through personal testimony, by the life of example, the preaching of the gospel and the creation of Christian institutions, to the end that the unbelieving will be reconciled to God through a personal faith in Jesus Christ; the organization of groups of obedient believers into churches of Christ, democratic in the processes and theocratic in the principles of their government, and the continued uplifting of human society through the Spirit of Christ and the ideals of His Kingdom, having as its final objective the establishment of the eternal, unchanging purpose of Almighty God in the hearts of men and the institutions of mankind.

Affirm the Competency of the Human Soul in Religion

The conception of the dignity of the individual, as held by Baptists, is grounded in the conviction that every soul possesses the capacity and the inalienable right to deal with God for himself, and to deprive any soul of his right of direct access to God is to usurp the prerogatives of the individual and the function of God.

Free Churches Within a Free State

Standing as we do for the principle of voluntariness in religion, grounded upon the competency of the human soul, Baptists are essentially antagonistic to every form of religious coercion or persecution. We admit to our membership only those who give evidence that they are regenerated, but we recognize gladly that the grace of God is not limited to those who apply to us, and that our spiritual fellowship embraces all who have experienced the new birth and are walking in newness of life, by whatever name they may be called. We hold that the Church of Christ, which in the Bible is called "the body of Christ", is not to be identified with any denomination or Church that seeks to exercise ecclesiastical authority, but includes all the regenerated whoever and wherever they are, as these are led by the Holy Spirit. This Church is a body without formal organization, and therefore cannot enter into contractual relations on any basis with the State. For this reason, Baptists believe in Free Churches within a Free State.

Today Baptists Feel Constrained to Declare Their Position

Since every session of the Congress considers legislation that raises the question as to the relation of the Federal Government to the institutions and the agencies of religion, and since recently many tendencies have appeared that involve the freedom of religion and conscience, and furthermore, since there are some state constitutions which do not have embodied in them the Bill of Rights of the Federal Constitution, American Baptists feel constrained to declare their position and their convictions.

The Trend Toward Paternalism

Today the trend of government, even in democratic countries, lies in the direction of greater centralization. The philanthropic activities of the churches within the United States are being taken over by the government. The defective, the indigent, and the dependent groups of our social order have long been supported from public funds. The greatest charity agency on earth today is our Federal Government. More and more the people are looking to the State to provide. As a nation we are becoming paternalistic. Efforts are now being made to place in the hands of the government the pensioning of those who are employed by the churches and the agencies that serve them: to grant to sectarian schools financial aid from tax-raised funds, and to support from public funds institutions that are established and managed by sectarian bodies.

Baptists Condemn the Union of Church and State

Baptists hold that the coercion of religious bodies through special taxes, the use of tax-raised funds for sectarian schools, and the appropriation of public money to institutions created to extend the power and influence of any religious body, violate the spirit of the First Amendment and result in the union of State and Church.

Oppose Special Favors Extended to Any Ecclesiastical Body

We oppose the establishing of diplomatic relations with any ecclesiastical body, the extension of special courtesies by our government to any ecclesiastical official as such, and the employment of any of the branches of our national defense in connection with religious services that are held to honor any ecclesiastical leader. All such violations of principle must be resisted in their beginnings.

Citizens of Two Commonwealths

We acknowledge ourselves to be citizens of two commonwealths, one earthly, the United States, the other heavenly, the Kingdom of God, and we claim the right to be good citizens of both. We recognize the sovereignty of the State and we give allegiance to the State, but we cannot give the State the control of our consciences. We must obey God rather than men.

The government resorts to coercion; we use persuasion. The government has authority over the acts of its citizens; we have to do with the motives. The business of the government is to make good laws; our business is to make good citizens who continue to demand the enactment of better laws, embodying higher and still higher ethical standards. The end of governmental administration is equal justice under law. The end of endeavor is the establishment of the will of God in the hearts and institutions of men. If one of us accepts an office in the government, he recognizes it not only as a public trust, but also as a divine entrustment; for the powers that be are ordained of God. In a democracy like ours, it is possible to be a loyal American and a devoted Christian. This is true because religious liberty is an essential part of our fundamental law.

Defenders of Religious Liberty

Believing religious liberty to be not only an inalienable human right, but indispensable to human welfare, a Baptist must exercise himself to the utmost in the maintenance of absolute religious liberty for his Jewish neighbor, his Catholic neighbor, his Protestant neighbor, and for everybody else. Profoundly convinced that any deprivation of this right is a wrong to be challenged, Baptists condemn every form of compulsion in religion or restraint of the free consideration of the claims of religion.

We stand for a civil state, "with full liberty in religious concernments."

4. Rights of Japanese Americans

One of the most unpleasant chapters of American history is that of the evacuation of all people of Japanese ancestry from the West Coast, following the attack on Pearl Harbor,

December 7, 1941, which brought the United States into World War II. Over 100,000 persons were uprooted and sent to "relocation" camps; the large majority of those so quickly evacuated were, in fact, American citizens. Representatives of many churches protested and provided comfort and help to the Japanese Americans in the time of crisis and in the resettlement process that followed. In 1943 the Joint Committee on Public Relations, representing Northern, Southern, and National Baptist conventions, adopted the following resolution at a meeting in Washington on April 27. *Source:* File, Committee on Public Relations, Records of the Baptist Joint Committee on Public Affairs. Archives, American Baptist Historical Society.

The Joint Committee on Public Relations, representing the Northern, Southern and National Baptist Conventions, views with grave concern the public statements of organizations and individuals making indiscriminate charges against all American citizens of Japanese ancestry linking them with those Japanese who are responsible for the outrageous execution of the American aviators who were military captives in Japan. The United States government had demonstrated its belief that no such indiscriminate condemnation of all American citizens of Japanese ancestry is justified by releasing many such citizens from detention camps for civilian employment and by organizing regular army units of such citizens for armed services abroad. As representatives of church organizations which have been working for many years with Japanese in America, we desire to make public record of our conviction that no blanket condemnation of all American citizens of Japanese ancestry is in any sense justified. We are convinced that loyalty to American democratic ideals and aversion to the purpose and practices of Imperial Japan among these American citizens of Japanese ancestry is comparable to that of other groups of American citizens and that they are patriotically desirous of the overthrow of the Axis powers for the sake of the peace of the world. We desire to declare our confidence in the competency of our government to discover and restrain all traitorous and subversive elements which exist among Japanese in the United States and its territories, differentiating between those that are loyal and those that are disloyal to our country. We likewise affirm it as our conviction that instead of aiding our government in this necessary undertaking, those who call upon the government to deny all civil rights to American citizens of Japanese ancestry are playing into the hands of the powers that are fighting against us by adopting their point of view in regard to race and in abrogating certain fundamental tenets of our democracy.

Adopted at a regular meeting of the committee on Public Relations, held in Washington D.C., April 27th 1943.

5. The North American Baptist Fellowship

The Baptist Jubilee Advance (see pages 415-417) terminated in 1964, but the experience was so fruitful for the seven North American Baptist bodies involved that continuing in some form seemed desirable. The project came under the wing of the Baptist World Alliance; its Administrative Committee took the action described in its records, and the North American Baptist Fellowship began its series of annual meetings. *Source:* Minutes of the Administrative Committee, 14, 15 March 1963. Records of the Baptist World Alliance. Archives, American Baptist Historical Society.

PROPOSAL OF NORTH AMERICAN BAPTIST FELLOWSHIP. At the meeting of the Joint Committee of the Baptist Jubilee Advance held at Valley Forge, March 12, 1963, the question was faced as to the possibility of a continuing fellowship among Baptists in North America after the final meeting of the Baptist Jubilee Advance in Atlantic City in 1964. Woyke read the following communication which the BJA Joint Committee had addressed to the Administrative Committee and the Executive Committee of the Baptist World Alliance:

In order to conserve the gains and values which have resulted from the Baptist Jubilee Advance and to increase opportunities for fellowship and for sharing of mutual concerns we make the following suggestions:

1—That the Baptist World Alliance give consideration to the creation of a North American Baptist Fellowship or Alliance.

2—That such an organization provide for an annual meeting of leaders of participating Conventions, Conferences, Federations.

3—That a general fellowship meeting of the North American Baptist Fellowship or Alliance be held midway between the Congresses of the Baptist World Alliance. (The meeting planned for Atlantic City in 1964 might serve as a pattern.)

All members present were in agreement that the fellowship begun in the Baptist Jubilee Advance should continue, and that the best sponsoring body for a North American fellowship would be the Baptist World Alliance. This would, of course, mean added duties for the Washington staff. The participating bodies have had provision for the BJA in their budgets over the past five years, and before this money is earmarked for other projects it should be spoken for again for the continuing fellowship group. Probably the same type of organization would be recommended as that of the North American Baptist Women and the European Baptist Federation. Concrete suggestions should be presented at Atlantic City so that upon the expiration of the BJA the forming of a North American Fellowship would naturally follow. MOTION was made and adopted that the suggestions of the Baptist Jubilee Advance Committee regarding the formation of a North American Baptist fellowship be approved in principle, and that the chairman appoint a committee to study means for its implementation and to report to the meeting of the Executive Committee in Waco in August.

At the close of the meeting Hargroves appointed Woyke as chairman of the special committee, and Adams, Moore, and Tuller as members.

6. American and Progressive National Baptists

The American Baptists developed a category of "National Associated Organizations" whereby certain national church bodies could enter into a relationship with American Baptists of mutual fellowship and voluntary cooperation. In 1970 the first such body to enter the relationship was the Progressive National Baptist Convention, a group that left the National Baptist Convention, Inc., in 1961 because of discontent with various administrative, organizational, and procedural matters. Within a few years the new denomination had just over a half million members. It entered the associated relationship with American Baptists in 1970. One of the outcomes was the Fund of Renewal, a campaign jointly sponsored by the two communions to raise a substantial sum (the goal was $7.5 million) to help meet some of the most pressing human needs of minority groups. A flyer issued by both conventions explained the policy concerning "associated organizations" in some detail; the introductory passages are provided. *Source: Progressive National Baptist Convention and American Baptist Convention in Associated Relationship* (n.p., n.d.), pp. 1-2.

In 1970 the American Baptist Convention and the Progressive National Baptist Convention each extended to the other an invitation to become an "associated organization." On May 14, the American Baptist Convention, in annual meeting at Cincinnati, Ohio, unanimously voted to accept the invitation to the Progressive Convention. On September 9, the Progressive National Baptist Convention at its 9th annual meeting at Kansas City, Missouri, in turn, responded unanimously to the invitation of the American Baptist Convention. Thus was completed a two-way relationship which had begun two years earlier when a joint committee of representatives of the two Conventions met on October 22, 1968, at the American Baptist Assembly, Green Lake, Wisconsin, under the chairmanship of Dr. Gardner C. Taylor, then president of the

Progressive Convention, to explore ways by which the two bodies might work cooperatively together in areas of mutual concern.

What does it mean to be "associated organizations"?

1. Associated organizations are autonomous national denominational bodies which acknowledge a mutual desire to be in close Christian fellowship and to witness together and cooperate in mission together wherever feasible.

2. It may also be described as providing a bridge across which the "associated organizations" can move freely in various forms of cooperation at all levels of their respective church life without losing identity as autonomous denominational bodies.

3. It provides a means by which the congregations of each "associated organization" are encouraged to enter into fellowship and cooperative endeavors in local communities with the other denominations as a further evidence locally of the "associated" relationship of the parent bodies nationally.

4. It is a means by which the program agencies of each "associated organization" can feel free to engage in joint projects which may require joint funding and sharing of personnel.

How does the relationship as "associated organizations" work?

While not being an organic union, it is a meaningful relationship by which the two bodies can address themselves to those matters which are of concern to all black and white people in the United States, particularly in areas of higher education, economic development, community organization, and a revitalized Christian witness. Illustrative of the aim has been the work of the PNBC and ABC Joint Fact-Finding Committee surveying the needs of most Black, Hispanic, and Indian churches of both conventions, as well as three national minority organizations (Council on Hispanic American Ministries, Opportunities Industrialization Center, and Southern Christian Leadership Conference) and seventeen educational institutions. In the light of the report of needs, a feasibility study was authorized by the ABC and PNBC in 1971, to suggest ways and means whereby two national bodies can engage jointly in a major fund-raising campaign for minority groups.

Suggestions For Further Study

Several recent titles help to introduce Baptist identity and mission in this period. Some of these books are denominationally oriented while others involve the larger American religious scene. A good, popular survey of Baptists is O.K. and Marjorie Armstrong, *The Indomitable Baptists* (New York: Doubleday, 1967) while Robert T. Handy, *A History of the Churches in the United States and Canada* (New York: Oxford University Press, 1976) places the group in the mainstream of American and Canadian Protestant issues and developments. Following the Baptist Jubilee Advance in 1963, Baptists of many persuasions produced *Baptist Advance* (Nashville: Broadman Press, 1964), which highlights a multiplicity of Baptist contributions in the twentieth century milieu. An important series of interpretive essays in the bicentennial context is James E. Wood, *Baptists and the American Experience* (Valley Forge: Judson Press, 1976). Robert A. Baker, *The Southern Baptist Convention and Its People 1607–1972* (Nashville: Broadman Press, 1974) presents the official history of the SBC in this century, while an older work, Samuel S. Hill and Robert J. Torbet, *Baptists North and South* (Valley Forge: Judson Press, 1964) focuses on the real issues dividing the two major conventions and the prospects for closer ties.

On American Baptist denominational life, Robert T. Handy, "American Baptist Polity: What's Happening and Why," *Baptist History and Heritage* (14 July, 1979) is a must. The author carefully traces the involved organizational history of Northern/American Baptists through the Study Commission on Denominational Structures in 1972. Another study, Paul M. Harrison, *Authority and Power in the Free Church Tradition* (Princeton: University Press, 1959) analyzed the American Baptist Convention at an earlier stage, using a sociological approach.

The advance of foreign missions is best illustrated in missionary ancedotes and biographies. Three representative personal accounts are: Catherine L. Mabie, *Congo Cameos* (Valley Forge: Judson Press, 1972); Gordon S. Seagrave, *My Hospital in the Hills* (New York: Norton, 1955); and John B. Hipps, *Fifty Years in Christian Mission: An Autobiography* (Raleigh: Edwards and Brighton, 1966). For solid, interpretive biographies, consult Leland D. Hine, *Axling: A Christian Presence in Japan* (Valley Forge: Judson Press, 1969) and Orville E. Daniel, *Moving with the Times* (Toronto: Canadian Baptist

431

Mission Board, 1973). A distaff emphasis that traces organizational integration is Louise Cattan *et. al., One Mark of Greatness* (Valley Forge: Judson Press, 1961).

American Baptist home missions have moved in several directions and through a number of changes in the past three decades. On the social problems confronting the churches early in this era, see Robert M. Miller, *American Protestantism and Social Issues 1919–1939* (Chapel Hill: University of North Carolina, 1958) for capitalism, oriental exclusion, and peace; on the urban scene, see Lincoln Wadsworth, *Mission to City Multitudes* (Valley Forge: Judson Press, 1954). Likewise, Clayton A. Pepper, *The Development of the Town and Country Church Movement Within the American Baptist Convention 1911-52* (Valley Forge: Judson Press, 1952) balances the urban strategy. Jitsuo Morikawa, *Biblical Dimensions of Church Growth* (Valley Forge: Judson Press, 1979) is suggestive of the ABC program thrusts in church development in recent years.

Billy Graham, as a symbol and a personality, has vividly influenced Baptist evangelistic styles since the 1950s. For the official biography, see John M. Pollock, *Billy Graham: The Authorized Biography* (New York: McGraw Hill, 1966); for a quite different interpretation, compare William G. McLoughlin, *Billy Graham: Revivalist in a Secular Age* (New York: Ronald Press, 1960).

A distinct home missions bibliography is available. William H. Brackney, *The American Baptist Home Missions Experience: A Bibliography and Resource Guide* (Valley Forge: National Ministries, 1981); and G. Pitt Beers, *Ministry to Turbulent America: A History of the American Baptist Home Mission Society 1932-57* (Valley Forge: Judson Press, 1957) in part survey the recent history.

On the subject of education, several studies or reports are useful in understanding Baptist contributions. In 1942 the Northern Baptist Board of Education commissioned a survey of seminaries and ministerial training and the result was Milton Froyd and Hugh Hartshorne, *Theological Education in the Northern Baptist Convention: A Survey* (Valley Forge: Judson Press, 1945), a book which profoundly influenced theological education for several years. A similar, individual effort was undertaken for the SBC and resulted in Edith C. Magruder, *A Historical Study of the Educational Agencies of the Southern Baptist Convention 1845–1945* (New York: Columbia University, 1951). Within the last two decades American Baptists have participated in several projects and studies. One of these produced Robert R. Parsonage, editor, *Church-Related Higher Education* (Valley Forge: Judson Press, 1978) which helped to redefine "church-relatedness." In the mission context, Earl H. Cressy, *Christian Higher Education in China* (Shanghai: China Christian Education Committee, 1928) reports on the status of mission schools at the peak of development on that field. Laurence T. Slaght, *Multiplying the Witness: 150 Years of American Baptist Educational Ministries* (Valley Forge: Judson Press, 1974) is the standard work on American Baptist educational programs in the era.

Beyond the histories relating to Northern and Southern Baptists, several reliable studies tell of the diverse Baptist groups in the present century. Frank Woyke, *Heritage and Ministry of the North American Baptist Conference* (Oakbrook Terrace, Ill.: Conference Press, 1980) identifies transitions in the German Baptist community, and Adolf Olson's *Centenary History* (Chicago: Baptist Conference Press, 1952) brings the story of Swedish Baptists up to date. Similarly, Joseph H. Jackson, patriarch of black Baptists, recounts that chapter in *A Story of Christian Activism: The History of the National Baptist Convention, U.S.A., Inc.* (Nashville: Townshend Press, 1980). Finally, two other books cover the General Association of Regular Baptist Churches and Conservative Baptists, respectively: Wilbur J. Hopewell, *The Missionary Emphasis of the General Association of Regular Baptist Churches* (Chicago: Regular Baptist Press, 1963) and Bruce L. Shelley, *A History of Conservative Baptists* (Wheaton, Ill.: Conservative Baptist Press, 1971). International Baptist life has seen advances both organizationally and numerically. In 1980 as the BWA celebrated its seventy-fifth anniversary, its story was retold in documentary fashion in Carl W. Tiller, *The Twentieth Century Baptist* (Valley Forge: Judson Press, 1980). Other typical and available works that detail Baptist development outside North America are Dean Kirkwood, editor, *European Baptists: A Magnificent Minority* (Valley Forge: International Ministries, 1981), Alan C. Prior, *Some Fell on Good Ground: A History of the Baptist Church in New South Wales, Australia* (Sydney: Baptist Union, 1966), and Erville Sowards, *et. al., Burma Baptist Chronicle* (Rangoon: Burma Baptist Convention, 1963).

The best biographies for the modern period are: Isabel Crawford, *Joyful Journey: Highlights Along the Way* (Valley Forge: Judson Press, 1951), Harry E. Fosdick, *The Living of These Days* (New York: Harper & Row, 1956), Edgar J. Goodspeed, *As I Remember* (New York: Harper & Row, 1953), William B. Lipphard, *Fifty Years an Editor* (Valley·Forge: Judson Press, 1963), Helen B. Montgomery, *Helen Barrett Montgomery: From Campus to World Citizenship* (New York: Fleming H. Revell, 1940), L. D. Reddick, *Crusader Without Violence: A Biography of Martin Luther King, Jr.* (New York: Harper & Row, 1969), Suzanne C. Linder, *William Louis Poteat: Prophet of Progress* (Chapel Hill: University of North Carolina, 1966), Robert G. Torbet and Henry Bowler, *Reuben E. Nelson: Free Churchman* (Valley Forge: Judson Press, 1961), Ridgely Torrence, *The Story of John Hope* (New York: Macmillan, Inc., 1948), and Leslie K. Tarr, *Shields of Canada: T. T. Shields 1873–1958* (Grand Rapids: Baker Books, 1967).

There is little doubt that the major controversy involving Northern/American Baptists from 1920 to 1950 was on fundamentalism in its various forms and expressions. Much has been written, thus any reading suggestions must be selective. In addition to several general histories, Norman F. Furniss, *The Fundamentalist Controversy 1918–1931* (New Haven: Yale University Press, 1954) contains a good introduction to the controversy among Northern Baptists and should be supplemented with C. Allyn Russell, *Voices of American Fundamentalism: Seven Biographical Studies* (Philadelphia: Westminster Press, 1976) on the major personalities. Two unpublished studies that deserve attention are Walter E. Ellis, "Social and Religious Factors in the Fundamentalist-Modernist Schisms Among Baptists in North America 1895–1934" (Ph.D. Dissertation, University of Pittsburgh, 1974) and Donald Tinder, "Fundamentalist Baptists in the Northern and Western United States" (Ph.D. Dissertation, Yale University, 1969). The pro-Fundamentalist view is expressed in two works by Chester E. Tulga: *The Case Against Modernism* (Chicago: Conservative Baptist Fellowship, 1949) and *The Foreign Mission Controversy in the Northern Baptist Convention 1919–1949* (Chicago: Conservative Baptist Fellowship, 1950). For the more recent strain of "independent, fundamentalist Baptists," see Jerry Falwell and Ed Hindson, *The Fundamentalist Phenomenon* (New York: Doubleday, 1980).

The liberal perspective, North and South, was expressed in several classics ranging in subject matter from biblical criticism to social justice. See, for instance: Shirley J. Case, *Origins of Christian Supernaturalism* (Chicago: University Press, 1946); Morton S. Enslin, *Christian Beginnings* (New York: Harper & Row, 1938); Harry E. Fosdick, *The Modern Use of the Bible* (New York: Macmillan, 1924); Conrad H. Moehlman, *The Christian-Jewish Tragedy* (Rochester: Leo Hart, 1933); Justin W. Nixon, *The Moral Crisis in Christianity* (New York: Harper & Row, 1931); and William L. Poteat, *Can a Man Be a Christian Today?* (London: Oxford University Press, 1926).

Another important concern, particularly for American Baptists, has been ecumenism. Investigations of the subject should start with James L. Garrett, editor, *Baptist Relations with Other Christians* (Valley Forge: Judson Press, 1974) and include also William R. Estep, *Baptists and Christian Unity* (Nashville: Broadman Press, 1966), which gives a good historical account. Robert Torbet, *Ecumenism: Free Church Dilemma* (Valley Forge: Judson Press, 1968) and Ernest A. Payne, *Free Churchmen: Unrepentent and Repentent* (London: Carey Kingsgate Press, 1965) both stress the need for Baptists to maintain dialogue with other Christians while holding fast to the autonomy of Free Churches. Additionally, Joseph H. Jackson, *Many But One: The Ecumenics of Charity* (New York: Sheed and Ward, 1964) addresses the issue for the black churches, as does Jarold K. Zeman *et. al.*, *The Believer's Church in Canada* (Waterloo: Baptist Federation, 1979) for Canadian Baptists in a broader Radical Reformation tradition.

Prior to World War II most American Baptists relied heavily upon the theological writings of A. H. Strong, W. N. Clarke, and E. Y. Mullins, supplemented of course with other theologians in the Reformed tradition. In the postwar period, much more diversity is evident as exposure to European theologies increased. The works of Emil Brunner, Karl Barth, and Paul Tillich have combined with Walter Rauschenbusch and Harvey Cox to add breadth to theology and ethics. The work of American Baptist conservative evangelicals like Carl F. H. Henry and Bernard Ramm and Southern Baptists Frank Stagg and Dale Moody have also achieved prominence in this generation. No one text satisfies the many persuasions found in any or all Baptist groups. Since its publication in 1963, the overwhelming standard guide to Baptist polity is Norman H. Maring and Winthrop S. Hudson, *A Baptist Manual of Polity and Practice* (Valley Forge: Judson Press, 1963), although a revised edition of the E. T. Hiscox *Guide* is still popular. An example of the special concern American Baptists have given to ecclesiological issues in the broader Christian context is E.P.Y. Simpson, *Ordination and Christian Unity* (Valley Forge: Judson Press, 1966).

The availability of twentieth-century primary sources continues to grow. For the Northern/American Baptist tradition, the *Directory* and *Yearbook of the American Baptist Churches in the U.S.A.* (separate volumes per year, replacing in 1972 the *Annual* of the American Baptist Convention) are the beginning reference points. For other Baptist groups, see the individual files of annuals under organizational names. The American Baptist Historical Society, as official archives of the American Baptist Churches, has recently arranged all organizational record groups into a convenient classification system with guides to specific agencies. Similarly, ABHS has arranged the records of the Baptist World Alliance and produced a comprehensive guide for materials housed in the official archives at Rochester, New York. ABHS also has extensive files for the General Association of Regular Baptists and the Conservative Baptist Fellowship.

Personal papers collections are available for most major figures of the era, housed in several repositories and under varying conditions of access. ABHS has substantial materials of the following persons: Alfred W. Anthony, Edwin T. Dahlberg, V. Carney Hargroves, Reuben Nelson, Justin W. Nixon, J. Frank Norris, Dores R. Sharpe, and Hillyer H. Straton. Andover Newton has a fine collection on Walter O. Lewis; Union Theological Seminary in New York administers the papers of Harry E. Fosdick; and Syracuse University collects the Carl F. H. Henry papers.

Among American Baptists, periodical literature since 1920 has been greatly reduced in quantity. The *Watchman-Examiner* ceased publication in 1970 and thus ended a distinguished independent editorial tradition. Regional and local news is covered in inserts to the national organ, *The American Baptist Magazine,* since most state and regional newspapers ceased independent publication in the 1970s; the *American Baptist News Service* has published weekly reports since 1976. For Southern Baptists, most state conventions continue to publish newspapers on at least a monthly basis; with other fellowships, monthlies are typical. For individual titles, consult ABHS.

Index

(Page numbers in **bold face** indicate reference to an illustration.)